The Other Side of Autism:

Famous Spirits Unveil Regressive Autism's Causes and Remedies

Written by Laura Hirsch

Channeling by Michael Parry

Spirit Artistry by Marti Parry

Cover art by Marti Parry.

Published by: Rainbow Books

The Other Side of Autism: Famous Spirits Unveil Regressive Autism's Causes and Remedies

ISBN: 978-0-9776653-2-7

To my sweet boy Trevor:
My love for you is the driving force that made all of this possible.

This book is dedicated to children with regressive autism
and the families who love them.

Contents

Prologue

"It has become appallingly obvious that our technology has exceeded our humanity."

— Albert Einstein

Foundation of Discovery

Before we begin, I need to give some background on the history of this book. I had written another channeled book about autism prior to this one, titled *Foundation of Discovery: The Cause of Autism – Channeled*, which actually became the stepping stone for this book. Here is the teaser from the back cover:

"What is Causing the Autism Epidemic? In 2006, a young mother of a child with regressive autism and her friend, a gifted psychic medium, are driving through a remote area of Nevada desert. The medium announces, 'There are military people working underground here.' One year later, the pair get together to channel information from the spirit world about the cause of autism. The horror of what is going on in the secret underground facility and its link to the autism epidemic is revealed to them. Discover the startling truth as you follow the incredible story of how the spirit world is stepping in to help solve the autism puzzle."

True story. This *former* friend, who is also a medium, had done lots of great readings for me over the years. She brought through information from my dead relatives that only the dead person and I knew about, and made predictions which later came true. So, I commissioned her to do a book project with me about autism. I would write, edit and publish it and she would do the channeling for it. To make a very long story short, we began the project in late 2007 and completed eight channeling sessions over the next seven months. I asked the questions pertaining to autism, and she channeled the answers from the spirit world.

For reasons only she truly knows, she stopped channeling and ultimately quit the project before we had finished. I felt obligated to my son to go forward on my own and put out there what was completed. I had done everything humanly possible to get her to continue and finish, but she had other intentions. I spent two years researching, writing, editing, talking to copyright lawyers and spent my own money publishing the book in January 2010, desperate to get this vital information out there to help children with autism, like my beloved child.

After the book came out, naturally, I began promoting it. I did a book signing at the Autism One/Generation Rescue conference in May, 2010. The conference wasn't very well attended because of the poor economy, but it was a great experience nonetheless. The following month, I was invited to be a guest on the Coast to Coast AM radio show with George Knapp. He was introduced to my book through a mutual friend. I was very nervous talking about the contents of the book, as you will understand when you read the upcoming book summary, but the interview went well. I received many supportive emails and validations through my website after my appearance. The information in the book was starting to create a little buzz, and plant some seeds.

As suggested by a copyright lawyer, to protect the medium's identity and for personal liability, I didn't use her name in the book, since she claimed that the reason she stopped doing the channeling was because she was afraid that she was going to be killed. After she learned that I was on Coast to Coast, she had a lawyer send me a demand letter based on fabricated charges and threatened to take legal action against me, claiming that the channeled material was hers, and that I was somehow infringing on her copyrights by publishing the information. Good one!

For those who got to read the book, I feel I owe a brief explanation as to why I temporarily took the book off the market and shut the website down shortly after its release. According to the lawyers that I consulted with prior to publishing the book, I owned the copyrights to the story, as well as the channeled material because the medium intentionally collaborated with me and then quit the joint project (which I have in writing). Her claim is that she never agreed to collaborate with me and that I used HER material without permission, claiming I infringed on her copyrights by publishing my book. Really? I have the original CD from our fifth session together (with her handwriting on it) which contains her voice saying and I quote "We are going to channel another chapter of the book. Right now, we are just referring to it as 'The Mummy.' Laura is here, and she's going to trigger the questions so that when I make the connection I can get the answers." (She accidentally made a duplicate copy of this session, which I found later in my car, I gave her back the other CD's after I transcribed them.)

This was five sessions into the process, mind you. Does this sound like I "stole" HER material against her will as she claimed in her malicious demand letter? Clearly not. I also videotaped a few of our channeling sessions in her home, which I still have. Did I break in and force her to speak against her will? Of course not. I am the one with a child with autism; she knows nothing about it. Why would she have any interest in the subject if not for her "friend" who asked for her assistance? The only reason she even has a copy of the transcripts is because I did all of the work, and uploaded it to her computer. Unlike her, I have a little something called proof.

It was pretty apparent that she wanted to use the channeled information for herself because it was famous spirits coming through, not just the usual dead relatives. She quit with the intention of keeping the material and using it for herself, and lied to me about her reasons, hoping I'd let it go. Guess again. Her demand letter revealed her true intentions. She wanted to use the material in her own book, and take all of the credit. Then she sent a second letter trying to extort money from me. Good luck with that, I have a child with autism, which means I'm broke.

The whole thing was downright laughable. The bottom line legally speaking is that because the words are channeled, they are not the original words of the medium, they are the words of the dead people, and therefore she is not eligible for copyright protection on them anyway. If she claims they're her words, she defrauded me by saying that they were the words of spirits. The truth is, because it was my idea, and my story which I wrote, researched and organized, and because she quit our collaboration, I owned the copyrights.

Sadly, because of the type of person the medium turned out to be (I'll spare you all of the colorful adjectives I've deleted), I wanted nothing to do with her and pulled the book off the market and shut down the website. I didn't have to do that, but if there was no book, I would have no ties or obligations to her. After a letter from my lawyer challenging her trumped up charges, she didn't proceed with her threats, but the damage had been done; actions speak louder than words. Her ego was bigger than her heart. Anyone who would threaten to sue me instead of talk to me is no friend of mine. There's more, but I'm going to take the high road here and leave it at that.

However, despite my personal feelings toward the medium, I still believed in the content of the channeled messages that came through in our sessions together. In fact, much of the research and testing that I did on my son afterward validated the channeled messages. If you had a healthy child who regressed into "autism" and learned of a possible cause of what happened to them and many other damaged children, could you keep it to yourself? I don't think so. At least my conscience wouldn't let me. I put myself in danger for a bigger cause. You will understand why as you read on.

Summary of Foundation of Discovery: The Cause of Autism – Channeled

First of all, I want to say don't kill the messenger! I mean me in this case. I feel a moral sense of duty and obligation to share this information. I am going to briefly cover some of the main messages that the spirits revealed during the channeling sessions for my book *Foundation of Discovery*. The main significance of sharing this information is because some of the same spirits come through again and some of the messages are restated through a different medium (Michael) three years later for the contents of this book, as you will see. Trust me, if I didn't have to mention it, I wouldn't, and I would have just started from scratch. Unfortunately, I need to start here. I'd like to thank the first medium for her role, and wish her the best.

The bulk of the important channeled information actually came through during the first two sessions, which were held less than a week apart. I truly believe in the validity of the information given during these sessions for two main reasons. First, because the medium was channeling and didn't know what she was saying at the time; she was repeating someone else's words. Second, the main spirit speaking to me hadn't identified himself until the second session and the medium's ego was not attached. She often got deep into a trance state when she channeled and didn't remember a lot of what transpired during the session.

Going into the first session, we basically just left it up to the spirit world to determine who would come through and share the best information to help understand the causes of and cures for autism. This was my intention. What happened next was very unexpected and unbelievable. The first spirit she picked up on was a male with wiry hair. My first question to him was about what was causing the increase in the diagnosis of children with regressive autism. After some talk about our contaminated drinking water, and corrupt government, the main problem was revealed.

4

This wiry haired spirit said that the soil in Nevada (where I live) was very contaminated and that it was coming from the creation of military weapons in a remote part of the Nevada desert. I asked if it was nuclear weapons, or what type of weapon it was. The reply was that there is a whole population of military living underground and they were working on techniques to kill people and have it appear that they died of natural causes (indicating biological weapons). It was in the form of a powdery dust and was meant to be dropped from the skies. This contamination also affected the food, as the wind was blowing it around and contaminating the topsoil. He said that it was new technology and unrecognized.

I was pretty confused; I had never heard anything like this before, and I thought I had read just about everything that had to do with autism. Then the wiry haired guy said that research needs to be done to pinpoint where these kids are because they are in concentrated areas, and it has to do with soil contamination and the food and water. He explained that if you combine the product that they are using that's going to be a future weapon with the vaccine, you have the reaction you're having now. Autism is not coming from vaccines alone. One triggers the other and that's what was causing these kids to get sick. He called it a neural attack. (The nervous system.)

He also said that their little bodies don't have the immune system to power through it. What allows the biowarfare to attack is a low immune system. He said to separate some of the shots because the current vaccine schedule downs their immune system so much that they can't fight what's in the environment. They are not considering the mixing of medicines or the receiver.

Then, he mentioned that eating potatoes and other root vegetables were especially bad. When I asked about organic farming, they said that it wasn't the answer because the contamination is still in the topsoil. He said in a later session that the future would be hydroponic gardening. I cried when he said that my child was not born that way, he was healthy and that this wasn't genetic. My son had what was going on because of two ingredients combining.

Next, the medium said that she kept seeing those underground military areas that she was sensing when she and I were driving together on a trip from Reno to Las Vegas a year prior. She said that she was seeing an X marked on that spot and said that is where it is going on, and where it was coming from. *(During our trip, she announced out of the blue that there were military people working in an underground city as we were driving through a military area in the desert.)* I looked it up after the session, and the military town is called Hawthorne, NV.

The wiry haired guy stressed that the military were just doing what they are told, and are under command. Because they are sloppy with it, the biological weapon, the dust, was coming out of the underground facility, and the wind was blowing it across the country. He said that the soil is not going to be able to be cleaned up, it needed to be removed or replaced and that we should eat from the ocean, because it is not contaminated like the land.

The wiry haired spirit said that these children are very psychic from an early age because they were forced to turn to another sense, their sixth sense. He compared these children to being mummified, trapped in their bodies, wrapped in a solution and that this will be unwrapped one day, but not until my son was in his 40's. That was 30 years away. I started calling the book "The Mummy" as a running title because of this reference.

In the second session, five days later, the wiry haired guy identified himself, but I didn't reveal his identity in the book because of his Publicity Rights. He is a very famous scientist, and his name and image are owned by a company. I didn't want any legal trouble, so I referred to him as The Wiry One, which is a name he said he liked in the second session. It doesn't take a genius to figure out who this is.

Also in this session, a few other spirits came forward. One was a medium, Edgar Cayce, and even though he didn't get to say much in later sessions (because the medium quit before we finished), he appeared twice. The other spirit said he was a President, and showed himself in a wheelchair. This could only be one person, President Franklin Delano Roosevelt. The Wiry One also talked about himself, obscure things which I validated later, for instance that he often didn't wear socks and that he went long periods without eating and would then eat like a bear. He also said that there was a friend there with him named John that he also worked with. I was fairly certain this was John Von Neumann, another physicist and mathematician who was also a professor at the same University as The Wiry One.

Some of the questions that the spirits answered for me were more specifics and clarifications about the biological warfare and vaccine connection to autism. They described the biowarfare in more detail, saying that they took something natural that biodegraded and added other things to it to make it a killer. In a later session, after doing some research, I asked if it was anthrax, and the answer was that it was a form of that, but that anthrax was primitive compared to what they're making. They also described how it is being made and handled; describing the plastic suits the military wore for protection looked as if they were working with bees. This dust is so fine that it can penetrate clothing and absorb into the skin as well as being breathed in.

They said that there are two vaccines affecting humanity. The first was the MMR vaccine (Measles, Mumps, Rubella), specifically the Rubella component. They said that this vaccine is given at age one, and is reacting with the biowarfare which they are exposed to through the air or dirt. Also problematic was the polio vaccine, which is the disease that President Roosevelt had which put him in the wheelchair. They told me to study the winds to see where the highest concentrations of these kids were and it should follow the wind pattern from the place they said it was being made in Nevada. They said that this stuff can go across the nation, blowing up the West Coast then across to the Great Lakes and then to the upper East Coast, and less in the South.

I asked how long they have been producing this biowarfare in Nevada and they said 11 years (Since 1996. I found out after the session that there was a 57% increase in autism in children born in 1996 than those born in 1994 according to the CDC.) According to what they were saying, it seems to reason that if a person was born before this time, they don't have this "disease." It's not the same thing. There were future predictions and other details mentioned during the sessions about autism, and if you'd like to read the book, it is still available online.

Unfortunately, in hindsight, based on the medium's litigious threats and other actions, I didn't know how much of the channeled information in our later sessions was coming from the spirits and how much was coming from her to suit her agenda. For example, during one of the sessions, she claimed that the spirits were saying that her name should be on the book as the author, but that part shouldn't go in the book. Please, how naïve did she think I was? The parts of the book that I am sharing are important to this story as you will later see. There are many parallels. But that's it in a nutshell. After these sessions, I did some research to try to back up what was disclosed. I still wasn't sure if I believed it at this point. If it was potentially true, I felt obligated to find out.

***

Foundation of Discovery – After the Sessions

I wasn't about to blindly believe what I was told without investigating it, especially given the severity of the accusations, and how ridiculous they sounded to me at the time. I began by studying the winds, as suggested by the spirits in the sessions. I found that in the Northern Hemisphere, the prevailing wind pattern is called the Westerlies, traveling from West to East. Often, the wind patterns change direction, in the case of the Santa Ana Winds, and the Diablo Winds, which originate in the Great Basin, which includes all of Nevada, and blows west toward the Pacific Ocean. This could explain why my son was contaminated, as we lived in Southern California from birth to age 3. Also, potato country is mostly in Idaho, which is downwind of Hawthorne NV, when following the typical Westerly wind pattern. From Hawthorne, NV, the winds typically blow to the Northeast, across the Great Lakes states and then to the East coast. You can see a live wind map at www.hint.fm/wind/.

When I looked up the Autism Statistics by state, and sure enough, the states with the highest increase in autism were all Northern states. Even current statistics show that for children ages 6-17, autism is highest in the Northeast and on the West coast and lowest among the Southern and Plains states.[1] Nevada was in the top five for cumulative growth of autism, even though the population is 35th in the nation.[2] All of the states around Nevada were at the top of the list for high autism rates and the other states with high autism rates followed the path of the wind from NV, as the channeled message claimed.

The autism rates were a conservative one in 110 at the time my book was published, one in 70 boys. The CDC reported that 40,000 children were diagnosed with autism in 2009. One percent of all children in this country have an autism spectrum disorder. This rapid increase rules out better diagnosis and genetics. In the history of written medicine there is no record of any developmental or genetic disorder remotely coming close

---

[1] www.graphics.latimes.com/usmap-autism-rates-state/
[2] www.statemaster.com

to a one percent number. Anything that affects one percent of a population is going to be a serious disease or medical illness.

Also validating was the discovery that the autism rate in the military population was double the rate in the civilian population. Everything that I looked up matched what was told to me in the channeling sessions. I didn't want it to be true, but I kept investigating to find out what really happened to my once happy, healthy son. I was even more intrigued, so I kept digging.

U.S History of Biological Warfare

I did a lot of research on biological warfare, and it left no doubt in my mind about the accuracy of the channeled information. It was not only plausible, but probable. I am going to share some of my research, which was partially included in *Foundation of Discovery* and let the reader come to their own conclusions. There is a lot of information in this section, but it is important because it drove me to discover things which ultimately led me to write this book. So, bear with me.

Biological warfare wasn't even on my radar when I did the channeling sessions for *Foundation of Discovery*. I vaguely even knew what it was. What little I knew about it came from what I had seen on TV after the fatal 9/11 anthrax mailings, but that's about it. When researching the history of biological warfare after the channeling sessions, I found that in response to Japan's full-scale germ-warfare program, the U.S. began research and development of biological in 1942. President Franklin Delano Roosevelt placed George W. Merck (former president of the pharmaceutical giant Merck & Co., who now manufactures the MMR vaccine) in charge of the effort to create a biological weapons development program at Ft. Detrick, MD.

On a side note, I learned that there was a series of letters written to President Roosevelt by "The Wiry One" and other scientists, warning him of the Germans potentially creating a nuclear bomb. The Manhattan Project was started after this, creating the U.S. nuclear bombs that were used on Japan during WWII. So, FDR and The Wiry One were also connected in life, which I didn't know. They were both involved, directly or indirectly with warfare activities. No wonder they were coming through in the channeling sessions to help.

I also discovered that under President Nixon, the U.S. initiated and signed the 1972 Biological and Toxin Weapons Convention (BWC). The

BWC prohibits the development, production, stockpiling, and acquisition of these weapons. The BWC thus supplements the prohibition on use of biological weapons contained in the 1925 Geneva Protocol. Opened for signature on April 10, 1972 and entering into force on March 26, 1975, The BWC is commonly portrayed as the first international treaty to ban an entire class of weapons. As of June 2000, it had 144 states parties, including the five permanent members of the United Nations Security Council, plus a further 18 signatory states. The United Kingdom, the United States and the Russian Federation are the depositaries of the Convention.

In the preamble to the BWC Convention it states, "Determined, for the sake of all mankind, to exclude completely the possibility of bacteriological (biological) agents and toxins being used as weapons, convinced that such use would be repugnant to the conscience of mankind and that no effort should be spared to minimize this risk." Article I states, "Each State Party to this Convention undertakes never in any circumstances to develop, produce, stockpile or otherwise acquire or retain: (1) Microbial or other biological agents, or toxins whatever their origin or method of production, of types and in quantities that have no justification for prophylactic, protective or other peaceful purposes; (2) Weapons, equipment or means of delivery designed to use such agents or toxins for hostile purposes or in armed conflict."

Did the United States stop its offensive biological weapons program after signing the BWC? I did more research about the history of biological warfare, and what I discovered was pretty appalling. One article I found was from the *Houston Chronicle,* titled. "Secret Germ Warfare Tests Produced Chilling Results."[3] This was just after the anthrax mail scare post 9/11, on Nov. 9, 2001. It said that "The Army kept the biological-warfare tests secret until word of them was leaked to the press in the 1970's. Between 1949 and 1969, when President Nixon ordered the Pentagon's biological weapons destroyed, open-air tests of biological agents were conducted 239 times, (in the U.S.) according to the Army's testimony in 1977 before the Senate's subcommittee on health. In 80 of those experiments, the Army said it used live bacteria that its researchers at the time thought were harmless, such as the Serratia that was showered

---

[3] Carlton, Jim, "Secret Germ Warfare Tests Produced Chilling Results" *Wall Street Journal.* (Nov. 9, 2001).

on San Francisco. In others, it used inert chemicals to simulate bacteria." The article went on to say, "The possibility cannot be ruled out that peculiarities in wind conditions or ventilation systems in buildings might concentrate organisms, exposing people to high doses of bacteria." Imagine how many tests they've done on an unsuspecting public since then! Many people became ill or died as a result of these experiments.

Further validation that the U.S. did not stop producing biological warfare was in a documentary by Dr. Leonard Horowitz called *The CIA, Hollywood, and Bioterrorism*. It was about the history of bioterrorism with lots of information. One article highlighted was from the prestigious scientific magazine *Nature* and said "In 1969, the use of biological warfare was renounced as a political ploy. By 1970, a year after Nixon ratified the Geneva Protocol; nothing had changed except the public's perception of chemical biological warfare risk. Rather than receive the promised annual cut in biological warfare research funding, the DOD's BW budget increased from $21.9 to $23.2 million. The stockpiled bioweapons Nixon pledged would be rapidly destroyed remained intact in Pine Bluff, Arkansas, and the announced transition of Fort Detrick from a BW testing facility to a solely defensive NIH run health research lab had not occurred."[4]

Even now, this offensive work continues. I found a damaging article titled "U.S. Corporations Aren't Disclosing Biological Warfare Research Work" from *Political Affairs* magazine from 6-22-07 states "A number of pharmaceutical corporations and biotech firms are concealing the nature of the biological warfare research work they are doing for the U.S. government. Since their funding comes from the National Institutes of Health, the recipients are obligated under NIH guidelines to make their activities public. Not disclosing their ops raises the suspicion that they may be engaged in forbidden kinds of germ warfare research. According to the Sunshine Project, a nonprofit arms control watchdog operating out of Austin, Texas, among the corporations holding back information about their activities are: Abbott Laboratories, BASF Plant Science, Bristol-Meyers Squibb, DuPont Central Research and Development, Eli Lilly Corp., Embrex, GlaxoSmithKline, Hoffman-LaRoche, Merck & Co., Monsanto, Pfizer Inc., Schering-Plough Research Institute, and Syngenta Corp of Switzerland. In case you didn't know it, the White House since 9/11 has called for spending $44 billion on biological warfare research, a sum unprecedented in world history, and an

---

[4] www.liveleak.com/view?i=377_1195303011

obligating Congress has authorized it. Thus, some of the deadliest pathogens known to humankind are being rekindled in hundreds of labs in pharmaceutical houses, university biology departments, and military bases." It went on to say that "In 2006, the NIH got $1.76 billion for biodefense, much of it spent to research anthrax."

I found a frightening article sourced from the *Wall Street Journal* titled, "Biological Warfare: Incredible, Deadly Viruses are Manufactured with Little Difficulty." It quoted a passage from the book, *"AIDS: The End of Civilization,"* by Dr. William Campbell Douglass which says, "With the advent of genetic manipulation (i.e., recombinant engineering), some most incredible and deadly viruses can now be manufactured with little difficulty. One devastating possibility would be to combine the highly contagious influenza virus with the genes of either the anthrax toxin, the botulism toxin, or the toxin from plague. If this type of designer virus were unleashed upon a population, infection of almost all of the populace would be certain, especially in the cities, and death would very quickly follow. There would be no treatment and diagnosis would be difficult. This is not science fiction. This is today's reality." The article went on to say, "The reports of chemical and biological warfare experiments that have allegedly been carried out against innocent American civilians by the scientists working in the defense industry and our own military are numerous and staggering in their implication. More and more of these stories are surfacing through declassified documents, leaks, and testimonials of some of the victims involved."[5]

The United States has a rich history of getting the world's top biological warfare specialists (war criminals) to come to our country and work for us. There is plenty of literature out there on Project Paperclip, including the book *Lab 257: The Disturbing Story of the Government's Secret Plum Island Germ Laboratory* by Michael Carroll. In the book, it says, "Nearing the end of World War II, the United States and the Soviet Union raced to recruit German scientists for postwar purposes. Under a top secret program code-named Project Paperclip, the U.S. military pursued Nazi scientific talent like forbidden fruit, bringing them to America under employment contracts and offering them full U.S. citizenship. The recruits were supposed to be nominal participants in Nazi activities. But the

---

[5] http://www.geocites.com/area51/Shadowlands/6583/project085.html?200719
.

zealous military recruited more than two thousand scientists, many of whom had dark Nazi party pasts." This was in 1945. Many of the Nazi scientists went to work at Ft. Detrick. They were given immunity from prosecution for war crimes and secret identities in exchange for work on top secret U.S. government projects, including biological warfare experiments.

One of these Nazi scientists was Dr. Erich Traub. He was a German Biological Warfare expert who operated a germ warfare lab in the Baltic Sea. In the book, *The Nazi Hydra in America: Suppressed History of a Century* by Glen Yeadon and John Hawkins, it claims that "In 1949, Nazi scientist Erich Traub applied to work under the Project Paperclip program. Within months, Traub was invited for a talk with Germ Warriors from Fort Detrick, the Army's biological warfare headquarters in Frederick, MD. A former declassified summary confirmed the meeting occurred, but the CIA denies the summary exists and claims that if it did, it would withhold it for reasons of national security. Almost all documents concerning Traub and the Army's biowarfare at Plum Island have been destroyed or remain deeply buried in the government's secret vaults. The few documents that remain show that Traub worked with more than 40 lethal viruses on large test animals. He was at Plum Island from 1949-1953. Reports of a Nazi scientist releasing infected ticks come from a former employee of Plum Island. Plum Island is two miles offshore from Old Lyme, Connecticut, home of Lab 257, where secret biological experiments were conducted with the most deadly strains of bacteria and viruses. Both Lyme disease and West Nile virus first appeared in the general area." There was also a three hour total power outage on Plum Island and a loss of negative air pressure, an important fail-safe mechanism at high containment labs. Birds and deer were the vehicles of transmission. Why am I bringing up Lyme disease in the context of this book? Many children with "autism" also have Lyme disease, caused by genetically engineered vector ticks from Plum Island.

But wait, there's more! The U.S. government also offered Japanese war criminals and scientists who performed human medical experiments salaries and immunity from prosecution in exchange for data on biological warfare research. The following disturbing information comes from an article by journalist Christopher Reed titled *The United States and the Japanese Mengele: Payoffs and Amnesty for Unit 731 Scientists*. "The Japanese Imperial Army group called Unit 731 was led by Army General Dr. Ishii

Shiro. He was the chief of Japan's well financed scientifically coordinated and government approved biological warfare program from 1932-45. Ishii rose to general and supervised deliberate infection of thousands of captives with deadly diseases. He also conducted grotesque surgeries, but the unique medical specialty of Ishii and his surgical team were dissections, without anesthetic, on an estimated 3,000 live, conscious humans." The article also stated that the Japanese performed "open-air germ tests on captured Chinese and Russian men, women and children. Some were bound to stakes in a large field and bombarded with anthrax. Others were subjected to germs of bubonic plague, cholera, smallpox, typhus and typhoid, and women to syphilis. Its biological warfare (BW) was also illegal, since all such experiments were banned by the 1925 Geneva Convention, which Japan signed but did not ratify."

The article continues to say "At Fort Detrick, Maryland, the main U.S. installation for BW, records remain on file of the thousands of tissue slides, preserved organs (some labeled 'American') removed from living bodies with medical schedules and reports on perverse surgical procedures on screaming and writhing human specimens." The most concerning thing in the article was "The disclosure of two documents previously marked Top Secret and dated July 1947. They show not only full U.S. participation in allowing the Japanese medical torturers who escaped to Tokyo to go free in exchange for information, but that the Pentagon actually paid them. As General Charles Willoughby, chief of U.S. Military Intelligence gleefully noted to his headquarters, these pay-offs were 'a mere pittance...netting the U.S. the fruit of over 20 years' laboratory tests and research' in this 'critically serious form of warfare.'"

There is a lot more disturbing and incriminating information in this article and others regarding this topic. The point is that after World War II, the U.S. paid and protected biological warfare experts from both Germany and Japan in exchange for information. But wait, it gets even worse.

I came across another historical incident involving anthrax testing and soil contamination that happened on Gruinard Island, a small Scottish Island, now referred to as "Anthrax Island." In 1942, during World War II, Gruinard Island was the site of a biological warfare test by British military scientists from Porton Down. The British government bought the island to test anthrax bombs on 80 sheep to see if the sheep would survive the anthrax bombs and to test the long-lasting contamination of anthrax spores in the soil.

The sheep became infected with anthrax and died within days of exposure.

After the tests were completed, British scientists concluded that a large-scale release of anthrax spores would thoroughly pollute German cities if used during the war, rendering them uninhabitable for decades afterward. The anthrax spores used on Gruinard Island remained viable in the soil for decades, 48 years to be precise. Decontamination attempts on the island following the biological warfare testing were unsuccessful due to the durability of the anthrax spores. As a result the island was quarantined for many years afterwards. Visits to the island were strictly prohibited, except by Porton Down personnel checking the level of contamination.

Starting in 1986, a determined effort was made to decontaminate the island, with 280 tons of formaldehyde solution diluted in seawater being sprayed over all 196 hectares of the island, and the worst-contaminated topsoil around the dispersal site being removed. [6] Some of these experiments were recorded on 16mm color movie film, which was declassified in 1997. You can watch it yourself on You Tube and other websites. The men are wearing full-body Biohazard suits with masks, you see the bombs explode, a cloud emerge, and the sheep dying. It is very disturbing.

For me, this information validated the fact that anthrax remains viable in the soil for decades and that they used seawater to decontaminate it. During the channeling sessions it was mentioned that saltwater would be used to decontaminate the soil in our country in order to grow food. They said that the topsoil is very contaminated with biowarfare, and that potatoes and other root vegetables were especially contaminated. This made more sense now, knowing that anthrax remains viable in the soil for decades!

Anthrax and the Soviet Union

Since it was mentioned in the channeling sessions that what they are creating in the underground military facility in Hawthorne is a form of anthrax, I did some more research specifically about anthrax. This led me to an article from the Canadian website CBC News Online from Feb. 18, 2004 titled *Red Lies: Biological Warfare and the Soviet Union*. The article said that during the Cold War, "While the world worried about the nuclear threat, the Soviet Union was secretly amassing the largest biological

---

[6] http://en.wikipedia.org/wiki/Gruinard_Island

weapons program in global history. It involved thousands of scientists, who spent two decades turning deadly diseases like anthrax and smallpox into weapons of mass destruction. It mentioned that the largest documented outbreak of human inhalation anthrax happened in Sverdlovsk, at a secretive military base called "Compound 19" in the Union of Soviet Socialist Republics in 1979. 68 people died. It was concluded that the escape of an aerosol of anthrax pathogen at the military facility caused the outbreak.[7] The Soviet government claimed the deaths were caused by intestinal anthrax from tainted meat for thirteen years, until 1992, when President Boris Yeltsin admitted, without going into details, that the anthrax outbreak was the result of military activity. All of the victims were clustered in a straight line downwind from the military facility. Livestock in the same area also died of anthrax.

Former first deputy chief for Biopreparat (the civilian part of the Soviet Biological weapons program), Dr. Ken Alibek, who defected to the U.S., says that the anthrax airborne leak had been caused by workers at the military facility who forgot to replace a filter in an exhaust system. He also says that if the wind had been in the opposite direction that day, toward the city of Sverdlovsk, that the death rate could have been in the hundreds of thousands.[8]

In the *Red Lies* article it stated that after the 1979 incident "During a scientific exchange visit to the United States, Alibek came to the unsettling conclusion that the U.S. was not engaging in similar biological weapons research. With the CIA's assistance, Alibek defected to the West, bringing with him firsthand scientific knowledge of the Soviet's secret program. Alibek says, 'They were shocked; shocked because you know they couldn't imagine that the Soviet Union had such an enormous, very powerful and sophisticated offensive program.'

In the years since the Sverdlovsk accident, Alibek and a research team had taken the Soviet military's anthrax and made it even more deadly. He developed a process to take ground up anthrax spores and coat each particle in plastic and resin. It kept the anthrax aloft four times longer, increasing its ability to infect people."[9]

[7] *Science* 1994, Volume 266, Pages 1202-1208
[8] http://www.pbs.org/wgbh/pages/frontline/shows/plague/sverdlovsk/
[9] http://www.cbc.ca/news/background/bioweapons/redlies.html

It gets worse. The article continued to say that "While scientists here (U.S.) were researching improvements to Russia's anthrax vaccine, they created a deadly invention. In the December 1997 issue of the medical journal Vaccine, the Obolensk (a Russian lab) scientists claim to have 'inadvertently' developed a new genetically altered strain of anthrax. Its most frightening attribute, this new strain overpowers Russia's anthrax vaccine, rendering it completely useless. America's vaccine is different. But if this new anthrax defeats one vaccine, there's a fear it could defeat the other. At Fort Detrick, the study set off alarm bells."

Then the clincher: "After scientists at Biopreparat created their new 'super anthrax' the U.S. government asked for a sample to test it against the North American vaccine. The Russians turned the request down flat. By 2001, the U.S. had still not received a sample. But on September 4, 2001 *The New York Times* ran an article titled "U.S. Germ Warfare Research Pushes Treaty Limits." It reported that the U.S. government was launching its own program to create genetically modified anthrax, at a laboratory of the Battelle Memorial Institute in West Jefferson, Ohio. In the article it says that "The 1972 biological weapons treaty forbids nations from developing or acquiring weapons that spread disease, but it allows work on vaccines and other protective measures. Over the past several years, the United States has embarked on a program of secret research on biological weapons that, some officials say, tests the limits of the global treaty banning such weapons."

It went on to say that "Earlier this year, administration officials said, the Pentagon drew up plans to engineer genetically a potentially more potent variant of the bacterium that causes anthrax, a deadly disease ideal for germ warfare." Then the part that really caught my eye, "At about the same time, Pentagon experts assembled a germ factory in the Nevada Desert from commercially available materials. Pentagon officials said the project demonstrated the ease with which a terrorist or rogue nation could build a plant that could produce pounds of the deadly germs."

Interesting that they choose Nevada to produce secret biological warfare, isn't it? Makes you wonder what else they are not admitting to. So, the U.S. recruited biological warfare specialists from Germany and Japan after World War II, and Soviet biological warfare specialists after the breakup of the Soviet Union. Do you still think the information given in the readings is impossible? Read on...

I found some information on the NTI (Nuclear Threat Initiative) website about a biological facility that the Soviet Union used for open-air testing of BW agents called Vozrozhdeniye Island in the Aral Sea. It said that "From 1936 to 1992, Vozrozhdeniye Island was the major proving ground in the Soviet Union for the open-air testing of BW agents developed at different Soviet BW facilities. A variety of BW agents were tested on the island, including the microbial pathogens that cause plague, anthrax, Q-fever, smallpox, Tularemia, and Venezuelan equine encephalitis, as well as botulinum toxin. Some of the pathogens tested in aerosol form were genetically modified strains that produce atypical disease processes and are resistant to existing medications, potentially complicating diagnosis and treatment. In addition to common pathogenic strains, special strains developed for military purposes were tested on the island."

This last description of what the Soviets were testing on the island seems more along those lines: aerosol form, genetically modified strains that produce atypical disease processes, complicating diagnosis and special strains for military purposes. Since then, I am sure that our advances in biotechnology have created an even more horrifying version than we can even imagine. Is it even detectable by today's biosensing equipment? The channeled messages for my book indicated that it was new technology and we didn't have recognition of it.

The following part of the article also got my attention because of the information given in the readings about why they are doing the BW work in the Nevada desert at a secret underground military base (they needed the heat and it was in the middle of nowhere). The article said, "Vozrozhdeniye Island was apparently chosen for open-air testing of biological weapons because of its geographic location and climate conditions. The shores of the Aral Sea are predominantly large, sparsely populated deserts and semi-deserts, which hindered unauthorized access to the secret site. The island's sparse vegetation, hot, dry climate, and sandy soil – all reduced the possibility that the pathogenic microorganisms would survive and spread."

There was more. "In 1998, information was revealed regarding viable anthrax spores on the Vozrozhdeniye Island, which caused a new wave of concern regarding the environmental condition of the island. It's also notable that during the late 1980's, large quantities of anthrax spores that had been mass-produced and stockpiled in Russia were transported to the island for decontamination and burial. In the aftermath of the September 11 attacks, the U.S. government recognized the urgency of decontaminating the anthrax burial sites to eliminate the threat of terrorist access. Moreover, because oil companies are interested in drilling on the island for petroleum and natural gas, these activities could stir up contaminated dust that could blow across to the mainland." [10] Contaminated dust, blowing... Sound familiar? I'm sure it doesn't stop at the border either.

In Ken Alibek's autobiographical book, Biohazard: The Chilling True Story of the Largest Covert Biological Weapons Program in the World-Told from Inside by the Man Who Ran It, he acknowledges the activities on Vozrozhdeniye Island, which they called Rebirth Island. He says that "Our teams would spend four or five months there, living in Army barracks and testing that year's supply of biological weapons." He describes how they would spray aerosol bioweapons on monkeys tethered to posts and how men in biological protective suits would retrieve them and examine them to see if they died of anthrax, Q fever, brucellosis, glanders, or plague. Genetic engineering of biological weapons has been going on for a long time.

According to Alibek, as early as 1970 in the Soviet Union, "Scientists had been studying peptides, strings of amino acids which perform various functions in our bodies, from regulating hormones and facilitating digestion to directing our immune system. One important group of peptides, called regulatory peptides, is activated during times of stress or heightened emotion – anger, love, fear– or to fight disease. Some regulatory peptides affect the central nervous system. When present in large quantities, they can alter mood and trigger psychological changes. Some can contribute to more serious adverse reactions such as heart attacks, strokes, or paralysis when overproduced. In a series of trailblazing experiments, the scientists found a way to duplicate in the lab the genes for a handful of regulatory peptides with known toxic properties. One of these was found capable, when present in large quantities, of damaging the myelin sheaths protecting the thousands of

---

[10] http://www.nti.org/e_research/profiles/Kazakhstan/Biological/facilities_vozro zhdenie.html

nerve fibers that transmit electric signals from the brain and spinal cord to the rest of the body. Unknown in the West, we called it myelin toxin." He continued, "As with all peptides, it was hard to obtain enough for useful experimentation. Genetic engineering solved this problem: scientists could synthesize the genes that code for the production of myelin toxin, reproduce them artificially in the lab, and insert them into bacterial cells. If a bacteria strain compatible with myelin toxin could be found, the transplanted genes would multiply along with the bacteria." They found a suitable bacterial host for myelin toxin in the bacteria *Yersinia pseudotuberculosis,* closely related to *Yersinia pestis,* the bacteria that causes plague.

They did successful tests on animals and found that a single genetically engineered agent had produced symptoms of two different diseases, one of which could not be traced. He says, "A new class of weapons had been found. For the first time we would be capable of producing weapons based on the chemical substances produced naturally by the human body. They could damage the nervous system, alter moods, trigger psychological changes, and even kill. The mood-altering possibilities of regulatory peptides were of particular interest to the KGB – this and the fact that they could not be traced by pathologists. Victims would appear to have died of natural causes." A few months later, they successfully transferred the gene for myelin toxin to Yersinia pestis. A toxin-plague weapon was never produced before the Soviet Union collapsed, but the success of this experiment set the stage for further research on bacteria-toxin combinations.

Did you get all of that? For decades, they have had the capability of combining genetically modified human toxins and bacteria that are untraceable. Imagine the possibilities today. During the channeling sessions, the spirits said that the biological weapon they are creating in the underground base in Hawthorne is a modified form of anthrax that is to be delivered in an aerosol form and that it will look like the victims died of natural causes. As you can see, this is entirely possible!

Just a thought here, if people died immediately after exposure to this BW, as they did in the Sverdlovsk anthrax leak, it wouldn't look like natural causes, would it? It isn't supposed to be immediately lethal. Maybe that's why our children aren't dying from exposure to what they are making now, but are being crippled by it, causing what they're mislabeling as autism.

Also in Ken Alibek's book *Biohazard*, in the biography section it says "Since he defected to the United States in 1992, (Alibek) has briefed the U.S. military intelligence and he is now working in biodefense." Are you following the time line? The man who weaponized and genetically modified anthrax for the Soviet Union defected to the U.S. with our government's assistance in 1992, and briefed our military intelligence. Then, according to the readings, the U.S. started creating a modified version of anthrax in a dust form in an underground facility in Hawthorne, NV in 1996. That is when the autism epidemic exploded in the United States. Still think it's a coincidence? Alibek's colleague, the late Vladimir Pasechnik, former Administrative head of Biopreparat in the Soviet Union and top weaponeer, defected to Britain in 1989. He worked at Porton Down, Britain's chemical and biological defense establishment until he died under mysterious circumstances. Britain has a comparable autism rate to the U.S.

In Ken Alibek's book he explains "The most effective way of contaminating humans is through the air we breathe, but this has always been difficult to achieve. Soviet scientists combined the knowledge gained from postwar biochemistry and genetic research with modern industrial techniques to develop what are called "aerosol" weapons – particles suspended in a mist, like the spray of an insecticide, or a fine dust, like talcum powder." He goes on to say, "Primitive aerosols lose their virulence and dissipate quickly. In our labs, we experimented with special additives to keep our agents from decaying when transported over long distances and to keep them alive in adverse weather conditions. These manipulated agents, more stable and more lethal, were our biological weapons."[11]

More Clues

After my book *Foundation of Discovery* was released in 2010, I found another incriminating book on biowarfare called *Germs Gone Wild: How the Unchecked Development of Domestic Biodefense Threatens America* by Kenneth King. On the book promo on his website, www.germsgone wild.com, Mr. King says that after the September 11, 2001 anthrax mailings, "The

---

[11]Alibek, Ken with Handelman, Stephen *Biohazard: The Chilling True Story of the Largest Covert Biological Weapons Program in the World- Told From Inside by the Man Who Ran It* (1999, Delta) pp. 20-21.

Government began funding a vast construction of risky new research labs specializing in potential bioterror agents. Many were located at American Universities. By 2007, there were at least 1,371 such labs, possibly hundreds more under the radar. No one in the Government was even responsible for keeping track. The new labs focus on scary diseases for which there is no cure or effective treatment. For diseases like anthrax, which kill if not treated promptly. Some researchers try to make existing germs more dangerous."

He goes on to say, "In 2007, a flurry of high profile accidents prompted a Congressional hearing and investigation by the Independent Government Accountability Office. The GAO experts revealed the startling proliferation which had occurred since 2001, testified that there is always a risk of accidents in such facilities, but said the labs were essentially regulating themselves. Just before the hearing, the Associated Press obtained secret documents with the details from over 100 lab accidents between 2003 and 2007. Most had been concealed from the public."[12] You can access the details of these accidents on the Germs Gone Wild website. Bioterror agents are even sent through the U.S. mail to these facilities, accounting for some of the "accidents."

What is especially troubling about this, according to Kenneth King, is that before the anthrax attacks in 2001, there were only 200 high containment germ facilities in the U.S., in 2007, there were nearly 1,400. Over 15,000 inexperienced people work with some of the most deadly pathogens on the planet with little to no oversight. Over $57 Billion has been spent on biodefense since 2001, originating from the 2001 anthrax attacks, which was created in our county's own biodefense complex. The Ames Strain, which was used in the mailings, was an anthrax strain originally created by the U.S. military at Ft. Detrick. Biodefense is an Academic-Military-Industrial complex. If you recall, they fall guy for the anthrax mailings "committed suicide." Makes you wonder, doesn't it? False flag ring a bell? Follow the money, I say. After reading all of this, the scenario described in the readings doesn't sound so crazy now, does it? Biological weapons could very well be a piece of the autism puzzle.

In addition to my biowarfare research, I also researched underground military bases. I had never heard of such a thing. The most credible witness

---

[12] www.germsgonewild.com

by far was the late Phil Schneider. Late, as in murdered for talking about what was going on in them. He was a former government geologist and structural engineer with 17 years experience working in government "Black Projects" who helped build the underground military bases. He called them D.U.M.B. bases, or Deep Underground Military Bases. He co-invented methods used in shaped charge explosives to facilitate underground bases and submarine bases. He worked at Area 51, S-4, and Los Alamos with a high-level security clearance. He quit his job in 1995 and broke his military security oaths to expose what the U.S. Government was hiding on a lecture tour. You can see these lectures on YouTube. They are very sobering and scary.

Phil Schneider claimed that in 1995, there were 131 underground bases in the U.S., 129 of them fully operational, and 1200 of them worldwide. They are an average of a mile deep and are about the size of a medium sized city. He claimed that 28% of the Gross National Product of the U.S. was spent building them, financed through the "Black Budget", hidden from Congressional view and oversight, and can't be audited by the U.S. Treasury System. It is totally illegal. He also claimed that he helped build the tunnels for the magnetic levitation train system that connects the underground bases, and reached speeds up to mach two. He said that the bases were used by different military organizations; the Army, Navy and Air Force. Half were used as research and development labs and the other half, he claimed, housed aliens. Creepy, I know. He also talked about the ventilation systems in the underground bases which are sometimes visible outside the mountain that they are built beneath. This piqued my interest because in the channeling sessions for my book, it was mentioned that the biowarfare "dust" they were creating in the underground base in Hawthorne, NV was getting out and into the air and blowing around.

Part of what the government was covering up was, as he put it, the "alien agenda." Phil Schneider was one of only 3 survivors of the infamous alien/human war at the Dulce, NM underground base where 66 government agents and workers lost their lives in August, 1979. He was missing 3 fingers on his left hand from this encounter, clearly visible in his videos. Thirteen attempts were made on his life during his lecture tour. In his final lecture, in November, 1995, that his soon to be released book would contain the latitude and longitude for each of the 131 underground bases. Two months later, in January 1996, he was found dead in his apartment, strangled by some type of cord. It was called a "suicide." Keep in mind this was a guy who was missing three fingers, had limited shoulder mobility and dying of cancer. He had told friends that if he ever "committed suicide" they would know that he had been murdered. According to his ex-wife, all of his lecture materials, photographs, alien metals, and notes for his book were missing, while things of value remained. His death was never investigated and his blood and urine samples from the autopsy went "missing." A lot of the websites about him have been shut down.

Another credible person on this topic is Richard Sauder. He wrote numerous books about underground and underwater bases and tunnels. He has lots of Public Domain documents such as patents and military contracts supporting his claims, many of which match Phil Schneider's accounts. There is plenty of hard evidence showing that these bases exist.

In addition, former CIA pilot John Lear claimed that there is an underground U.S. Navy submarine base at the Hawthorne Army Depot. He says that there are deep underground tunnels that lead to and from the Pacific Ocean from the base. There is a sign on the main road there that says "Naval Undersea Warfare Center." I've seen it myself. In the middle of the desert, mind you. He seemed like another credible former government employee exposing what they're hiding. I've seen John Lear interviewed on the TV programs *UFO Hunters and Decoded* exposing other government secrets such as Area 51. He had a lot of incriminating evidence to share.

As if all of this wasn't enough to convince me, I also met a retired former high-ranking government employee for the state of NV who told me that he had been in the underground facility in Hawthorne when he worked for the government. It was totally random, I met him at a social gathering, making small talk, and asked him where his favorite vacation spot was and he said "Hawthorne" because he went there a lot as a child and then proceeded to tell me this story. When I asked him if by "underground" he meant the bunkers or the underground city, he specified that he was taken on a tour of the underground city.

In addition, I have a friend who has a child with autism who told me that she was at a social get-together with some military friends who worked at the base in Hawthorne. One of the guys told my friend that his wife had recently worked there and had to wear a biohazard suit and had to be hosed off with water before she left. This description matched that of the protective suits described in the channeling sessions. Although I hadn't been in the facility personally, I had heard more than one anecdotal story of its existence. Another person I know randomly told me that her son trained at Hawthorne before he went over to fight in the Middle East, and said that he told her that they were using anthrax over there. Still another friend whose husband did a few tours in Iraq and Afghanistan also trained in Hawthorne, and acknowledged to his wife that underground military bases are everywhere. I believed them.

After my appearance on Coast to Coast, I received a contact via my website from a gentleman which said "I work at the Hawthorne Army Ammunition Plant and have for the last forty years. You have only scratched the surface on what goes on there. The truth would scare the hell out of you." George Knapp, who interviewed me, is also a reporter in Las Vegas, and told me that he investigated bioweapons at Hawthorne after 9/11 and found a huge stash of anthrax and other bad stuff that was carted off to Tooele, Utah for incineration. He and his photographer were taken into custody by military security for investigating. So, here was another person validating that there was anthrax in Hawthorne.

In addition to all of this research, I had to try to prove this theory medically by testing my son somehow. I couldn't exactly take him to a Western Medicine doctor and ask them to test him for exposure to biowarfare, now could I? Ha! Of course not! To my knowledge, no such test even exists. So, to make another long story short, I tested him with energetic forms of testing that check for the resonance of energy signatures in the body. One type is called Quantum Biofeedback, a computer program, and the other is called BioSET, which uses muscle response testing, or applied kinesiology as the testing modality and vials containing the energetic signatures of pathogens and toxins. During BioSET, the body is then cleared of the pathogens and toxins using acupressure or acupuncture afterwards. Our practitioner also transferred the energy signatures into a homeopathic remedy to continue the detoxification afterwards.

Trevor tested positive for exposure to dozens of bacteria and viruses, many that were on the list of Pathogens and Toxins with Biological Weapons Potential including *Bacillus anthracis* (anthrax), *Clostridium botulinum* (botulism), *Clostridium perfringens* (a foodborne pathogen), *Rickettsia prowasecki* (causes Typhus), *Rickettsia rickettsii* (Rocky Mountain spotted fever),

Dengue fever virus (Break-bone fever), *Lassa fever virus* (a hemorrhagic fever virus), *Monkeypox virus, Smallpox virus,* and aflatoxins (fungal mycotoxins). This was the tip of the iceberg. He also tested positive for *Borellia burgdorferi (causes Lyme disease)* many mycoplasma varieties, as well as the SV-40 Simian virus from the polio vaccine.

I even drove to Hawthorne and got a local topsoil sample to test with, using my dog as a decoy, pretending to pick up dog poop in a bag and grabbing the dirt instead. My son showed a weakness to it during muscle response testing (As did some of my friends' children with autism). He became very upset and was even hitting his head during this clearing session from the dirt. We cleared him of the aforementioned pathogens as well as numerous others using acupressure and homeopathy, and he improved dramatically afterward.

In spite of all of these validations, something else happened during these sessions with the medium that was driving me to find a way to finish what was started. The Wiry One instructed us to get a chalk board, and during a few of the sessions, he used the medium in a physical way by manipulating her arm to write on the chalkboard. If I hadn't seen it with my own eyes, I probably would think that this sounded far-fetched myself. He said that he was going to lay down the formula for the cure for autism. Playing devil's advocate, could this have been her making this up and I was just gullible enough to believe it? Perhaps. But what if it were true? What if this was leading me toward something that could ultimately help heal the world of autism? Or at least a certain subset of people with "autism," like my son. I couldn't just let this go unfinished.

***

Introduction

"For an idea that does not at first seem insane, there is no hope."

— Albert Einstein

Where do I begin? Before I just cut to the chase, I will give you a brief background on myself. I had a very normal Midwestern upbringing. I was one of five children in a middle class Catholic family from Wisconsin. I was a normal kid, and was not raised by a band of gypsies or hippies. I was a shy kid and a bit of a prankster and believe it or not, was considered the funny one in the family. My friends would describe me as the cute, tomboy jock. I excelled in competitive gymnastics, my favorite sport, which I also taught to children for years. I was a bit of a goody-goody, and always followed the rules. I love rock music; heavy metal, hairbands, alternative, all of it. I am afraid of clowns and spiders. I enjoy crude, juvenile humor. I am a college graduate with a BA degree in Speech Communications. As a child, my biggest aspiration in life was to get married and be a mom. Given the subject matter of this book, I feel it's important to show that I am a very relatable person, not a freak show. And I like to talk to dead people, big deal. You'll see why shortly.

Currently, I am the proud mother of two beautiful boys. My older son, Trevor, born in 1998, was diagnosed with autism at the age of three. I am talking specifically about regressive autism. The not born with it variety. This is not exactly the path I thought I'd be on when aspiring to be a mom, but most of my life has not exactly gone according to plan. Trevor wasn't born with autism; he became autistic, if that's what you want to call it. There are different kinds of autism, but a lot of people with similar symptoms get lumped into the category of autism without knowing what is causing those symptoms. The kind of autism I am talking about is regressive autism, where a child was born healthy, and then something changed. Sick children, not neurodiverse people who are also labeled with autism. Hundreds of thousands of parents report the same story of regression.

The new autism statistics came out in April, 2012, just as I was finishing this book. The new statistics according to the U.S. Centers for

Disease Control are that 1 in 88 U.S. children has autism, which is up 78% from 2002. Boys have it 5 times more than girls. Autism in boys is 1 in 54, an increase of 82% from 2002. Autism in girls is 1 in 252, an increase of 63% from 2002. Now, keep in mind that these conservative figures are for 12-year-olds from 2008, like my son, who are at the beginning of the autism tsunami. These rates are going to go up in coming years. An estimated 1 million children has autism. The autism rate doubled in the last five years. Autism costs U.S. taxpayers $137 billion dollars a year, which is only going to increase.

It is not just my opinion that my son was healthy and then regressed, or the delusions of multitudes of parents who are in denial of their child's condition. Research is finally catching up to parents' intuition. Most recently, at the Autism One/Generation Rescue conference in 2012 that I attended just before publishing this book, Keynote Speaker Dr. Luc Montagnier, co-discoverer of the HIV virus, and the 2008 Nobel Laureate in Medicine stressed how autism has its roots in infections. He presented data on ill children recovering health and lost skills after treating the bacteria, viruses and heavy metals that were causing the symptoms and behaviors. He uses antibiotics in his practice, which have other side effects. However, it was great to see a highly respected scientist validating what many parents already knew, that regressive autism is a disease.

In another recent study announced in September, 2011 called the Autism Phenome Project, UC Davis's MIND Institute identified for the first time two biologically different subtypes of autistic brain development. One group – all boys – had enlarged brains and regressed into autism after 18 months of age; another group had immune systems that were not functioning properly. They compared this major breakthrough to the discovery of different forms of cancer in the 1960's. This study is validation for many parents who already knew this. Their child does not have classic autism, or what any adult with "autism" has. This is different. This is not genetic; their child wasn't born this way, the acquired this condition.

Another new study that threw a monkey wrench in the decades-long "autism is a genetic disorder" fallacy, based on outdated 20-year-old data was the California Autism Twin Study (CATS) which reported its findings in July, 2011. It was the largest and most rigorous twin study ever conducted and proved that the majority of autism cases stem from shared environmental causes, and is not 90% genetic as the old data suggested. The twin study found that the concordance rate (both twins have autism) among fraternal twins is considerably higher than previously reported (about 35%). All statistical models demonstrated that both genetic and shared environmental components are significant with regard to ASD, an estimated 38% for genetic heritability and 58% for the shared environment. Roughly 60% of the cause of autism is environmental? But what are these environmental causes? This was a groundbreaking study again validating what many parents already knew. Their child wasn't born this way. So what happened to their bright, happy, healthy children?

Down syndrome, Fragile X, Angelman syndrome and other disorders have a testable genetic link, are evidenced from birth, and their rates have remained stable over the past 50 years. In contrast, autism rates have increased rapidly across the world, affecting childhood populations in similar numbers to past medical epidemics of a pathogenic origin, such as the Bubonic plague. There is also congenital autism, or infantile autism, where there was a problem with the child evidenced from birth. This is your classic autism, or Kanner's autism. In the literature from the 1940's, 50's and 60's describing Dr. Kanner's autism, these children were not affectionate, (children with regressive autism are), they did not have fine or gross motor skill abnormalities (children with regressive autism do), nor did they have seizures (40% of children with regressive autism do). Again, regressive autism is not the same thing and needs a new name, quite frankly.

Many people who pick up this book are going to think that this story is fictional because of the skepticism surrounding mediumship. I assure you it's not, it is 100% true. Any parent of a child with regressive autism will back me up on this; my time is too precious to waste making up fictional stories. Every wasted moment takes away from my child's recovery. This book is about the bigger picture. The channeled information in this book was not given just to help my child; it was given to help all children with regressive autism. It's about using all possible resources to change the future for these children and to prevent what happened to them from happening to the next generation. Desperate times call for desperate measures, and it appears that we need some guidance. Our brightest minds can't seem to figure this out, thanks in part to the pharmaceutical cartel and our government. Did I say that out loud?

I understand how unbelievable the information contained in this book is going to seem to the average person. Trust me, I know where many of you are coming from, I was raised Catholic; remember? Talking to the dead to get information to help solve the autism puzzle? Skeptics are going have a field day with this! Before you judge, just remember that we don't see things as they are; we see things as WE are. We all have a lens that we see the world through, based on our life experiences. If you haven't had any experience with talking to dead people, you will probably ridicule it.

There are many factors involved in a person being open to the subject matter of talking to dead people. First, you must believe in life after death. Second, you must believe in the ability to communicate with the dead. Third, you must trust the information transmitted by the spirits. Religious beliefs are also a huge factor here. Despite all of these hurdles, I do believe and trust, with good reason, or I wouldn't be staking my reputation on this. My motive in sharing my story is to do my part to help children with regressive autism and their families. If this material has the potential to help solve the autism puzzle, I am willing to deal with the scrutiny and ridicule that comes with the territory. It would be extremely selfish to keep this to myself, but I didn't, so behave.

Until you have had personal experience with something, human nature causes you to be skeptical of unfamiliar things. But for the sake of the future of children with regressive autism, I challenge you to let go of your preconceptions and with an open mind and heart, listen to another viewpoint that may contradict your own. Perhaps for now, you will have to live vicariously through my experiences. For those of you who have a child with regressive autism that said you would leave no stone unturned to help your child, here is a new stone for you.

Over the years, I have seen many theories about the cause or causes of autism come and go, with no conclusive answers. I have attended the biggest autism conferences in the country and listened to the leaders in the field on what the latest scientific research shows. From what I've seen, it is pretty much the blind leading the blind, but I believe some of them are on the right track. I hope that this information can be an adjunct to true science. I am not a doctor or a scientist. I'm a mom, trying to help my son. Although this mom's methodology may seem a bit unorthodox, there is much to learn here. Science and spirituality are two sides of the same coin.

I would like to propose a theory based on these sessions, that in many, dare I say, most cases, **regressive autism is a disease**, and not a developmental disorder, as it is currently categorized. Because it is a disease process, it can potentially be cured. Again, I'm not talking about adults with autism. This is a modern disease. I'm not talking about children born with other problems, and mislabeled with autism. I'm specifically talking about children born in the 1990's and later, who were born normal, healthy children and then regressed and were subsequently also mislabeled with autism. There needs to be a different diagnosis for these children. It's not autism. This can only be explained by a disease process.

The current paradigm needs to change in order for these children to recover. My intention is to share my incredible story along with the science to support my theory in order to stop this tragedy. This story contains new information which will hopefully encourage unbiased independent scientists, if there are any left, to take action to prove or disprove my hypothesis about the causes of regressive autism, which will be revealed throughout the story. Each chapter adds more pieces of the puzzle, both causative and curative.

I am going to begin by giving a crash course in mediumship, then explain a few things about my personal interest in the topic, and finally get into specifics of this book and how it all came to be before we dive into the story. Here we go...

Mediumship

Much of the information contained in this book is "channeled" by a medium and a spirit artist. For those of you who are still evolving spiritually, you may be asking, what does "channeled" mean, what is a medium, and what the heck is a spirit artist? A medium, or psychic medium as they are often called, is a living person who can receive messages from a dead person (spirit). These messages come to the medium in the form of any or all of the following: "Clairvoyance" (clear seeing), "Clairaudience" (clear hearing), "Clairsentience" (clear sensing) or even physical mediumship, where the spirit actually enters the physical body of the medium and uses the medium's body in a physical way. When a medium receives messages from a spirit, that information is considered "channeled." Channeling is the process in which the medium receives messages from a spirit. A spirit artist is also a medium and gets information from spirits, but instead of verbally transmitting the messages as a traditional medium does, they draw pictures based on the messages they receive from the spirits.

I often call the spiritual dimension "The Other Side," hence the name of this book, *The Other Side of Autism*. Get it? Others call it heaven. Whatever you call it, it is merely another state of consciousness, where the eternal part of us comes from before we incarnate into a physical body and where it returns to after the physical body dies. When a medium channels, they connect to a stream of consciousness in this dimension.

I like to think of a medium as a psychic interpreter. They understand the language the spirit is speaking and can translate it back to the person on the other end of the conversation who doesn't speak the language. It is a telepathic exchange with the spirit and a verbal exchange with the living person. The medium can ask questions for the living person and receive the answer from the dead person. The medium is usually in an altered state of consciousness while channeling. However, they may also receive messages from spirit when they are not "on", for instance, during a meditative or dream state. Often information is "downloaded" to them, and they just have a knowing about something without understanding why or where it came from.

Michael Parry, the medium who is channeling the information for this book is a conscious medium, as opposed to a trance medium; meaning he is conscious during the telepathic communication and not in a trance state, as some mediums are. He is able to converse with both the living and the dead at the same time, and often many spirits at once.

It is a pretty simple process to understand, but until you've had a good, valid reading in which your own dead loved ones tell you things that the medium couldn't possibly know, it is easy to be skeptical of this process. I know because I used to be a skeptic. Once you have however, you are changed forever. I learned firsthand that mediumship is a legiti-mate service to bring solace to the bereaved, not a purposeless pastime for naïve believers.

Typically, when you have a session or a reading as they are sometimes called with a medium, you are somehow connected to the spirits that come through to talk to you during the session, and can often instantly validate their messages. They are generally relatives or friends that you shared life experiences with, and the messages are often things that couldn't be investigated, as I will later demonstrate.

The sheer odds of a good medium getting the names, dates and places correct that are associated with you and the dead people should be enough to convince even the biggest skeptic that there is something beyond guessing or detective work at play here. During a session with a medium, there are usually lots of tears shed, but above all, profound healing occurs.

Personal Interest

Why am I so interested in mediums and channeling, you ask? I am an intelligent, completely sane person who happened to have some devastating life experiences a bit earlier than most people do. In 1995, I was forced down the spiritual path after the sudden death of my first husband, Darren. Again, not exactly the path I thought I'd be on, being widowed at the age of 27. After his death, I was on the fast track to find the answers about life after death.

Understand that this was in the mid to late 90's, before all the popular TV shows were out on the subject. As I mentioned, Catholic girls from Wisconsin didn't talk to dead people. This was unchartered territory that I was catapulted into. When Darren unexpectedly died, I desperately needed to know for certain that we don't just cease to exist when we die. Moving to California and questioning my religious upbringing were also part of shifting my perspective.

So, years after Darren's death, as part of my grief process, I investigated mediumship. If people claimed that they could talk to dead people, I wanted in. I was also fully prepared to prove it as a sham. I was stubborn and skeptical and needed a lot of convincing, so I began by reading every book I could find on the subject and then decided I needed to have a personal experience to truly believe that communicating with the dead was possible. Not someone else's story, my story, my deceased loved ones.

I spent lots of money on numerous sessions with lots of different mediums to prove to myself that they weren't all in cahoots trying to pull a fast one on me. I was still in shock over Santa Claus, the Easter Bunny and the Tooth Fairy. Finding out that angels weren't real and that we became worm food when we died would have been too much to handle in my fragile state. Too bad I didn't know then how expensive having a child with autism was going to be, or I would have saved some of the money. I shudder to think of how many hours of therapy I could have purchased for my son instead of myself, but I digress. I suppose I did get my money's worth because it has come full circle and I have learned invaluable life lessons, and can hopefully help others through my experiences.

NEWSFLASH! There is no death! That's right, I said it. We don't die! We merely enter another dimension, another plane of existence after our physical bodies stop working. How do I know this for certain? Because I have had countless readings with more mediums than I'd like to admit over the past 16 years who were all able to connect with my late husband and other loved ones in the spirit world and told me things that only the dead people and I knew, and made predictions that later came true. So there! There is no other explanation, believe me, I have thought of all of them. They were talking to my dead loved ones. For a complete stranger to come up with obscure facts that could only have come from the person in spirit left me no options but to believe. Trust me; I didn't just jump on the paranormal bandwagon right away. It was a long, epic battle to convert me from a skeptic to a believer. Now I am a huge proponent.

So, as you can see, I have a little bit different perspective on life and death because of my frame of reference and experiences. While most of you partied in your 20's and 30's, I was investigating spiritual topics and talking to dead people. Ok, I partied a bit too; my friends have the blackmail pictures. And by party, I mean drink alcohol; I have never done drugs, in case you're thinking that I have to be "on something" to believe in this stuff. I'm the girl next door, except I enjoy talking to dead people, what's weird about that? I find them to be more enlightened, supportive and interesting than the living in many cases, and it beats therapy for healing grief any day. Knowing we don't die changes the way you live.

Trevor

On with the rest of the story. Let's fast forward a few years. I was living in Southern California, happily married to my second husband Matt, and in 1998 we were blessed with our first son, a blond-haired, blue-eyed beauty whom we named Trevor. I would have laid down my own life for him in a heartbeat. He scored a perfect 10 on his Apgar score at birth, meaning he was in the best possible condition. He was born 10 days late, by natural childbirth, and was a healthy 7 lbs., 11 oz., and 21 inches long.

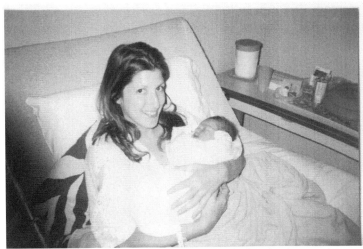

July 14, 1998, Trevor and I in the hospital, the day he was born.

Some of the "red flags" for autism include: by 6 months – no big smiles or other warm, joyful expressions; by 9 months – no back and forth sharing of sounds or other facial expressions; by 12 months – lack of response to name, no babbling or baby talk, no back and forth gestures such as pointing, sharing, showing, reaching or waving; by 16 months – no spoken words.

In Trevor's baby book, I kept track of everything. Here are his milestones: I first smiled – 1 month old, laughed – 3 months old, grasped a toy – 3 months old, slept through the night – 6 weeks old, then stopped when you ate solids, held my head up – 2 months old, rolled over – 3½ months old, sat up – 6 months old, crawled – 6½ months old, stood up- 7½ months old, walked – 9½ months old, my first tooth – 5½ months old, my first word – dada, just under 9 months old. In the notes, I wrote that the doctor said he was doing 12 month old skills at 8 months, and that he was very advanced, physically very strong and agile. I also wrote that at 9 months he said "lalala" "mamama" and "dadada" but first understood and said "dada." On his 9 month page, it says that he says mama and dada, waves bye-bye, and understands the words no, outside, bye-bye, mommy, daddy, grandma, grandpa, doggy, Elmo, Barney, bottle, cheerios, goldfish, hungry, bath, and home. On his first birthday page under "sayings," it says, mama, dada, dog, car, what's that? (while pointing). He was clearly doing all of the things that are considered "red flags" for autism if a child isn't doing them.

Trevor was developmentally ahead of schedule; he walked and talked when he was just nine months old. I have home videos of him between 6 months and 12 months playing peek-a-boo with me with his blanket, dancing in his toy car and laughing at our dog, pointing to an airplane in the sky when asked "Trevor, where is the airplane?," blowing kisses, looking at the camera when his name was called, tackling a stuffed Barney wearing his #4 Brett Farve Green Bay Packers jersey, playing with toys, laughing hysterically at his dad, shaking his head "no" when I ask him for a kiss, repeating sounds and facial expressions, laughing and smiling as I tossed him in the air and spun him in circles, babbling and making baby talk, showing advanced large and small motor skill mastery, and interacting with numerous family members. He was a chubby, happy, healthy, delightful baby.

The thing that stands out the most in our home videos when Trevor was a baby is how happy we all were back then. We were always laughing. He couldn't have been more loved. He was doted upon by his parents, his live-in grandma/nanny, my brother, Matt's parents and two brothers. He was the light of our lives. We all laughed and played with Trevor every waking moment. Refrigerator Mom? Bite me, Bettelheim.

Going back and reading my pregnancy journal, it was evident how much in love Matt and I were. I gushed about how much in love I was and how happy I was. Once Trevor was born, I felt like I grew a new heart, I loved him so much. I took so many pictures and videos of him in different outfits and locations. He was so perfect and beautiful. I felt as if my life was now complete. I could die happy. A picture is worth a thousand words, so here are some pictures of him as a baby before he became "autistic":

2 months old, so cute.

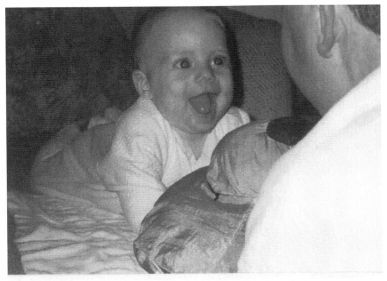

5 months old, smiling and laughing at dad.

6 months old, playing with Dakota. Parasites, anyone?

9 months old, crawling and laughing. He started walking this month.

11 months old, walking everywhere, a happy boy.

Trevor's first birthday present.

Then something changed. Between ages one and two, Trevor stopped looking at the camera when I was videotaping him. I jokingly said on the video that he was in an "Elmo trance" because he ignored me when I repeatedly called his name while he was watching "Elmo's World." He started walking on his tiptoes; he started lining up his toys and became upset when they didn't touch. He made elaborate patterns with his match-box cars. We thought it was so cute at the time, and bragged about how smart he was. His language seemed to stall. He lost skills he had previously mastered, like holding his silverware. On his first birthday, he fed himself his cake, on his second birthday, I fed him his cake and he ate with his hands.

Trevor's first birthday cake, using his own fork.

Lining up his toys, everything touching and matching, age two.

Matchbox car obsession.

More matchbox cars lined up.

Trevor began pulling people to get them to get what he wanted instead of talking. We said he was just spoiled and called him "The Prince." He didn't show much interest in playing with other kids. In his baby book, on his second birthday page under "sayings," it says "Not much – you do everything you can not to talk, like opening the refrigerator yourself or tagging someone until they follow you." Does this sound like a child born with autism? No, because he wasn't born with it, he regressed and acquired it. Between ages one and two, he regressed.

It was easy to reason away his oddities at the time and as a first time mom, I wasn't overly concerned. When I asked neighbors and friends about his delay in language they'd give me an example of someone they knew who didn't talk until they were three and were perfectly fine, or I'd hear the old "boys talk later than girls" explanation. He was spoiled, he was a boy, early walker, late talker; blah, blah, blah. These well-meaning pacifiers only satisfied my worries temporarily.

At the time, I was a very compliant mom who wanted to do the best for her children, and protect them from harm. So I did what I was told by his pediatrician, like any responsible mom would, and followed the recommended vaccine schedule; even though my husband's family practiced Christian Science and didn't believe in vaccinating for religious reasons. To them, I was the Anti-Christ. Just kidding...sort of... I am quite sarcastic at times. I paid to ensure that he was healthy and naively held him down myself as he received vaccination after vaccination, believing that the "medical experts," the doctors, knew best. My instincts questioned it, but I followed the rules. If only I had done the research myself, he would not have had his childhood stolen.

As a baby, he used to eat anything we gave him, and then between one and two he started limiting what he would eat to mainly wheat and dairy products. He always wanted to drink a bottle, and didn't give it up until he was three. He was very difficult to get to sleep, and woke up a lot during the night. We had to drive him around in the car to take a nap. I cringe now when I see what he was eating and drinking, but I'll address that later.

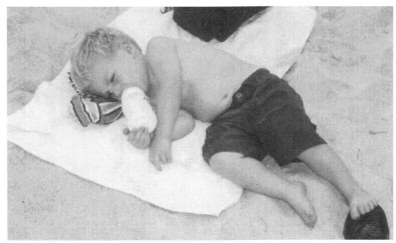

Two years old, bottle on the beach in North Carolina, visiting my dad.

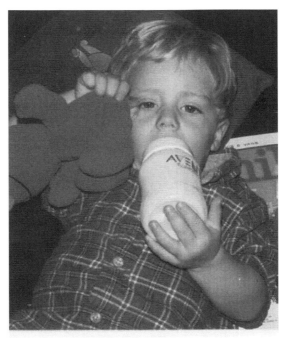

Rubbing Elmo's tag on his eye.

In the "Elmo trance," eating macaroni and cheese (ugh!),
and not looking at the camera.

The wrapping paper was more fun to him than the toys.

Lining everything up in the bathroom too. I cringe now at all the chemicals in those products.

Shortly after Trevor's diagnosis, Damon is two months old. Trevor is rubbing a plastic ribbon Christmas ornament on his mouth, and not looking at the camera.

Trevor became very sensitive to everything around him. He didn't like certain clothes, and we had to cut all of the tags off of them or he'd whine. He didn't like to walk on grass with bare feet. He covered his ears a lot when there were loud sounds. He smelled things, and rubbed things on his lips. He always had to have a toy or two in his hands, or other objects. He looked at things really close to his eyes, and often closed one eye and looked at things moving by his eyes. He made "hand puppets" with his fingers and looked at his hand out of the corner of his eye. He would get anxious and "freak out" for no apparent reason. Pictures only tell part of the story because I have plenty of pictures of Trevor during this same time period where he looks happy and normal and you wouldn't know that anything was wrong. But here are some pictures showing some "autistic" behaviors:

Running through the sprinkler in our yard with his shoes on.

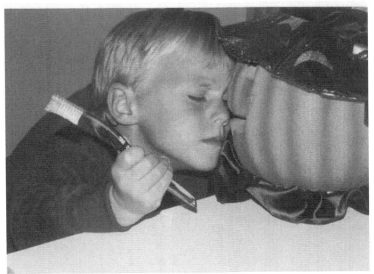

The pumpkin had lights that he was stimming on, and holding a toothbrush.

Covering his ears on dad's motorcycle. I don't blame him there.

Making his "hand puppets."

Anxiety "freak out" during photo.

At Sea World, visually stimming on his Shamu toy, 3 years old.

When Trevor was two, I became pregnant with our second son, Damon. But when Trevor regressed instead of progressed when we went to his three-year check up, his pediatrician was concerned and referred us to a developmental specialist. I was eight months pregnant, and on the infamous September 11, 2001, we had the appointment which led to Trevor's diagnosis of autism. My personal world also imploded and crumbled down around me on that fateful day. Damon was born a month later. Not only was I struggling with post-partum depression, I was also grief-stricken over Trevor's diagnosis that I did not accept, as well as post traumatic stress watching other young widows deal with losing their spouses on 9/11. It was a dark time for me.

I thought I knew everything there was to know about grief after surviving the loss of my first husband, I even wrote a book about it. Boy was I wrong. The pain of having a child diagnosed with autism is a chronic state of grief. It is grieving for the living dead. Aside from the typical stages of grief: shock, denial, bargaining, depression and acceptance, there are new emotions and phases mixed in as well. There is a lot of fear and worry that parents of children with autism face as well as blaming others or ourselves. There also hopeful phases when we see a therapy working well for our child. It is a total roller coaster of emotions. We all deal with grief differently. My husband and I certainly did, and

49

were never in the same phase at the same time. Many parents don't even acknowledge it as grief, and don't take care of themselves or their spouse.

During this time, I was also writing my first book called *Widowed Too Soon: A Young Widow's Journey through Grief, Healing, and Spiritual Transformation*. The book chronicled the grief process along with my experiences with various mediums and my own direct after-death communication from my late husband and others. Unlike most books about mediumship and grief, mine was from the perspective of the bereaved.

Our family moved from Southern California to Reno, NV when Trevor was three, and his little brother Damon was seven-months-old. Having a child diagnosed with autism is absolutely devastating to a family and a marriage, and mine was no exception. My husband I were both grieving and fighting about everything constantly. Two years after moving to Reno, Matt and I divorced (temporarily). Even though my mom lived with me and helped me with the boys, our split made things more difficult because, among other things, I had to go back to work. I got certified and started teaching Pilates, which was my sanity at the time, and published my book to try to earn extra money and help others at the same time. Mainly I was on a mission to fix my son.

***

Chapter One

The Beginning

After I published *Widowed Too Soon*, I began going to Psychic and Healing Arts Fairs to promote the book. It was a great place for me to be because I was learning about alternative healing modalities, energy healing, and finding products that were helping Trevor. I was hardly ever at my booth; I was desperately searching for ways to heal my baby. Often during the sessions I had with the various mediums at the fairs, they would bring up Trevor, and my loved ones in spirit would tell me he was going to be okay, gave me suggestions to help him, as well as let me know they were guiding me. What a great way to help him, I thought, ask the dead people!

On March 13, 2005, I was at one of these fairs in Santa Barbara, CA. This is where I met and had my first session with Michael Parry and Marti Baker (she later used her married name), a husband and wife team who combine the mediumistic abilities of Michael with the rare psychic artistry abilities of Marti. I had many sessions in the past with other mediums, but this was a new twist that I had to check out. I put my name on the waiting list and looked through Marti's impressive portfolio of portraits that she had drawn next to an actual picture of the person before they died that clients sent her later. There were also examples of her "doodle page" that she draws of smaller, significant pictures. Michael and Marti looked like a totally normal middle-aged couple, not like some of the eclectic individuals you meet at some of these fairs, wearing odd clothing and accessories, acting all mystical.

Before I get into the details of my session, I want to explain a few things about this process. First, I just met Michael and Marti for the first time on the spot, so they have no time to investigate me, as some skeptics believe is what happens before a session, and how they get their information. You can't rig a live event like this. Second, during the session, Marti put on headphones so she couldn't hear what was being discussed during the session with Michael. So, she was not eavesdropping and drawing who and what was coming through in the session with Michael. In fact, she often draws a completely different person than the spirit Michael is talking to. Third, understand that this work is very difficult because what the medium is seeing, hearing, feeling, smelling or tasting has to be described to the person, who is usually a complete stranger sitting in front of him. Often things get lost in translation. It doesn't mean he was "wrong", only that his interpretation was off. You will see examples of this during the sessions. He's still getting it; he just doesn't know what it means to the other person. That's part of this process, figuring out what the clues mean. Also, as I later learned, Michael often will pick up on something or someone in spirit and he asks the person questions about what he's getting in an effort to understand it. This doesn't mean he's "fishing" for information as some skeptics would have you believe; he's trying to understand and clarify the information he's getting from spirit.

That being said, I was nervous and excited as I sat down for my 30-minute session with Michael and Marti. I was separated from my husband Matt at the time, and was feeling very unsure of my future and what I was supposed to be doing and was hoping for some guidance. I also wanted to connect with my late husband Darren because the ten-year anniversary of his death had just passed and I was feeling a bit nostalgic about it.

(NOTE: I am going to try to condense the session as much as I can and summarize most of what came through, but I will highlight some of the "big moments" of Michael's channeled material verbatim in **Bold** print, what I said in regular print and the validations and my explanations afterward in parenthesis and *italics*. This will be the pattern for the rest of the book also.)

When Michael started talking to me, I immediately noticed his charming British accent. He took a few minutes to get "connected" by listening to some music on a headset. He needs to figure out who he is talking to first, so he begins a telepathic conversation with the spirit or spirits that show up for the person having the session before he begins. Michael had a piece of paper in front of him and began writing some things on it. He wrote down D, R, and N, three of the letters in my late husband's name (Darren) and also the number three. Marti had her headphones on and was doing her thing in the corner of the booth.

When Michael started my session, the first thing he came up with was that there was a younger man there that felt like a boyfriend and that he was showing him a ring. Then he said:

Michael: "I don't know if you were engaged or…"

Laura: "Married."

Michael: "Oh, you were married. Wow, blimey. Did he cross quickly? Because I felt like (snaps his fingers) and I'm gone."

(He died at the scene.)

He went on to say that he asked Darren if he did this to himself and he said "No" and that he told him that it was an accident. Michael started rubbing his neck and said that he felt a mess all up here. *(Darren died of head and neck trauma as a result of a car crash.)* Then he told me that the number three that he had written down was for how many years we were married *(we were together for eight years but married for almost three years)*, and shocked me with this next gem.

Michael: "Why is he holding a baby here? Did you lose a child?

Laura: "I have two kids, but lost one in between."

Michael: "He's got the child over there, that's what I thought."

I was on the verge of tears. He continued with more hits. He said that Darren was showing him a black or dark colored SUV. *(The car he was killed in was a dark purple SUV that looked black.)* He said that he wasn't alone in the accident; his best friend was with him. Michael got choked up with emotion as he explained to me how Darren was feeling. He then asked me if I was at the beach recently and thinking about him, and that he crossed around now and that I was feeling particularly sad. I told him I was just at the beach a few days ago *(I was visiting my brother in Southern California)* and that the ten-year anniversary of his death was the previous month. It was comforting to know that Darren was aware of that. Then he shocked me with this:

Michael: "Who is the light-haired person he's showing me? If I said Ricky or Richard would you understand that?"

Laura: "Yes, Ricky. That is an ex-boyfriend of mine who died."

Michael: "Did he have fair hair?

Laura: "Yes."

Michael: "I said, 'Who are you? I know you're there, I can see you.' And he said 'Ricky.' They're comparing notes."

Laura: "Oh yeah? Darren and I broke up a few times and I dated Ricky. Then Darren and I got back together and got married."

(Oops, I said Darren's name before he got it. For him to say "They're comparing notes" was amazing to me and made me laugh because there was a short time where I was dating both of them, and only I knew that fact. I guess they both knew it now.)

Michael: "Ok, well he's over there with Ricky. Did Ricky cross sudden also? Cuz I feel like (snaps fingers) and he's over there as well."

He continued talking to both of them and accurately described how Ricky died *(He was stabbed in the chest and died right away.)*. Then he said that they looked different and described what Darren looked like; saying he had heavier eyebrows than Ricky, that he had deep set eyes, high cheekbones and a very straight nose. All were true. He said that they both liked to impress people *(True)*. Then he asked me if I knew anyone gay who had crossed because they were showing him his brother, who is gay. Then he understood the reason they were showing him his brother was to get him to say his name, Darren. So, he misinterpreted why they were showing him his brother, thinking I knew someone gay in spirit, but instead, it was because they shared the same name. Next, he accurately described my Darren's accident:

Michael: "I don't know if he just lost control of the vehicle. I don't know if there is an intersection where this happened or a bend. But I'm feeling a bend and (he flips his hand over.) Understand? He told me he flipped, the car flipped so it was on its roof. Was it kind of on one side almost? I feel like the roof is smashed to one side."

Laura: "His side."

Michael: "So his end was down like this. He's showing me the roof. That's why his friend survived. Understand?"

Laura: "Yes."

(His friend was at the wheel and lost control of the vehicle and it flipped and landed on the roof on Darren's side, and there was a bend in the road.)

Then Darren told Michael that he was saying sorry to his friend, even though he was the one who died and said, "I had to go, I had to go." He told me that I was going round and round trying to figure it out and that some things are just beyond my control and when I got over there I would understand why. It had something to do with the past. He explained that sometimes you think something is a mistake, and actually you are playing something out. This karmic explanation was strangely comforting to me.

He continued with more validations; that they were on their way home when the accident happened after being out drinking and that Darren was 6 feet tall. Then he said something funny:

Michael: "Why is he showing me shoes? Was he buried?"

Laura: "Yes."

Michael: "I think this has something to do with the funeral. I have a whole time around the funeral. Like his shoes are on or something."

Laura: "Yes."

Michael: "He did, didn't he? Is that normal?"

Laura: (Laughing) "I don't know."

Michael: "He's insisting that he had on black shoes. He's showing me a pair of shiny black shoes. Are they like his best shoes or something? Who put them on him?"

Laura: (Almost in tears, laughing) "Me."

Michael: "He thinks he looked pretty hot when he went. Is he funny?"

Laura: "Yes."

Michael: (Laughing) "He's lifting his feet and showing me these shiny black shoes and I said, 'What's that got to do with?' And he showed me in the coffin. The things they bring up, you know?"

(He was dressed in a nice dress shirt I had bought him for Valentine's Day, but never got to give to him and was wearing shiny black shoes in the coffin.)

Next, he told me to say "hi" to his parents, mentioning that his dad was in denial, which was true. Then he mentioned my younger sister and said he wanted to rib her about her big hair. *(She had huge curly hair and we used to tease her and call her 'Brillo'.)* My time was almost up and he mentioned that I have been in an on/off relationship with a guy for a while. I explained that I was married for eight years and we just separated two weeks ago.

Marti showed me the picture she had drawn during the session and said that she felt that it was a Native American woman who was one of my relatives, and that now she is a guide of mine. She said she doesn't usually get guides. I told her that I am part Native American. Michael often intuitively knows what Marti's pictures are about, and often gets their name if she doesn't. They work together that way. He told me that this lady was definitely connected to me. Since my session was shorter than their usual hour sessions, I didn't get a doodle page this time, just this portrait:

I thanked them and told them how amazing the session was. I told them that I had recently written a book about grief, including sessions with other mediums and that I wished I would have met them before I published it because it was the best session I'd ever had. I felt like I was walking on air all day.

Now, for all of you skeptics out there, use your logic here. There is no possible way that Michael could have known that I was a young widow just by looking at me, or that he could accurately describe all of the things he did, including the physical descriptions and personalities of my late husband and ex-boyfriend. Odds are a young girl who looked to be in her 20's wouldn't be there to connect with her dead husband. Perhaps a grandparent would be dead at my age, not a husband and an ex-boyfriend.

Michael also accurately described the car accident Darren was in: the color and make of the vehicle, what exactly happened, the fact that his best friend was involved, that he died instantly, the bend in the road. You can't research stuff like that! The reason I knew was because I went to the scene of the accident and saw it, and his friend explained what happened to me. Only the dead person and I knew that information, not Michael. For him to be able to hone in on these details with absolute accuracy is astounding. Just to get the name "Ricky" correct is against all odds. I had a baby name book with 30,000 names in it. I'm no statistician, but come on now!

Also, I accidentally said Darren's name during the session, but Michael had written three letters of his name on his paper before he said a word to me. Darren is not a very common name. He was also shown his brother named Darren to get the name another way. Probably the biggest validation was the shiny black shoes in the coffin. Unless you were there, you couldn't possibly know that. Even if you were there, only the top part of the casket was open, so his feet were not even visible. And for Darren to say he looked hot in the coffin was totally his goofy sense of humor. I can't tell you who the woman in the portrait is that Marti drew, but I am part Native American, so for it to be a relative of mine is a validation in and of itself.

So, this is how my relationship with Michael and Marti began. I was just a client, impressed by their talents. I wanted to give this example to show what a typical session with them is like and what kind of information can come through. Over the next five years, I had four more sessions with them that were equally impressive, which I will share some highlights and pictures from as well.

Our Second Meeting

In September of 2005, six months after my first session with Michael

57

and Marti, they came to Reno, NV, where I live to do some private sessions at a metaphysical bookstore I frequented. When I learned that they were coming, I jumped at the chance to have another session with them. This time, it would be a full hour. I was so excited! Now, just to be clear, they have many sessions each month and don't remember the details from their past sessions unless it is something truly extraordinary. My first reading was pretty run-of-the-mill for them. The following is a summary of my second session with them and the incredible portrait and doodle page from Marti.

When I arrived, Michael mentioned that I looked familiar, and I told him that they did a session for me six months earlier. He listened to his music and connected, seeing who was there for me. When my session began, the first thing he said was that I had a husband in spirit that was here, a guy with dark hair that died in an accident. He also said that there was somebody with a skin condition, like eczema or arthritis with him, like a grandparent and then said it was my mom's mom. *(My maternal grandmother was in spirit and had Rheumatoid arthritis.)* He also said that there was another lady there who met him when he crossed over, as well as two other men; one was a friend of his, and another guy.

Michael knew that I had two children and an ex-husband, and said that my late husband, Darren loves my kids and wants to connect to them. He also mentioned that his hand was tingling and his neck hurt, validating Darren's neck injury in the accident. He told me that Darren said I was in great shape and knew I had been working out a lot lately. *(I was teaching Pilates and very fit.)* He also mentioned that I'd been using hand weights, small solid ones and that Darren said that he was watching me. *(I just taught a weight training class that morning, using small hand weights.)* He also said that I lifted stuff with my legs too, a leg press machine that you press in and out. I told him it was the Pilates reformer. Michael didn't know what that was, but that's what he was being shown.

He mentioned that I was going to be going on a trip to visit relatives soon, and I said yes, and that Darren's mom was one of them. *(I was driving from Reno to Wisconsin for my High School reunion and to visit friends and family the following month.)* Darren wanted me to say 'hello' to his mom from him and tell her he loves her.

Next, my grandmother jumped in again and said that she had a stroke, and that she made him feel a pain in his arm. *(She did have a stroke shortly before she died.)* She said that she is around a lot, and is very close to me. I told him that my mom, who is her daughter, lived with me. Then he said that Darren was going on talking about two houses. I told him that I was looking at buying a house and I was debating between two houses. He accurately described the layout of the one he thought I should get and mentioned that he wanted to thank my brother Joe for helping me out with the house. *(My brother Joe offered to help me pay the mortgage.)*

Next, he brought up my sister and said that she recently did something cool and said "Way to go, sis." She recently published her own book on prenatal exercise. He said that he liked my sister. It was nice to know that he was still aware of what was happening in my sibling's lives.

This next part was pretty interesting. He asked if there was someone named Stephen. I told him that Darren was adopted and that his birth name was Stephen. Michael said that Stephen was his brother's name, and he changed it to Darren. I mentioned that this came up in my last session six months ago. So, both his brother and my late husband were named Stephen at birth, and then had their names changed to Darren. Again it was a way to get him to say his name. Since I blurted it out the first time, he came up with a clever way to say it was him in a different way that I would understand.

He mentioned that I recently changed my diet, and that I had been juicing stuff, and was happy about that. Even though I was thin, I wasn't the healthiest eater at the time, but recently started juicing. Next, Darren said that he wanted me to find love again with someone else and that I was ready, and that he was going to shove some people my way. He told me that I was shy but that I'll know it when I feel that fluttering feeling.

He brought up my trip again and said that I was going East on a road trip, and brought up the 13th of the month at the end of the year. *(His mom's birthday is on November 13th.)* He said that it's important that she knows that he will be there on her birthday. *(His mom called me after her birthday and told me that she had a vivid dream visit from Darren on her birthday. I told her about what he said to me in this reading. She was very comforted.)*

The most incredible part of this session was the pictures Marti drew. First, when she showed me the portrait, I said that it looked like my maternal grandfather without his glasses. I always remembered him with dark glasses on. Michael told me that my grandfather just said to him "My name is Edward." *(My maternal grandfather's name is Edward.)* Michael suggested that he must have been one of the other fellows he saw earlier. Below is the portrait that Marti drew followed by an actual picture of my grandfather. Keep in mind that she's obviously never met the man or seen a picture of him.

Next to Marti's portrait is an actual picture of my maternal grand-father. Imagine him without the glasses. My mom recognized him instantly in Marti's picture, gasping and exclaiming "That's my dad!"

The doodle page is particularly interesting because at the time of the session, most of it made no sense to me. Here it is:

Doodle validations: I understood the school on the hill, because I was going on the trip to my High School reunion. Get it? A school on a hill? A **high** school. Marti explained that the umbrella had to do with me dating and that she heard the song *"It's Raining Men."* She said that the hula girl was symbolic of Hawaii, and the ring was a wedding ring and there was also a picture of a plate of sushi. I didn't like sushi; I had never been to Hawaii and had no plans of going there.

After the session, I dated a lot of guys before finding a steady boyfriend. Two years after this session, my old college roommate got married in Maui, Hawaii, and my boyfriend and I went to the wedding. He surprised me and proposed to me on the trip, and the ring looked very similar to the one in the picture. It was a band with diamonds going around the middle, and the ring manufacturer's name was inscribed inside the ring. He also introduced me to sushi, which I now like, and we even had some in Hawaii. After the trip, I dug out the doodle page and was stunned at the accuracy of Marti's pictures. My ex was a skeptic, but he was even shocked.

The engagement didn't last long; I called it off about six months later. I actually ended up getting back together with my ex-husband, Matt, and remarrying him. We called it "I do, Part Two." The point is that even though the pictures didn't make sense to me at the time of the session, they did later on. Two years later, I finally knew what the pictures meant. This is significant to the rest of the story. You don't always know what everything means during the session, but you have to trust that it is important or the spirits wouldn't be bringing it up. Or, you attach a different meaning to it at the time, and then later, something else happens that makes more sense.

More Sessions with Michael and Marti

I had two more sessions with Michael and Marti, a year apart, prior to the fateful session that started our book project. I am going to give a condensed version of these two sessions, because they aren't the focus of the book; but I do want to share a few highlights from them and show some of Marti's psychic artistry from the sessions.

Session One

The first of the two sessions was a year later, on October 6, 2006, and was held at the same metaphysical bookstore in Reno, NV. I was feeling very lost and sorry for myself because I was divorced, not finding anyone I really liked, and was doing three different jobs and not very happy. I wanted some guidance basically. This session was held two months before I met the guy that proposed to me in Hawaii.

The session felt more like a therapy session than anything. The first spirit to come through was my maternal grandmother. She named her daughter, Sally, my mom's sister, and accurately said that she had recently been in the hospital. My grandma also told Michael the names of my aunt's three sons and her husband by name at some point during the session. There was also a man that Michael felt was a grandfather who was there for my ex-husband at the time. The grandfather accurately told Michael my ex-husband's name, Matt, and his age, 33.

My grandma took center stage and talked about me having no direction and said that I was just drifting along. She said that I had a lot of gifts, I just wasn't using them. Michael asked me what I did. I told him that I did three things; taught Pilates, was a healer, and a writer. What followed was the cool part of the session:

Michael: "So you are a healer. I thought you were. Do you like working

with children?"

Laura: "Yes."

Michael: "Have you ever worked with children who have disabilities? They're showing me you doing this (uses his hands like he's doing hands-on-healing) and they say you're very good at it."

Laura: "My older son is a special needs child, that's why I got into healing."

Michael: "I think that's really where your calling lies. That's what they're telling me."

Laura: "What do I do with it? Children with autism are sick and can't handle our toxic world."

Michael: "Our world is very toxic. Whatever you know and whatever you feel you can do, you must do."

Laura: "I've been holding back those gifts because I'm alone."

Michael: "Your grandmother is saying you need to step up to the plate. You're a strong person and have a lot to offer. Don't make your love life your focus and you'll see what happens."

The rest of the session was kind of funny, talking about some of the guys I had dated over the past year. Michael was talking to me and getting psychic impressions at the same time. He knew some of the guy's names that I had dated, their professions, and even what they looked like. Marti chimed in too and they were both giving me dating advice. I sounded pretty pathetic, listening to it years later. At the end of the session my late husband and paternal grandfather made a brief appearance.

The doodle page was particularly interesting. Even though Matt and I were divorced at the time, the doodles were all about his family. When presenting me the doodle page, Michael said that his grandfather in spirit was named Louie or Louis and died a long time ago. (*Matt's maternal grandfather's name was Louis and he died when his mother was a child.*) I thought that the portrait might have been of him, but Matt's mom said it didn't look anything like him. Since I don't know who the man in the portrait is, I am only showing the doodle page, which I can validate. Maybe Louis sent Marti the impressions for the doodle page to show that he's still around and aware of what's happening.

At the time, I remember being upset that the pictures were for Matt, since we were divorced. I paid good money for the session, and the pictures were for my ex-husband, whom I was very angry with and barely spoke to. In hindsight, maybe he needed some convincing about all of this, since he was always a big skeptic, or they knew something I didn't since we got back together a few years later. Here is the Doodle Page:

Doodle validations: Matt's parents owed two VW Beetles, one original 1967 and a new one, they were big into tent camping, they are musicians and sing, and Matt, his dad and brother fly fish and wear fishing waders when they go. Marti felt that the prim and proper hand holding the tea was describing my mom, who has good manners, and that it was from her mom in spirit. This was true.

Session Two

The second session was held a year later on October 19, 2007 at a different bookstore in Reno, NV. The woman who owned it was a tarot card reader, whom I had a few sessions with at the fairs over the years, and she told me about her bookstore opening. I found out about Michael and Marti's upcoming appearance when I went in to check out her store and signed up for a session.

This session was really great for many reasons, so I am going to share a little bit more of it than the previous one. The first spirit to talk to Michael was my paternal grandfather. He validated that it was him by saying that he was my father's father, that he was there with his wife (*she was also in spirit*), that he committed suicide by shooting himself, and that he had come through before to say 'hi' to me. (*He did shoot himself and he came through briefly a year prior in my last session.*)

Darren came through next and gave Michael more details of his accident. They like to tell him new things each time evidently. Among the new details were that someone fell asleep at the wheel (*his friend Dave did, who was driving*), that the other guy survived, that Darren hit his head and was thrown from the vehicle, and that he didn't have his seatbelt on but his friend did. (*Dave told me the details of the accident and all of these things were correct. I was a bit fuzzy about if he was thrown from the vehicle, but this confirmed it for me.*)

Darren also brought up the names of two of my siblings and my brother's wife's name, and said to say 'hi' to them. He knew about my recent engagement, even though it didn't last, and described the guy down to the location of one of his tattoos. Then he brought through a few friends of mine who had crossed over. The first one was my old neighbor, Tony. Michael described the age and circumstances of his death. He said it was a quick crossing and that it wasn't his fault. I called my brother, who was his good friend, to find out the specifics of Tony's accident and he said that he was driving by himself and that his car went off the road and crashed. My brother always suspected that an animal or another car ran him off the road. For Michael to say that the accident wasn't his fault validated his theory.

The second one was the brother of my friend who got married in Hawaii. Michael said his name was Mike and that he was dressed in biker leathers, he was killed on his bike, and he had light brown hair and blue eyes and was about 6 feet tall, which were all true. Michael said to tell your friend that he showed up and said 'hi' to her, and to tell her I know she just got married, and that he was at the wedding. He also talked about her having a baby, and a few other personal things. (*Her wedding was a month earlier, and she does have a son now.*)

The next part was really heartwarming for me. Earlier in the session Michael asked me if Darren and I had one child together, and I said no. I was thinking a human child, but we did have a dog, a Siberian husky named Dakota, who was like our child. I had to have her put to sleep the year before because of declining health at age 14. I always wondered if Darren had her now and was watching over her. Here was the exchange:

Michael: "Did you just get a dog, a small one?

Laura: "Two years ago we got a Pug. Does he have our dog?"

Michael: "This is a bigger dog. He says 'Yes.' But it's a bigger dog. It's not like a Husky is it?"

Laura: "Yep."

Michael: "He says it's a Husky. I said 'She looks like a Husky. You've got her there?' He said, 'Sure do.' It's a nice dog. I love Huskies, they're my favorite dog. Well, this dog is here. It's not a demonstrative dog, but its tongue is out and it's right there next to you and it's nudging you. It just kind of leans against you, that's what it's doing. It's all alert. And it likes the Pug, that little dog you've got."

Laura: "They were both alive together for a little bit."

Michael: "It likes that dog; it says to say 'hi' to that dog." *(Dakota did like Yoda, the Pug.)*

This made me happy to know that my furry kid was with her daddy. I could actually feel her there next to me when he told me she was there. Kind of an energetic vibration is how I would describe it. It's nice to know that our pets survive death as well and that we will be with them again also. Think about this for a minute skeptics, how many dog breeds are there? Hundreds. So for him to get the breed right is pretty incredible. Siberian Huskies are not the most popular dog breed either.

Next, I asked about my son Trevor, the one with regressive autism, who was nine years old at the time. Here are some of the messages I received:

Michael: "Is he with it? Because they tell me that there is something wrong with his head. That's why I'm doing this." (He was rubbing his head.)

Laura: "He was diagnosed with autism. He was poisoned with mercury and other toxicities." *(That's what I thought at the time.)*

Michael: "Have you done detox with him?"

Laura: "Yes."

Michael: "What's he like now?"

Laura: "He's getting better all the time."

Michael: "He will improve. You are doing the right things. I feel a problem with his head, with his brain. Yeah, that's it. Like he has attention deficit, like he can't focus. It's not just mercury you know; it's all sorts of stuff."

Laura: "He's got a lot going on; Lyme disease…"

Michael: "Lyme disease? What's that?"

Laura: "Tick bite, a systemic bacterial infection. He had a fungal infection, all kinds of stuff."

Michael: "So you're looking after him, aren't you?"

Laura: "Yeah."

Michael: "Maybe that's why I thought you were a nurse." (At the beginning of the session, he asked me if I was a nurse, and I said no.)

Laura: "Yeah. And I do energy healing, so when you said nurse, I thought 'Well, I'm a healer.'"

Michael: "No, no, you are like a nurse. You are; that's what that was." (I have basically nursed him back to health over the years on my own.)

Just then, Marti showed me her Doodle Page. I will explain what the images mean after the pictures.

Doodle validations: Marti said that when she was drawing it she was confused if it was massage or hands-on-healing because of the hands by the fire. Michael asked if my hands got hot when I did healing. I told him that I used to do Reiki, and my hands got hot then, but when I started doing Reconnective Healing, it was done with the hands off the body and my hands sometimes felt cold. Michael told me he did healing work too. The business card picture also had to do with healing work; I started working at a new place and had to make new business cards. The golf club was for my late husband, who was an avid golfer. The shoes Marti felt were Vans, which my kids wore.

The portrait that she drew I instantly recognized as my paternal grand-father. The mouth was a bit off, but she said he had dark wavy hair, which he did. Michael, who was talking to him at the beginning of my session, said the portrait was him as a younger man. Here is Marti's portrait, next to my paternal grandfather at age 18:

Again, keep in mind that Marti had never met or seen a picture of him before; she was just seeing it in her mind basically and drawing a picture based on what she was seeing. This is pretty darn close. Her portfolio contains even more incredible similarities than mine, but I was in awe. And as far as the doodles go, would those things mean anything to you? No, because they were meant for and made perfect sense to me.

Marti's Spirit Artistry

Here are a few examples of some of Marti's other portraits. The first one is from a session they did where famous UFO abductee Betty Hill showed up and posed for Marti. There was a whole story that went along with that too, which is in Michael's blog, www.mysticmikemysticmike. blogspot.com. The following portraits are more examples of striking resemblances that she's drawn. Keep in mind that the people having the session sent her the actual picture of the person after the session. She just draws who is posing for her in spirit at the time of the session and she has no idea who it is many times. The validations come later.

Heritage Junction

I hope you are beginning to see how talented these two are and the possibilities that exist by connecting to those in spirit. There is nothing more valuable in healing grief than connecting to your loved ones after they have passed on. When they are able to share information that the medium couldn't possibly know, giving names, dates, and describing things that have happened after they've died leaves little room for skepticism. It is truly life affirming and life changing. Michael and Marti are not psychics who predict the future, it is the spirits who bring forth the messages, but as you can see, they often share future information as well as validations from the past. Now, let's get down to business, shall we?

***

Chapter Two

"Certainly there are things worth believing. I believe in the brotherhood of man and the uniqueness of the individual. But if you ask me to prove what I believe, I can't. You know them to be true but you could spend a whole lifetime without being able to prove them. The mind can proceed only so far upon what it knows and can prove. There comes a point where the mind takes a leap—call it intuition or what you will—and comes out upon a higher plane of knowledge, but can never prove how it got there. All great discoveries have involved such a leap."

— Albert Einstein (From "Death of a Genius" in Life Magazine)

A Prayer Answered

After I received the first of the two demand letters from the original medium's lawyer, something incredible happened. I had been desperately praying to find a way to finish the book somehow, either with a new medium, or I thought that perhaps the original medium would come to her senses and agree to finish it with me. After receiving the first demand letter, I knew the latter was out of the question. I just couldn't let this go, knowing what I knew. I was on to something here, I could feel it. They had more to tell me, so I had to find another way.

It was the beginning of October, 2010, and I received a phone call from the woman who owned the metaphysical bookstore where I had previous readings with Michael and Marti. The bookstore had closed, but she called to tell me that they were coming back to town and to contact them directly if I wanted to book a session with them. I hadn't had a reading with them in three years. It seemed so out of the blue and random, that I figured perhaps this was a sign that I needed to go, so I booked a session at the last minute.

On my way to the session, I said a prayer to the Universe, to whomever was listening, that if Michael said The Wiry One's real name during my session, in any way, shape or form, then I would ask him if he would be interested in finishing the book with me. It would be a definite sign. He didn't know that I made this request, so if by some miracle, The Wiry One's name came up, I would have my answer. It had never happened before, so why would it now? Because he was so good, I had thought about calling him and asking him to do it, but this would be the true test.

My session was on October 19, 2010, ironically three years to the day of my last session with them. A lot had transpired in my life in those three years. My father died of cancer, Matt and I got remarried, and of course all that transpired with *Foundation of Discovery*. My first session with the medium that channeled the information for *Foundation of Discovery* was a month after my last session with Michael and Marti in 2007. Three years of drama ensued and I was brought back to Michael and Marti. I will share the highlights from our incredible session.

This time, the session was held at a hotel just a few blocks away from where I worked at the time. After teaching my Pilates classes, I stopped by for my session before I had to pick my kids up from school. Imagine if I told my students, "Yeah, I'm going to talk to some dead people now, see you tomorrow." I was leading a double life. Anyway, I was very anxious going into our session, wondering if my secret wish would somehow come to fruition, and hoping that my late father would stop by talk to me. The grief was hitting me hard and I really missed him, as the second anniversary of his crossing was less than two weeks away.

I knocked on the door, and Marti answered, looking pretty and happy. Her long, platinum hair made her look extra ethereal that day. Michael came into the room, smiled at me and said hello in his familiar British accent. After some initial chit-chat and formalities, we began my session.

The first spirit out of the gate was my dad. He told Michael that he was my dad and that he died of cancer, which was true, followed by some personal validations that really let me know it was him. Then my late husband Darren's grandfather named Frank came through, and said that he was like a granddad to me. Frank then brought Darren through.

Michael said that he had a sudden crossing in a vehicle accident and that they had a good chat last time I came to see him, which they did.

Michael asked me if I had a nine-year-old. I said yes, and I told him that he just turned nine four days earlier. He said that both Darren and my dad wanted me to know that they were at the party on Saturday. His party was on Saturday. Both of my grandmothers were also there, along with Frank's wife, Helen, who Michael also named.

Next, he talked about some drama that was going on with our family living situation and gave me some insights on that. My dad took center stage again and told Michael that I said something to him before he died like "I'll see you again, or I'll see you later or something like that, and that he was grateful to you for that." I told Michael about the phone conversation I had with him the day before he died. He was living in North Carolina and I was in Nevada. He was a fear-based Catholic, who served in the U.S. Marine Corps as a "rifleman" and he was afraid that he was going to hell when he died. I instinctively knew this would be the last time I talked to him. I told him that when he died, he could still talk to me; I told him that I still talk to Darren, and both sets of grandparents, and I know people who could connect us, and that I was open to it. I told him he wasn't going to hell, and that I would talk to him soon. I told him not to be scared and that I loved him. He died the next day.

(This meant a lot to me because Michael could not have known about this conversation. I actually talked to my dad through another medium the very day he died. He couldn't talk and his friend called to tell us what was going on. I called my friend, Terri Jay, a local medium who can talk to people in comas and animals and people with autism, and we set up a session for later that night. I wanted to see what my dad wanted us to do since none of us lived near him. He died that afternoon, but we still did the session that night with my mom and brother included as well. My dad thanked me for what I said to him before he died, and said that it helped him let go. So, this was the second medium that gave me the same message from my dad.)

Darren came back into the conversation and Michael asked if I had any questions about my children. I told him yes, about my older son. *(The one with regressive autism.)* He said:

Michael: "Is he a pain?"

Laura: "Well, he has autism."

Michael: "I feel like he's difficult. Oh, he's difficult only because he's autistic. Well, there are different types of autism."

After talking about another child in spirit that would have come in if she could have and validating Darren's birth date, the 18th, Michael said the following:

Michael: "Was there a breathing issue with one of your kids when they were born? Does anyone suffer from an oxygen deficiency or is anyone on oxygen at the moment?"

Laura: "No."

Michael: "This is wild. I'm asking him (*Darren*) **about your son with autism…and he keeps telling me about this oxygen thing."**

Laura: "Well, one of the therapies for kids with autism is Hyperbaric Oxygen Therapy."

Michael: "Is it? I have no idea, I know nothing."

Laura: "That's what I thought he was talking about. Kids with autism often improve after doing Hyperbaric Oxygen Therapy."

Michael: "Well, he's telling me oxygen, pure oxygen. I said, 'To do with the autistic kid?' He said, 'Yeah.' Really?"

Laura: "That's what I thought you were getting at, but I didn't want to tell you."

Michael: "No, no, no. I don't know anything about autistic kids. You know the movie with the two brothers, *Rain Man?* Isn't he supposed to be autistic?"

Laura: "He's a savant. It's different."

Michael: "In my head, that's what I think of an autistic person."

Laura: "Well, this is another part of what I wanted to ask about."

I proceeded to tell Michael that I had written a book, and part of it was channeled by another medium that I was having legal issues with. I told him that the book was about autism and that the cause of what happened to my son and many other young children came through in the sessions. I told him that the medium quit halfway through and I had to put it out there by myself because the information was so critical. He asked me what we came up with as the cause, and I told him that it had to do with biological warfare. He said that he tended to think that it was a chemical thing too.

He asked me if a friend of mine had come to see them for a session yesterday, and I said yes. *(I referred a friend to go see them.)* Next, this unbelievable exchange happened:

Michael: "This is what I'm going to tell you. Listen now. Fluoride in water isolates the pineal gland. It forms a barrier around it, a deposit around it. That's your uplink to your higher self. When people don't have that, they get very angry and depressed. That's one thing that happens to people who drink a lot of fluoride in the water. The Nazis used it in war. Einstein's brother was a chemist, and wrote an entire...oh that's interesting here, because Einstein showed up in a session."

(I was almost in shock that he said "The Wiry One's" name.)

Laura: "He's the main author of my book."

Michael: "Yeah, well Einstein was here. Einstein was here for your friend. I don't know, he didn't tell me that *(about the book)*. I just told him that Einstein was in the room."

Laura: "When I came here, I said that if you brought up Einstein; and I had this condition..." *(I didn't get to finish my story here.)*

Michael: "Well, I did. I told him that Einstein was in the room, that he was the scientist that was present. This scientist showed up and I said 'You know, I've spoke to Einstein before.' I started talking about Einstein and said this guy is a scientist and he absolutely wants to talk to you, but you don't know him. He says something about he's famous, he's well known, and blah, blah, blah. Anyway, the thing is, Einstein's brother was a chemist and he did this whole thing just prior to the war and during the war about the use of fluoride by the Nazi's to subdue people and it makes you passive because you have no uplink. It shuts you down and makes you subservient, 'Oh, well, we'll all just go in the oven.' It makes you like that, like sheep. That's why fluoride is in the water."

Laura: "We don't drink tap water."

Michael: "I don't either. That's one thing. But there are dozens of things that they do. So there is this chemical stuff, and why a lot of these conditions happen. And on top of that, you have all of this nuclear dust all over Nevada, and that has impacts too. All of these things; yes, you're on the right track."

(I didn't know it at the time of the session, but Einstein didn't have a brother, but that

didn't matter, Michael said his name! Holy Crap! I also found out later that fluoride does affect your pineal gland according to an article I read by Dr. Joseph Mercola, so that part was accurate.)

I told Michael that my book wasn't finished and I wanted to ask spirit what I should do to finish it. He asked me why the other medium bailed, and asked if she had an ego problem. He hypothetically asked me how someone can be true to themselves when their ego is so big. Before I could answer him, Marti told me that on my friend's doodle page, she started drawing a formula, a square root of something and the number 24. I was stunned. I asked Michael if I should get someone else to finish the book with me, or what I should do. This was his reply:

Michael: "Here's what I'm going to say. I tell you what we'll do, ok? Because this is something that is so cool, I'll just do this with you. Just because we can. I'll do this stuff with you, no money involved; I'll just pursue this with you."

Laura: "Really?"

Michael: "Yeah, I will do that; I'll do that for you."

(Marti says "The only thing is… I'm getting that the world is not quite ready for this.")

Michael: "Don't think about money. We'll just do it. I saw Albert *(Einstein)*. I told you that I talked to Albert before, didn't I?"

Laura: "With my friend?"

Michael: "No, several years ago. I had a full-old conversation with him."

Laura: "No, you didn't tell me."

Michael: "I didn't tell you that? Well, I'll tell you. I have a recording of it at home. This is what happened; I'll quickly tell you. This guy, who is a friend of someone we know, came over to the house for a session. He was 30-something. I looked over and there was this old guy *(in spirit)* with a pipe and he looked German to me. I said 'Is your grandpa German? Smoke a pipe?' 'No,' he says. 'Oh, ok. It's not your grandpa?' 'No.' I said 'He's German.' Somebody else came in for a minute and I came back to this guy and said, 'What's your name?' He said, 'I'm Al, Albert.' I said, 'This guy is Albert, do you know who this is now?' 'Yep,' he said. 'Who are you to him then? What relative?' He said, 'I'm not.'

'Are you a friend of his?' He said, 'No, not really.' 'He's not a relative and he's not a friend, I don't get it.' 'Well, he's sort of famous,' he said. *(To the spirit)* 'Well, who are you? I don't get it.' 'I'm Albert Einstein.' I just laughed and said, 'He says he's Albert Einstein.' He said, 'That's right.' I said, 'What? Hold on a second. You don't know Albert Einstein, you're too young. You've never met him. Hold on a second, this doesn't make any sense.' I said *(to the spirit)*, 'If you're Albert Einstein, then why are you here?' He said, 'Well, this young gentleman asked me to come to his session and answer some questions and I'd be delighted to do so.'"

Laura: "Really?"

Michael: *(Laughing)* "When I told him this, he said 'That's right.' I said, 'You asked Albert Einstein to come and talk to you?' And he said, 'Yeah.' So, this is what happened. And then he brings out this whole list of questions. I said, 'You have a whole list of questions for him?' And he says, 'Yeah' and brings out this list. I said, 'Holy cow, this is amazing. Well, he's going to do it for you.'"

Laura: "Were they scientific questions?"

Michael: "Some of them. I don't remember what he said to him, but when he left, he said he answered all of his question."

Laura: "This is so unbelievable. When I said that I had a condition, I said that if Michael mentions the name Albert Einstein in my session, I will see if he would be interested in finishing this project with me."

Michael: "Well, there you go."

Laura: "And you said it before I did."

Michael: "Yeah, well that's why."

Laura: *(Voice cracking)* "I'm ready to cry right now."

Michael: "This was the furthest thing from my mind when I looked at you. I thought we were going to have an ordinary session, talking to some grandpa or something. Funny, huh? I'd like to pursue it; I'd like to do it. Let's do it."

Laura: "I would love you to. This has consumed my life for three years. I'm going to cry, this is so huge to me." *(Sniff, sniff.)*

Michael: "Well, there you go. Cool, hit the nail on the head."

Wow! Not only did Michael mention Albert's name numerous times, fulfilling my secret request, he offered to help me with the book project before I even had the chance to ask him if he'd be willing to help me! Spirit works in mysterious ways sometimes that absolutely humble me. When one door closes, another door opens. I was crying and so happy the way this session turned out. When Marti showed me the portrait she had drawn, I wasn't sure who it was. It was a young bald guy, perhaps a friend of my brother, who said he wanted to help out. Maybe someday I'll figure it out. It didn't really bother me because the doodle page that Marti had drawn totally blew me away. Here it is:

Doodle validations: The snake in the desert symbolizes the military up to no good in the desert, the premise of my book that we were talking about. The child's face with the bandages is "The Mummy," was running title of my other channeled book, as I explained in the last chapter. They compared children with autism to being mummified. Marti said she felt like it was a child dressed up as a mummy. The fact that Michael brought up Albert Einstein and Marti drew a picture of a mummy child was proof enough for me that the same spirits were intervening.

The other pictures she drew were about my dad. I set aside part of my back yard as a memorial to him. We used to have a Japanese garden in our yard when I was a child, which my dad, who was an architect, designed and built. There was a large Buddha statue in it, along with a pagoda and a pond with a bridge and waterfall. So after my dad died, I planted a Japanese maple tree with a small Buddha statue and a pagoda under it in his honor. My mom had just bought me a swing for Mother's Day, five months earlier, that looks identical to Marti's picture, which sits adjacent to the memorial area. It has a wooden base and a two seated swing which hangs from ropes. Here is a picture of my swing with my boys and our dog, Gizmo. Compare it to Marti's drawing, it's an uncanny resemblance. The Buddha statue and pagoda are not visible in the photo, but they're over to the left of the swing.

We talked for a little while longer, discussing the details of the book collaboration. Michael asked me who the medium was who did the channeling, and before I could answer, Marti guessed who it was. I laughed and asked how she knew that. She said, "I just knew" and added that some of what the other medium was saying wasn't channeled. Michael agreed and said that she was putting her own stuff in there and that her ego took over. It was good to have them validate that my intuition was correct about what happened. Most of the things she said that I thought weren't legitimate; I didn't put in the book. She was not the only vehicle the spirits could use to get this information out, obviously.

Michael said that he didn't want to read the book and be tainted by what she said. He said that the spirits would have to tell him very precise things. We agreed to just start over, start a new book. Michael was the perfect channel because he didn't have any children and didn't know anyone with autism. Also, they both have an enormous amount of integrity, and genuinely want to help others, as I do.

I'd like to just share the final part of our conversation before I left. This was not channeled, just us talking.

Michael: "I had this weird feeling for a long time that I'd meet Albert again. Albert is like Winston Churchill and a lot of people like that. They are really trying to help with things that are going on here on Earth."

Laura: "That's what he said. *(In the channeling sessions for my other book.)* He wants to help humanity once again."

Michael: And Albert is absolutely in that category. He's one of those people that are just determined to make sure that we make it."

Laura: "He said because they used his discoveries for warfare."

Michael: "For wrong-doing. That's right."

Laura: "People think of the nuclear bomb and him, like he created it, and he didn't. He said that he wants to make that correction."

Michael: "He didn't, no. I know that's part of why he comes through. That's why he's there, I absolutely know that."

***

After the Session

As I drove to school to pick up my beautiful boys, I said a prayer of thanks to Albert for what had just happened. I had tears of joy streaming down my face, feeling immense gratitude for another opportunity to help my son and others like him. It proved to me that I didn't need the other medium; The Universe had a Plan B. I would get another chance to help finish what spirit started.

A week later, I could only laugh out loud when I received the second demand letter from the first medium's attorney, this time attempting to extort money from me to prevent her from suing me. One word: karma. I wish I didn't have to mention her at all, but since the information was the springboard to this book, the story wouldn't be complete without the prequel.

The reason I am now going to use Albert Einstein's name instead of calling him The Wiry One is that Michael and I discussed it and he doesn't care about the legalities, he knows he's talking to him; and he feels that they'd have to prove otherwise. According to my lawyer, there is no case law on channeled material. Plus, the Right of Publicity must yield to the First Amendment, which ensures that the public is constitutionally entitled to know about things that affect it. Also, editorial writing does not require clearance, quotes fall under fair use, and all of the photos used are mine or are in the public domain. This information is intended for educational purposes, which does not violate publicity rights, and above all, it is commissioned and authorized by the man himself. It's really sad to me that you can't just tell a story without worrying about stuff like this. We are not trying to infringe on anyone's rights, we are merely trying to help people.

***

Chapter Three

"Only a life lived for others is a life worthwhile."

— Albert Einstein

Starting Over – Session One

A month after our last session, Michael and I started our book project. We decided to do the sessions by phone and we would both record them, in case something malfunctioned on either end. Since we lived in different states and didn't know how many sessions there were going to be, this made the most sense. Michael thought it would be best to approach it like he does a regular session, just see who shows up and see what they have to say. This wasn't Dial the Dead, the spirits were in charge of who talked to us. I also had a list of questions written down, just in case. Marti wasn't able to be there this time.

The date was November 17, 2010. We both started our recorders and I nervously waited to see who showed up. Michael mentioned to me that earlier that morning a deceased doctor (in spirit) came to him. This spirit doctor has been helping him during healing sessions with people for years. He didn't know his name, but he helped with diagnosing what was wrong with people he was doing healing work on. How cool is that?

The first person that Michael brought through was my dad. He said a few things that I validated, for example how he died, his height, the fact that my parents were split up. Then my dad said that Albert *(Einstein)* was there. The first validation that it was him was really interesting:

Michael: "He's saying that he won a prize in 1922."

Laura: "He won the Nobel Prize."

Michael: "1922."

Laura: "1921." (I had a Biography DVD about him that I was looking at and it said that he won the Nobel Prize for Physics in 1921.)

Michael: "1921?"

Laura: "Yeah, uh-huh."

Michael: "Oh, I had no idea he had won it."

Laura: "Yeah, the Nobel Prize in Physics."

Michael: "1921?"

Laura: "Uh-huh."

Michael: "Hmm. Like November?"

Laura: "I don't know, I'm just reading, I have this DVD sitting in my room and there are a few things on the back of it and that is one of them."

(After our session, I researched online because Michael was confused as to why my DVD said 1921, because Albert told him 1922 and November. To my surprise and delight, I read that in November of 1922, he learned that he won the Nobel Prize in Physics for the previous year, 1921. They announced the winner the following year evidently. Who knew?)

Next, Albert mentioned a few names, George, Henry, and Werner, whom he said was a friend of his. George and Henry were pretty common names, but how many Werner's could there be?

(After the session, I searched for a friend of Albert's named Werner, and came up with Werner Heisenberg, who was born in 1901 and died in 1976. He was a Nobel Prize winning German Nuclear Physicist, who was the pioneer of Quantum Mechanics, and formulated the Uncertainty Principle. He also attended the Solvay Congress in Brussels along with Albert Einstein and other esteemed physicists and chemists of the time. He also wrote a book, titled "Encounters with Einstein." I'd say this is the Werner he was referring to that was coming through with him.)

The following photograph is from the Solvay Congress in 1930. Because it is in the public domain, anyone can use it for any reason without permission. Werner Heisenberg is in the back row, the last person on the right, and Albert is in the front row, fifth from the right.

Herzen, E. Henriot, J. Verschaffelt, C. Manneback, A. Cotton, J. Errera, O. Stern, A. Piccard, W. Gerlach, C. Darwin, P.A.M. Dirac, E. Bauer, P. Kapitsa, L. Brillouin, H. A. Kramers, P. Debye, W. Pauli, J. Dorfman, J. H. Van Vleck, E. Fermi, W. Heisenberg. Th. De Donder, P. Zeeman, P. Weiss, A. Sommerfeld, M. Curie, P. Langevin, A. Einstein, O. Richardson, B. Cabrera, N. Bohr, W. J. De Haas.

Next, Michael started talking about some issues that children with autism had. First, he asked if I knew if they had problems with their bones, or bone marrow, a condition that starts in the bones, and mentioned Leukemia. In the last channeling session for my other book, *Foundation of Discovery,* Albert had mentioned the bones being affected also. I mentioned to Michael that a friend of mine has a son with autism who was later diagnosed with Leukemia. Then he says:

Michael: "He's talking about the back of the head. Something that goes inside, behind the pineal gland and the thalamus gland."

(This comes up again in a later session and is clarified.)

Laura: "Ok."

Michael: "Like a poison or toxin."

I told him that I had questions, and he asked me to give him one. I directly asked him what was causing regressive autism, where the child was normal, and then they weren't. He said "He keeps showing me breathing and lungs, something in the air." The something in the air made me think of the biowarfare that was discussed in my other book. Then he jumped to another subject, but later came back to this one and added, "He keeps saying it's like a poison, it's inhaled."

Michael asked me if I knew if Albert was diabetic, and I told him that in our other sessions for my other book, he mentioned that he thought he was diabetic, and described how he would go for long periods without eating, and then eat like a bear. Michael said that Albert was telling him that he was diabetic. Then Michael asked if Albert was fun, because he was chuckling. I told him yes, and Michael said:

Michael: "Did he come through that way in the sessions with her?" *(The medium that did the channeling for my prior book.)*

Laura: "Yes, funny, laughing, giggling."

Michael: "He says he's not commenting about her. He doesn't want to. I asked him why she didn't pursue it. He's talking about the details, making me feel like the specifics were a difficulty. Am I correct?"

Laura: "Yeah, it was kind of…"

Michael: "Difficult."

Laura: "Yeah, I had to ask questions over and over, it was hard to really get the answers."

Michael: "He's saying something about that, about it being difficult."

Laura: "Yeah."

Boy was I glad that I didn't have to bring up the subject, he answered it for me. Obviously Albert was aware of all the issues. Next, Michael said that Albert said that he's met with me ten times. I told him we did eight sessions before. Michael said "Plus the last one I did, plus this one makes ten." He was right, which also validated for me that Albert was there during the last session when Michael mentioned his name.

He went back to the guy named George again, and added that he also won a Nobel Prize.

(After the sessions, I looked up all of the Nobel Prize winners named George who knew Albert, and there were a few. I wasn't sure who this was, but the name George comes up again in a later session and is identified. Unless this was a different George, in a later session Nobel Prize winner George Bernard Shaw shows up.)

My dad jumped back in and said that he liked fishing. I confirmed that, telling him that we had a cottage on a lake and he taught me how to fish. He also said that my dad was very smart. It was interesting how someone in spirit that I knew, my dad, kept popping in to say things that I could validate, followed by things that Michael, and often I, had no idea about until after the session. It seemed like their way of showing us that if this fact is true, then this other fact is probably also true.

After that, Michael went back to some more problems with kids with autism. He said, "Is there epilepsy with some of these kids? I felt like I couldn't stay in my body, like with epilepsy, true?" I confirmed that. (Up to 40% of children with autism have seizures. Mine didn't.) He added that "It manifests in different ways, and one of them is epilepsy." Then Michael asked if they had skin problems, which I also confirmed and he said "Wow, Albert is holding his pipe, and is smiling at me now." I'm sure he was pleased that Michael was getting what he was telling him.

More things came up that I, as a parent of a child with autism would know, but Michael wouldn't. Just to give an example of how it was coming through, this is part of the exact transcripts:

Michael: "Are these kids nervous?"

Laura: "Yes."

Michael: "Like anxiety?"

Laura: "Yes, very much so."

Michael: "This brain thing, in the back of the head, it's in the brain and spinal fluid."

Laura: "Ask him if it's viral."

Michael: "It's almost like a reaction to chicken pox or no, smallpox, mumps, measles. Is it a virus that's dormant?"

"Do you know if there is anything like Septicemia?"

Laura: "Septicemia? What is that?"

Michael: "It's like a septic condition in the body."

Laura: "I don't really know what that is. What is that?"

Michael: "It's a poison."

Laura: "Yeah, they're all super toxic."

Michael: "In what way are they toxic?"

Laura: "Lots of different ways. Lots of these kids have to go through major detoxes from different bacteria, viruses, metals, allergies, tons of stuff."

Michael: "Oh, really?"

Laura: "Yes."

Michael: "Is there an improvement after they do it?"

Laura: "Yes."

Michael: "Really?"

Laura: "Yes, they're always doing different detoxes, parasites, tons of different infections, always."

Michael: "I think what they're calling autism is so many things. Why do they call it autism?"

Laura: "Because they don't know what they are talking about, pretty much."

Michael: "I don't understand why they call it autism."

Laura: "Yeah, they just lump it into a category because they don't know what else to call it. If they have speech problems, social disorders and sensory dysfunction, they put them into the category of autism. They don't look for the cause."

Michael: "Eyes, something to do with the eyes."

Laura: "Yes."

Michael: "The eyes don't work right."

Laura: "Well, they look out of the corner of their eye; they call it stimming, where they look at things back and forth really fast."

Michael: "Huh."

Laura: "Yes, that's one of the symptoms they look for."

Michael: "There is toxicity in the system."

Laura: "And where is it coming from?"

Michael: "I don't know if it's injected or inhaled?"

Laura: "Or a combination of the two."

It was interesting because we were both learning through this process. I had to look up certain things afterward, for instance the term Septicemia. I had no idea what that was. It means the invasion and persistence of pathogenic bacteria in the bloodstream; blood poisoning. In return, I was validating the things that I knew about autism that Michael was being told by spirit, which he knew nothing about. This fact alone proved the legitimacy of the information in my eyes. Unless you have a child with autism and read everything out there like many of us parents do, you wouldn't know these things. Autism means Rain Man to most people, including Michael.

Back to the session. Michael asked me when kids received shots. I replied from the day they're born and they get some every few months, over 30 by the age of two. He said that their immune systems can't handle these things when they're young, and said that they were compromised. Then he asked if they repeated things a lot. I said, "Yes, it's called echolalia, and they repeat things they hear over and over or repeat a question instead of answering it." He was in disbelief.

Then he said they were bringing up Vitamin C, and that there was a deficiency and that it was also good for detoxification. Next, he said, "He's telling me that there is an aversion to loud noises." I told him yes, they have major sensory issues and that my son often has to wear noise blocking headphones in class because of it and covers his ears a lot. Next, he brought this up:

Michael: "They're showing me a dusty old filing cabinet. It goes back to war times. It's like a dusty old filing cabinet. I don't know if it has anything to do with DDT? There were some sort of studies done then and the conclusions they arrived at. Definitely a compromised immune system."

(According to an article on www.vactruth.com called "7 Trivia Facts about Polio" during WWII and into the 1950's, massive amounts of pesticides including DDT were sprayed on crops. These chemicals were found to increase viral infections in hosts. Also, there is a lot of evidence showing that the polio outbreak had to do with DDT in cow and human milk supply, see www.nccn.net/~ wwithin/ddt138.htm. Additionally, Dan Olmsted and Mark Blaxill from "Age of Autism" wrote a series of articles called "Age of Polio: How an Old Virus and New Toxins Created a Man-Made Epidemic" going into great detail about how polio was linked to DDT and that the polio vaccine did not eradicate polio, as vaccine proponents would have us believe.)

After that, Michael brought up bone loss, and calcium deficiency. I confirmed that and told him that a lot of kids are allergic to dairy and don't get enough calcium. Adding that these kids are very sick, but nobody but the parents addresses their physical issues. Then he said:

Michael: "I am asking how we can correct this and he said you have to do it holistically, using several different methods, on a case by case basis. Some kids are going to respond to light therapy; some kids are going to have to be in an environment where it's very, very quiet. You know sort of like sound therapy. Very subtle things. They're talking about their environment and the need for color and light therapy."

He was off to a great start. He continued, "They have a lot of fear, like something sets them off." I said "Oh, yeah, lots of tantrums." Then he said, "He's talking about a Center for Advanced Disease Control or something like that. A research center." And then this came up:

Michael: "I'm asking about this viral thing. Is it in the ground? The food?"

Laura: "It's in the ground and the food? That's awesome! He told me that last time."

Michael: "Oh, really? Wow."

Laura: "Yes."

Michael: "What he's doing is he's making me look at the floor in front of me, so I look at the floor and it turned to dirt."

Laura: "Oh, my God. Yes."

Michael: "And he put his hand in the dirt and let it pour out of his hand onto the ground."

Laura: "Yep."

Michael: "Well then I asked him if it was worse in certain areas than others, with the dirt. There's a pattern where there are certain areas, it's in the dirt in the food and water. He's talking about a poison in the ground."

Laura: "Mmm-hmm."

Michael: "So, you have to discriminate about what they eat. It seems to be a combination of like 3 dozen different things, you know."

Laura: "Mmm-hmm."

Michael: "Their immune systems are all compromised, more than their parents."

Laura: "Mmm-hmm."

Michael: "Then we have toxins getting in the system, multiple things going on. So it is showing up in several different ways. You have to address it, there needs to be a center where they evaluate each one, and have a regime set up for each one."

Laura: "Yeah, they all present differently."

This whole segment reminded me of what was said in my last book about the biowarfare contaminating the dirt, water and food. Although it wasn't specifically mentioned what the "poison in the ground" was at this point, I felt that's what he was referring to because it came up when Michael asked him about the "viral thing." It made me feel that it really was The Wiry One again. But Michael also said that there were multiple things going on with these kids, which I am a firm believer in. The other medium didn't finish the job, so who knows what else might have come through had we finished?

Michael continued by correctly saying "He's *(Albert)* telling me that they scream like they are in pain, but they don't know where the pain is coming from." He added that the pain is at a cellular level, and that it is nerves in various places in the body, an internal thing. Next, Michael said, "He keeps showing me a center dedicated to curing this, with scientists. Something like the Cancer Treatment Centers of America. He's talking about having detox, holistic; they're talking about the nervous system. He said that doctor's understanding of this is sparse. They don't know."

Then Michael began talking about chemicals in the environment and I asked if there was a military connection. He replied that the military had a blatant disregard for human life and added:

Michael: "He is talking about breaking down chemicals in the ground and water; something biochemical carried by the wind. A dispersant, something dispersed over a city."

Now I really felt he was talking about the biowarfare agent. He continued bringing up some more symptoms associated with autism, including allergies, and a Vitamin A deficiency. He started questioning me again about the shots, and how many they got and which ones. When I mentioned the MMR, he asked if it was German measles and said that it's too strong. He asked, why do they need all of those shots? Those diseases won't kill you if you get them, it's not a pleasant thing to have, but it builds you up. Then Michael said "Albert is saying, 'Sadly, it's big business, the vaccine business.'" (It's a $17 billion/year business.)

Much to my delight, the next thing he said was "He's talking about homeopathy." I said, "Ha, ha! That's what I do with my son." Michael added, "He's also talking about Bach Flower Essences." To which I replied, "Yep, I use those as well." He said, "They work, they need time and the right environment." I was a huge proponent of homeopathy, and flower essences are also an extension of homeopathy. That is how I detoxed and treated Trevor for the most part. I took classes, read tons of books and tried many different remedies. Bach's Rescue Remedy was a life saver for me when Trevor was upset.

Next, Michael asked me if these kids hurt themselves. I said yes, and told him how my son would just flip himself down the stairs, and kick a hole in the wall when he was angry. Michael was stunned and said that he was seeing a room with cushions, a soft environment, and pillows with a velour covering, like being in the womb. He added, "Their system is in shock. Their immune system is in a state of shock, that's what's going on. And they can't quite recover. It's too much, it's madness, Albert says it's too much. That's basically what's going on." Then Michel said "He's saying the name Arthur."

(After the session, I looked up people that were associated with Albert, and the name Arthur Stanley Eddington stood out. He was a British Astrophysicist whose 1919 eclipse observations dramatically confirmed Einstein's prediction of how much gravity bends light. He also wrote articles which explained Einstein's Theory of General Relativity to the English speaking world.)

Some more autism idiosyncrasies were mentioned next, including that they were worse at night, which I jokingly called "The Witching Hour." He also mentioned that they had sleep problems. He asked if they had an aversion to water, because they were showing him water and he didn't know why. I told him that drowning was the number one cause of death, and most don't know how to swim.

Next, Michael said, "He's talking about hypersensitivity," and was showing him things he could relate to, like his own bad childhood allergies. I said, "Yes, very much so. All of their senses are heightened." Then he said that they were talking about a lot of trouble with the teeth, and problems with the heart. All true. Then he says, "He's saying there is a propensity to run, like they just take off." They're showing me my childhood and how I loved to run. They're showing me a parallel so I understand. I told him that they did run, and had no sense of danger. It is actually called elopement. I've experienced it firsthand, and it is very scary indeed.

Our session was winding down, and Michael finished the session with, "He's saying keep up the good work and we'll make an appointment soon." I said, "Ok, thank you!" I told Michael how incredible I thought that session was because I asked Albert *(mentally)* to tell me things that you wouldn't know anything about. He said, "Was I right?" I answered, "Yeah, you hit everything, all of the things that he talked about in the first sessions that we had together. The dirt, the wind, and the virus stuff, the compromised immune system, and all of the little things about autism that you know nothing about." Michael confirmed "No, I don't."

***

Session One After the Session

<u>**Featured Spirits:**</u> Albert Einstein, Werner Heisenberg, Arthur Stanley Eddington

Part of what made this initial session so validating for me was the fact that Michael had not read my other book and didn't know what was brought up by Albert in our sessions together. In addition, I also had a list of questions to ask during the session and I secretly wrote a request on the very top of the page that said "Prove to us who this is. Tell us something that I *(Laura)* know from the last sessions *(from my other book)* that they *(Michael and Marti)* don't know." That request was answered by Michael talking about the bones being affected, the dirt and water being poisoned, the biochemical agent carried by the wind, and the fact that Albert was diabetic. All of those things came up in my other sessions with Albert. We went into this with no expectations, as a trial run to see what would happen, and we were both pleased with the outcome.

Plus, as I mentioned earlier, Michael doesn't have any children, and he doesn't know any kids with autism to know what they're like, much less the hidden physical issues they have. He wouldn't know about their nutritional deficiencies, hypersensitivity, screaming, elopement, seizures, toxicity, and all the other things kids with autism commonly have. This was the tip of the iceberg, but it was exciting start. I couldn't wait to see who would come through next and what they had to share.

Another thing I want to mention about Michael here is that he trusts what spirit tells him over and above what people tell him. For instance, just because I mentioned to him that the other medium came up with biological warfare as the cause of autism, unless the spirit people tell him the same thing, he doesn't blindly believe it. As you will see in some of the upcoming sessions, he actually gets much more specific things than I could have imagined regarding autism. I felt truly blessed and grateful that he was willing to do this with me.

One of the most challenging parts of all of this was the fact that neither one of us personally knew Albert nor the other spirits that he was bringing through with him. This meant that I had to do research afterward to try to validate who these people were, and if they were connected to Albert or the subject matter in some way. Michael just had to trust what they were saying and left it up to me to look it up later. I think that's why my dad was part of the session, to give Michael the confidence that he was getting things right. I could validate what my dad was saying, and the stuff about autism that I knew, but the other names and associations I had to look up afterward. As you'll see, sometimes a name would come up in one session, and then in a later session, they'd come through again and give more details once we figured out who they were. The game of Psychic Who's Who was just beginning.

I added some of the validations within the story to make it easier to read, instead of having to read it at the end of the chapter. Just know that I had to look up all of the names and bits of information after the session. Then, I would call Michael to tell him what I found, and he would get very excited. We were constantly in awe of the discoveries made after each session and it drove us both to continue. I felt like a detective, taking the clues they were giving me to solve the autism mystery.

I'd like to share some other validations from this session. A few weeks after this session, I took Trevor to do a BioSET session, which uses muscle response testing and ergopathic vials of substances with the energetic signature for testing. We were testing for nutritional deficiencies including

Vitamins, and Minerals. He was deficient in Vitamins A and C as well as calcium. These items were specifically mentioned in the channeling session.

I also looked back at the last Quantum Biofeedback (QB) session Trevor had done, which was done two weeks prior to this session and one of his acute deficiencies was Vitamin C. In the session he had done the month prior, on October 1, he showed a deficiency in Vitamin A, and Beta Carotene, the precursor of Vitamin A. Trevor also did a QB session four months after this session, and his practitioner ran a nutritional report, and it still showed a Vitamin A and C deficiency, among others. In addition, in the "Special Report Nutrition" section, the Pineal, Pituitary, and Hypothalamus scored high, meaning there is a deficiency there as well. The point is, dead people brought it up and then I validated it medically, to the best of my ability.

Keep this in mind; neither Michael nor I had any idea who these scientists were. We obviously both knew who Albert Einstein was, who didn't? But unless you run in scientific circles, who knows who Werner Heisenberg or Arthur Stanley Eddington were? These men were all connected in life, and apparently in death. I was a communications major in college; I didn't take physics or higher math classes. I chose to be a speech major in order to avoid higher math classes. I was a Pilates teacher and a mom who liked to talk to dead people. Michael was a medium, not a doctor or scientist. You couldn't make this stuff up. If we were making it up, don't you think we'd pick dead people that everybody knew? As you'll see later on, I never even found out who some of them were. I'm hoping that someone else with connections to them or greater research skills might figure some of it out.

***

Chapter Four

*"You may object that by speaking of
simplicity and beauty I am introducing
aesthetic criteria of truth, and I
frankly admit that I am strongly
attracted by the simplicity and beauty
of mathematical schemes which nature
presents us. You must have felt this
too: the almost frightening simplicity
and wholeness of the relationship,
which nature suddenly spreads out
before us."*

— Werner Heisenberg

*(In a letter to Albert Einstein. From
Ian Stewart's, "Why Beauty is Truth")*

Session Two

It was December 7, 2010 and Michael and I had our second session. This time, Marti felt that she was supposed to look things up on the computer as they came through instead of drawing. This wasn't your typical session talking to someone's dead relatives. We had an agenda, and were hoping for some answers to help my son and other children with autism and I promised that I would share our findings with the world when we finished, no matter what it was.

This session began with Michael asking me if I knew if Albert had any heart related problems when he died. I said that I didn't know.

(After the session, I learned that on April 17, 1955, Albert went to Princeton Hospital complaining of chest pains and died of an aneurism the next day. He also had heart problems earlier in his life, requiring surgery.)

Next, Michael asked me if Einstein ever lived in New Jersey. After thinking about it momentarily, I said, "Yes, he lived in Princeton, New Jersey." Albert told Michael that he was in New Jersey and Michael had written down New Jersey on his paper when we started. I told him that Albert taught there, and that was also where he died.

Michael had also written down spring 1943 on his paper at the beginning of the session along with the number 10. It's a form of automatic writing. The spirit is actually writing through him. During the session Michael pondered why he had written down that date, and said "I wonder what Albert was doing then, unless he was working on the Manhattan Project."

(After the session, I researched what was happening in Einstein's life in 1943 that had to do with the Manhattan Project. It turns out that beginning in the spring of 1943 he worked as a consultant with the Research and Development Division of the U.S. Navy Bureau of Ordnance, Section Ammunition and Explosives. A series of letters he wrote to Lt. Stephen Brunauer beginning on May 17, 1943 can be seen online in the U.S. National Archives and Records Administration or on the Wikimedia Commons website.)

Next, Michael said that Albert was talking about a Hyperbaric Chamber and it had to do with my son. I told him that when I went to see them in Reno two months earlier, my late husband brought up Hyperbaric Oxygen Therapy for my son and I was wondering if I should do it as a therapy for him. Michael said, "It's to put pure oxygen into the system right?" I answered yes, and said that they were getting good results using it with kids with autism. He said, "I am totally positive with that." "Cool" I replied. Michael stated, "Albert is saying 'definitely' to the Hyperbaric Chamber."

"Now he's saying that iron is an issue, or something to do with iron." I mentioned that some kids with autism have high levels of iron, and they even keep it out of some supplements designed for them. He responded, "Because iron is the transporter of oxygen in the body."

(I researched this more after the session, and confirmed that excess iron is common in autism. There is plenty of information online about Iron Overload Disease, also called Hemochromatosis, which if left untreated, can lead to organ damage and cancer. However, iron deficiency is also common in autism. I also found out that parasites eat iron in the body, and our kids have lots of parasites, including mine. So, parasites could be causing an iron deficiency and hence, less oxygen.)

The next thing that came up was Michael stating "And now he's showing me gold, but as a therapy of some sort." I told him about a story I was familiar with about a guy diagnosed with autism a long time ago who claimed to be cured with gold salts, and that homeopathic gold, Aurum metallicum, was also a remedy being used in autism. "Well that works too, he's telling me. Ingest gold or you take gold, ok?"

(This was particularly interesting to me because mercury is used to extract gold in mining, so the gold would be used to extract mercury in the body. Many of the vaccines that children received contained Thimerosal, a mercury-based preservative. A few years earlier, I was having a reading with another medium, and she also told me that gold would help my son. I used the homeopathic remedy Aurum metallicum for about a year. More comes up on this in a later session.)

Then he brought up a few more excesses and deficiencies common in autism. First he said "He's bringing up copper." I mentioned that a lot of kids have high copper and they also keep it out of some supplements for that reason. Then he said "And he's making me feel like there's some sort of electrical property to all of this where it's almost like there's short circuiting going on." Again, he brought up the teeth, and said, "I don't know if we brought this up before, but are they low in calcium?" I answered "Yes." Then he said "He's saying they are low in magnesium" which I affirmed.

This next part was pretty interesting. Michael said that Albert was saying a name like Fitzgerald to him. Marti began searching on the computer for a Fitzgerald and autism and Einstein. She interjected that she found a psychiatrist named Michael Fitzgerald who theorized that Albert Einstein had a form of autism. I mentioned that I had asked Albert this question in my other book and he replied that he did not have what my son has. Michael insisted that he was telling him that he did have a form of autism. Michael said that he can only go by what he was getting, and that there are different forms of autism and that Albert was telling him that he had a form of autism and that's why he was interested in helping with it.

He followed this up by saying that Albert would go for days without eating, sometimes three days with only drinking fluid, and that he had issues with being cold, having a low temperature. He added that Albert would get angry, have outbursts, lose his temper and fly off the handle, and then later have to apologize to people, explaining that he wasn't angry at them. Michael said, "This is what he's telling me. I know nothing about him. I don't know where he lived; I don't know how he died."

(Michael Fitzgerald, Simon Baron-Cohen, Tony Attwood and many other autism specialists all theorized that Albert Einstein had Asperger's Syndrome, which was added

to the Diagnostic and Statistical Manual in 1994 as a mental disorder and is currently considered to be on the autism spectrum. After this session, I read many articles and book references to Albert's major tantrums, which Michael mentioned. It was interesting that he validated this fact about himself as well as the distinction of the different types of autism. He reportedly didn't talk until he was 3 or 4 years old.)

Next, Michael mentioned the name "Werner" again, and said that he wants to go back to this person. Marti looked up the name on the computer and mentioned Werner Heisenberg, which was the same name I came up with during my previous research from the first session. Michael got all excited, and said, "Werner Heisenberg, that's it! He says that he's a friend." Michael added that he wanted to put an "H" in the name, but spelled it W-E-R-N-E-R and said "He's telling me how pleased he is and how happy he is and that we seem to be getting through very well." I guess it was Werner Heisenberg last time.

Then, Michael asked me if I had made an appointment yet for the Hyperbaric Chamber for my son. I told him that I was looking at a couple places in town and comparing pricing. This must have been very important for him to bring it up again.

Next, he said "Now he's also talking about sea salt or salt. This is weird, but he seems to attribute an electrical current to this, what I'm getting is low frequencies, tiny currents, he's talking about. Like a soothing...almost something so that maybe you can set up theta waves in the brain."

(After the session, I looked this up and indeed sea salt has electrical conductivity to it. Kids in school do science experiments where they put a light bulb in salt water and the bulb lights up. A practitioner I know that treats children with autism uses Quinton hypertonic marine plasma, a special ocean water as part of her protocol. It also kills pathogens. Marine plasma mirrors that of human blood plasma. I used Himalayan salt in my son's bath, but had never had him drink it.)

Then Michael brought up the Kangen water filtration system I had recently bought for Trevor, that makes alkaline, ionized water, and said that it was very good for him. I was happy because it was a big purchase that I was still paying off. It helps alkalinize and detoxify the body.

He also mentioned a form of visual therapy that would be helpful. He said he was seeing visual patterns that looked like Mandalas. He said that my son needed order, and that people with autism have a hard time making sense of what appears to be a random world. They don't like random things, and that these visual patterns help them find order and allow them to not be afraid. Anyone with a child with autism knows how important routines can be, and if you change their routine, a full-blown tantrum is often the result.

(After this session, I went online and printed up some different Mandala patterns, and let Trevor pick out some that he liked and showed them to him when he became upset. It seemed to calm him down. Some of them are very beautiful and would make great decorative art.)

Then Michael said that Albert had another scientist with him named Oscar, whom he also called a friend.

(After the session, I looked up scientists connected to him and found Oskar Klein. He was a Swedish Physicist who along with Theodor Kaluza formulated the Kaluza-Klein concept, which later re-emerged as String Theory. Oskar Klein also wrote to Albert Einstein to explain his ideas about how to unify Einstein's Theory of Relativity with Maxwell's Theory of Light.)

After that, Michael asked me if Trevor had any reactions to the color orange. I told him that the previous day, he wore and orange shirt and had a really bad day at school. He said that orange was not good for him; it jumbled him up and was too active for him. He said to put him in blue instead. He said that he was very sensitive to color, as were a lot of autistic kids. He asked if he liked pink, and if there was something pink in the bathroom. I told him I didn't know. He said to show him pink when he got angry. He said that pink would pacify him, that's why they dress little girls in pink. It's a defense mechanism so that nobody can get angry at or attack them. He added that green would also be good for him, for emotional balance, and that blue is the color of the throat center, and he'd probably be most talkative when wearing blue. He added to have him wear yellow occasionally to stimulate his mind. He said "You're just dealing with hypersensitivity, you see."

(Interestingly, after the session, I found a pink rose quartz candle holder in my bathroom, and the next time he became upset, I had him hold it and he calmed down. I was amazed. I also had a small rose quartz crystal stone that I gave him to hold when he got angry. Also, the next BioSET appointment he had, I noticed that his practitioner had a box of vials of all the colors. We muscle tested him for them all, and the two that he was weak to were violet and ORANGE. I told Michael, and he laughed.)

Next, Michael asked me if my son had any skin problems, like rashes. I told him yes, and explained that when he was younger, he had an oozing rash on his outer calf that he now has a scar from, and that he has little bumps on the back of his arms, which I thought was *Molluscum conta-giousum*, and that he took a homeopathic remedy for it, but they didn't go away. Michael asked if they were little white bumps on his shoulders and felt that it was a nervous thing. The final part of the session was the following:

Michael: "Oh, I wanted to know what your 10th question was."

Laura: "The 10th question was...Well, this had to do with vaccines. Can any vaccine, or combination of vaccines, or a lowered immune system, leave a child vulnerable?"

Michael: "Yeah, the answer to that is 'Yes.'"

Laura: "Ok, because in the last session, he was talking about the poison in the dirt and in the water and in the food, and about vaccines. And I was trying to connect it all. And he mentioned the immune system being compromised, so that was the question, was it a specific vaccine or any combination of vaccines?"

Michael: "Also, I feel like, what I'm getting is I'm seeing a mother and the womb, and I'm seeing a transmission from the mother to the child."

Laura: "Hmmm."

Michael: "So it's possible for toxins to go to the child, you see, through the parent, and also through their immunizations. Which brings up the next time we do this, probably you'll get into the symbiotic relationship."

That was the end of the channeling session, but our conversation continued as we summed up the session with the following:

Laura: "Alright, this is great! There were more validations of people he brought up last time. He brought up that Werner Heisenberg, or the name Werner, and I thought that was who he was talking about, and he validated it today."

Michael: "Yeah, so he brought up Werner last time?"

Laura: "Yeah, the name Werner, and I looked it up in a book, and there was a Werner Heisenberg and now Albert's saying it was a friend of his."

Michael: "And was he?"

Laura: "Yeah, he's in this book."

Michael: "Oh, I see, he wrote about him as a friend, did he?"

Laura: "Well, he's one of the "Main Characters" in a book about Einstein called *His Life and Universe*."

Michael: "Oh, I see. So, he was someone that was in Einstein's life, so to speak?"

Laura: "Yep, while he was alive. He was another physicist."

Michael: "Alright, cool."

Laura: "Yeah, so that's great. And lots of other little things about autism."

Michael: "Yeah, he brought up quite a bit, really."

Laura: "And Princeton, NJ!"

Michael: "That's the first thing he wrote down. And spring of 43, I don't know what he was doing then."

Laura: "And then the hyperbaric chamber again. Which is interesting, because it was my late husband who was talking about it the first time, and now he's talking about it again, so I am definitely going to try that therapy."

Michael: "Alright."

Laura: "I'll look up a few of these things."

Michael: "Do you keep records of what you do?"

Laura: "Yes."

Michael: "Like a kind of a diary?"

Laura: "A little bit, yeah, I have a whole folder full of things and I've written down a lot of different therapies and how they've helped him, yeah, so I keep records."

Michael: "On what you've noticed, and the improvements you've noticed, and things like that."

Laura: "Yeah."

Michael: "Ok, because all of this is kind of like chronological; it's almost like a chronicle. Do you have any film of your boy when he was younger?"

Laura: "Yeah."

Michael: "I think that the film is the most important thing, because you can see the difference."

Laura: "Yep, you can see the before he changed..."

Michael: "These are before and after, you see."

Laura: "Yeah."

Michael: "Otherwise, people might not believe you, no matter what, do you know what I mean?"

Laura: "Yeah, I have them all under his dresser in a box."

Michael: "You know, you have to validate it through visual behavior."

Laura: "Mmm-hmm."

Michael: "That's the only way you can really chronicle it."

Laura: "Right. Yeah, well you can see how he changed from when he was a baby, in the first year of his life, until the second, third and fourth. He would laugh and point. You'd say, Trevor where is the airplane? He'd point to the sky. He was tackling things, totally aware and alert. And then the next year, he wouldn't even look to the camera when you'd call his name. He'd just wander around like he didn't know you were there."

Michael: "Oh, well hopefully Albert will address that exact thing the next time. I'm pretty comfortable now that he is coming and talking to us."

***

Session Two – After the Session
Featured Spirits: Albert Einstein, Werner Heisenberg, Oskar Klein

I know the verbatim talk gets to be pretty monotonous, so I try to summarize a lot of it, but the reason I added the last section verbatim is to emphasize a few things. First, and I don't know if this is a good thing or a bad thing or a little of both, but Michael has a horrible memory of what happens during a session. It is kind of an inside joke between us. He doesn't remember a lot of it and then when I tell him something or someone came through last time, or a few sessions earlier, he is in disbelief. It's good because I know it was genuine if it comes up again, for example the name Werner. Similarly, as you will see, often a first name would be given in one session, and then the middle and/or last name comes through in a later session. The same thing happened with certain information; it was expanded upon in a later session. It let us know that we were correct or that we were on the right track. It was very exciting for both of us. I couldn't wait to see what was going to happen next.

There was some interesting synchronicity going on during these sessions. I had no idea who Werner Heisenberg was prior to him coming through to us. Then, afterwards, I'd be watching TV, and he would be on. I learned that he was the head of the nuclear weapons program for the Nazi party from random TV shows that "just happened" to be on when I'd walk in the room. The Military History channel (which I don't watch) happened to be on in my room after coming home from dinner one night, and a show from 2003 called "Dead Men's Secrets: Hitler's Nuclear Arsenal" was on. I saw Heisenberg, and taped the show. It was a fascinating look back at Hitler's race to develop an atomic weapon and deploy it on San Francisco. This plan was narrowly averted by the Allied bombing of Hiroshima. But, Heisenberg was a key player in attempting to build Germany's atomic bomb. I wonder if this is why he was coming through to help us.

Michael and I agreed that it would be best if I did the research after the sessions, because he didn't want to be influenced in any way. He is a very authentic and highly ethical medium, and I have great respect for him because of that. He wants to do it the right way, and not know anything beforehand. Now a skeptic would say, "Oh, he just looked it up ahead of time." Could he? Yes. Did he? No. He is true to his gift and the process. I wouldn't trust just anyone to do this sacred work this time.

During this session, after information came through Michael, Marti looked it up on the spot, but this technique turned out to be a bit distracting. It broke up the session and disconnected Michael. But for this particular session, it was good because she looked up the name Fitzgerald, which led to Albert insisting that he did have a form of autism. Not what my son has, but today, it would be called Asperger's Syndrome. That diagnosis didn't exist in his time.

The other thing I want to emphasize here is that you can see by our dialogue that I did the research after each session to try to validate the information that came through, and then I would report my findings back to Michael afterward. He told me that he felt ridiculous saying some of the things that the spirits told him, but he said it anyway, and when it turned out to be accurate, it motivated us both even more to continue. This becomes truer later on. If the things he said turned out not to be accurate, I don't think either of us would have wanted to keep doing it.

During this session, Hyperbaric Oxygen Therapy (HBOT) was brought up again for my son with autism. This time by Albert, the first time was by my late husband. After the session, I began aggressively researching HBOT, calling around and interviewing numerous local HBOT providers, and going on a tour of one facility. I didn't have the money to pay for it, but I volunteer for a local autism organization, which graciously provides financial assistance to many families with children with autism to pay for therapies that would normally be financially out of reach. I applied for the funding to pay for HBOT and it was approved! I signed him up to start when he was off from school for break two weeks later. Michael and I had another session prior to that.

***

Chapter Five

"The discovery of natural law is a meeting with God."

— Friedrich Dessauer

(Philosophie der Technik, 1927)

Session Three

Our third session was on December 15, 2010. It was only Michael and I again this time. I am going to use a lot of exact dialogue in this chapter because it was all pretty important. The session began with Michael saying:

Michael: "Ok. There's a man that I'm looking at that's standing in front of me here. He's giving me the name Friedrich. Friedrich De, Dyna that's what it sounds like. I'm asking if Albert is here and he says, 'Yes, he's standing over to your right,' and I said, 'Ok.' And he's saying something about Austria or Austrian."

Laura: "Mmm."

Michael: "I don't know if this Friedrich guy is the Austrian guy. (His last name) sounded like Dinear. He's talking about studies done on children back then. I believe by the German government. So they're talking about these studies done. Austrian or German? Well he's definitely got a German sounding accent, this guy."

(After the session, I found Fredrich Dessauer, 1881-1963, a German born physicist and professor who was a distinguished pioneer in German medical radiology. When the Nazis came to power, he fled to Turkey as an Émigré Professor where he established The Institute of Radiology and Biophysics. Albert Einstein unsuccessfully tried to help Dessauer immigrate to the United States via personal requests and recommendations.[13] They knew each other and corresponded. A March 29, 1954 letter from Dessauer to Einstein can be found in the Einstein Archives, Document No. 301148.)

Laura: "Ok."

Michael: "It's not Albert talking to me at the moment; it's this other man

---

[13] www.easst.net/review/sept2007/namal

who'd like to help here. So, we don't just have Albert here. I think this man is a friend of Albert. Talking about being of help to Albert. Maybe sort of a mentor or someone like a mentor to Albert and he's saying a name like Johann to me."

(Fredrich Dessauer was a professor at the Johann Wolfgang Goethe-Universität in Frankfurt, Germany from 1921-1934 and again from 1953-1963. He was the director of what is now known as the Max Planck Institute for Biophysics in Frankfurt.[14] The Institute is part of the Kaiser Wilhelm Society, whose other Institutions were directed by Albert Einstein and Werner Heisenberg.[15])

Michael: "Are these kids highly active?"

Laura: "Yes."

Michael: "Well he said a propensity towards high activity."

Laura: "Yes."

Michael: "I think he's taking about the studies that were done. That's exactly what he said 'a propensity towards high activity.' He's talking about the kids seem to be exhibiting subconscious activity. It's almost like they're in a trance a little bit."

Laura: "Mmm-hmm."

Michael: "The man I'm looking at has strong, wavy black hair; a good head of hair on him. He seems to be about 6 feet. A robust looking man. I don't know if this is Friedrich. He's nodding at me, so I think it is. He's talking about his research. So this is a research scientist."

Laura: "Ok."

---

[14] www.biophys.mpg.de/en/institute.html
[15] www.en.wikipedia.org/wiki/Kaiser_Wilhelm_Society

Friedrich Dessauer

Michael: "I don't know if they tried doing brain wave oscillation back then. He's talking about measuring brain wave activity. He's talking about the brain wave oscillations and then it dips he said, there were these dips that they would notice and lack of response on the subject's part. So, there was speculation that something in the brain like the neurons were not interacting as they should like something was getting in the way or something wasn't allowing the transmitters to work."

Laura: "Mmm."

Michael: "Cornea... Are autistic kids very sensitive to light?"

Laura: "Yes."

Michael: "I mean do they try to shut their eyes in bright light more than an average person."

Laura: "Yeah. They are very sensitive to a lot of stimuli of all kinds, motion, color."

Michael: "In his research he found that using light in some way on the subjects through the visual cortex to try and stimulate the brain. He says patterns are very important. That's interesting. He says, 'as you know, light is sound and sound is light, so it's the frequency of the light, the frequency of the patterns would induce a calming effect.' Boy he's getting into some stuff here. He says in effect they were trying to produce a result; he calls it a healing result, upon the brain through the visual cortex using light. And he says in certain cases proved very effective. You know a lot of the studies were destroyed or...this must be prior to the war or just preceding the war because he talks about the Nazis as 'them.'"

Then, a new spirit made an appearance.

Michael: "So he must be Austrian, this man, from Austria. And he's saying a name like "Wolfgang" and it almost sounds like "Plutz" or "Pulse" Wolfgang...is there a P? It sounds like a P."

Laura: "Okay."

Michael: "I think he had to flee Germany eventually, this man. I think he also came to America. He might be like a professor this guy."

Laura: "Is this Wolfgang or Friedrich?"

Michael: "I'm not sure which one. I think it's Friedrich I'm talking to, but he's mentioning this Wolfgang... I can't quite get this last name."

(From Wikipedia: Wolfgang Pauli, 1900-1945, was born in Vienna, Austria. He was a theoretical physicist who won the Nobel Prize in 1945, and was nominated by Albert Einstein. He studied at the University of Munich, Germany where he met his lifelong friend and colleague Werner Heisenberg. He also studied at Göttingen University in Germany. He came to the United States in 1940 and joined the faculty at the Institute for Advanced Study in Princeton, New Jersey as a Professor of Theoretical Physics, where he was a friend and colleague of Albert Einstein. Wolfgang Pauli can also be seen in the Solvay Congress photograph in the back row in Chapter Three.)

Michael: "Now, he's making me think of your questions."

Laura: "Ok."

Michael: "I think he thinks he's done enough to identify himself to me and what he does. He's putting like...they look like pills. He's showing me five pills here. Do you know a medicine called Dervocet?"

Laura: "I know there's a Darvocet."

Michael: "Yeah, it's like Dervocet. Darvocet. Is there?"

Laura: "Yeah, it's a pain killer."

I told Michael that I was prescribed Darvocet during my pregnancy with Trevor when I had an upper respiratory infection. I was coughing so much that my ribs bruised. I was also prescribed Darvocet after childbirth for pain by my OB.

Michael: "He put five pills in front of me, and I said what are the pills? Are they five different pills? And he said, 'Say this name 'Darvocet, ask her...'"

Laura: "What about it?"

Michael: "Well it must have done something here. He said it's detrimental."

Laura: "Oh, lovely."

Michael: "Ok, what's in the pills? Ah, this is interesting. You weren't getting oxygen."

Laura: "Ahh."

Michael: "You yourself were starved of oxygen. How interesting. Hold on. Ok. He's certain that the chamber will work, ok?" *(Hyperbaric Oxygen Therapy)*

Laura: "Ok."

Michael: "He's telling me you will see a marked improvement."

Laura: "Awesome!"

I told Michael that it was the sickest I had ever been in my life and that I was also prescribed antibiotics, which I didn't want to take, but my doctor insisted that it wouldn't cross the placenta. My son was born with thrush, which is a white coated tongue, indicating a systemic fungal infection, caused by antibiotics. They wipe out all the good bacteria in the GI tract, allowing the yeast to proliferate and lower the immune system.

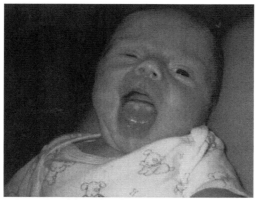

Trevor, 3 weeks old, with a fungal infection on his tongue.

Michael continued:

Michael: "Well, there you go then, so now you know it does cross the membrane and did affect him."

Laura: "I always thought that being on those antibiotics is what did that to him, gave him thrush."

Michael: "And also he wasn't getting the oxygen he needed."

Laura: "Probably because I couldn't breathe very well."

Michael: "Exactly, because your lungs were not to capacity."

Laura: "Yeah, and that was at the end of the pregnancy. I'll have to go look it up, but I know I was really sick when he was due, and he was 10 days late. So if I would have gone into labor at his due date, I probably wouldn't have been able to have natural childbirth, I would have had to have had a c-section because I was so sick. But then I got better."

Michael: "Ok, he's saying the 14th. What happened?"

Laura: "That's the day he was born! July 14th."

Michael: "He was born on the 14th? That's what this man is saying to me."

Laura: "Oh, my God!"

Michael: "This isn't Albert, you know. This is…"

Laura: "Fredrich?"

Michael: "Listen, he seems almost like a more like a doctor to me. He's more of a medical research person, but he calls himself a scientist, you see? And I'm sure he knows Albert, and he says 'I do.' So, he's very precise, this man. But great energy, I like him. He's very old fashioned in the way he speaks. So, he's very deliberate. See, I asked him for the date to convince you that he knows what he's talking about."

Laura: "Yes."

(On December 3, 1933, Albert Einstein wrote a letter to David L. Edsall, Dean of the Harvard Medical school in an attempt to free Dessauer from prison after being arrested by the Nazis on trumped up charges. According to Einstein's letter, "I am referring to Prof. Dr. Friedrich Dessauer, University of Frankfurt who has made a name for himself in the field of experimental physics applied to medicine.[16]" So, yes, they did know each other, and Dessauer was both a doctor and a scientist, like Michael said.)

Michael: "He doesn't want you to go away thinking that there was anything that you did, not to have any thoughts that it was in any way your fault. Do you understand this?"

Laura: "Well, thank you for saying that." *(I still felt some blame.)*

Michael: "Well, this is what he says. And you need to take his word for it, okay?"

Laura: "Okay. So, did that set him up somehow for what happened?"

Michael: "To a degree, he said, yes. It didn't help."

Laura: "So, what happened then?"

Michael: "Oh, boy, I've got to listen to him here. He says his understanding of it is that something triggered it later. That his system was already compromised and that the things that were taken or given to him? I'll get to that in a second. He says, but what happened to him later triggered it, like triggered a response, or triggered a, like a latent thing."

(After the session, I looked in Trevor's baby book and was horrified to learn that I was sick not once but twice while pregnant with him, once in the fourth month, where I was sick for two weeks and put on antibiotics, and again at the very end of my pregnancy, where I was sick for three weeks and put on Darvocet and antibiotics. Even more

---

[16] Albert Einstein Archives, Hebrew University of Jerusalem, Document 49 476-1 and 2.

horrifying was the discovery that Darvocet was recalled by the FDA a month prior to this session in November 2010 because of serious heart risks! I also learned that respiratory infections are usually viral, not bacterial, so the antibiotics I was prescribed probably did nothing for my lung infection, but did cause thrush in my son. He also had cradle cap, which is fungus. Notice what comes next in this session following the previous comment about what it was that triggered what happened to my son later.)

Michael: "Did your son have any food poisoning? Or did you suffer food poisoning?"

Laura: "I think he did. We do this energetic testing called QXCI *(aka Quantum Biofeedback or QB)* and it's come up that he's had food poisoning."

Michael: "Food poisoning, like when he was little?"

Laura: "I don't know if it was when he was little. It's not that I had to ever take him to the hospital or anything for it, but I think that he's had a lot of different poisons."

Michael: "This sounds crazy, but I don't know what Botulism is."

Laura: "It's food poisoning."

Michael: "Oh, is it?"

Laura: "Yeah, Botulinum toxin. Yeah, that's one of the toxins he had in his system."

Michael: "Oh, I said, 'Botulism? That sounds a bit extreme.' I had no idea what that is. Then he said, 'Food poisoning.'"

Laura: "The bacteria Botulinum toxin."

Michael: "Now why is he bringing this up?"

Laura: "I don't know."

Michael: "Botulism, that's what he said. Alright, I'm going to have to take him very, very seriously. Botulism, food poisoning."

(After the session, I looked up botulism and learned that it is caused by the botulinum toxin produced by the spore-forming bacteria Clostridium botulinum, and is the most poisonous substance on Earth. Inhalation botulism is caused by aerosolized botulinum toxin that could be used as a biological weapon. It is a neurotoxin and has seven types, A-G. Botulinum toxin is also what is used in Botox. Hear that ladies? The CDC has designated Clostridium botulinum as a Category A bioterrorism threat, which are

considered to pose the greatest threat to U.S. health and security.[17] My son had tested positive for it during QB as well as BioSET sessions previously. On the QB printout, it says BOTULISM- CLOSTRIDIUM BOTULINUM, bacteria, attacks nerves, Biological Warfare Variations.)

Michael: "It seems he was talking about the effect on your son's stomach, you know, the antibiotics, right? And how he had a weakened system, and then he starts talking about botulism and food poisoning, ok?"

Laura: "Ok."

Michael: "Now, perhaps we're dealing with a couple of different issues and they're not directly connected. It could be a couple of different things, you see, like we said before. There might be different causes to similar things, follow me?"

Laura: "Mmm-hmm."

Michael: "So, he appears to be talking directly about your son. There seems to be similarities in other cases. So there may be other people who went through similar things as you. A lot of this isn't looked at, you see? People overlook things."

Laura: "Mmm-hmm."

Michael: "They're not looking at what was going on while the person was pregnant. Because, you see, if they believe that nothing interacts with the placenta, then they are going to dismiss it."

Laura: "Yeah. They have birth drugs that they give to women to induce labor, I didn't have any of that, but a lot of women think that it also harmed their child."

Michael: "Oh, I didn't know that. They give drugs to women?"

Laura: "Oh, yeah. Epidurals, Pitocin, all kinds of stuff."

Michael: "What do they do all of that for?"

Laura: "To schedule the birth, so the doctor can golf."

Michael: "Oh, that's what it's about. Let's see if he can give me some names, because I don't know them, if he comes up with that, it would be great."

---

[17] www.cdc.gov Facts about Botulism

Michael mentioned the names of two more spirits that were there to help. The first one was a professor with a first name that started with an "A" that sounded like "Aberon" and a last name that sounded like "Plex" with a "Z" sound in it. He was having a hard time hearing the name, so I looked for names in the book *Einstein: His Life and Universe* by Walter Isaacson, which had I recently bought to try to validate some of the information that was coming through. I saw the name Abraham Flexner, who was an American Education Reformer. He founded the Institute for Advanced Study in Princeton, and recruited Einstein there. Michael got all excited when I told him.

Earlier in the session, a guy named Philip showed up that Michael said sounded French like Phillipe. As I was reading about Abraham Flexner in the Einstein book, the name underneath his was Philipp Frank. I told Michael and again he got excited, "Philipp! Yes!" I told him that the book said that Philipp Frank was an Austrian Physicist who succeeded his friend Einstein at German University of Prague and later wrote a book about him. Michael said, "I couldn't get the last name, but I knew it was Philipp. Oh, absolutely. This guy is Austrian, the one who is talking to me."

(After the session, I looked up Philipp Frank a bit more, and found that Albert Einstein recommended him as his successor for a professorship at the German Charles-Ferdinand University of Prague, which he held from 1912-1938. His book about Einstein is called "Einstein: His Life and Times." I also found that Abraham Flexner, aside from personally inviting Albert Einstein to the United States and the Institute for Advanced Study, also helped reform American medical education. I could see why he would be interested in the subject matter.)

Michael added, "Philipp is one of the people here. In fact, I don't think Albert has said anything to me yet. He's brought his friends, he said. I think they all have something to say on the subject, you see? They describe themselves as like a group of friends who all are extremely interested in helping, ok? So they're like a group of friends, but they're sort of scientists, medical people, there are a bunch of them, you see? And they are working together to solve problems, they said. To try and help solve some of the problems."

Next, Michael asked me what other questions I had. I replied:

Laura: "Well, since they just brought this up, I want to know what happened to my child. What triggered what happened to him? Because I know he wasn't born that way."

Michael: "No, he wasn't born that way. But some of the things that happened to him, weakened him, and it's like it set him up for something that happened. They said something was given to him. Something he took. They said he was given something or he took something that caused this. That's what they said. So let me narrow that down, let me see if I can find out what that is."

"They are showing me metal, but I don't know if they are showing me mercury, but they are showing me metal. What looks like some shiny metal? Now I can't imagine he swallowed metal."

Laura: "No, but there was mercury in the vaccines he received as a child."

Michael: "Did you notice a difference after that?"

Laura: "It was a gradual thing. It was between ages one and two that he started losing skills."

Michael: "They said at one year."

Laura: "Mmm-hmm. Did a vaccine trigger this?"

Michael: "I think so?"

Laura: "Which one? Or was it a combination?"

Michael: "Was he given 10 shots in that space of time?"

Laura: "At the one year appointment, I think there are 3 different shots given with 3 different things in each one. I'll have to look up his record, but I know he got the MMR, Polio, HiB, and I forget…"

(After the session, I looked up Trevor's vaccination record and cringed to find that at 13-months-old, he received the MMR vaccine and the Chickenpox vaccine on the same day; this is Measles, Mumps, Rubella, and Varicella; four live viruses all at once. Two months later, he received the HiB, [Haemophilus Influenza Type B], the IPV, [Inactivated Polio Vaccine], and the DtaP, [Diphtheria, Tetanus and acellular Pertussis] vaccines. All three of these vaccines contained Thimerosal at the time, a mercury-based preservative, containing nearly 50 percent mercury.)

Michael: "Every time I look, I see shimmering metal. Looks like fluid metal. It's got to be mercury. Every time I look toward them, that's what they show me. They're talking about it impairing brain function. Mercury

will impair brain function."

I mentioned that they claimed to have taken Thimerosal out of the vaccines in 1999, but the autism rate increased. We discussed how they use fear to manipulate people into doing what they want, like getting the flu shot, which still contains mercury. He gets pretty passionate about the government and what they're up to. Michael began channeling again:

Michael: "He's talking about poison. So, I don't know if he means the mercury or if he's talking about some other additive or some other thing that is like arsenic, but it seems to be like a poison, ok?"

Laura: "Ok."

Michael: "He said it's like a poison, but it's called something else. It almost acts like an oxygen depletent. So it's something that has an effect on iron or something or causes the blood to not carry oxygen. I know it sounds crazy. I have no idea what I'm saying to you right now. I just have to go with it. You have no idea how foolish I feel when I'm doing this stuff, especially when I don't understand it."

Laura: "No, just say what they're saying and I'll look it up."

Michael: "Well that's what they're talking about, ok? It seems to be something that over a period of time causes the blood to not carry oxygen."

Laura: "Ok."

Michael: "It causes things like asthma, bronchial infections, and poor digestion. It causes an array of things; skin conditions, hypersensitivity, especially to touch."

Laura: "Yes."

Michael: "So, I don't know if some of these kids don't like to be touched or picked up."

Laura: "Yep. They can't stand tags on their clothes; they don't like to be hugged. Where is this poison that does that coming from?"

Michael: "It could be in an array of things, you just have to identify the poison, but it's almost like they are overdosing on arsenic or something. Ok, let me tell you this, this is what they're saying. When people are getting this sick, or this messed up, en masse, they're telling me it's like

a pointer to a greater problem."

(After the session a lot of information came my way about sources of arsenic. For instance, apple juice, because the seeds have arsenic in them and are blended into the juice; rice, mainly rice grown in the Southern U.S., used in infant formula, rice milk and many gluten-free products; and conventional chicken, because chicken feed has arsenic in it, and then the arsenic filled chicken poop is used to feed cows. Interestingly, HBOT is used to treat arsenic poisoning.)

Next, Michael asked me if I had done any detoxes for metals on my son. I told him yes. I did homeopathic detoxes numerous times. Then he brought up the name Arthur again. I was thinking it was Arthur Stanley Eddington again, but then Michael asked me if I had any questions. I told him:

Laura: "I'm just now a bit more confused here. Are they saying that mercury, or all these shots in one day triggered what they're calling autism in my son, or is it other poisons added to it?"

Michael: "What I get from them is what you call autism is many things. It's obviously brain damage of some sort, ok?"

He mentioned the hypersensitivity in these kids, and added. "Now, that is where mankind is heading. That is the future. We are going to be super sensitive as a race. Now, normal, the regular people, there are insensitive, so we'll call it a negative condition. In a way, it's like autistic kids are not prepared to deal with their super sensitivity, or their hypersensitivity. They can't control it because they're not adults." Continuing to try to answer my question, he said:

Michael: "It could be something that's in the air that maybe works in conjunction with mercury and some of the medicines. Because every time I look, they show me the bloodstream. So there must be something in the blood, or that stays in the blood. This definitely seems to be part of the immune system. Almost like the immune system is on like overload. So, anything that makes it worse than it already is, and it can be many things."

Then he brought up Hyperbaric Oxygen Therapy (HBOT) again. I told him that I had just made an appointment for Trevor to start the following week to do 30 sessions of HBOT after receiving some funding to pay for it through a local autism organization. Michael said "This gentleman that's been talking to me the whole time, he says he's cautioning you against expecting immediate results, but he's confident that you will notice a marked improvement from the chamber. You should notice a difference in a week, he said. Wait and see what happens with the hyperbaric chamber. That's really going to improve oxygen flow in the blood and everything and I think you're going to see some major results." I was so excited to try it out and see what was going to happen.

Before the session ended, Michael brought up the fact that mercury is still in the flu shots given to children. I mentioned that there is also mercury in the Rhogam shot, which women get during pregnancy and again after the birth if they have a negative blood type, as mine is. Marti said that she even got that shot forty years ago because her blood type was also Rh negative. Then he channeled a few more things about my son, for example that when he was a baby he curled up in the fetal position and had a lot of stomach problems. This was true, he was colicky and could curl his knees up to his chest and I later learned that he had fungus, bacterial infections, parasites and food allergies. Michael said that most children with autism are overly acidic and need to be more alkaline. He added that we breathe in a lot of acidity from pollution in the air, and that the oxygen content in the air is very low.

Michael finished the channeling and we talked about some of the political issues surrounding autism. Michael said "A lot of the research has been done and swept under the rug. Doctors that do research that goes against the AMA get thrown out, they get ostracized and they're history. They lose their license. This goes on all the time or they mysteriously die if they bang heads with the government. The government wants them to say one thing, they're saying no, that's not what my research says and then they mysteriously jump out of a window or something. This stuff goes on all the time; I've been watching it for decades. So this is what we're dealing with."

He added, "The government at the end of the day is a collection of people, and we don't really know who half these people are. It's not like our elected government. It's a collection of individuals with ulterior mo-tives, people behind the government. Just because the guy is the Presi-dent, he has all these cronies around him, his buddies and pals. They get elected into these lifelong positions, and they bring in their people with their agendas. So, you're dealing with a vast corruption, and it's all about money and agendas."

***

Session Three – After the Session

Featured Spirits: Friedrich Dessauer, Albert Einstein, Wolfgang Pauli, Abraham Flexner, Philipp Frank, Arthur Stanley Eddington

Now, remember, during the session, I did not know yet that the names mentioned were actual people. It wasn't like Michael telling me my family member's names, which I could instantly validate. No, I had to look them up after the fact, and was both shocked and delighted to see the dots connect. This is very crucial to the credibility of the story. I was given names of people I didn't know by dead people, and didn't find out until after the session that they even existed. Not only that they existed, but what they said about themselves, and their connections to one another were totally true! Don't you think that if we were making this up, we would pick people that everyone knew? I'd never heard of them. The point is, these people were all real, and connected.

Trust me, the research was exhausting. Thank God I'm a good speller. If you get one letter wrong, you might not find what you're looking for. Foreign names are especially challenging, which many of these were. I miraculously looked in the right places and found the validations. When I called Michael to tell him about Friedrich Dessauer and Wolfgang Pauli and all of the other validations I found afterward, he was so encouraged and happy. Accuracy is a big deal to a medium.

I really couldn't wait to start HBOT now! This was the third dead person that brought it up in the past few months in regards to my son. First was my late husband, then Albert, and now a medical physicist, Fredrich Dessauer. Here is another interesting part of the HBOT saga. When I was researching which place to take my son to do HBOT, there were a few options. I went to check out one facility and talk to the director and the building was called the Center for Advanced Medicine. I had to look back at my notes after hearing that name because it rang a bell. Sure enough, in our first session for this book, Michael said "They're talking...something about a Center for Advanced Disease Control or something like that." Medicine is disease control. This was a sign to me that I was in the right place.

Like all therapies, there are numerous options. I chose the hard chamber over the soft chamber because it is 100% medical grade oxygen done in a medical facility using a specific protocol facilitated by trained profess-sionals; not a blow up oxygen chamber with only partial oxygen and forced air facilitated by amateurs or by me. This was a medical procedure, and I wanted to do it the right way. After the name of the building had come through in a channeling session, I felt confident with my choice. With the cost of a lot of treatments, and what's at stake, you have to do your research. Time is of the essence. No one wants to waste precious time or money on treatments that don't benefit their child. If I hadn't received the funding for our sessions, we never would have been able to afford HBOT. We paid $150 per session for 30 sessions. You do the math. I felt that I had angels looking out for me, helping me line up the funding for my son. I will discuss our experience with HBOT in a later chapter, be-cause he did another series of 40 later on.

***

Chapter Six

*"The nation that destroys its soil
destroys itself."*

— Franklin D. Roosevelt

Session Four

This session was done three days before Christmas in 2010, so Marti was out shopping when Michael and I did our phone session. Michael didn't know this at the time, but I had written at the top of my note page "Is Biological Warfare causing regressive autism?" I was hoping some spirit would read it and give Michael the answer for me. I felt I still needed some clarity on this since it was brought up in our first session of the book and again in the session before this, as well as three years prior during the channeling sessions that I did with the other medium. I felt that there was more to talk about on the subject. Michael began by saying:

Michael: "There is another new person here with the name "Franklin." I said "Franklin?" And he said "Yes."

Michael didn't know this at the time either, but in addition to Albert Einstein, President Franklin D. Roosevelt was one of the spirits that came through to talk to me via the other medium for my other book, *Foundation of Discovery*. So, naturally I said:

Laura: "I was thinking Franklin Roosevelt when you first said it."

Michael: "Yeah, I thought of that for a moment, but I thought, nah, why would he be here?"

Laura: "Because he had come through to me before."

Michael: "What?"

Laura: "He did."

Michael: "Are you serious?"

Laura: "Uh-huh."

Michael: "Roosevelt?"

Laura: "Yes, FDR."

Michael: "That's who I first thought it was."

Laura: "Yeah, FDR. See if that's him."

Michael: "Did he have orthopedic problems?"

Laura: "He had polio."

Michael: "Oh!"

Laura: "He was in a wheelchair."

Michael: "Somebody said something about an orthopedic doctor, or orthopedic surgeon to me. Alright, hold on a second. Let's see if, oh blimey."

(Orthopedics is the study of the musculoskeletal system. Orthopedic treatment is used for poliomyelitis to prevent deformities.)

Michael: "Ok, let's see. This is a weird one; I don't know how I'd prove it was him. Why would he be here? I know he's here to help. I wonder if he passed any laws for children, concerning medical care for children."

Laura: "He did have a lot to do with special needs laws."

Michael: "Did he?"

Laura: "Yes, and he founded the March of Dimes."

Michael: "What's that?"

Laura: "It's for disabilities, it's a fundraising…"

Michael: "This might be him because he's talking about what he did for children. Cuz I'm asking him why he's here and some of other people in the room said it's because he had a lot to do with helping children. I said, "Really?" And they said, "Yeah.""

Laura: "Yeah."

Michael: "I had no idea he did that. Ok. Funding, he's talking about funding."

"Hmm. He keeps repeating "Missy" to me. It seems to be the name of someone immediate to him, like a nickname but it sounds like "Missy.""

Laura: "Ok."

Michael: "He's going to have to say some things that we're not going to know, that we'll have to find out."

Laura: "Yeah, I don't know who "Missy" is, I'll look it up."

(After the session I looked this up and found that President Roosevelt's personal secretary was named Marguerite "Missy" LeHand. There were rumors of a romantic involvement between them as well. This was a huge validation that it was really him.)

Michael: "Did he smoke a pipe? Do you know?"

Laura: "I don't know if he did."

(After the session, I found that FDR smoked a pipe occasionally but was well known to smoke cigarettes in a cigarette holder.)

Michael: "Interesting. They're going back to the blood converting again. So, I think the biggest issue is the thing we discussed about the blood not carrying the oxygen, or there is something blocking it. Like a beta-blocker, whatever that is. They're saying Beta Blocker. Ok?"

"You know, I think it is FDR."

Laura: "Yeah?"

Michael: "Yeah. I just heard somebody say it is, so I think it is. That's interesting. I didn't know he was so much into kid's stuff."

Laura: "Yeah, he also was a patron of the Big Brothers/Big Sisters Foundation."

(I knew these things about him because I looked him up three years prior.)

Michael: "Now, he says 'I'm here today to talk not just about your child, but all children.'"

Laura: "Ok."

Michael: "He says ever since he's gone over there, he's had a great interest in helping children. Even greater than when he was here. He says, 'There is definitely brain damage, but it's not irreversible.'"

Laura: "Oh, awesome!"

Michael: "So, there's hope for a lot of these kids out there. 'It's not irreversible,' he says."

Laura: "Ok. How do you reverse it?"

Michael: "Well, he's taking about the right nutrition as one of the main

key factors."

Laura: "Mmm-hmm."

(This sounded a lot like how he came across in the sessions for my other book, very strong willed and determined, and wanting to help children.)

Next, Michael asked me if we could listen to music while we were in the Hyperbaric Chamber. I told him that there was a TV above us that the sound from it came into the chamber. I was in there with him during his sessions. He suggested that we play a CD of elevated music, like classical music to help facilitate a deeper healing. I told him that I had all of the Baby Einstein DVDs which has classical music playing. He said that it would be good, because he was hearing classical music playing in the background. Then he said:

Michael: "Is there any difference in the brain barrier? The membrane around the brain of kids with autism?"

Laura: "I don't know. I've just heard a lot about things crossing the blood brain barrier."

Michael: "They're talking about the blood brain barrier, ok?"

Laura: "Ok."

Michael: "It seems to me that there's a blockage, or certain things don't reach the brain. It's like the brain is stifled. Starved as it were, one of them is saying to me. Maybe it's particularly fatty? It seems to be a deal to do with fat, though."

Laura: "I know the brain is a very fatty organ."

Michael: "But it's in the fat. Something's like collecting in the fat."

Laura: "Is it mercury?"

Michael: "Well, it's like it short-circuits it, or it just doesn't allow it to perform its function. I think it's mercury, is the biggest problem."

Then Michael said that they were talking about a virus. I told him that a lot of kids with autism had a lot of viruses and when they went on antivirals they got better. I asked him if it was a brain virus, because I had recently heard about a doctor who claimed that he detected a virus in the brains of children with autism and was using a series of frequency-based patches to treat the virus. Michael said that they were talking about the brain and now they were talking about a virus. I told him that they named the virus R1H2 and it is of unknown origin and was detected in 90-some percent of all children with autism that they tested.

(Ricky Hunt, the creator of the Aura Patches passed away in 2011. He found the virus in over 90 percent of more than 300 children with autism using an energetic form of testing. I had recently started using them with Trevor on a recommendation by our QB practitioner. She tested Trevor energetically using the patches and he had the virus.)

I told Michael that one of my questions was about where this virus comes from. He responded:

Michael: "I think it's a genetically engineered virus."

Laura: "Ok."

Michael: "I just asked them flat; I said where does it come from? Is it a genetically engineered one? That's what I think, am I correct? And they said, 'Yes.'"

Laura: "And how are they getting it?"

Michael: "I'm asking. They're testing it. On what? For what purpose? Oh, boy. Is this like a weapons program? They're talking about it's a virus that was used, that they are messing around with; they're testing for a weapons program."

Laura: "Yep."

Michael: "And I don't know if it just got out or they're deliberately experimenting with it? Testing, I'd say testing. So this is a covert thing that they're doing under the guise of normal procedure."

He said it was being created in a lab, but couldn't pinpoint where. He also mentioned something being in the shots and something in the air. Also that it didn't show up straight away. Then Michael said that they were talking about Chromium and Bromide. I asked if it was a combination of the vaccines and something in the air.

Michael: "Well it may be, maybe one is a trigger, and maybe that's why it doesn't happen immediately. It could be a combination of the things, you know, working in conjunction with one another."

Laura: "Hmmm."

(I also learned after the session that Chromium-6, also known as the Erin Brockovich

chemical, is present in the majority of U.S. cities, according to a study done by the Environmental Working Group. Chromium-6 or hexavalent chromium is a cancer causing toxic metal which can be released from steel, pulp mills, metal plating and leather-tanning facilities. Bromide was harder to pinpoint which one they meant. It is used in treating water, and can be in drinking water. It is also used in bread in the U.S. And it is supposedly one of the chemicals released in Chemtrails, spread by planes in the air.)

Michael: "And they're also saying Chlorine."

Laura: "Oh, okay.

Michael: "Do autistic kids, does their skin absorb things quicker than other kids?"

Laura: "I don't know, but they can get Chlorine from the water in the bath through their skin, was what I was just thinking, because there is Chlorine in the water."

Michael: "Well, I'm trying to narrow this down, you know. There are lots of things, because we are not dealing with just one thing, that's the problem. But it's this virus thing that's getting me."

Laura: "Mmm-hmm."

Michael: "It does appear to be a virus, or act like a virus."

Laura: "I'd like to know more about this virus too."

Michael: "I wish I had a scientist on hand so I could ask about this stuff. Apart from these guys, you know. Is it in the air? It's a combination, is it? Does the nervous system get attacked?"

Laura: "Yes."

Michael: "They are talking about the reaction to all this, is that the nervous system comes under attack."

Laura: "Yep."

Michael: "Whatever this is causes the body to attack itself."

Laura: "Ok."

Michael: "And the nervous system comes under attack, that's what they're telling me, ok?"

Laura: "Is it like an autoimmune response?"

Michael: "Yeah, yeah, it has to do with the immune system, because the immune system is very weak and highly susceptible, so hence you have various conditions. So, you don't have just one, you see, because different people react in different ways. Their bodies react in different ways depending on their constitutions, how they are made up."

Laura: "Ok."

Michael: "They are talking in old terms, some of these people. So, it's kind of weird."

Next, Michael asked me if my son's skin itched. I told him yes, and that he liked to be scratched a lot. Michael said that his skin itched and he asked the spirits why they were making his skin itch, and they said because her son's skin itched. Then he said "You see, your skin is the outside of your insides. Your stomach and your intestines and your insides are simply the skin as well, you follow me? Your skin is an organ. And it's inside and outside. So whatever is going on inside, is going on the outside, and whatever is going on outside is affecting the inside. So, because the skin is the biggest organ, and you look at it like an organ... This hypersensitivity thing, we're back to this again." Then he asked if my son was allergic to dust, had a fast heart rate, and had high sugar levels. I answered yes to all of them.

Then Michael started talking about opiates and didn't know what they were getting at. I told him that lots of kids with autism are allergic to wheat and dairy, which have an opiate effect on them because they don't digest them properly. He said that's what they are talking about. He added "This is kind of weird, I've never done this before, but they're using the back of my pen, and I'm wearing corduroy pants, and they are sketching something on my pants and it looks like a stalk of wheat. It looks like the top of a piece of wheat. And that's what they are sketching up. And they're going on about opiates." I told Michael that gluten is the protein in wheat that becomes like a drug to them, and that when I took it out of Trevor's diet, he got better. To that Michael said:

Michael: "Wow, this is interesting. Well you know they've been messing around with, what do you call it? Changing the DNA of different foods."

Laura: "Yeah, Genetically Modified Organisms, GMO's."

Michael: "I've got to find this out, hold on. Is the wheat not wheat any more, is it altered wheat, or is it something in their bodies that is altered and is reacting to the wheat? It's altered wheat. Is the wheat we're getting more modified than we realize? Every time I ask them, the answer is 'Yes.'"

(I learned after the session that wheat has not been genetically modified yet, although Monsanto has a patent on it. Wheat has been hybridized to the point that the body doesn't recognize it. So, it isn't the same wheat anymore. I will explain more in the summary about the extremely scary things I did learn about GMO's after this was brought up in the session.)

Michael: "You know who owns most of it is chemical companies."

Laura: "Monsanto."

Michael: "And the chemical companies are putting patents, if you can believe it, on every seed and plant that you can think of so that nobody else can use it. How you can patent a plant, I don't know, but that's what they're doing, they own a patent on it."

Laura: "Right, I know."

Michael: "But if their genetically modified seed lands on your land, it belongs to them. Can you believe this crap? But that's what they're up to."

Laura: "I know, it's ridiculous. So, don't feed them any Genetically Modified foods, is that what we're getting at?"

Michael: "Yeah. I'm trying to figure out their purpose for this then. What are they up to? All I can think of is that they're seeing what the effects are on people with genetically modified products. They seem to be messing around with a lot of different things, genetically, and the general population is like an experiment."

"They keep making me think that the virus doesn't act like a normal virus."

I asked Michael how all of this fit together and he said that they're doing so many different things that it is hard to figure out which thing is causing what, that's the problem. He mentioned that several countries are altering the weather and using weather as a weapon. He ended the session with "It's like a giant puzzle, isn't it?"

***

Session Four – After the Session
__Featured Spirit:__ President Franklin Delano Roosevelt

This session was very interesting for numerous reasons. First of all, the fact that similar information via a different medium came through three years apart referring to a virus in the brain that is genetically engineered and had to do with a "weapons program" shows me that there is definitely a need to investigate this possibility further. What if this were true? It would change the whole concept of certain types of autism from being a "developmental disability" into being a "disease" which means it is potentially curable. But how do you treat a virus in the brain?

The blood-brain-barrier (BBB) is a shield of tightly packed cells which protects the brain from blood-borne intruders such as bacteria, but also keeps out most large drug molecules. Most medicines and supplements don't cross the blood-brain barrier, which is why it is hard to treat brain disorders and diseases. According to the website for ArmaGen, a Biotechnology company trying to create pharmaceuticals to treat brain diseases, "In order to cross the BBB, small molecules must have a molecular weight of <400 Daltons and must also be lipid soluble." [18] Less than two percent of all drugs have these properties. This means traditional antivirals, antibiotics and antifungals which are large molecule drugs, don't cross the BBB. Oxygen, which is a gas, as in HBOT, crosses the BBB; repairs damaged brain tissue, and awakens neurons. Does it kill pathogens in the brain? More on this topic later.

The energetic patch system that I was talking about during the session was the only way I had heard of (at the time) that could potentially reach the virus in the brain. The founder of the company, the late Ricky Hunt, said in an interview that I listened to that he discovered a parasitic virus of unknown origin that had an affinity for the brain. Most viruses have a specific part of the body that they live in, and in this case it was the brain. The patches were encoded with bio-resonant energy meant to restore the body's energy system. People with the same disease had the same missing frequencies, and the patches were supposed to bring back these energies

[18] www.armagen.com/about-bbb.php

to the level of a healthy person. It expanded on the concepts of home-opathy. I used the patches on Trevor for a year and saw some improvement, but certainly not recovery. Another company makes the patches now. Again, more on this topic to come.

Another huge component of this session was that FDR came through again! Michael did not know that he had come through to me before, and then when he asked for proof that it was really him, FDR gave the name "Missy," the nickname of someone connected to him. I didn't find out until after the session that his personal secretary's nickname was Missy. Let that sink in for a second. A dead person gives us a name that is later validated to be true. Again, go back to the odds of getting a name correct. Plus, how many Franklin's and Missy's are there? Add to that the mention of Orthopedics, helping children, and smoking and it all adds up. For FDR to come through again for me validates the fact that it was truly him the first time around. So, not only did the same information come through two different mediums about biological warfare being involved in autism, but the same spirits brought through the information, without prior knowledge of the second medium. Ponder that for a moment. When just one medium said it, it was questionable. But when the two most accurate mediums I have ever known say the same thing, it becomes much more valid.

Michael wondered why FDR would be coming through in our session. Besides the fact that he had come through to me before, FDR was the President that started the Biological Weapons program in the U.S. in 1942 at Ft. Detrick, MD. It made perfect sense to me why he'd be coming through. He could see what a mess things had become regarding biological warfare. The question I had written on my note page was addressed during the session. Biological warfare was not the only cause of autism, but it was a contributing factor in many children, including my own.

After this session, I did a lot of research into Genetically Modified Foods, and was completely horrified at my findings. So much so, that I read the labels of every food in our house and threw away bags of food that possibly contained it. I did the same thing with Trevor's foods when I decided to put him on a gluten-free diet. This time, it was for the entire family. Certain people in my family probably thought I was a nut job I'm sure, but I was not budging on this one. I will explain why.

For those of you who don't know what Genetically Modified (GM) or Genetically Engineered (GE) foods are, also known as Genetically Modified Organisms (GMO), I will give you a brief overview. Genetically Modified or 'transgenic' crops are created in a laboratory by moving genes into a plant from another species to obtain a desired trait. In many cases the genes used to create transgenic crops come from bacteria or viruses. The majority of transgenic crops contain one of two genetically modified traits: an insecticidal toxin from the Bt bacterium (*Bacillus thuringiensis*), or resistance to an herbicide (Glyphosate, commonly known as Roundup), owned by Monsanto. In plants modified with the Bt toxin, the plant produces its own pesticide, killing target insects. Roundup Ready plants can be sprayed with the herbicide, killing weeds, but not the GE plants.

We are not talking about hybridization or cross-breeding techniques here. You can't cross a plant with an animal by hybridization, only through Genetic Engineering. Some of the techniques used include using viruses or bacteria to "infect" animal or plant cells with the new DNA and coating DNA onto tiny metal pellets and firing it with a special gun into the cells.

What's so bad about GMO? Where do I begin? I am going to focus for a moment on how Genetic Engineering could have affected a healthy child who would later be diagnosed with autism. First of all, the autism epidemic that we are facing exploded in the 1990's. In 1994, rBGH (Recombinant Bovine Growth Hormone) was a Genetically Engineered growth hormone injected into cows to make them produce more milk. If your child drank infant formula, like mine did, it was Frankenformula, with many GE ingredients from milk, soy and corn products. Regressive autism is twelve times more common in formula fed infants than breastfed infants. Red flag!

Then, if your child was sensitive to the formula, as mine was, you were probably advised by your pediatrician to switch to a soy formula. Also Frankenformula, as the majority of soy was and is Genetically Engineered in the U.S. Then, when your child turned one, your pediatrician probably recommended that they switch to cow's milk, also Genetically Engineered thanks again to rBGH. By then they were eating GE foods as well that were snuck into the food supply.

Guess what they feed the GE injected cows? You guessed it, GE corn and GE alfalfa. Unless the cows were grass-fed and the milk was organic, chances are your child was ingesting GMO. GE corn is altered to produce its own pesticide, *Bacillus thuringiensis* (Bt). It destroys the guts of the insects that ingest it, causing death. It is designed to create holes in the digestive tract of insects. Does leaky gut ring a bell? What do you think happens to an infant's gut when it ingests it? Nobody knows, because no human testing was done prior to putting it on the market.

Even worse, a recent study from the University of Sherbrooke, Canada have detected the presence of Bt toxin in the blood of 93 percent of pregnant women and in 80 percent of their unborn babies blood. Promoters of GE crops have maintained that Bt toxin poses no danger to human health as the protein breaks down in the human gut. The presence of Bt toxin in maternal and fetal blood shows that this is not true. GE crops are banned in 80 countries or require labeling; the U.S. and Canada are not among them.

Now here is where it gets even scarier. Remember when I said that in the sessions for my other book; the spirits mentioned the biowarfare blowing across the country? The world actually, the wind patterns go across the planet. They mentioned that it was also genetically engineered and made up in part with *Bacillus anthracis.* In my new research, I learned that there are three Bacillus bacteria species which all live in the soil and are so closely related that they may as well be regarded as a single species. *B. anthracis* causes anthrax, *B. cereus* is linked to food poisoning, and *B. thuringiensis* is of course the biopesticide in GE crops. The three readily mate with one another and exchange plasmids (circular pieces of DNA) carrying specific toxin and virulence genes.[19] Dangerous recombinants could arise between the Bt plant debris and the *B. anthracis* bacteria in the soil.

In another article I read titled "Bad Medicine" from the *Bulletin of the Atomic Scientists* from Nov. 1998, Professor Emeritus Conrad A. Istock writes "The genes for the anthrax toxin do not reside on the bacterium's main chromosome, but on a smaller secondary DNA molecule called a plasmid. In laboratory experiments, these plasmids have transferred from *Bacillus anthracis* to other species of bacteria. One transfer was to *Bacillus thuringiensis*." He added "The transfer of plasmids occurs naturally among many bacteria. Massive releases of anthrax spores could easily lead,

---

[19] www.badseed.info/resources/anthrax.php

through the infection of animals, to spontaneous transfers of the plasmids to other bacteria as well. While anthrax does not spread from one human to another, it can propagate in the soil." He also states that "Were a large quantity of anthrax spores to be dispersed, the soil, vegetation, local animals, equipment, supplies, clothing and personnel would be contaminated with dormant spores. Spores that adhere to objects or collect in recesses or on fabrics will readily become airborne again. They will remain viable for a long time." My thoughts: What happens when a person eats food grown in this soil? Could these recombined bacteria be in the food? Is the Bt toxin in GE crops recombining with and becoming weaponized anthrax or a new mutated version?

In the sessions for *Foundation of Discovery,* the spirits mentioned that root vegetables were especially bad, mainly potatoes. They likened eating them to cannibalism, because the body attacks itself when it eats self. I found out after this session that between 1995 and 2001 Monsanto introduced a range of GM potatoes in the U.S and Canada, called Newleaf and Naturemark with resistances against the Colorado potato beetle with pesticide producing Bt toxin in them. In 1998 and 1999, Monsanto received full regulatory authorization in the U.S. and Canada for additional genetically modified potatoes: the NewLeaf Plus for Russet Burbank and the NewLeaf Y for the Russet Burbank and the Shepody varieties. These new products provided crops resistance to the potato leafroll virus and the Y virus, respectively, in addition to insect protection. Farmers started to grow these potatoes on about 50,000 acres in Idaho, the East, Northwest, and Midwest, representing about 3.5% of the Nation's potato acreage. Major companies such as McDonald's, Wendy's and Frito-Lay refused to use GM potatoes, primarily due to consumer skepticism regarding the unknown environmental and health consequences of GM foods, and they were taken off the market in 2001. What happened to the soil that grew these GE potatoes, and to the new non-GMO potatoes that took their place? Currently, one third of all cropland in the U.S., or 165 million acres contains GE crops. Scared yet?

Although classified as a pesticide, Bt is actually a protein, and in the case of the Bt potato, the protein is meant to bind to receptors in a beetles stomach, inhibiting its ability to digest food. Children with autism have problems digesting their food. Most of them take digestive enzymes because of this common problem. My son with autism was born in 1998, during the time GE potatoes and other foods were snuck into our food

135

supply. I'm sure he ate his fair share. My other son, who was also allergic to milk, actually drank a popular milk substitute made from gulp, potatoes. Luckily, he wasn't born until 2001, when they took the GE potatoes off the market, but who knows?

Now, take the GE foods a child is eating and drinking, and add to it a genetically engineered bioweapon that children are being exposed to, via air, food and water. Michael mentioned in the session that there was a genetically engineered virus that was part of a weapons program. The medium from my other book also talked about biowarfare in the air combining with the MMR vaccine. Guess what? Vaccines are also genetically engineered. So, now we have GE foods, GE bioweapons, and GE vaccines bombarding our innocent babies. Are there recombinations and viral mutations happening in their bodies with exposure to all of these items? Are our children becoming genetically altered? Does anybody know the ramifications of all of this? No, I don't believe so.

In my research on GMO, I came upon the work of Jeffrey Smith, author of the 2003 book *Seeds of Deception: Exposing Industry and Government Lies About the Safety of the Genetically Engineered Foods You're Eating,* a landmark exposé regarding Genetically Engineered foods we are all unknowingly eating. I watched his speeches on the internet and was flabbergasted. He also wrote the 2007 follow-up book *Genetic Roulette: The Documented Health Risks of Genetically Engineered Foods* in which he identifies 65 health risks associated with GE foods, including offspring mortality, sterility, allergies, organ defects, and childhood diseases; effectively shattering the safety lies from the biotech industry. He also runs the Institute for Responsible Technology. I highly admire his work and passion to warn people and correct this problem.

One of the most interesting things to me that Jeffrey Smith brings up, that my autism mom brain picked up on, was his assertion that ingested Bt toxin from GMO foods is transgenic and can transfer to the bacteria in our gut, thus creating Bt pesticide producing bacteria within the body. How many kids with autism have gastrointestinal problems? It is made to puncture holes into the guts of the bugs that eat it. Why would it not do the same to humans? Maybe leaky gut is not caused from yeast, but from GMO. I know that my son muscle tested weak to Bt toxin and Roundup during a BioSET session. Not a surprise to me.

Jeffrey Smith actually sees the connection between GMO's and autism, and spoke at the Autism One/Generation Rescue conference in May, 2012. His presentation was titled "Are GMO's promoting autism?" You can download it for free on the Autism One website, www.autismone.org or www.responsibletechnology.org/autism. He gives great scientific evidence to show the correlation using animal studies and symptoms in children with autism. I actually introduced myself to him at the conference, and told him how going non-GMO has helped our whole family, including my son with autism. I did a video testimonial for the GMO documentary he's putting together. GMO is definitely a major part of the autism puzzle.

It's not just the plants themselves that are problematic; the pesticide, glyphosate (Roundup) they are using is also linked to many problems. Another person I came across in my GMO research was Dr. Don Huber, an agricultural scientist and microbial ecology expert. He has discovered a new fungal pathogen linked to glyphosate (Roundup) causing Sudden Death Syndrome in plants; as well as warning us of other GMO related problems including glyphosate resistant superweeds and superbugs, destroyed soil quality, damage to human and animal gut flora, and an 80-90% reduction of micronutrients in GE plants, not to mention cross-contamination via the wind. Animals fed GMO feed have compromised intestinal flora, just like children with autism do. You can't change the gut flora back to normal unless you stop feeding them GMO-containing foods.

In addition, Dr. Huber warns that cattle are now dying of *Clostridium botulinum*, that means botulism, because their beneficial gut bacteria has been altered by glyphosate. Glyphosate is patented as a microbiocide, meant to kill intestinal microorganisms. In cattle, these beneficial bacterial normally control the growth of botulism. Is it possible that human's gut flora is also being destroyed by GMO's and glyphosate, increasing their susceptibility to dangerous pathogens like—say, a genetically engineered military grade bioweapon made in part with *Clostridium botulinum*? Call me crazy.

Genetically engineered crops are being grown in other parts of the world as well, causing horrible birth defects on local residents. According to Dr. Joseph Mercola's website, one Argentinean scientist confirmed what other scientists had already found—that glyphosate can potentially cause birth defects, sterility, and neurotoxicity—but they attempted to silence him by threats and public ridicule. According to the Environmental Working Group, US Geological Survey (USGS) released a report showing that air, rainwater and rivers across the Midwest US agricultural belt are routinely contaminated with high levels of glyphosate. There is a lot of concern about glyphosate ending up in local drinking water as a result of this study.

In addition, Robyn O'Brien wrote a wonderful book called *The Unhealthy Truth: How Our Food is Making us Sick- and What We Can Do about It*, which outlines some of the very problems I am talking about here with GMO's and much more. She also founded the Allergy Kids Foundation, whose goal is to protect American families from the additives found in our food supply. She reminds me a lot of myself, doing detective work to find out what happened to her child after a severe allergic reaction. Her work is very commendable and detailed. She asks the obvious questions, sees through the BS, and connects the dots. This is a must read for all parents. You will never look at food the same way again. Robyn is a prime example that there really are humanitarians out there who genuinely and selflessly want to help other people. Bravo, Robyn. I love the saying on her website that our children represent only 30 percent of our population, but they are 100 percent of our future. This future isn't looking so bright to me.

It made me angry to learn that many other countries have banned GMO's or at least have labeling laws, while here in the U.S., our food has been full of GMO's for years without our knowledge or consent. Most consumers in the U.S don't even know what GMO means, much less that they have been eating them and feeding them to their children for years. Because of corporate greed and collusion with government regulatory agencies, as well as scientific fraud, the American people are blissfully unaware that their food supply has been tainted. It should come as no surprise that the incidence of not only autism, but food allergies, asthma and ADHD have skyrocketed in the past two decades. One in six children in the U.S. has a "developmental disability." Houston, we have a problem.

So, you ask, what foods contain GMO's? Virtually all packaged foods in the grocery store in the U.S. In our busy society, we have become so reliant on convenience foods. To avoid GMO's, you must read labels and know what to look for. If a food is 100% USDA Organic, it cannot have any GE ingredients in it, or if it has a Non-GMO Verified label. The top foods to watch out for are non-organic corn, soy, canola, cottonseed, and sugar (from sugar beets, not pure cane sugar). This includes all derivatives, including high fructose corn syrup, soy lecthicin, etc. GMO's are also used in the feed for various animals; so meat, dairy, fish, and eggs that are not organic may be GMO. This also means that fast food is also Genetically McModified.

There are comprehensive Non-GMO shopping guides that can be found online at www.responsibletechnology.org and www.truefoodnow. org. They even have free apps for your smart phone that tell what brands are safe to buy. There are so many reasons why GMO's are bad; I encourage you to do your own research at the aforementioned websites. Here is a breakdown of GM foods in the U.S:

Currently Commercialized GM Crops in the U.S.:

Soy (93%), Cottonseed (93%), Canola (93%), Corn (86%), Sugar Beets (95%), Hawaiian papaya (more than 50%), Alfalfa (at Supreme Court), Zucchini and Yellow Squash (small amount), Tobacco (Quest® brand).

Other Sources of GMOs:

• Dairy products from cows injected with the GM hormone rBGH

• Food additives, enzymes, flavorings, and processing agents, including the sweetener aspartame (NutraSweet®) and rennet used to make hard cheeses

• Meat, eggs, and dairy products from animals that have eaten GM feed

• Honey and bee pollen that may have GM sources of pollen

• Contamination or pollination caused by GM seeds or pollen

Some of the Ingredients That May Be Genetically Modified: Vegetable oil, vegetable fat and margarines (made with soy, corn, cottonseed, and/or canola)

Ingredients derived from soybeans: Soy flour, soy protein, soy isolates, soy isoflavones, soy lecithin, vegetable proteins, textured vegetable protein (TVP), tofu, tamari, tempeh, and soy protein supplements.

Ingredients derived from corn: Corn flour, corn gluten, corn masa, corn starch, corn syrup, cornmeal, and High-Fructose Corn Syrup (HFCS).[20]

Aside from the GMO problem, in this session, Michael also mentioned

---

[20] http://www.responsibletechnology.org/gmo-basics/gmos-in-food

the opiate properties of wheat, and that the wheat we eat is altered. To validate this, Dr. William Davis, a preventative cardiologist, author of *Wheat Belly* states:

"Wheat is not the same as it was 50 years ago. It is 2 ½ feet shorter. The stockier plant can support a much heavier seed bed, and it grows much faster. It is not genetically modified; when a plant is genetically modified a gene is inserted or deleted. What has been done is that the plant has been hybridized and crossbred to make it resistant to drought, fungi; and vastly increase the yield per acre. Agricultural geneticists have shown that wheat proteins undergo structural change with hybridization, and that the hybrid contains proteins that are found in neither parent plant. Thousands of 'Frankengrains' have been created over the past 50 years, using extreme techniques, and their safety for human consumption has never been tested or questioned."

In addition to these foreign proteins, The Opioid Excess Theory, speculates that peptides with opioid activity cross into the bloodstream from the lumen of the intestine, and then into the brain. These peptides come from incomplete digestion of certain foods, in particular gluten from wheat and certain other cereals and from casein from milk and dairy products. Further work confirmed opioid peptides such as casomorphines (from casein) and gliadorphin, aka gluteomorphin (from gluten) as possible suspects, due to their chemical similarity to opiates.

The fact that Michael mentioned opiates and wheat together during the session validates this theory in my eyes. Some people poo-poo the gluten-free, casein free diet for children with autism, but I saw in my own child a huge change when we took wheat and dairy out of his diet. It was as if he felt pain for the first time in his life. He had self-limited his diet to only foods with wheat and dairy, where he used to eat anything we gave him. Was he addicted to them like a drug? If you don't think that things you ingest can affect your brain, drink a few beers and see what happens. What do you think happens if a baby's gut is ravaged by Bt toxins and then eats altered opioid producing wheat? Nobody really knows, do they? I know plenty of adults, myself included, who suddenly become allergic to wheat, dairy and other foods. Why? They are not the same foods that I ate growing up.

One of my favorite Native American quotes is "We do not inherit the Earth from our Ancestors; we borrow it from our children." Bioengineering is a very big problem, and will be an even bigger one in the future if something isn't done to correct it now. Messing with Mother Nature is not a good idea. Aside from GMO's, there are also synthetic chemicals, additives, preservatives, artificial colorings and flavorings, neurotoxic sweeteners, pesticides, heavy metals, and numerous other carcinogens in our food supply that have not been tested for safety. It makes me wonder if the cause of all of this is greed, stupidity, or worse, deliberate genocide.

We have to take matters into our own hands. It is imperative that we learn about these hidden dangers, read labels and make informed choices. Believe me, I used to drink Mountain Dew and eat Ho-Ho's for breakfast, I wasn't always this conscious about the food I ate. I am now a self-professed Food Nazi. I was always an athlete and believed that as long as I was thin, I could get away with eating whatever I wanted to. Not true. I am wiser because I wasn't always so wise. Ignorance isn't bliss; it is harming our children. Blind faith on the part of parents is another part of the problem. The fox is guarding the hen house, people. You must learn what ingredients are bad, clean out your cupboards, and start over. Read labels, and go cold turkey. If other adults around you are ignorant and addicted to certain foods, as people around me were, try to educate them, but demand that your children only eat what you choose to feed them; healthy, non-GMO food. Their health depends on it. If you think organic food is expensive, you should price out cancer and autism.

Because the subject of a genetically engineered virus as part of a weapons program that is in the air came up again in this session, I did a bit more research on what happens when you inhale a virus. I read an article in *Scientific American* from December 28, 2011 called "When Viruses Invade the Brain: Neurodegenerative diseases may result from a nasal infection." It explains a new way that viruses infect the brain. In the article, Stephani Sutherland writes that viruses rank among the environmental factors thought to trigger brain-ravaging diseases. Neuroscientist Steven Jacobson and his colleagues at the National Institute of Neurological Disorders and Stroke have determined that viruses make their entry to the human brain through the olfactory pathway, right along with the odors wafting into our nose.

Researchers found evidence of live HHV-6 virus in the olfactory bulb of patients with MS, which reactivates inside the brain. He further explained that the virus appears to invade the brain by infecting a type of glial cell called olfactory ensheathing cells (OECs), which nourish smell-sensing neurons and guide them from the olfactory bulb (the brain region involved in detecting odors) to their targets in the nervous system. These targets include the limbic system, a group of evolutionarily old structures deep in the brain, which is where viruses like to reactivate, Jacobson explains. He points out that olfactory neurons and their OECs are among the few brain cells known to regenerate throughout our life. This neurogenesis may keep our sense of smell sharp, but at the cost of providing the virus the opportunity to spread.

The way this virus entered the brain had remained a mystery, as the seat of our intelligence is largely protected by the blood-brain barrier, which filters out many germs and drugs. However, researchers had known that other viruses, such as influenza and rabies, apparently could use the sensory network hooked up to the nose as a kind of highway into the central nervous system. Moreover, in experiments, scientists demonstrated that HHV-6 could infect lab-grown versions of the olfactory ensheathing cells, which help olfactory neurons grow and establish connections in the brain. The researchers believe the virus might use these cells as a bridge across the blood-brain barrier, the first time scientists had evidence these cells could be a route of infection. They were going to research if other viruses could use this route as well. That explained the disease pathway for me, how inhaled biowarfare could infect the brain.

Another thing that I am going to mention here is that many children with autism have also been "diagnosed" with what used to be called PANDAS (Pediatric Autoimmune Neuropsychiatric Disorder Associated with Streptococcus). If your child exhibited sudden onset and severe obsessive/compulsive (OCD) type behaviors, they called it PANDAS. My son suddenly began lining up all of his toys, especially matchbox cars, into intricate patterns on the floor, and if they didn't all touch, he'd get upset. Everything had to be "just so." Even if we were driving in the car, and we didn't turn where he thought we should, a tantrum would ensue. No one called it PANDAS back then, although he did have strep a few times when he was older.

Currently, there is a much greater understanding about how many different bacterial and viral infections can attack the parts of the brain that are responsible for movement control, obsessive thoughts and compulsive behaviors, and the extreme emotional and behavioral ups and downs exhibited by children whose brains are infected and inflamed. Because it is now known that multiple infectious agents are involved in the clinical presentation of an autoimmune brain attack, they no longer refer to the syndrome as just PANDAS. Many children with the same symptoms were not exposed to strep. Instead this group of neuro-immune disorders is now referred to as PANS (Pediatric Acute-Onset Neuropsychiatric Syndrome). Confusing, right?

One question: Isn't it possible that this biowarfare that Michael and the other medium have been talking about could be another source of an infectious agent attacking the brain, causing the same symptoms that we are calling PANDAS/PANS? Just because a child has had strep, staph, Lyme, mono, or mycoplasma, which are other infections leading to a PANS diagnosis, doesn't necessarily mean that those agents are the cause of the OCD symptoms. How do you know what is causing the symptoms? Especially if it is something that is not detectible in blood tests at this time. We did energetic testing for my son and there were so many infectious agents that he was "positive" for, including many biowarfare agents. Were they sub-clinical, and didn't cause symptoms? Were they genetically engineered not to be virulent? What agents were causing what symptoms in him? Were there mutations or recombinations occurring in him? What about all of the other toxins he was exposed to? Was there synergistic toxicity from multiple exposures? Ok, that was more than one question, but you see where I'm going with this.

***

Chapter Seven

"Marie Curie is, of all celebrated beings, the only one whom fame has not corrupted."

— Albert Einstein

(As quoted in "Madame Curie: A Biography" by Eve Curie, 1937)

Session Five

This session was on December 29, 2010 and Marti joined the session this time with her spirit artistry. We had lots of surprise guests show up this time. We never knew who was going to make an appearance or what they had to contribute. It began with Michael saying that there was a lady there this time and they were saying a few names and dates to him. The dates were 1915 and 1951 and the names were Rose, and Marie and what sounded like Curr or Car to him. Then the session continued:

Laura: "I wonder if it's Madame Curie."

Michael: "Well then I got the name Marie as well."

Laura: "Marie Curie. That might be her."

Michael: "I know she's a scientist, but this is who I'm thinking it is."

Laura: "Marie Curie. C-u-r-i-e, I think."

Michael: "Oh, is it?"

Laura: "Yeah."

Michael: "C-U-R-I-E. Marie Curie. Huh, well there's a name Rose as well."

Laura: "Ok."

Michael: "Unless that's her middle name, or someone immediate to her, but there's also Rose. Has she ever shown up?"

Laura: "No. But I've seen her actually in a picture with Einstein during this, what I've been looking up recently."

Michael: "Did he know her?"

Laura: "Yeah. They're in that Brussels conference together. And she won the Nobel Prize also."

Michael: "Oh, very cool. So, he knew her. I thought I saw him in the room here, but he wanted me to talk to this lady first."

Laura: "Ok, cool."

Michael: "Ok, now, there's someone else here. I don't know about this. I'm not sure if it's Jack or Jackie. But my thought is that it's Jackie Onassis. But, I don't know why she would be here."

Laura: "Hmm."

Michael: "Jackie. I think she just said "hello" to me. Talking with Albert ... she says she's working with Albert to try to find the solution."

Laura: "Is it Jackie Onassis?"

Michael: "No, I think I'm talking with Marie."

Laura: "Oh, ok."

Michael: "A chemist? Is she?"

Laura: "I'm not sure what her specialty is, I'll have to look it up. She a scientist of some sort."

(Marie Curie won the Nobel Prize in Chemistry in 1911. She had previously won a shared Nobel Prize in Physics with her husband Pierre Curie in 1903.)

Michael: "And she's saying a name like Brunton, or Brightoned...Byron ...Sounds like that. I wonder if she has a sister who is a nurse? She's talking about a nurse, but I kind of feel like it might be a sister. Marie Curie. She's talking about nursing to me. Maybe she knew nuns, or maybe she was like a Catholic or something."

(Marie Curie's older sister's name is Bronislawa or Bronya for short. They helped each other pay for their higher education. Bronya studied medicine at Sorbonne in Paris and then helped Marie pay for her schooling. Marie later founded the Radium Institute in their native Warsaw, which was headed by her physician sister, Bronya. During World War I, Marie used mobile radiography units, which became known as "Little Curies" for the treatment of wounded soldiers, and she trained 150 nurses to use them. Also, their mother was a devout Catholic, and the deaths of her mother and another sibling,

Zofia, caused Marie to give up Catholicism.)

Michael: "She keeps saying my name, but I don't think she's saying me, but she's saying Michael. So it's someone immediate to her. She's saying yes to that. It's someone immediate to her, ok."

Laura: "Ok."

(Marie Curie's granddaughter, Hélène Langevin-Joliot, was married to the late Michel Langevin, who died in 1985. Hélène's parents are Marie's daughter Irène and Frédéric Joliot-Curie, who together won a Nobel Prize in Chemistry in 1935 for their discovery of artificial radioactivity. Michel Langevin was the grandson of Marie's colleague and love interest, physicist Paul Langevin. Marie and Paul are seated next to each other in the Solvay Congress photograph in Chapter Three.)

Michael: "They have to do this, they have to identify themselves. You know I won't do a session when I don't know who I'm talking to, you see?"

Laura: "Yep."

Michael: "So, you have to do this every time. Now she's saying… It could be a French name, it sounds like Bouton, Bouffant? They're talking about how they're trying to improve the communication here. They're saying how well it's going. So, I suppose it is going very nicely."

Laura: "Oh."

Michael: "Maybe her birthday is in January. And she brings up the 22nd."

(After the session, I was looking up the birthdays of the spirits that were coming through, and although it wasn't her birthday, the day Rose Kennedy died is on January 22nd, which is still accurate to me. She is Jackie Onassis' mother-in-law. I called Michael right away to tell him about that one. He couldn't believe it. Sometimes it's hard to tell who is doing the talking.)

Then, Michael jumped back to trying to figure out the name Marie was trying to get him to say:

Michael: "Sounds like Bousson. Or Marty Bouffant. I can't understand what she's saying here. A fellow scientist. Someone else that she knows, I believe. Also, like a mentor."

(One of the professors that Marie studied was the French physicist and mathematician,

Marcel Brillouin. He also attended the Solvay Conference in 1911 with Marie Curie and other noted physicists and chemists.)

Michael: "Hmmm, she also got some sort of award from England."

Laura: "Ok."

Michael: "She's talking about this to me and she must have gone there, or she must have gotten an award from there, like the Royal Academy or something, of Science, or something."

(Marie and her husband Pierre were the recipients of the Davy Medal in 1903, which is awarded by the Royal Society of London "for an outstanding important recent discovery in any branch of chemistry" for their research on radium.)

Michael: "And she's saying the name Stark, like S-T-A-R-K."

Laura: "Ok."

Michael: "And it's John. She said, 'Ok, and now let's get down to business.'"

(Johannes Stark was awarded the Nobel Prize for Physics for his "discovery of the Doppler effect in canal rays and the splitting of spectral lines in electric fields". Both Marie Curie and Johannes Stark were recipients of the Matteucci Medal, an Italian award which was established to award physicists for their fundamental contributions.)

Laura: "Alright."

Michael: "Here we go."

Laura: "I like her."

Michael asked me if I had been doing anything with the color therapy that was suggested in a previous session. I answered that Trevor has been carrying around a pink rose quartz stone a lot, that he's been wearing blue and green clothing, and that he received an orange sled for Christmas, which I exchanged because it came up that orange was not a good color for him. Then Michael said "Oh, that's interesting, because she's talking about color and vibrations." Then he asked if he was dry, because they were showing him my son's mouth and that his lips have been very dry, and recommended that he needed more water.

Next, he asked who Kris was. I said that it is my mom's name. He said that her dad was here. He followed that up by asking if someone cuts my son's food up into really small bites. I laughed and told him that my mom did. That was just a validation that it was my Grandpa and he sees what's going on. Michael said that my Grandpa said "hello" and said that he thinks my boy is doing better. He said that he's been working with the alphabet more and reading more. Then he asked if my Grandpa had cancer. I told him "yes." Michael asked my Grandpa if he had any insights, and then he said:

Michael: "That's weird; I keep seeing people banging their heads. Do some of these kids bang their heads against walls?"

Laura: "Yes. Yes, or the floor, yep. That's one of the signs of autism, head banging."

Michael: "Remember I talked about that brain barrier?"

Laura: "Yes."

Michael: "I get this itching feeling on my head too. Like a burning sensation, almost. A kind of itchy, burning feeling. Do any of the kids complain of that?"

Laura: "Well, they don't really talk. I think that there is something happening in their head or their brain and they bang their head to relieve what's happening, is my theory."

Michael: "I feel like that's why they're doing it."

Laura: "So what's causing that to make them bang their heads?"

Michael: "She was talking about a virus, Marie."

Laura: "Right."

Michael: "Did she work with Plutonium or something?"

Laura: "I'll have to look her up. I've seen her though in a lot of the pictures, she's the only woman."

(She was famous for her work with radioactivity, for isolating radioactive isotopes, and the discovery of two new elements, polonium and radium.)

Michael: "What she keeps showing me is that she's doing a lot of research with sound and light on viruses."

Laura: "Ok."

Michael: "To see how they react to certain frequencies of light and sound. I

almost feel like they are ultrasonic sounds, though."

Laura: "Oh."

Michael: "Like ultrasounds, but certain frequencies, you know."

Laura: "Ok."

Michael: "I don't know if she's saying 20 Hertz or 20,000 Hertz?"

Laura: "What's the virus?"

Michael: (Asking her) "What kind of virus? Are there viruses that affect your nervous system? Or they make you catatonic, they paralyze you? She keeps talking about nerve toxin."

Laura: "Alright."

Next, Michael talked about an Angstrom, which I found out later is a unit of measure to express the size of atoms, lengths of chemical bonds and measures the wavelengths of electromagnetic radiation, and then he said "20,000 angstroms." I have no idea what this is referring to, but it is an old term, not used much anymore. Perhaps it will make sense to someone. Then the name David Mazer came up. I couldn't find who this is, but again, perhaps later on it will make sense. Next, he began talking about electromagnets:

Michael: "It's something you wear, right? Around your neck, around your wrist, where? It's round. Like a magnet? An electromagnet. What I'm seeing is magnets, she's showing me magnets, but they seem to be like electrically charged magnets, they're not just regular magnets."

Laura: "Ok."

Michael: "But they're little electromagnets. So they have like either a battery that can be worn on various parts of the body. It's like magnetic therapy, but they charge the magnets. I don't know if magnets can be charged so that they're different, or what? Maybe they can. Magnets have like different..."

Laura: "Strengths or something? Is that a type of therapy?"

Michael: "Yeah, it's something they're working on they said."

Laura: "To have an effect on the virus?"

Michael: "Well it affects the blood, but it may affect the virus. I know this ok. I know that when space people come to Earth, they have suits that give off like a musical note. A kind of a frequency that keeps bacteria away from them and viruses. It's innate in the suit."

Laura: "Oh."

Michael: "So, they're thinking of the similar lines, you see? What appears to be like a patch, or an ornament that you wear around your neck, around your wrist. But I'm seeing it primarily around my wrist. I know they have these magnets that people wear, but it seems to be a little more than that, because it seems to be either moving, or it has a moving part to it. Almost like it's spinning."

Laura: "Is this in existence now?"

Michael: "So it's sort of tied to the frequencies of the Earth. They've buried me, this is not areas I'm not really, I'm not a scientist, and I don't understand what it is that they're showing me here."

Laura: "Mmm-hmm."

Michael: "You can't tell somebody scientific terms, how to build something or make something. Maybe somebody's already thinking along these lines and they're...Something in the brain. Or it's worn around the wrist or the neck. Do you know anybody called John Henry?"

Laura: "I don't think so. John Henry...Is he connected to this?"

Michael: "Maybe, maybe. You know obviously we're in an area where they might say a lot of things we don't understand at the moment. But it seems like somebody called John Henry. It might have to do a lot with sound, this John Henry, sound frequencies, by what they're drawing here. And this Mazer guy or Mezer, it sounds like David Mezer, Mazer, or Mezer. Let's try another tactic. Do you have any other questions tonight?"

Laura: "Yeah, well I wrote a question down on the top of my page and I'm just wondering how do all of these pieces fit together? They've told us a lot of little pieces. Mercury, vaccines, biowarfare, chemicals, food. How do all of these pieces fit together to cause regressive autism?"

Michael: "Well, they're talking about the motor skills being affected."

Laura: "Yes."

Michael: "Ok."

Laura: "Especially small motor skills in the hands."

Michael: "They're talking about the motor skills, and these things are acting like a switch, and they switch off the motor skills, the part of the brain that the motor skills...They seem to block it you see."

Laura: "What exactly is blocking it? Is it the virus?"

Michael: "I think it's a virus. But it seems to be, it's like it's amplified or made worse by the toxins. You see you don't just have one component, you've got several components, you see?"

Laura: "Ok."

Michael: "You've got 2 or 3 things all working in conjunction."

Laura: "Ok."

Michael: "It's a dance. It's like they're all working together, all of these things."

"Madam Curie is saying 1951. This must have to do with her, but I didn't think she lived that long. I don't know what the significance of that is, but she's bringing that up."

Laura: "Ok."

(In 1951, the name "Centre of Oncology- Maria Sklodowska-Curie Memorial Institute" was officially given to the Radium Institute, founded in 1932, in Warsaw, Poland, her native country. Marie Curie died in 1934.)

Michael: "And somebody called Jean, or Gene, and what sounds like Seteur. It might be a little bit of me tonight, because I'm having a hard time accepting that I'm talking to her. So, just bear with me, if it's a bit bumpy tonight. If some of this is validated, I'll be way happy, ok?"

Laura: "Ok."

Michael: "Somebody is absolutely saying this name Mazer or Mezer, Mazer to me."

(I haven't figured out who these people are just yet, or their significance. There are dozens of people in the U.S. alone with these names, so I am including it in case it makes sense down the road. As I've shown, things don't always make sense right away, or can be misinterpreted.)

Michael: "Does (your son) like hot water?"

Laura: "Yes. My son has a hard time distinguishing hot and cold. He'll be in a hot bath and not feel pain. It's like the pain receptors don't work right."

Michael: "It's really weird, cuz he can have the water really hot."

Laura: "Oh, yeah, he'll be bright pink and not even flinch. He turns it all the way hot if I'm not watching him."

Michael: "Oh, wow, cuz that's what I thought. He likes it hot, but he doesn't actually feel it."

Laura: "Yeah. And then he'll like it extremely cold and laugh and think it's funny. He'll put his head right under the ice cold water in the bathtub."

Michael: "Oh, my goodness. So, he can't feel?"

Laura: "Yeah, that's part of it…"

Michael: "So, the nervous system, it's not getting to his brain, the nerve signals."

Laura: "Is that what that is?"

Michael: "Yeah, absolutely. The nerve receptors are blocked. His receptors, he could be feeling it, but it's being blocked from the pain receptor in the brain."

Laura: "Yeah, it's very common with these kids."

Michael: "I didn't know they had these physical characteristics like this. I thought they were just more of an emotional, like mental issues."

Laura: "No, it's very pervasive. So, is this virus the engineered virus that they brought up earlier?"

Michael: "Uh-huh, I think so."

Laura: "Dang. Can they tell us what it is? What it's made with? If it's genetically modified, it could be anything. But, what is it?"

Michael: "Hold on. They said something about T4."

Laura: "T4? I know that the thyroid gland produces T4."

Michael: "What? I don't know what that is, what is it? What is T4?"

Laura: "It's a hormone."

Michael: "Oh, it's a hormone. Somebody said something about T4."

Laura: "Ok. Yeah, a lot of their thyroids are dysregulatory."

Michael: "Ok. Then, maybe this same virus is affecting their thyroid or their glandular system as well."

Laura: "Ok."

Michael: "Somebody said it's to kill people, I said, yeah I know that, but how? With what? It's meant to happen slowly. It's something that they want people to think it's just normal, and it's ordinary. What I'm sensing then is that these things that they're putting out there are just meant to be, it sits in such a way that you can't put your finger on it, basically. That you can't know what's causing it. You can't point your finger, you can't blame anyone, because you can't figure it out, you see?"

Laura: "Yep."

Michael: "But it's like, they're back to this nerve, it's like a nerve toxin, or a nerve virus. Like a bio-mutated virus. The funny thing is, I see it on my skin. It's like; it's almost like a nerve agent."

Laura: "You see it on your skin?"

Michael: "Yeah. It's like a nerve agent. Is it escaping from like a...has there been a release that maybe they've been talking about and they're covering it up? Oh...There seems to be a release that took place that they're trying to cover up or hide. You know, like not make public."

Laura: "Mmm-hmm."

Michael: "It could have been a mistake on their part, or deliberate, but they're trying to cover it up, you see?"

Laura: "Where did it escape from?"

Michael: "I believe a military compound of some sort."

Sound familiar? Something escaping from a military facility that is designed to kill people and make it look like they died of natural causes! It was referred to as a bio-mutated virus and a nerve agent that he could see on his skin. That would imply that it is in the air. It also affects the glandular system, including the thyroid. This becomes clarified even further in a later session. Next, Michael asked me if my father or grandfather were in the military. I told him my dad was in the Marines. He continued:

Michael: "Ok, then I must be talking to him then, cuz he's a military guy, see? Well, maybe he's saying this to back up what I was saying you see? Because we were talking about a military release, aren't we?"

Laura: "Mmm-hmm."

Michael: "And all of the sudden, your dad started talking to me and made me feel like they were in the military and that they should know, you see? Is there anything like Botulism?"

Laura: "Yeah, they brought that up last time, and they said if my son had food poisoning. And Botulinum, the Botulism toxin comes up in his system when we do different types of testing."

Michael: "Is it still there today?"

Laura: "I don't think so. Is that part of the genetically engineered stuff? Is there Botulinum toxin mixed in there or something?"

Michael: "Well it might be, because I'm puzzling this, and that's what they threw in my head, Botulism."

Laura: "Hmm."

Michael: "I reckon it's like a cocktail, of different things you know."

(It's interesting that he used the term "cocktail" to describe the biowarfare which included botulism. A Russian Doll Cocktail is a biowarfare agent named after the Russian nesting dolls, in which you find a smaller doll inside each doll. A Russian Doll Cocktail is a camouflage system incorporating a combination of organisms, which could pass through a population unnoticed, making it harder to detect what it is, and where symptoms are coming from.)

Laura: "Mmm-hmm. Is there Anthrax in it? Cuz you mentioned your skin…"

Michael: "Oh, the big A!"

(He had written a big letter A on his paper at the start of the session.)

Laura: "Yeah, and you said something about your skin." (Weaponized airborne anthrax can penetrate clothing and skin.)

Michael: "Anthrax! I was trying to think of what it was. I bet that's it,

anthrax."

Laura: "Ask them if that's part of it."

Michael: "That's it."

Laura: "Yeah?"

Michael: "I bet that's it. I knew it was the name of one of the weapons. I don't know if it is a virus or what. It's strange."

Laura: "Well, they genetically modify it and add chemicals to it, and who knows what it is now? It's all military-grade."

Michael: "That Island off of England that nobody is even allowed onto to this day was used for Anthrax testing."

Laura: "Yeah, Gruiniard Island off of Scotland, they exploded all the anthrax bombs there."

Michael: "Gruiniard Island, yeah."

Laura: "Yeah, I've read about that. So, there is anthrax in it, are they validating that."

Michael: "I think so. Well there's no real way to contain it, you see? Once it's out. They didn't just test it in England, they tested in America too."

Laura: "Mmm-hmm. So then what happens when it is released into our country and it's in the air and everywhere else?"

Michael: "Well, ok. Here we go back to something, ok."

Laura: "Ok."

Michael: "You know when people take cyanide, little tiny, are poisoned, I mean the reaction to it is extraordinary, isn't it?"

Laura: "Mmm-hmm."

Michael: "I mean, cyanide is instantaneous, right?"

Laura: "Mmm-hmm."

Michael: "Now what is it about cyanide that causes instant death? You know what I mean? What is it that can kill you almost instantly?"

Laura: "I don't know."

Michael: "You see what I'm getting at?"

Laura: "Mmm-hmm."

Michael: "It's almost supernatural in a way, the effect it has. It's obviously a reaction on one level, like a mental level or vibrational level to whatever that vibrates at, when they get that. You know sleeping gas, how can it put you out of your body? It sort of forces you out. It's like also when people have epilepsy and they flash a light at them, and they go into an epileptic fit. It's a frequency, see what I mean?"

Laura: "Mmm-hmm."

Michael: "So, this frequency is causing them to have an epileptic fit. So everything basically has a frequency, and you just have to know how to nullify that frequency, or have something that resonates to the frequency that will combat the toxin or the virus, you see what I mean? This is the area that we are going to in the near future. So we are dealing with is that these are very high sound frequencies that vibrate, that affect these viruses or toxins or force them out. See what I mean?"

Laura: "Mmm-hmm."

Michael: "Or nullify them. I think that's the only way forward really. I just had a thought. If he can't feel pain, hot or cold, but you could function really well in every other way, you'd be pretty damn hard to kill, wouldn't you?"

Laura: "Probably."

Michael: "You could tolerate a lot. You could tolerate extreme cold, extreme heat; as a soldier, I mean."

Laura: "Yeah, but not if your nervous system was screwed up and you screamed all the time and you couldn't talk."

Michael: "Yeah, but you said he was immune to it, or he didn't feel it."

Laura: "Oh, the pain? Yeah, but I'm just kind of saying some of the other things that are affected by this also."

Michael: "It's very strange, isn't it? So, what things make him scream?"

Laura: "Sometimes, no one knows. Something just sets him off, and he just freaks out and runs, or flips himself around. In the middle of the grocery store, he'll just scream and throw a fit. You never know when it will happen or what sets him off. It's very troubling."

Michael went back to T4 again, asking if I had problems with my thyroid before he was born. I said no, but now I am hypothyroid and had/have Wilson's Syndrome too, which is a T3 problem, how the body uses T4. It started after childbirth, which it often does. Michael continued:

Michael: "A lot of these things are exacerbated by this preexisting condition. Not that it's the cause, but he's hypersensitive to everything now. What appears to be a virus is making him hypersensitive to everything, and it's very hard to pinpoint what's going on because he's just so sensitive to everything, and sometimes insensitive. It's a constant fluctuation. Of course, your glandular system is mostly responsible for the balance of the body, and if something throws that off, you can't get balanced."

Laura: "Uh-huh."

Michael: "Well you know, this whole thing is a bit like a puzzle because none of us are scientists, we're not trained scientists, and we don't know even what half this stuff means. So for them to try to tell you exactly what's going on, I'm not sure that they know exactly how to fix this."

Laura: "Mmm-hmm."

Michael: "I think what they're trying to say is that this stuff, the causes of this are things that are not easy to rectify. I don't think you can take a pill and that's it. You know what I mean, it's not like that, it has to be combated by doing things that boost the own defense mechanisms and maybe stimulate the body's healing process. All you can do is kind of fix this in various ways, you know what I mean?"

Laura: "Mmm-hmm."

Michael: "Sometimes using external means. The body is very good at repairing itself, you just have to bring balance back to the body, and maybe we can figure out how to nullify some of the effects of what's going on. It's clear that your boy and a lot of these kids are suffering from a sort of poisoning. That's the simplest way to put it; it's a sort of poisoning."

My late husband made an appearance next. Michael said that he had blue eyes, and a "D" name (Darren) and was showing him a ring. He was talking about my puzzle piece ring, which he said he sent to me. I bought it at an autism conference, and wear it every day. I found it very interesting how again the people in spirit that I personally knew kept popping in to tell Michael things that I could validate in between the things we didn't know anything about. Again, it made me think, "Well, if this is true, then this other stuff may also be true." The conversation continued:

Michael: "Generally, people might think that there is a simple solution to this, and I'm not sure there is."

Laura: "Mmm-hmm."

Michael: "I think there are certain ways to try to heal the body, to kind of boost the body's own way of healing itself. Get rid of the virus or the toxins and things like that so that the body can function again. It's acting as an inhibitor to the body, you see?"

Laura: "Yep."

Michael: "I think that anything can be healed, but some things are harder than other things."

Laura: "Yeah, but if you don't know what you're looking at or what's causing it, that's half the battle right there."

Michael: "Well, look, this virus that's in the brain, you said that people have identified this virus?"

Laura: "Yeah, there's this guy that's a homeopath actually, in Henderson, NV."

(The company is closed down, and the guy died shortly after these sessions.)

Michael: "Well, what does he call it, what is it?"

Laura: "Well, they named it, and they said it is a virus of unknown origin, it's a very active, parasitic virus and they named it R1H2, because it's not a known virus, it's an engineered virus."

Michael: Oh, it's a parasitic virus. Oh, how interesting, because briefly I did see like a parasite. Oh, then that's what it is, a parasitic virus, I think that's absolutely what it is."

Laura: "Yeah, and it lives in the brain. Most viruses have a propensity for certain organs, some live in the heart, some live in the eyes, this one lives in the brain."

Michael: "All of these parasites are kind of creepy looking when you

look at them. The viruses, they almost look like little entities or like little robots and stuff. They're bazaar looking. You look at them and they look like little machines that somebody's manufactured."

Laura: "Well, they pretty much have."

We chatted for a few more minutes before the session ended. Marti had drawn a portrait as well as a doodle page during the session. Here they are:

The portrait on the left is the one Marti drew, and the picture on the right is an actual photograph of Marie Curie. Notice the similarity in the eyes, nose, mouth and hair. There is also a mole on her cheek. She's even wearing a collared shirt! Marti didn't know what Marie Curie looked like, even after she drew it, she wasn't sure if it was her until she saw this photograph of her. Here is the doodle page Marti drew:

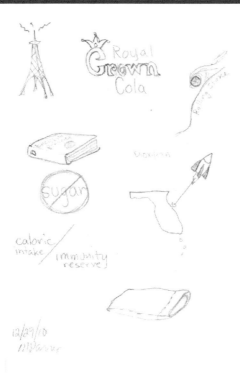

Doodle Validations: Remember my earlier example of a doodle page from Marti and I didn't understand what some of the doodles meant until years after they were drawn? Well, I don't know what all of these doodles mean, so maybe they will mean something later. Marti is shown or told what to draw, but she doesn't know what they mean every time either. Sometimes, I will think it means one thing at the time, but then later on, a better explanation comes forward. The same thing happens with messages given during the session. There have been times during a regular session where I thought that a medium was talking about a certain person, or couldn't remember who they were at the time, and later on I remembered or someone else clarified it for me. (I've heard this called "Psychic Amnesia.") I'm sure this is going to be the case with people I don't know. I do my best. So, I will just describe the meanings of the things I think I understand.

In this case, during the channeling session, some of the Kennedy family made an appearance, Rose (President Kennedy's mother) and Jackie (his wife). When Marti was drawing the doodles, she felt that the picture of the state of Florida had to do with Cape Canaveral, where the rockets are launched. None of us remembered this at the time of the session, but the

NASA Space Center in Cape Canaveral, Florida is known as the John F. Kennedy Space Center. Wow!

As I was researching possible meanings of Royal Crown Cola, I discovered that famous NASA astronaut, John Glenn, a close friend of the Kennedy family, was the President of Royal Crown Cola! When Robert Kennedy was assassinated, John Glenn was in Los Angeles helping him with his campaign. He was actually one of the pallbearers in his funeral. I also saw him receiving awards by President Kennedy at the Kennedy Space Center and at the White House. John Glenn is still alive, but the Kennedy family was mentioning him in a way to further validate the fact that it was them coming through. There is more from this family in further sessions, so keep reading!

Marti also felt that the tower with electricity had something to do with Nicola Tesla. I know that he and Albert Einstein knew each other in life. On the Tesla Society website, there is a picture of the congratulatory letter that Einstein had sent to Tesla on his 75th birthday. Tesla invented so many things in his day, and didn't get the credit he deserved. He revolutionized power generation and transmission. He also worked with frequencies and created wireless energy. He worked with electromagnetic energy. Interestingly, many of the suggestions that have come through or come through in later sessions are among Tesla's inventions, including frequency based energy and healing and electromagnetic jewelry. Some copper jewelry on the market uses Tesla technology. Michael had talked about copper electromagnetic bracelets at one point. This area clearly needs more research.

Marti also felt that there was a toxin in the pillow stuffing, and that sugar was bad for children with autism. I have read about chemical flame retardants in mattresses and pillows that are problematic for children, especially sensitive children, which is why I buy hypoallergenic bedding and pillows for my son. Pillows are often filled with petroleum-based, highly toxic chemicals. We spend a third of our day sleeping (most of us), so it's important to be aware of what our sensitive kids are breathing in during this time.

As far as sugar goes, sugar feeds yeast, which many children with autism have, among many other reasons to keep sugar out of their diets. Sugar is considered a toxin; it suppresses the immune system and decreases brain activity. Also, as I mentioned earlier, sugar beets are genetically engineered, and is included in many foods. If it just says "sugar" and is not organic, it is probably GMO. In addition, high fructose corn syrup is genetically engineered, has mercury in it and has been implicated recently as a cause of autism comparing the diets of children in the U.S to children in Italy.

I'm not quite sure what Dioxipan is. I read that it is a biodegradable polymer Poly (1, 5-dioxipan-2 one) which are carriers for controlled drug delivery, with various medical uses, including vaccines. Is that it? I don't know for sure. I looked in the Encyclopedia Britannica under "D" like the doodle shows, and the only word remotely similar is "dioxin" which is an herbicide toxic to humans used in Agent Orange, a military defoliant. Dioxin is also in plastic, including baby bottles. It is carcinogenic, especially when heated. Who hasn't heated a bottle in the microwave at 2am? After the session, I talked to Michael and he said that he felt that the word was supposed to be dioxin, not Dioxipan.

It is hard to speculate unless the meaning is very clear sometimes. Perhaps some of these things will mean something to someone else or make sense later on. This is part of the challenge of this work, getting the correct meaning of things across. We were all trying our best.

The rolling stone down the hill, if I had to guess, could be referring to the fact that in psychiatry they use metaphors to help diagnose mental illness. "A rolling stone gathers no moss" is a commonly used metaphor to see if people take the meaning literally. Children with autism have a difficult time with abstraction.

Last, but not least, I'm guessing again on what caloric intake slash immunity reserve means. I read many articles stating that reduced caloric intake lowers immunity. It makes me think of my son self-limiting his diet to certain wheat and dairy based foods. He didn't grow much for three years and has always been small for his age. Maybe some of these things will become clearer in the future. I don't claim to know everything. I'm just trying to make some sense of it all.

***

Session Five – After the Session
Featured Spirits: Marie Curie, Rose Kennedy, Jackie Onassis

I had to look up a lot of names and dates to validate all of the people that came up in this session. I had heard of Marie or Madame Curie, but didn't know anything about her except that she was some kind of scientist. All of the names she brought up were related to her or were scientists who worked during her time. The mere fact that she accurately gave the names of people in her life, that none of us knew about should be enough to prove it was her, but to top it off, Marti drew a dead-on picture of her. Most of the information brought through in this session came through Marie Curie.

She talked about kids with autism banging their heads, and that they had an itchy burning sensation in their heads. Then she started talking about a virus that affects the nervous system, and about using frequencies of sound and light to affect the virus. She even used old terminology, angstroms, which I had to look up. I already knew about Rife Technology, started by Royal Rife, who used a frequency based machine to affect pathogens in the body. There are also other newer technologies that I read about after the session. The Quantum Biofeedback sessions I do with Trevor is also does frequency based distance healing specific to the pathogens in the person.

Marie also talked about electromagnetic jewelry as a therapy that can affect the virus. She said that the virus is made worse by toxins and that they all worked together. These kids have a sort of poisoning. I looked up electromagnetic jewelry after the session, and there are some that claim to affect bacteria and viruses. I bought a Q-Link necklace for Trevor and have him wear it especially if he's on the computer, because it also is supposed to block the harmful electromagnetic frequencies. EMF can increase the production of toxic microbes and endotoxins according to what I read from Dr. Dietrich Klinghardt. There are many other forms of frequency based jewelry out there. I also recently bought Trevor a cool copper cuff bracelet with 6 magnets in it from www.magneticjewelry store .com. There might be something more advanced out there, but this is what I've found so far.

She went into more details about the virus and where it's coming from. Michael called it a bio-mutated virus and said that it is escaping from a military compound, and being covered up. He specifically mentioned botulism, which is used as a bioweapon. He said that the virus is made to slowly kill people and make it look normal, like natural causes. This even further clarified and validated what I already knew.

Although it was just a brief appearance in this session, both Rose and Jackie Kennedy showed up. One date was given, January 22nd, and after the session, I learned that it was the day of Rose Kennedy's death. That was pretty significant, proving it was her. These two both show up again in later sessions, but this was their first appearance.

***

Chapter Eight

*"For years we have heard the experts
say that autism is a lifelong
disability,*

this is simply not true anymore."

— Bernard Rimland

Session Six

Our next session was on January 5, 2011. Marti was able to join us again with some of her Spirit Art. As a mother of a child with autism, this was one of my favorite sessions. Michael began:

Michael: "I think I've got Albert in front of me here, it looks like Albert anyway."

Laura: "Ok."

Michael: "So, he's saying 'hello' to you."

Laura: "Hello."

Michael: "He's going on about Amino Acids to me. He's showing me bottles that at first I thought was acid, and he said they're Amino Acids."

Laura: "Ok."

Michael: "Ok, he says they're very important."

Laura: "My son takes them."

Michael: "He says there are five main ones."

Laura: "Ok."

Michael: "Bernard, Bernard, he keeps saying to me. There's somebody else here with him. I don't know who it is, it's this guy called Bernard. I don't know if he suffered with autism, or did research on autism, I don't know."

Laura: "Oh, my gosh, there's this guy named Bernard Rimland, who started the Autism Research Institute, and had a son with autism."

Michael: "Oh, he's deceased though, right?"

Laura: "Yeah, he just passed away a few years ago, I think."

Michael: "Yeah, this guy's here called Bernard."

Laura: "Oh, my God!"

Michael: "Who says he dealt with autism."

Laura: "Yeah."

Michael: "Oh, cool. Oh, yep, that's who it is; he's saying 'hello' to you."

Laura: "Oh, my God, he's like a hero in our community."

Michael: "Is he?"

Laura: "Yeah."

Michael: "Well that's what he's saying; it sounds like Bernard or Bernerd."

Laura: "Wow, I'm honored."

Michael: "His son is alive correct?"

Laura: "Yes."

Michael: "Does his son do research as well?"

Laura: "I don't know a lot about his son."

Michael: "No, no, he says not. Hold on. He's involved in a way, but kind of indirectly, I think."

Laura: "Ok."

Michael: "He says he's here with Albert to help. Albert brought him along."

Laura: "Wow."

(Michael had no idea who Bernard Rimland was, or anything about the Autism Research Institute. I was a bit star struck because Bernie was a hero to the autism community, especially to the moms. He single handedly changed Bettelheim's false perception of autism being caused by uncaring "refrigerator mothers" long before the autism epidemic exploded and devoted his life to helping families affected by autism. Rimland's son attends ARI's conferences and other events.)

Michael: "Yeah, I totally got disconnected from Albert, cuz there's somebody else here, you see. And I said tell me who this is, where'd

you go? He said, well, there's someone else, his name's Bernard. And this guy called Bernard showed up in front of me and he said he was dealing with autism, I thought he had autism himself, and he was telling me that his son had autism. Does he have a daughter also?"

Laura: "I don't know."

(After the session, I learned that he has two sons and a daughter.)

Michael: "This man seems...is that you I'm looking at? I'm not sure if this is him, there's a guy with like black hair, dark hair, and it's kind of swept back."

Laura: "Ok."

(If you look on the Autism Research Institute's website, you will see a picture of Bernard Rimland with swept back dark hair.)

Michael: "He keeps saying Charles. There's someone called Charles here as well."

(I don't know if he has a relative named Charles, but I found it interesting that when Bernard Rimland was in the Navy, he worked for the Navy Personnel Research and Development Center and there were a few research articles that he co-wrote with a guy named Charles H. Cory.)

Michael: "And there's a name like M-A-R, Mar...what's this name?

(I found out after the session that Dr. Rimland's son with autism is named Mark.)

Michael: "I think this guy had cancer, that's how he died, this Bernard guy."

Laura: "Ok, I'll have to check."

(I learned after the session that he died in 2006 after a long battle with prostate cancer.)

Michael: "Did he do this thing for about 20 years?"

Laura: "A long time."

Michael: "It was a long time."

Laura: "I'll have to see, but he was a pioneer. His son's a little older, but he started this because of his son. It's called the Autism Research Institute, and they run the Defeat Autism Now! protocol. They have doctors, it's huge."

(He started the Autism Research Institute, or ARI, in 1967, and in 1995, he along with Drs. Sidney Baker and John Pangborn began the Defeat Autism Now! program, a biomedical approach to treating autism.)

Michael: "He keeps insisting on this person called Charles. And there is another name but every time I go to write it, it seems like it's Mar, Mar something. Mar, M-A-R. Well, he's written Marti. Maybe you're drawing him."

(Marti said, "I don't know.")

Michael: "Ok, this is weird, I said I don't know why I'm writing Marti, and he said, 'Look, she's drawing a man.' Maybe she's drawing him. Anyway, he's got dark hair."

(His son is Mark, as I mentioned, but Marti was drawing a picture at the time, so I think he was validating that she was drawing him.)

Laura: "I know what he looks like, but I'm not going to say anything."

Michael: "Hold on. Is this the person who's going to speak to me, is this Bernard? Bernard is saying Michael."

Laura: "I'm not sure, I'll have to look."

(Marti interjects that the guy she was drawing was Jewish.)

Michael "Oh, you felt he was Jewish, ok."

(I found out after the session that Bernard Rimland was in fact Jewish. There is a 2002 magazine article about Bernie from the San Diego Jewish Journal titled "A Mensch Among Men: Dr. Bernard Rimland Won't Rest Until He Defeats Autism." It can be viewed on the ARI website. In the article, he discusses his Jewish heritage and upbringing. None of us knew this at the time of the session. Michael and Marti didn't even know who he was, only I did.)

Next, Michael brought up the name of a researcher with the name Levi. He said that Albert was bringing this up. This name and more information regarding this Levi person comes up again in a later session. I was having a hard time figuring out who it was after the session.

Then, he started talking about nutrition, bringing up Vitamin D. Vitamin D3 plays an important role in many bodily functions including calcium absorption, immune system regulation, brain function, anti-inflammatory, and blood sugar regulation among many other things.

The next part of the session had to do with my ancestry, including past lives. It was very interesting for me personally. It began with Michael saying that he just drew a Roman numeral five next to the word Charles on his paper. He got the feeling that it meant Charles the Fifth, the French king. He asked me if I ever lived in France, and I told him that I am part French. He said that they were talking about my connection to France, going way back to the 15th or 16th century. That's where he felt they were taking him with this. He mentioned someone three generations back by the name of Henri. I didn't know my heritage that far back.

Next, Michael said that they were talking about Scottish ancestry for me also. I affirmed that I'm part Scottish as well. He mentioned the name William or Bill and a place that sounded like Dunfry. I found out after the session that there is a city in Scotland called Dumfries. Who knew? My maternal great grandparents came to the U.S. from Scotland. Then Michael said this interesting tidbit:

Michael: "Ok. This is strange. Is this your third book?"

Laura: "Yep, it's the third one."

Michael: "You've written before, you know. You've done writing in the past."

Laura: "Really?"

Michael: "In another life, yeah."

Laura: "Hmm."

Michael: "They're talking about... you must have lived in England before."

Laura: "I don't know."

Michael: "In Tudor times. Way back. That's interesting. I got the whole Henry the Eighth feeling going on here."

Laura: "Oh, really?"

Michael: "Apparently you lived in those times, and that's when you wrote. You were some sort of scholar, like in English or something, or English Literature."

Laura: "Weird."

Michael: "Yes, it's weird, I know. They're talking about it as though they're utilizing your skills now. This is where it comes in handy, you see."

Laura: "Wow."

Michael: "They're going on about this French king. This is the Charles guy that they're talking about... A Monarch... Yep, yep, they're saying everything to do with a king here. So, it's like a Monarch. I don't know if you're somehow connected. Maybe they're telling you something so cool, that later on you'll find out, and you'll go 'Oh, my God.' Maybe it's going to be one of those moments, you know what I mean? Have you ever wanted to totally research your family history?"

Laura: "Yeah, I started trying to when my kids were born."

Michael: "Did you?"

Laura: "Yeah, but didn't get too far."

Michael: "Were you wondering if there was any genetic predisposition or something?"

Laura: "No."

Michael: "Just doing it purely out of a fascination with it?"

Laura: "Yeah, cuz we always thought we were part Native American, we'd been told both ways, yes and no, and I was mainly trying to find that, validate that."

Michael: "Well that's hard to validate, there's not much written down about that kind of stuff."

Laura: "It was validated in readings with different mediums, but I never had any paper trail."

Michael: "Any ties to North Dakota?"

Laura: "Ah, that's funny. One of my good friends is from the Dakotas, and we both think we were twin sisters in a past life in Native American times."

Michael: "They're telling me you were Indians in North Dakota."

Laura: "Oh, my God, I'm totally getting chills right now."

Michael: "They'll only usually tell you these things if you sort of already know. When you've had inklings of it, you know what I mean?"

Laura: "Yep."

Michael: "Then they're ok telling you, affirming to you that it's correct, follow me?"

Laura: "Yep, that's awesome."

Michael: "I said where in America? And they said North Dakota."

Laura: "Yep. The Ojibwa Tribe."

Michael: "Yeah, I wouldn't have even known that. It felt northern somewhere, and they said North Dakota."

Laura: "Oh my gosh, I can't wait to tell her that."

Michael: "Apparently, it was a very happy incarnation. A happy life, you had a good life."

Laura: "Mmm."

Michael: "And apparently you've had a few incarnations in America, that's why you feel so at home here."

Laura: "Hmm."

(This was a huge personal validation for me. My friend Melanie, whom I consider my big sister, is one of my few spiritual friends. She is also part Ojibwa. People think we are sisters all the time. We met through our Reiki teacher, and I ended up facilitating her Reiki Master attunement. The day before the attunement, she woke up out of a dream/ vision about us being Native American twin sisters, who lived in the Dakotas. She described something that happened, and cried and apologized to me for her actions back then. It was very healing for us both. I wasn't sure if I believed this until another psychic friend of mine, upon first meeting Melanie said, "You two were twin sisters in a past life." We just laughed. Now with Michael saying this, it was more intriguing. Interesting how I named my first dog Dakota, isn't it? Long before I was interested in this stuff.)

The subject changed again, Michael said:

Michael: "They're saying a name that sounds like Steven, but it almost sounds like Stephan."

Laura: "Ah."

Michael: "Let me find out who this is and what this is about."

Laura: "Ok, I think I know."

Michael: "Stephan? Finnish or Swedish? Finland. Well is it like a new kind of thing? Who is this guy? So this Foundation with Bernard has grown exponentially?"

Laura: "Yeah."

Michael: "Apparently it's getting bigger and bigger. Do they support these, the stuff he's doing with your boy, with the tank (HBOT) and the other programs, or are they not at that stage yet?"

Laura: "Yeah, they do a lot of alternative therapies. And Stephen Edelson now runs the Autism Research Institute."

Michael: "What's that?"

Laura: "Stephen Edelson, it's spelled like Stephan, is the new Director of the Autism Research Institute since Bernard Rimland died."

Michael: "That's it, that's it. Cuz they're talking about this guy called Steven, but it sounds like Stephan."

Laura: "Yep."

Michael: "And all of the sudden I'm back to Bernard again and he's talking about the Research Institute."

Laura: "Yep. He's the new Director."

Michael: "Well, he wants to say 'hello' to him."

Laura: "Oh, my God."

Michael: "Ok?"

Laura: "Ok."

Michael: "Whether he gets to hear it personally or through the book, but he's acknowledging him and saying how grateful he is to him and then saying 'hello' to him."

Laura: "Oh, my gosh."

Michael: "But it's spelled like Stephen, isn't it?"

Laura: "Yes."

Michael: "Yeah, that's it. That's it."

Laura: "Oh, my gosh, that's awesome."

(How many dead people are there named Bernard, who ran an Autism Research Institute that would bring up someone named Stephen, emphasizing the spelling, to thank them? Answer: one. Bernard Rimland. Remember earlier when Michael said that Bernard was saying the name Michael? Stephen Edelson's middle name is Michael. Coincidence? I don't know, but it's worth mentioning.)

Michael got quiet for a moment and then mentioned that his "master" as he referred to him, George King, his teacher for many years was coming through and giving him personal information. After this, Michael said that they were talking about us doing some travel abroad after the book gets published. There was going to be some travel ahead. Then Michael mentioned that my dad was in the room, and a Jack or Jackie and that Bernard was back too.

Michael: "Back to Bernard again. Bernard seems to be the most important person here today to talk. Jackie? I don't know. There's somebody else here apparently. Did we talk about Jackie Onassis before?"

Laura:" Yeah, last time. You thought she was in the room."

Michael: "I am back to this again. It's a woman who's in the room. And I said it sounds like Jackie, not Jack, and they said it is. But I can't get her out of my head. I think it's Jackie Onassis. But I don't know what she's got to do with any of this."

Laura: "Maybe one of their relatives has autism now?"

Michael: "I have no idea. There has to be a connection to autism somehow. Maybe you're going to find this out, I don't know. It's weird; I can't understand why she'd be here."

Laura: "Ask her?"

Michael: "Wasn't she married to that Greek Millionaire? Have I got the right person?"

Laura: "Jackie Onassis Kennedy."

(Marti explains to us how Jackie was married to former President JFK, also known as Jack and then later married the Greek Millionaire, Aristotle Onassis. Remember, Michael did not live in the U.S. until the 1990's, he lived in London, England, and I

wasn't even born yet when JFK was assassinated. We were not the most knowledgeable people about their family.)

Michael: "Oh, it is the same person. That's it. That's it, that's who it is. Cuz she said Jack and then John, and then Jackie. It is! It's Jackie Onassis, holy cow!"

Laura: "Ha, ha."

Michael: "I don't know why she's here, I don't understand. It almost seems to have to do with financial aspects."

(Marti says, "That's what I was thinking, maybe it's funding.")

"It's like funding, or there's some kind of funding going to come from this. She's working on that aspect."

Laura: "Oh, that would be cool."

Michael: "Ok, with all of her connections financially. So there's some kind of financial connection as well, ok?"

Laura: "Ok."

Michael: "So it is Jackie Onassis."

Laura: "Wow."

Michael: "Well, I just heard her say "hello" to you."

Laura: "Oh, my gosh."

Michael: "So, she's saying 'hello.'"

Laura: "'Hello.'"

Michael: "Yep, she said, "I'm here to help too." I said, "Ok, very cool." What about your husband, the Greek Fellow, where's he?" (Marti asks if he's dead, Michael says, "Yeah, I'm sure of it.")

(I found out after the session that Jackie was widowed for the second time when Aristotle Onassis died in 1975. Jackie Kennedy Onassis died in 1994.)

"Was there an Oskar Klein?"

Laura: "Yes."

Michael: "It is Oskar Klein isn't it?"

Laura: "Well, that was someone who came through before. He gave the name Oskar, I thought it was Klein."

Michael: "So there is an Oskar Klein?"

Laura: "Yep, he was connected to Einstein, and was another scientist."

Michael: "I don't know what he spoke about, but he's also here again."

Laura: "He didn't speak last time; he just brought up the name Oskar."

(This is an example of how I did research, and thought it was a certain person, and then it was validated in a later session by giving the last name this time. Last time an Oscar was mentioned, this time the first and last name were mentioned together.)

Michael: "Well, he's here. Ok. I feel a little overwhelmed actually. There are so many people in front of me. What does Jackie have to say? Is Oskar going to speak to me or Jackie? You know, I feel that Jackie is very connected to children as well. So, I don't know if she started some funding for kids in some way, or was helping children, but I feel that as well with her, ok?"

Laura: "Ok. She was married to JFK, right?"

Michael: "I didn't know it was one in the same person, I couldn't put the two together, although I had the weird feeling that it was. Because I was thinking of JFK, and then I was thinking of his wife, and then suddenly I was thinking about Jackie Onassis, and I was thinking, I don't know who that is."

(Again, the Jack, John, Jackie Kennedy, Jackie Onassis confusion. We sound brilliant, don't we? History was not my favorite subject in school, can you tell? It's probably a good thing, because I had to look all of this stuff up later.)

(Marti says, "I keep thinking of the name Ari.")

Laura: "Ari?"

Michael: "Yeah, like Aritstotle."

Laura: "Yeah, well the place that Bernard Rimland worked at, the initials are ARI, Autism Research Institute."

Michael: "That's it, that's it."

(Marti says, "It's also Aristotle Onassis.")

Michael: "They called him Ari as well? How interesting."

(I looked this up after the session, and Aristotle Onassis was indeed called "Ari" for short.)

Laura: "How funny."

Michael: "I know what this means then, what they're doing is they're tying the funding in with the Institute. Do you understand?"

Laura: "Oh, ok."

Michael: "So the ARI is the Institute, but Ari is also this Millionaire."

Laura: "Oh, Aristotle Onassis."

Michael: "Got it? Because they're talking about funding. Now, they're talking about Senators. So, there has to be some sort of, maybe some Senators have kids with this."

Laura: "Yeah, there are a few."

Michael: "They said that there are some Senators that have children with autism. So, there's going to be a means to get things passed or funding. So there's going to be a lot of interest in this, ok?"

Laura: "Ok."

Michael: "See, we may not be talking about things we've been talking about before, in the other sessions today. They may be talking about other aspects of this, see?"

Laura: "Mmm-hmm."

Michael: "Weird. Julian Law? Jude Law? Julian Law? Are you saying Jude Law? Is he going to be doing a movie about this or something? Huh, I wonder why they're talking about; I think they're talking about Jude Law. But he's an actor."

Laura: "Right."

Michael: "I don't know if he's going to be doing a movie about this or what?"

Laura: "Huh."

Michael: "That's weird. Calisto. Calisto, CAL-isto. Bear with me because they get into some pretty far out stuff sometimes, and I just have to make sure where we're going with what they're talking about."

Laura: "Mmm-hmm."

(I was thinking of the actress Calista Flockhart when he was saying this, or the city of Calistoga, CA. Who knows?)

Next, Michael brought up some names that they were saying that he was having a hard time with. Sometimes the names run together and are two different names, or parts of two names. Foreign names are particularly difficult to get. What he thought was a first and last name of a person, turned out to be two different people.

Michael: "I'm sure they're saying a name like Frederic von Stock, or Frederic von Strap, some kind of name like that. Frederic. This sounds like at the turn of the century, did he know Curie? Madam Curie. Connected there with her?

(Frédéric Joliot-Curie, a French Physicist and Nobel Laureate, was married to Marie Curie's daughter. He was also Marie Curie's assistant at the Radium Institute. I also found it very interesting that Frédéric Joliot-Curie was one of the scientists mentioned in the letter from Albert Einstein to President Roosevelt as one of the leading scientists on the course to chain reactions.)

"It's an 'S' name, like Stapp, Staph? Staph, or Steph, hmm. They made me feel like the research into chemical warfare really began in the WWI, because they're showing me mustard gas."

Laura: "Hmm."

Michael: "And so I think all their research began then, around the time of WWI, with mustard gas."

(After a bit of research, I'm fairly certain that the name of the spirit Michael was trying to get here was Wilhelm Steinkopf. In German, W's are pronounced with a V sound, and the "St" beginning and "ph" ending of the name Steinkopf also came through. Wilhelm Steinkopf was a German Chemist and a friend and colleague of Albert Einstein at the Kaiser Wilhelm Institute, where Steinkopf co-developed a process for mass producing mustard gas, the first bio-chemical weapon for war use during WWI. Mustard gas was also know as LOST, parts of the names of co-develpers Lommel and Steinkopf. At Germany's Fritz Haber Institute between 1914-1918 they did research and production of chemical weapons, including mustard gas, according to their website.[21] There is a photo on the website from 1915 of a young Albert Einstein with

---

[21] www.fhi-berlin.mpg.de

Fritz Haber. A few years later, Einstein became director of the Kaiser Wilhelm Institute of Physics. The use of chemical weapons in WWI killed 92,000 soldiers and injured 1.3 million. Einstein's pacifist views sharply contrasted Haber's, saying "Warfare cannot be humanized. It can only be abolished.")

Michael: "Now they're showing me green leaves and stuff. Why am I seeing leaves? It's on the leaves? It's back to Botulism. There's botulism, is it a kind of soup? Or is it...is it like a food poisoning? Spores on the leaves."

(Again, just like anthrax, which produces spores which remain viable in soil for decades, Michael was seeing botulism spores on leaves. This makes me think of airborne biowarfare contaminating the plants and soil, poisoning the food. When he said a kind of soup, I believe that means a bunch of things mixed together, including this.)

Michael: "Ok, do you have anything you wanted to ask them, or do you have anything written down that you wanted to ask them?"

Laura: "Well, I wrote down on the top of my paper today more about give us more details about the cause. They've been giving us little bits and pieces, so a little more specific."

Michael: "You know, it's strange they can't identify this virus."

Laura: "Mmm-hmm."

Michael: "If it's a genetically engineered virus, then they're not going to identify it, cuz there's nothing to go by, do you follow me?"

Laura: "Mmm-hmm."

Michael: "I mean, it's a new thing, you got me?"

Laura: "Mmm-hmm."

Michael: "I mean, somebody just has to put a name to it and work out, you know, like its properties."

Laura: "Mmm-hmm. I want to know how the kids are getting it. They're talked about a few different things, and I'm just a little confused."

Michael: "Well, you see, it's introduced in different ways. It's in the air, so it's airborne. It's injected. And it's taken orally. That's why you have different kinds, because you're not just dealing with one kind, it's like variants on it."

(Marti said that she also felt rain, and saw like the acid rain. She drew a picture of rain.)

Michael: "Marti drew rain. So, it could be like, from the atmosphere in the water, you know? We're dealing with these toxins and viruses that are all around us, it seems. It's a bit like a soup, ok? That's how they put it. It's a bit like a soup. You just keep adding all these ingredients, and you end up with a certain soup."

Laura: "Ok."

Michael: "You see, as time goes on, more and more souls from higher realms are going to be coming in. The more they come in, the more sensitive they're going to be, ok?"

Laura: "Mmm-hmm."

Michael: "They're going to have more and more sensitive children incarnating, ok? And they're going to be more succeptible to a lot of things because this is a very toxic environment that we are now in. More toxic than it's ever been. Due to all of the things that are present."

Laura: "Uh-huh."

Michael: "Maybe Rose is connected to Jackie; it's like Jackie's mother or something?"

Laura: "I think there's a Rose Kennedy."

(Marti says yeah, it's on the Kennedy side.)

Michael: "Who is that to Jackie?"

Laura: "Mother-in-law, I think."

Michael: "Is it her mother-in-law?"

Laura: "Yeah, I think Rose Kennedy was JFK's mom."

Michael: "Rose Kennedy is John Kennedy's mom."

Laura: "I believe so."

Michael: "Oh, that's what they're telling me. Rose is connected to Jackie."

(Marti had been looking online to see if Jackie had any sort of charitable foundation, and found that there was one in her own name set up.)

179

Michael: "I don't know how it is, but she says it's through her. And it's for autism?"

(Marti answers, "Yes.")

Michael: "I don't know why though. Is it unrelated to any autistic children to her though?"

(Marti answers, "Yes.")

Michael: "Well that's interesting. How funny, I wonder who started it. Does she have a daughter, Marti?"

(Marti says, "Yes.")

Michael: "Is it through her daughter?"

(Marti says "Not that I know of, Caroline is her daughter.")

Michael: "I don't know."

(Marti says, "She's the only one left.")

Michael: "Oh, she's the only one left alive, Caroline."

Laura: "Hmm."

Michael: "What is this R name she keeps saying to me? Is it like a last name? What is the name? Oh, Robert, just Robert."

Laura: "Hmm."

(Marti mentions that Robert Kennedy Jr.'s article is about autism and mercury.)

Laura: "Oh, I've read that article. It's a great article."

(Robert Kennedy, Jr., son of JFK's brother Robert Kennedy Sr., wrote an article for Rolling Stone magazine and Salon.com alleging a government conspiracy to cover-up a connection between the vaccine preservative Thimerosal and autism.)

Michael: "Who's the one who died in the plane crash with his wife?"

(Marti says, "That was Jackie's son.")

Michael: "Jackie Onassis's son. That's it. Oh, well he's here too."

(Marti says, "That's John John.")

Michael: "John John, Yes, he's here. Oh, ha, ha. Oh, cool. I can't even

think right at the moment. So, he wrote an article for Rolling Stone about mercury. There you go. What more do you want?"

Laura: "Yeah, I totally forgot about that. I knew he was a Kennedy, but I didn't know which one he was."

Michael: "There is totally a connection to autism with them. And they're saying, 'See I told you it was mercury.'"

Michael starts talking about the need to condense the research, not have it so scattered, mentioning that Albert was great at unifying people and bringing them together. He said there was a need for serious research into this adding:

Michael: "I don't think that there are too many things that are not known. You follow me?"

Laura: "Except the Biowarfare."

Michael: "Yeah, but like I said to you, you're not going to know those kinds of things. If I told you it was xyz, you probably wouldn't be able to find it anywhere, because it's not written up. If they come up with a new virus, they're going to categorize it with a name that nobody's even heard of; nobody would know what it is, because it's secret. You follow me?"

Laura: "Yep."

Michael: "So, you're not going to be able to look it up or find it or even know anybody who would know what it is, you see?"

Laura: "Mmm-hmm."

Michael: "So that's a kind of a waste of time in a way. That's the sense they give me here of that. They may come up with something, but it could be a couple of decades before you find out that it was correct."

Laura: "Mmm-hmm."

Michael: "What is important is that they're giving you pointers as to what can cure it. You see, you can't take this stuff out of the atmosphere. You can't get rid of mercury out of the ocean right now, it's full of it."

Laura: "Mmm-hmm."

Michael: "So, how do we combat it, that's the thing. What are the things

to combat it? What are the things that get mercury out of the body? What are the ways we can prevent absorbing and taking these things into the body?"

Laura: "Right."

Michael: "It's preventative measures and clean-up efforts. These are the things that matter."

Laura: "Mmm-hmm."

Michael: "Look at BP with that oil disaster. Look at the millions of gallons of toxic chemicals they've poured into the ocean. Nobody stopped them, nobody did anything about it. Now we have all of that toxin in the ocean now. God knows what's in it. It just seems no end to the stuff that people pollute our world with. I don't know how to stop it all. People have to just get in the game, you know? If you've got Senators that have kids that they love who have disabilities due to chemical poisoning, whether it is mercury or whatever, then you have got some clout."

Laura: "Mmm-hmm."

Michael: "You have to get people in positions of power, who have a direct connection to some issue like this, and then they'll get involved. Then they'll do something about it, see? That's the only way we are going to change things. There's no other way. I mean, you know if people just don't care, then nothing is going to get done."

Laura: "Yep."

Michael: "You know there's a research center that's on an island that's off the East Coast, it's on a little island and nothing gets on or off it, it's totally isolated. Just before Bush ended office, he was trying to get it put on the main land."

Laura: "Is that Plum Island?"

Michael: "I think so, it's like a little research center that's been on that island forever."

Laura: "Yeah."

Michael: "Got me? And they were trying to put it on the main land! What are you frickin insane?"

Laura: "Yeah, they're still trying to do it; it's going to be in the middle of the United States."

Michael: "Exactly. What lunatic wants to put that on the main land?"

Laura: "Yeah, right in tornado alley."

Michael: "Yep, but some lunatic wants to put it on land. Oh, wonderful, yeah, just wonderful." (Sarcasm.)

Laura: "Yeah, it's in the works."

(The Department of Homeland Security's National Bio and Agro Facility would be the country's second largest biodefense facility, and would have BSL-4 labs for experiments with killer diseases with no effective treatment or cure. It is going to be in Kansas, and takes over what they were doing on Plum Island. Wizard of Oz, tornado, Kansas; Auntie M!)

Michael: "It's a huge kind of picture in a way. Once people see the links, how it's all linked together, you know? I mean the FDA, I don't know where there heads are at, but I don't even think they are a legitimate organization, I think they're a front for corporations. Understand?"

Laura: "Yep."

Michael: "You can't trust what they say. 'Oh, the FDA approved it.' Really, you mean some corporation approved it?"

Laura: "Who will make money off of it."

Michael: "Make a bunch of money, and if somebody doesn't agree with what they say, they off them, or throw them out of a window or something. That's what happens with them."

Laura: "Mmm-hmm."

Michael: "Botulism. They're back to this again. I think that's one of the keys here. It doesn't make any sense to me how mercury and botulism can be linked, but they are."

Laura: "Ask them if Botulism toxin is in the biological warfare they are talking about, the genetically altered stuff."

Michael: "It is. It is. They're saying affirmative. Yes, Yes."

Laura: "I knew it!"

Michael: "Let's do the pictures Marti's drawn here."

Laura: "Ok."

Here are the two pictures that Marti drew. First the portrait and then the doodle page:

The following picture is of Bernard Rimland when he was older; he is the second from the right. There is another reason I chose this photo, as you will see later on in the book. Now remember, Marti has never even heard of Bernard Rimland, much less seen a picture of him. She was seeing an image of him in her mind and drawing it. It is an artist's rendition, not a photograph. The fact that it resembles him at all is incredible. I didn't really think it looked like him at first; I always picture dark hair, glasses and a beard when I think of him. Imagine him without glasses and a beard and look at the picture; he has the same hair, eyes, lips, and ears. Marti saw and felt an older Jewish guy and said that he was thin. After she faxed me the picture, I had her go to the ARI website to look at a picture of him. Immediately upon seeing it, she said, "Yeah, that's him."

Here is the doodle page Marti drew:

Doodle Explanations: Before Marti faxed me the doodle page she explained the pictures to me over the phone, and what she thought they meant. Michael and I added some insight as well. As she mentioned earlier during the session, she drew a picture of rain. I told her about reading a recent study that showed that states with a lot of rain and precipitation have higher incidence of autism. The rain brings what is in the atmosphere down to Earth. Marti also got that to be careful where you buy your vegetables. Know where they come from. Michael said they were showing him the leaves, and botulism spores settling on the leaves. Marti said, even organic, you need to know where they come from. Michael said his vision of the future is things that are grown in greenhouses with... all three of us say "hydroponic" at the same time. Michael emphasizes that hydroponic is the future. This is the same information that I was given in the sessions for my other book. With biowarfare, nuclear radiation, GMO and Roundup contaminating the soil, it seems like that is going to be our only option.

Marti explained that the picture of the shake with the vegetables around it was a juice drink to be mixed in a blender. The vegetables are specific, she asked on each one. They are onion, tomato, blueberries, ginger, and asparagus. Asparagus was one of the most important ones, and raw. Kids may not like the taste of ginger, just add a little bit, she said. The blueberry might sweeten it a bit. Nutrition is so important to children with autism. Maybe this combination has special benefits. I looked up each item separately, and they all have nutritional and health benefits for the body including the brain, immune system, digestion, blood, and kidneys. Some are anti-inflammatory, anti-bacterial, anti-oxidant, anti-cancer, among other things. You can find nutrition information and facts about these and other foods on the website www.juicingforhealth.com.

Marti said that the picture of the child bundled up meant that the cold really bothers some of these children and that you have to really bundle them up. I know my own son has issues with weather. He especially hates the wind. He likes really hot and really cold water, or doesn't notice how hot or cold they really are.

Marti explained that the microscope she drew has a plug inside and was electronic. Perhaps that means an electron microscope which has the highest magnification capability, with magnifications of up to 10,000 times. Or perhaps a dark field microscope used live blood analysis which could allow one to see the virus/biowarfare agent coming up in the sessions. Could it be detected in the cerebro-spinal fluid?

The book with "Top Secret- FYEO" on it, means "For Your Eyes Only," Marti said. Michael added that some of this was Top Secret, meaning government and military secrets. I'm assuming it is referring to the genetic-ally engineered virus they were talking about again.

In the final picture of the hand, Marti said it had stubby fingers, a child's hand. Michael added that he was feeling it had to do with a Bio-scanner. I have a friend who tested my antioxidant levels using a Pharmanex Bioscanner, in which you place your hand on a device which reads your levels in a few minutes. My levels were low I remember. Then, she recommended some supplements for me. That was my only reference for a Bioscanner, maybe there is another kind as well for detecting other things.

***

Session Six: After the Session

Featured Spirits: Bernard Rimland, Albert Einstein, Frédéric Joliot-Curie, Wilhelm Steinkopf, Oskar Klein, Jackie Kennedy Onassis, Rose Kennedy, President John F. Kennedy Jr.

I was so excited to find out the validations to the things that Bernard brought up. I had forgotten his son's name during the session, but Michael said the letters M-A-R, and his name is Mark. Also, that he did die of cancer as Michael said. I also learned that Bernie was a technical advisor on the movie "Rain Man" and that the actor Dustin Hoffman, who plays an autistic savant in the movie, modeled his performance on Mark Rimland. I called Michael to tell him some of these validations, and when I told him about Rain Man, he said, "You're kidding me. I almost said that he was showing me the movie Rain Man, but I thought it was just a reference for me because that's how I know about autism." He said he wished he would have said what he was seeing. But that was another validation that Bernard was showing Michael the movie during the session. I had no idea.

I found it interesting that during this particular session they talked about the engineered virus again, specifically botulism and affirmed that it was part of the biowarfare. More details were brought up when Michael saw botulism spores on the leaves. Bernie spent his whole life trying to find the causes and ways to treat autism. He organized Think Tanks of the top scientists and doctors in the country to share their findings and train other doctors to help more children. The fact that the information on this topic came up during Bernie's session gave it even more credibility to me.

As I was looking up information about Rose Kennedy, I discovered that her daughter Rosemary Kennedy, born a year after JFK, had some intellectual disabilities. At age 23, her father, Joe, had a lobotomy performed on her, hoping to fix her problems. Instead, it left her permanently incapacitated and she had to be institutionalized for the rest of her life. When I called Michael to tell him about this discovery he told me that he had been thinking about lobotomies a lot lately, even dreaming about them, and had no idea why. Now it made sense to him.

Her sister, Eunice Kennedy Shriver, started the Special Olympics in Rosemary's honor. I could not believe what I was reading. I also learned that her father, Joseph P. Kennedy was the U.S Ambassador to the United Kingdom during FDR's presidency. Rosemary, prior to the lobotomy, even visited the White House and met FDR. The Kennedy's and FDR were also connected in life, and were both assisting us in our sessions!

It was also interesting that while Jackie Kennedy Onassis was talking about funding for autism, the name "Ari" came through to Marti; which is both the nickname of her second husband, Aristotle Onassis and the abbreviation for Bernard Rimland's Autism Research Institute, ARI. Then, during my research after the session, I went onto the ARI homepage which lists Important Links, and much to my surprise, the first link says "The Eunice Kennedy Shriver NICHD Brain and Tissue Bank for Developmental Disorders." My jaw about hit the floor as I read this.

As if that wasn't enough to get my attention, I also found that within the Albert Einstein College of Medicine in New York (which I didn't know existed), there is also the Rose F. Kennedy Intellectual and Developmental Disabilities Research Center (IDDRC), which broke ground in 1966. There is a picture on their website with Rose and Bobby at the groundbreaking ceremony holding shovels. Currently at the Rose F. Kennedy Center, they have an Autism Spectrum Disorders Research cluster, a multidisciplinary effort looking into novel treatments and interventions, as well as an autism evaluation center. What a legacy! What the Kennedy's started there was out of the love of a special child.

Here was another parallel, having a beloved family member damaged because of a botched medical procedure/trusting bad medical advice. (Like thinking that injecting an infant with 9 diseases and numerous toxic chemicals in one day is a good idea.) I believe that having loved one with a disability was another reason the Kennedy family was interested in what we were trying to do. The stigma of mental illness in those times was much different than it is today, especially for a family with political aspirations such as the Kennedy's. I cried when I read about what happened to Rosemary. They kept her hidden away for a long time. Having a loved one permanently damaged and living with the aftermath is a heavy cross to bear.

That is what all parents with children with regressive autism are dealing with today. The truly sad part to me is how the medical community denies their disease, blaming genetics. I'm afraid to see what happens when they become a financial burden to countries that have to take care of them when their parents no longer can. I know without a shadow of a doubt that when Trevor and I are both on The Other Side, he will not have autism anymore, and I will understand the reasons for all of this. But for now, it is my job as his mom to make his life here on Earth the best it can be. I am his guardian, his protector, his voice. I only pray that I can fix him or outlive him.

***

Chapter Nine

"I think back to what Camus wrote about the fact that perhaps this world is a world in which children suffer, but we can lessen the number of suffering children, and if you do not do this, then who will do this? I'd like to feel that I'd done something to lessen that suffering."

— Robert F. Kennedy, Sr.

(In an interview shortly before he was killed, responding to a question by David Frost about how his obituary should read.)

Session Seven

This session was held on January 12, 2011. Marti sat in on the session and drew some pictures. Here are the highlights of the session:

Michael: "I think I've got Bobby here with me."

Laura: "Bobby Kennedy?"

Michael: "They're saying Bobby Kennedy and his mother."

Laura: "Bobby would be Robert, right? Robert Kennedy?"

Michael: "Is he Robert Francis?"

(I learned afterward that Robert F. Kennedy's middle name is Francis.)

Laura: "I don't know. Rose is Bobby and JFK's mom."

Michael: "Oh, Rose is their mother."

Laura: "Uh-huh."

Michael: "It's got to be her then."

Laura: "Ok."

Michael came up with a few names they were saying, and I couldn't definitively say what they meant since I don't know the family personally,

I don't want to speculate the meaning. Next, they gave the name Schneider. My first thought was that it was Phil Schneider, the murdered geologist who worked for the government building underground military bases which I researched during my investigations for my book, *Foundation of Discovery*. However, after the session, I found out that there is a book called *Robert F. Kennedy* written by a man named Steven Schneider. I guess I'll never know for certain who this Schneider person was because my late husband jumped in to say "hello" to me. He reminded me of the time that he broke his arm, which was true. It was before I met him but he had the scars and told me what happened. Then Michael said:

Michael: "They say there are a lot of people here today ready to talk to me."

Laura: "Ok."

Michael: "He said I hope you can hear us well. I said, I can hear that pretty well. He said, good, we'll begin then. Is Albert here? Yes, ok. He says mostly the Kennedy's."

Laura: "Hmm."

Michael: "Oh, you know the one who just died?"

Laura: "Edward?"

Michael: "Yeah."

Laura: "Edward Kennedy is there?"

Michael: "Edward, yeah the one that just died."

Laura: "The Senator? Oh yeah, that was like in '09 or something."

Michael: "Yeah, the late Edward Kennedy."

Laura: "Wow, I watched his memorial. Neat guy."

Michael: "Oh, he's talking about a big event; you watched his memorial, did you?"

Laura: "Yeah."

(Senator Edward "Ted" Kennedy died on September 25, 2009. I watched his memorial service on TV, and learned a lot about the whole family. I was impressed with all that he did while in office to help others, especially people with disabilities, including directing the passage of the Americans with Disabilities Act of 1990 and fighting for No Child

Left Behind.)

Michael: "Is there anything dedicated to people who are blind connected to any of the Kennedy's?"

Laura: "I'm not sure."

Michael: "Or had to do with Einstein? They're going on about blindness. It has to do with someone who was blind. Or technically blind, but I think blind. Now they're saying something about DuPont. Oh, Alfred. Alfred? Not Albert. Alfred. Oh, there is somebody here called Alfred, not Albert."

(After the session I learned that Alfred I. du Pont, a member of the influential du Pont family was missing an eye from an accident and gave money to help people with disabilities. He dedicated his fortune to the Nemours Foundation in Jacksonville, Florida, dedicated to the health of children. Interestingly, the company DuPont now is a big chemical manufacturer and is involved in the biotechnology industry/genetic engineering as well; some of the very things implicated in being causative factors in autism.)

Michael: "They are showing me copper. Hmm, they never brought that up before. What connection does copper have then? It's like copper around the body? They're talking about copper being very helpful too. I feel like they're on the wrists."

Laura: "Some of the bracelets have copper in them."

Michael: "Are they a copper/silver mix?"

Laura: "Some of them are, yes."

Michael: "Cuz they're talking about that."

Laura: "Oh."

Michael: "You know what's weird, it's like they hum. I don't know if they've tuned them?"

Laura: "Oh."

Michael: "But they're talking about tuned, like you tune an instrument."

Laura: "Right, I wonder if it is the resonance."

Michael: "It would have to be tuned somehow."

Laura: "Hmm."

Michael: "Hmm, how interesting. I don't know if you do that electrically, or mechanically."

(Marti says, "I think it's electric, cuz as soon as you said copper, I saw electrically, what they zap them with, with the copper around it so it must be something to do with that.")

Michael: "I think that it's like some sort of electrical pulse or frequency that they put into the copper, almost like an electromagnet. I don't know exactly how it works, but I see it charged."

Laura: "Ok. What will those bracelets help with specifically?"

Michael: "They're more to do with the virus. I think it's got more to do with affecting a virus or viral conditions in the body."

Laura: "Ok. It could be used for lots of different things."

Michael: "Do some of them use Platinum? Is Platinum used at all? Are they Platinum coated?"

Laura: "I don't remember."

Michael: "I think this is pretty new technology they're talking about."

Laura: "Ok."

(After the session, I read that copper jewelry has many health benefits, notably that copper is an antifungal and antibacterial agent according to copper.org. It has been used for thousands of years to help heal wounds by stopping the growth of harmful organisms. Also, the Greek physician, Hippocrates, who is called the father of medicine, wrote that silver had beneficial healing and anti-disease properties. Silver is known to have a toxic effect on some bacteria, viruses, algae and fungi. I have seen some copper bracelets with magnets in them, and bought one for Trevor.)

Michael: "Does your boy get out in the sun everyday?"

Laura: "At recess at school, and in summer, he loves being outside."

Michael: "Does he take his shirt for 10 minutes in the sun?"

Laura: "Not usually, should he? That's vitamin D."

Michael: "Yeah, but he needs to get a certain amount of exposure to the sun, ok?"

Laura: "Oh, ok."

Michael: "Ok? That will help him."

Laura: "Ok."

Michael: "Is your son very pale?"

Laura: "Yeah, he's got light hair, blue eyes, and really pale skin."

Michael: "Pale. Now see, pale is a lack of D. Lack of Vitamin D makes you very pale.

So, whatever assists in the uptake of D."

Laura: "Ok."

(This is the second time they've brought up the importance of Vitamin D. I put him on a Vitamin D3 supplement.)

The next part of the session was very interesting. Michael started talking about Michaelangelo. I assumed he meant the painter and didn't know what he was referring to. Then he said that it was a place or a center, maybe in Italy. I told him that I was looking up a Brain Center in Italy recently when I was researching the name "Levi" that came up in a past session. I found that there was a Nobel Prize winning woman who runs a Brain Center in Italy with Levi in her name. The conversation continued:

Michael: "It is in Italy that they are talking about. It's a place in Italy."

Laura: "Maybe that's it, cuz I was looking it up online, but I couldn't understand it because the website was in Italian."

Michael: "Yeah, it's Italian, it's not here they said, it's in Italy. It's a place that they're doing research in Italy."

Laura: "I didn't know if it was her, because she's still alive, she's like 100 and something."

Michael: "Yeah, that's fine. They can talk about people who are still alive, remember?"

Laura: "Ok, I was just thinking she was dead (because they were talking about her), so I thought I might have had the wrong person, but maybe not."

Michael: "No, no, they could be referencing someone alive, you see?

And maybe there is some connection, and Michelangelo, or someone with the same kind of name. Maybe you can find that out."

Laura: "Ok."

Michael: "There is a connection there."

Laura: "Ok."

Michael: "Ok. And they're saying "valid" so I must be on the right track."

Michael: "There is definitely somebody with the name like Alberto, it's not Albert. But there is somebody with a name like Alberto. I think this is all connected to this Italian thing, ok?"

Laura: "Ok."

Michael: "Well she must be doing important work then?"

Laura: "Yeah."

Michael: "Well, her work must be groundbreaking, if they're pointing you in that direction, then she must be. Maybe you can get a translation somewhere of her stuff."

Laura: "Yeah, she's all to do with the brain, and Neurology. Ok. I guess I was on the right track."

Michael: "Yeah, yeah you were. I know it's difficult, cuz you can't read it, but that's who they're talking about, I believe."

Laura: "Ok."

(The woman I thought "Levi" was from the other session was possibly Rita Levi-Montalcini, who started EBRI, European Brain Research Institute in Italy. However, she was still alive and had Levi in her name, not her first name, so I wasn't sure. Since the spirits brought it up again in this session, I looked up the website again after the session, and noticed an English translation button. Voila! I looked up the researchers names, and of the 7 group leaders listed, one was named Michelangelo, and another was named Alberto! The exact two names that Michael mentioned. They are doing important brain research at EBRI including metabolism in brain diseases, focusing on mitochondria. One of these two researchers even won the Marie Curie Fellow award. The connections just kept coming.)

Michael: "Yeah, they are cautioning you about, you know, don't over expect, don't expect like huge results, you understand?" *(My son's improvement.)*

Laura: "Mmm-hmm."

Michael: "It will be a slow progress, you understand?"

Laura: "Mmm-hmm."

Michael: "I think you're seeing gains, but I think it's going to take a bit of doing, you know?"

Laura: "Mmm-hmm."

Michael: "They're saying the gold will help. So I think that getting the mercury out of the system with the gold, I think that's really going to work."

Laura: "Ok. Now should it be gold salts, or homeopathic gold? And what potency if it is homeopathic?"

Michael: "Oh, well you can find that out with a pendulum. You can dowse it. Have you ever used a pendulum?"

Laura: "Yeah, I know how to do that."

Michael: "Well, just douse it; you can dowse it for the strength. They're saying 3 or 30. Ok?"

Laura: "X or C or LM?"

Michael: "X"

Laura: "30X, funny. I had him on 30X, and I stopped."

Michael: "What was it, gold?"

Laura: "Homeopathic gold, aurum metallicum it's called."

Michael: "Aurum metallicum, yeah. Well, don't stop."

Laura: "Ok, I'll get it again, I have to order it."

(After the session, I also learned about colloidal gold. From the website purest colloids.com, it says "Colloidal gold is nanoparticles of pure gold suspended in pure water. The gold nanoparticles in Mesogold are a few nanometers in diameter (a nanometer is a billionth of meter). These particles are so small they can only be seen by the most powerful electron microscopes available today. An atom of gold is about 0.288 nanometers in diameter, so the gold nanoparticles in Mesogold are only about eleven

times the diameter of a single gold atom. These particles stay suspended in pure de-ionized water and do not fall to the bottom. It is these suspended particles that make Mesogold a true colloid. Ionic gold is what some producers call their non-colloidal gold supplements. Ionic gold is a gold salt that is dissolved in water. Products labeled as ionic gold are really gold chloride, also called Chlorauric acid, a water soluble gold salt. The reason you don't see gold chloride on the label or mentioned in the ads is because gold chloride is known to be potentially toxic to humans. Gold chloride has been known to cause Peripheral Neuropathy." So, colloidal gold or homeopathic gold is what you'd want, not ionic gold, which is a gold salt, and is potentially toxic. In a pilot study on colloidal gold and cognitive function, there was a 20 percent increase in IQ scores in 4 weeks. The study can be seen on the purestcolloids.com website.)

Michael: "They all work together. You're not going to achieve results with just one thing; you're going to have to use a number of things on him, and homeopathic stuff just takes a while to work. You're not going to notice it straight away, generally. It's more subtle. It takes a while. You're like building it up, you see."

Laura: "Can they tell me how long should I have him on it?"

Michael: "Well you may have to take it for a couple years or something. But you're not going to see it immediately, or over a few months necessarily. It may take 6 months, a year, before you start noticing. But used it in conjunction with what you're doing now, with the chamber, and some other things, then you may notice more results, you see?"

Laura: "Mmm-hmm."

Michael: "But you mustn't stop using it."

Laura: "Ok. Thank you."

Michael: "Well, they're saying you were doing the right thing with the 30X."

Laura: "Ok."

(A few years prior to this I was having a reading with another medium that I know. She started talking about my son and autism and said that he needed gold as a therapy. I asked if homeopathic gold would work, and she said yes, but to have him take it for 18 months and in a 30X potency. Now Michael was saying the exact same potency and for a long time. I had used it for a year previously, and then moved on to something else. After this session, I started up again.)

Michael: "There's also a lady called Janette, I think it's Janette. It sort of sounded like Janet, but I think its Janette, with an F last name. Almost sounds French, like Janette Furher, Furrer. She seems to be some sort of like a chemist, but she may be a homeopath. Maybe it's Janette Francis, or Francois. Yeah, it sounds like Janette Francois. Maybe this person is a homeopath. She may also be a doctor."

(I haven't figured out who this lady is, but I left her name in here in case some day it makes sense to me or someone else.)

Laura: "Hmm."

Michael: "Are you using any flower remedies on him?"

Laura: "Yeah, I use one for anger and I use the Bach Rescue Remedy."

Michael: "Do you use Rose on him?"

Laura: "No. Should I?"

Michael: "I see like a tincture, you see. I see it in water, like drops in water."

Laura: "Ok."

Michael: "You should use Rose on him."

Laura: "Ok, Rose Flower Essence?"

Michael: "Yeah, Rose Flower Essence. He gets like anxiety attacks, you see?"

Laura: "Yeah."

Michael: "That's what he basically suffers from is anxiety, and that's why he gets upset, cuz he gets anxious and anxiety, you see?"

Laura: "Yeah."

Michael: "It's like he doesn't feel safe."

Laura: "Yeah. And the Rose will help with that?"

Michael: "Mmm-hmm."

(After the session, I bought a Rose flower essence remedy for Trevor and gave it to him when he was upset and anxious. It really helped. Also, Rock Rose is one of the flower essences in Rescue Remedy, used for natural stress relief. I've been known to use it myself.)

Michael: "Hold on. Somebody is talking about forensic pathology to me. I never really thought about that, but somebody must have done some work afterwards, you know once people have died, on certain conditions. I never thought about looking into that. What they've found, you know, related to certain conditions. They keep saying the word 'pathology.'"

Laura: "Ok."

(Forensic pathology is the "what happened" specialty, studies done after the person has died. There have not been many studies done on children with autism post-mortem, mainly because of a lack of subjects, but now there are brain banks for autism research. Some of the post-mortem studies I have found on people with autism show viruses in the brain and brain differences. One post-mortem study showed pathogens in the brain that were resistant to any known antibiotics. This is an area worth further investigation.)

Michael: "You know, a lot of the things are being worked on. People are on the right track with a lot of things, you know. It's just getting people to take you seriously, the general public, you know what I mean? A lot of these people are on the right track with the things they're doing."

Laura: "Yeah."

Michael: "When Robert (Kennedy) was first talking to me, I felt this kind of battle, kind of mentality. Like they were in a war, you know what I mean, with other minds while they were here. They looked at it like they were at war, fighting."

Laura: "Mmm-hmm."

Michael: "With established order, you know, that's how it felt to me, when he connected with me. Almost like a fight to the death, you know, like do or die."

Laura: "Mmm-hmm. Well, he was assassinated."

Michael: "Yeah, I know, I never really felt this with him before."

Then we talked about the pictures Marti had drawn. She didn't draw a portrait, only the doodles this time. Here they are:

<u>Doodle Explanations:</u> The boy with the cone on his head – Both of them felt that there was a copper wire inside the cone. It is a shape-power hat. Michael compared it to a dunce cap that children wore in school as a punishment. It was supposed to make them smarter. The copper wire spirals inside or outside the cone, and it energizes the brain. Maybe the copper has an effect on the virus in the brain, as the jewelry they were talking about during the session suggested. Michael said that he has a copper device with gold plates on it that was devised by his master, which he lays in and it energizes the etheric body and aura. This works in the same way. I have yet to try this only because I'm not very crafty.

The xylophone had to do with sound therapy. Pure sounds like the xylophone, and Michael was feeling something about the musical notes C and E. The kite had to do with Benjamin Franklin, who was famous for his kite and key experiment with lightning. What I didn't know was that he also invented a musical instrument called a glass armonica. Michael said that it also had to do with sound therapy. The armonica incorporates the principles of wet fingers on glass. It is an instrument of tuned glasses in a long cylinder, which you turn and use your fingers to play it. Again, he felt that this had to do with music therapy for kids with autism.

The bloomers, after a three way discussion, had to do with children with autism and their toileting issues. Michael asked me if my son had any kidney problems, and was linking anxiety to the kidneys. I told him that he used to wet his bed for a long time, and peed a lot. He suggested that what Marti was picking up on represented a diaper, and perhaps being a "late bloomer." I told them I how grateful I was that Trevor did not do what many children with autism are known to do, which is smear their own poop on things. I joked that they made artwork out of it. Many of my friend's children displayed this behavior. Michael said that he was feeling that by smearing the poop on the wall, they were trying to show their parents that something was wrong; there was something in it that the parents needed to see. Marti compared it to a cat that won't use the litter box when they are having a problem; they want you to see it. To a child, poop is just waste, they don't attach to it their parent's ideas of it being nasty. Michael made the parallel of this to when a child sees the spirit of a deceased person, and the parent layers their own fears on the child because of the way they were raised. The parents just don't understand what is going on in either case. The parent puts their own judgments onto the child out of ignorance when the child experiences something outside their parent's sphere of understanding. I never thought about it that way.

I'm not sure what Dunsmuir or Dunsmoor means or the finger with the band-aid means. Michael felt that the finger with the band-aid had something to do with my late husband, but I can't think of what he was referring to. Maybe it is one of those things that will make sense later on.

***

Session Seven – After the Session
Featured Spirits: Robert "Bobby" Kennedy, Rose Kennedy, Edward "Ted" Kennedy, Alfred DuPont

I actually gave most of the validations that I discovered after the session within the chapter. I found it very interesting that even more members of the Kennedy family were showing up. They seemed to be very interested in helping us in this endeavor. They seemed to bring up new things each time.

I wish I would have been able to find out who the French sounding woman named Janette was. Maybe someone else will be able to figure out who she is by the description. She gave some good advice about flower essences, which I actually use for my son. It will be interesting in the future to see if forensic pathology can shed some light on the pathogens in the brains of children with autism. Perhaps the Eunice Kenny Shriver Brain Bank will be utilized for this endeavor.

***

Chapter Ten

"Those who have the privilege to know have the duty to act."

— *Albert Einstein*

Session Eight

This session was held on January 19, 2011. Marti joined us again for the session. It actually ended up being a very short session because Michael was having a hard time connecting. There were a few things that were very important, and Marti's pictures were a premonition of a future event.

Michael mentioned that there was a drug researcher present that died under mysterious circumstances, an apparent suicide. He mentioned a few names that I didn't understand; William Hirsh, Henry, and Lawrence. Marti had been busy drawing. She said to Michael that she saw a nuclear facility with a crack in it. She asked him where Chernobyl was, he said Russia. She drew a picture of two beaker shaped nuclear reactors. Michael had also drawn a beaker on his paper. They were both feeling like there was going to be a nuclear accident, like a Chernobyl. Michael said that many of the reactors are not shaped this way, but are square and encased in cement, but the beaker shape are what the original ones looked like.

Michael said that he was talking to this scientist, wearing a cream colored suit with a wide brimmed hat, sitting cross-legged in front of him. Then he blanked his mind, and the first thing he saw was a beaker in front of him, swirling or moving and vibrating. He felt that they were going to talk about something unrelated to autism today. Something even more dangerous and pressing. Michael says:

Michael: "I think they are talking about something in the near future that hasn't happened yet. I think that's what they want to talk about."

Laura: Ok.

Michael: "A great threat. He's showing me iodine."

Michael knew it was an accident at a nuclear reactor, but couldn't pinpoint where it was. Next Michael asked if I had a question concerning Botulism again, because they were saying it to him. I told him that I was looking it up, and there were different types, maybe they could tell him what type it was. He said that they put an "A" next to it. I told him that there was a botulism type A. He confirmed that they said Botulism A. (*I learned after the session that Botulinum type A is the most toxic.*)

Then Michael changed the subject and said:

Michael: "There's a place that looks like either Oklahoma or Arkansas."

Laura: "Ok."

Michael: "In one of those places. Fort Smith. I don't know what that is."

Laura: "Probably a military facility."

Michael: "Well, it's between Oklahoma and Arkansas."

Laura: "Ok. What's the connection there?

Michael: "Now they're saying Henry again."

Michael also said that my dad was there and said the name Jim and Jack. I thought he meant Jack Kennedy again. He asked if Jack was in the room and then said:

Michael: "Is it an attack, or is it an earthquake? I think there's going to be...Oh God."

Laura: "Hmm?"

Michael: "You know I think there is going to be an attack on a nuclear facility; I'm just trying to understand where though."

Laura: "Great."

Michael: "I don't know about you Marti, I'm having a hard time. I have this very far away feeling.

(Marti said she felt scared.)

Laura: "Hmm."

Michael: "I'm not doing very well today. Marti, I can't get into it. Let's not speculate."

We decided to call it quits for the day, but here is the picture that Marti drew:

Doodle Explanations: You see, even mediums can have an off day. Every session isn't Earth-shattering. They're all different. As short as it was, this session was still valuable. As I mentioned, the two beaker-shaped items in the top left are nuclear reactors. Notice how one has a crack in it? The picture to the right of the reactors looks like a hot poker in a fireplace. Michael felt that it had to do with the nuclear rods heating up or over-heating. Marti said she felt that the stars were fluorescent. Michael mentioned that anything fluorescent is radioactive. Marti also drew a kilt. Michael thought it had to do with nuclear accidents that they have covered up in Scotland, which gets half of their electricity from nuclear power, and is also a base for many nuclear powered submarines, I later learned. I am also part Scottish.

Marti felt that Alzheimer's had to do with President Reagan. She said "I was getting the Alzheimer's and it had to do with Reagan. To tell you the truth, I got a really a weird thing on Reagan, that he was given Alzheimer's because he knew too much." Michael agreed saying "I do believe that Reagan was poisoned and he was just a puppet. He became like a puppet."

***

Session Eight – After the Session

After the session, I looked up Ft. Smith and Oklahoma and Arkansas. To my surprise, I found that there is a nuclear reactor in Arkansas, just over the Oklahoma border, not far from Ft. Smith, a military facility, that has a beaker-shaped nuclear reactor called Arkansas Nuclear One. It is actually two units. Michael also mentioned earthquakes. There is a fault line called the New Madrid fault line that runs through Arkansas and much of the Midwest. After what happened in Japan less than two months after this session, I believe that they were talking about two different incidents here. I believe that this area in Arkansas is ripe for an accident, because of all of the earthquake activity on the New Madrid fault line, but what was referred to during the session as "Something in the near future that hasn't happened yet" I believe was something else.

Two months later, on March 11, 2011, the Fukushima nuclear disaster occurred, resulting from a 9.0 magnitude earthquake and tsunami. It was the largest nuclear disaster since Chernobyl in 1986. There were over 15,000 casualties, with thousands more injured and missing. The reactors experienced full meltdowns and released radioactive materials, and there were several explosions from overheated nuclear fuel rods. The buildings were the square concrete type. After hearing the news about Fukushima, I called Michael and Marti in disbelief. We agreed that this is what they must have been referring to. Michael validated it further by telling me that Marti had drawn another picture during another session for someone else in May of 2010 of a nuclear power plant explosion and wrote the word "Boom" above it, and "Power Plant?" below it. This was 10 months before Fukushima's nuclear power plant accident. Here is Marti's drawing, with the date written on it. (The other pictures meant something personal to the person having the session.)

5/20/10
Parry

Also during our session, Michael brought up iodine. One of the main radioactive isotopes released in the Fukushima explosion was iodine-131. Immediately after hearing the news, I had some potassium iodide compounded for my entire family because radioactive iodine (iodine-131) attaches to iodine receptors in the thyroid gland, irradiating your thyroid, leading to thyroid cancer. I learned about this during my research after the session, so I was somewhat prepared when it actually happened. We already had thyroid issues.

One person I found to be quite enlightening during my research on this subject was nuclear whistleblower Leuren Moret. She worked at the Lawrence Berkeley and Lawrence Livermore nuclear weapons labs in California. She also had experience at the Nevada Test Site, where they blew up thousands of nuclear bombs. She also visited Hiroshima and Nagasaki Japan to see the damage from nuclear weapons. Some of the more shocking things she says are about nuclear power plants and depleted uranium weapons. Radiation is a boomerang weapon, she says, it goes around the planet and ends up in your own backyard. It contaminates the troposphere, the first 10,000 feet of atmosphere and is transported around the world in a few weeks. Rain and snow bring the nanoparticles down to Earth. She also states that we are all Gulf War veterans because of the use of depleted uranium weapons. She says that in 10 years, the number of radioactive atoms released in the Gulf war is equivalent to blowing up 400,000 Nagasaki bombs. The Middle East is radioactive rubble, uninhabitable forever, she says. She even believes that the autism increase has something to do with nuclear radiation.

The greatest impact from nuclear radiation is on unborn babies and newborns. It has the ability to mutate our DNA, and pass it down to the next generations. The half-life of some of these isotopes is billions of years. The entire planet has been affected by radiation exposure. The fallout from atmospheric testing has been replaced by nuclear power plants. Even though Michael felt that this information wasn't directly about autism, I felt after my research that nuclear radiation indirectly contributes to damaging vulnerable children. Nuclear radiation is carcinogenic. Michael feels very strongly about banning nuclear weapons and energy. It is the biggest threat to our planet. Because of atmospheric testing and the use of depleted uranium weapons, we have essentially already had a nuclear war on this planet trying to prepare ourselves against a nuclear war. This subject comes up again later, and I will share more of my research at that time.

***

Chapter Eleven

"How can I save my little boy from
Oppenheimer's deadly toy

There is no monopoly of common sense

On either side of the political fence

We share the same biology

Regardless of ideology

Believe me when I say to you

I hope the Russians love their
children too."

— From the song "Russians" by Sting

Session Nine

We had our next session on January 26, 2011. Again, this was a very short session. Marti drew some great pictures again this time.

Michael: "There is a man here, a new person, he's called George, and he is Russian. But it is the Russian spelling of George. *(Yuri)* He is wearing dark, heavy, glasses that are squarish. He is a scientist. And he's saying a name like Jowski, or Kowowski. I am hearing Lenin, and he said he worked in the nuclear establishment. He worked during the Brezhnev period and was part of the nuclear program."

(I could not find this person for the life of me, but learned afterward that George in Russian is Yuri. There were lots of Yuri's in the Soviet nuclear program, but couldn't pinpoint who this guy was.)

Laura: "Ok."

Michael: "He's saying a name like Kursk. This is a place. He has concerns over this place. He spoke some English, but he lived in Russia, on the Poland border."

Laura: "Is there a reactor there?"

Michael: "Yes, he says. And he has concerns over Chernobyl still."

(After the session, I learned that there are 3 nuclear reactors at the Kursk facility, using the same obsolete technology as Chernobyl. Kursk has 6 units; Kursk NPP II has one unit. Chernobyl is still emitting nuclear radiation.)

Michael: "I don't know if this is his wife, but there's a name that sounds like Mina, or Minya. He's saying he had published papers or articles that we could find him. He's saying they did research on children in Russia to show the effects of radiation, they worked with Doctors.

Laura: "Ok."

Michael: "There's another man here called Boris and a name that sounds like Kupov. Boris Kupov. He is a fellow scientist or friend."

(After the session, I found a Boris Gubanov – Soviet Rocket Engineer, who was the chief designer of the Energiya rocket, the most powerful rocket successfully used. His wife's name was Nina Gubanov. There is a book called "Energiya-Buran: The Soviet Space Shuttle" that details it.)

Michael: "And there's a man named Karl, Karl Warner or Werner. He was a friend of Einstein."

(After the session, I learned that Werner Heisenberg's middle name is Karl. Werner Karl Heisenberg, giving more validation that it was him in the other sessions. He was a friend of Einstein, and Einstein actually nominated Heisenberg for a Nobel Prize.)

Laura: "Ok."

Michael: "I'm hearing an L name, Linkya, sounds like Linsky, a place, Lilynkya? Two L's?"

Laura: "Ok."

(I'm not sure what this city is, but I found it interesting that Russia had a network of secret cities designed for nuclear weapons production and detonation. Some cities have never even been listed on maps, and employed millions.)

Michael: "They're showing me drilling way, way, way down, like miles down. This sounds crazy to me, but this is the Russian George, and he's saying his colleagues were crazy. He's saying the name Kursk. Kursk. It's near Poland, near Ukraine."

(Kursk, Russia in near the Ukraine Border, Poland is north of there. The city of Kursk has radioactive contamination from the Chernobyl nuclear accident.)

Laura: "Ok."

Michael: "He's saying he worked on rockets as well. This is Boris talking."

(As I mentioned, Boris Gubanov was a soviet rocket engineer.)

Michael: "He says they are going to detonate another device on the moon, a nuclear device. Is this the Russians and the Americans?"

Laura: "Hmm."

Michael: "I'm feeling a sense of disbelief. There are repercussions here. The moon is a beam. I'm seeing them as naughty children, doing it out of spite, disobeying because they can. I am seeing an explosion on the moon in the future."

Michael was being told a lot of Russian names of places he didn't understand and it drew him to go to a map of Russia, and have the spirits point out places to him on the map. I went to my computer to look them up as he pointed them out. These were the Russians speaking, showing other places of concern, regarding nuclear activity. The places Michael was drawn to on the map are listed below, followed by things I discovered later:[22]

Novaya Zemlya– An Island that was the main test range where they detonated nuclear bombs underground including Tsar Bomba, the largest nuclear bomb ever detonated. There is also a nuclear weapons production complex located here. When Michael said he saw them drilling miles down, that is what they did on this island before detonating Tsar Bomba.

New Siberian Islands– The arctic waters around these islands were dumping grounds for nuclear waste from Russian submarine fleets and nuclear reactors with their fuel rods still inside.

Tiksi– Located on the Laptev Sea, nuclear powered icebreakers are docked here. It is also a staging base for soviet bombers to reach the U.S. Military bases located here. There is also a floating, barge mounted nuclear power plant planned for Tiksi.

Irkutsk– North of Irkutsk– Nuclear bomber base located here, with airfields to the northwest. There is also a radioactive waste processing center located here.

---

[22] www.globalsecurity.org/wmd/world/russia/nuclear_fac.htm

<u>Olenek</u>– A nuclear bomber base is located here.

<u>Lake Baikal</u>– There is a nuclear research facility nearby, and a there is a proposed uranium enrichment plant to be built nearby. Lake Baikal is the world's deepest and largest lake and holds nearly a fifth of the world's fresh water, as much as all of the Great Lakes combined. There is also severe water pollution at the lake from pulp and paper plants as well as agricultural and industrial waste.

<u>Magadan</u>– Near the Bering Sea, it is contaminated with Radioactive Cesium. There is also a problem with radioactive waste disposal here, as well as being a port for the Pacific Fleet of nuclear submarines.

This was really interesting because Michael didn't know the names of these cities they were trying to tell him, so he went to the map and was shown certain cities. I never would have been able to pronounce them or find them if Michael didn't spell each one for me from his map. When I looked them up, there was nuclear weapon or nuclear contamination activity related to each place he mentioned. Russia was a huge nuclear weapons manufacturer and after the break-up of the Soviet Union, there was a big problem in dismantling nuclear weapons and nuclear submarines, as well as getting rid of nuclear waste. I see why these Russian spirits who worked in this industry were concerned, especially after the recent Fukushima accident. They lived through and are still living with the repercussions from Chernobyl.

Here are the pictures that Marti drew:

Doodle Explanations: Marti's picture of the red leaf was for Rooibos tea to put in the bath for skin conditions. She said to just float a bag of tea in the bath water. Rooibos is also a liver regenerative substance, I found. And she also said mint bath salts would be good.

She felt that the Tiger and Ganges had something to do with India. I'm not quite sure what the reference meant here because I found conflicting information. On one hand, I learned later that the Ganges River, which flows through India is very polluted with bacteria from human waste and dead bodies and many people die from water-borne illness after drinking or bathing in it. There is a very high autism rate in India as well, which is downwind from the Middle East, who the U.S. is at war with.

On the other hand, I also read that for thousands of years the native population of India has used the water from the Ganges River for healing. Gallon jugs of this water from the Ganges have been stored for over half a century at the University of Calcutta, and are still completely free of bacteria. It used to be considered sacred water that had miraculous healing ability. It flowed down from high in the Himalayan Mountains. However, now it is very polluted and lots of money is being spent on clean-up efforts. So, I'm not quite sure what the message was there.

There was also a picture of a hand and a foot with acupuncture needles in it, but she specifically got the message to not use the needles on the sole of the foot or the palm of the hand. I had some experience using acupuncture to remove allergies on myself, and in Trevor, we used acupressure. It really worked to remove food allergies. There was also a picture of the sun. I'm not sure if this meant Vitamin D again or something else.

***

Chapter Twelve

"The world is a dangerous place, not because of those who do evil, but because of those who look on and do nothing."

— Albert Einstein

Session Ten

This session was on February 2, 2011. Marti drew both a portrait and a doodle page this time. It was another shorter session. It began with Michael saying that Albert was there, and he was getting a bunch of other names. One was Yuri again, and a name that sounded like "Kopov," but it ended in "ov." He was also getting the name Alexander or Alexei. He said the way they put it was "Albert and friends" were there and mentioned that Werner was also present. I asked if it was Werner Heisenberg, and they said "yes." Michael said that there seemed to be a lot of Russians, and didn't know where to begin. He said they were saying a name like "Yelzi" with a "Z" sound or "Yelzki." Marti had started to draw a portrait of what Michael said looked like a Russian guy.

Next Michael brought up the name of an American scientist who worked with nuclear powered rockets. He brought up the names of his wife and son, as well as a friend of his. I have yet to find this person, plus he didn't really say anything significant, so I'll leave it at that.

Then Michael said that he felt like John Wayne was in the room and that he was looking at his cowboy boots. He wondered what he was doing there. At the same time, Marti was drawing a picture of dueling guns, further validating that it was him. Michael had done a session in the past where John Wayne came through, because the person was connected to him, so this wasn't his first encounter with him.

(After the session, I did some research to see what John Wayne could have to do with the subject matter. Interestingly, he was an anti-Communist and Joseph Stalin ordered his assassination due to his anti-Communist politics. It didn't happen, of course. Also, I found that the filming of his movie "The Conqueror" in Southwest Utah was downwind from where they detonated nuclear weapons in Southeast Nevada. Radioactive fallout contaminated the film location and 41% of the cast and crew later had cancer, including

John Wayne. There was even a movie made about this.)

Michael was having a hard time figuring out who was talking to him. There were three or four guys all going on about cold fusion. I knew it is a way of making energy. Michael apologized and said that he had a total blank. So, we talked about Marti's drawings. Here they are; first the Russian guy, (awesome picture, not sure who he is) and then the doodle page.

Doodle Explanations: Marti drew lots of little rabbits on a hill. It reminded her of how they introduced rabbits to Australia to kill something else and the rabbits took over the place. They have a real problem with rabbits there. That was the feeling she got. Like an upset in the ecosystem. Nature should not be messed with. It brought to mind the story I had recently read about genetically engineered mosquitoes being introduced into the wild, and all of the problems involved with it.

She drew a rainbow with clouds on each end with a plane flying over it, and also a child's pinwheel blowing. She felt this had to do with rain pulling toxins down to Earth, and wind blowing them around. Interesting that there was a plane in the sky, isn't it?

We started talking amongst ourselves for a bit and a few interesting things came up. I mentioned that they've given us a lot of information, but I still wanted to know how it all ties together. I told them that I recently had an epiphany about the similarities between Gulf War Vets and children with autism. Marti said that she gets the feeling they want to expand on more than just autism. In a way, it's all tied together, cancer and other illnesses. I said that I felt that Gulf War Vets who are exposed to nuclear, chemical and biological warfare and untested vaccines get sick when they come home and degenerate. Children, exposed to the same things, are more vulnerable so they get it the worst; it affects them differently than an adult. They are still being exposed to these things in the environment. Michael mentioned the horrendous birth defects in Iraq from depleted uranium. He said that they're messing with so many things that they shouldn't be messing with. They've pointed out different co-factors, so now that we know this, how can we fix it?

He was asking the spirits that question. He asked them how we can clean up the mess in Iraq? They kept showing him heat; it has to be very high temperatures. You have to go shovel up the surface that's contaminated and then melt it somehow at very high temperatures using certain methods and gasses. It's very costly and a lot of work, but maybe the by-product could be used for something else, so maybe it's not totally cost prohibitive to clean it up.

***

Session Ten: **After the Session**
Featured Spirits: The Russians, Werner Heisenberg, John Wayne

After this session, as it often happens, I had a synchronistic event occur, which gave me further understanding of what Michael was talking about here at the end of the session. During an episode of UFO Hunters, which I regularly watch, they were talking about a process called "soil vitrification" where the soil is heated from 1500 to 3000 degrees Fahrenheit. It can occur naturally when lightning strikes, but now it is used to clean up toxic waste sites. Four electrodes are put into the area and then an electric current passes through the electrodes to create heat to melt soil and create a glass-like rock that contains contaminants, making it safe for transportation. It is expensive and fairly new technology only now beginning to be utilized. Months later, I learned that the Russians have been using this technology for a long time for nuclear waste disposal.

I also did more research on Gulf War Syndrome and came across some very interesting studies by Dr. Garth Nicolson. His step-daughter was in the Gulf War and when she came home she became very ill with fatiguing symptoms. After some testing on her and other Gulf War vets as well as their family members, including many children with autism, he also came up with some similar conclusions to my previously mentioned epiphany. The vets he tested, as well as their spouses and children test positively for *Mycoplasma fermentans*, which is a government created organism, as well as other Mycoplasma species. He discusses the nuclear, biological and chemical exposures that lead to this illness. His website is full of studies and testimonials he has given to the military to help veterans. The website is www.immed.org. There is too much to go into here.

After reading all of this, I was still wondering if Trevor had been exposed to depleted uranium and *Mycoplasma fermentans*. A week after this session, I took Trevor to a BioSET session. He tested weak to *Mycoplasma fermentans* and other *Mycoplasma* varieties as well as uranium 238, which is depleted uranium, and other radioactive isotopes, showing exposure to them. The question I have is, what are the other biological agents that people have been exposed to that can not currently be tested for in a blood test? When tested energetically to the other bacterial and viral agents that can be weaponized, my son shows a weakness to many of them during muscle response testing. There is no current test that can detect genetically engineered bioweapons in a person's brain, or in the environment for that matter. I'm sure that the Gulf War vets and their families would test positive for other biological agents if there was a way to test for them. The anthrax vaccines they received didn't do them any favors either.

Another Doctor who shares my hypothesis that the same exposures show up differently in people depending on when they are exposed to them is Dr. Michael Goldberg, the author of *The Myth of Autism*. He concluded that the only explanation for regressive autism is that it is a disease process, specifically an infectious agent (viral, bacterial or other agent) in the brain. When presenting his preliminary NeuroSPECT work, Dr. Goldberg suggested that "If this disease process hits you as an adult, you get CFS or the new idea of adult ADHD. If it hits you as a teenager or older child, you get ADD/ADHD variants or CFS/CFIDS. But if this process hits you as a young child, with an immature brain and immature immune system, you get autism/PDD."

NeuroSPECT is a way of looking directly at cerebral blood flow in the brain and directly at brain activity. Dr. Goldberg says, "In using Neuro-SPECT for many years now, it has become obvious that 'scattered' areas of dysfunction, vasculitis with either increased or decreased blood flow, was occurring in areas that could not be correlated to existing tracks or pathways in the brain. The findings over many years now are only consistent with the idea of a virus scattered, living in/irritating the brain, and/ or the immune system attacking those or other scattered areas of the brain."

Let me connect the dots for you and say it in plain English. If you are exposed to the biowarfare in the environment, it affects you differently depending on your age. A child whose brain is not developed stalls or regresses. An adult exposed to the same stuff shows different symptoms. Dr. Goldberg assumes that the viral agents in the brain are some of the viruses in the herpes family, which may be true for some people. What if you inhale a genetically engineered bioweapon that goes directly to the brain designed to kill people slowly and make it look like they died of natural causes?

It gets better. NeuroSPECT scans on children with autism show decrease in blood flow in the temporal and occipital areas, which is consistent with past reports of temporal lobe dysfunction in such children. The right temporal lobe correlates with social skills, and the left temporal lobe areas with speech and auditory processing, all of which are compromised in children with autism. Dr. Goldberg has also found the cerebellum to have less blood flow, which controls fine and gross motor skills, also affected in autism.

In *The Myth of Autism,* Dr. Goldberg also says that "Autoantibodies to neurofilament axonal proteins (NFAP) have been noted in autistic children and have been reported in neurotropic 'slow virus' diseases, Kuru (from cannibalism) and Creutzfeldt-Jakob disease (Mad Cow disease) in adults. Other studies suggested an association of an infectious agent (slow virus) in the etiology of these diseases. This is considered indirect evidence that some cases of autism may also be associated with the concept of a slow virus." He says that we are looking at a slow but insidious immune/viral phenomenon, not an acute, fast moving infectious disease like the flu.

While I fully agree with Dr. Goldberg's assessment of autism being a disease process, he's still a doctor who is trained to use pharmaceuticals to treat patients. Although I agree with him on many of the things he says, he lost me when he stood by vaccines and thinks mercury has nothing to do with autism. By his own admission he also says "Antivirals are not neurotropic agents and don't work on the brain." Then why treat a virus in the brain with antiviral medication that doesn't even cross the blood brain barrier? More on this later.

***

Chapter Thirteen

*"The most beautiful thing we can
experience is the mysterious. It is
the source of all true art and all
science. He to whom the emotion is a
stranger, who can no longer pause to
wonder and stand wrapped in awe, is as
good as dead —his eyes are closed."*

— *Albert Einstein*

Session Eleven

This session was held on March 9, 2011. Marti was there to draw as well. Michael began by connecting with my late husband along with his grandfather Frank. Autism related issues started coming up right away. He mentioned my son having an aversion to milk, he saw excess sugar, borderline diabetic, and said that he was more acidic than alkaline. He also mentioned that he said things backwards, didn't like to play games or play with toys the right way, and that we had some drums that hurt Trevor's ears, which were all true. This picture is from eight years ago, when my brother bought Damon a drum set for his third birthday. That's Trevor holding his ears.

Next, my friend's brother, also named Michael, who died in a motorcycle accident, came through. He had come through in the past. He mentioned a few names, including his mom's nickname, Lou, and his dad's real name, which I only knew by his initials. He said that he died young and in an accident. These things were all accurate. He said he was very close to his sister and that he was here to help, and also to help Michael connect. After this session, when I told my friend about her brother's appearance, she told me that her brother's former girlfriend, whose name came up during the session, has a son with autism.

After Michael's appearance, my ex-boyfriend Ricky came through and gave me some validations that it was him. He told Michael that his name was Rick and that he was my ex. Michael said "I think Albert's here because I saw someone emptying his pipe, tapping out his pipe in front of me. But I'm having too hard a time connecting to him for a minute." He continued with Rick, saying that he was fun, that he had a sudden crossing, and felt something going in his body. I told him Ricky was stabbed. Michael added that he was stabbed in the chest, which was true. He asked me if he was 23 when he died. After the session, I had to look up his age, and he was right again. He said that he was a muscular guy (true), and that he was standing there with a big smile on his face. Then Michael asked if Ricky did drugs. I told him yes. Michael said that Rick showed him a cop car, and Michael asked if he wanted to be a cop or something, and he said "No, I was doing drugs." I helped him straighten out his act. He knew I didn't date guys that did drugs. The subject switched back to my son again:

Michael: "Is there any swelling in your son? In his brain? Did he ever have any kind of swelling?"

Laura: "I think so, yes."

Michael: "How do you know that?"

Laura: "Just things that I've read about other children with autism that have had neuroinflammation. Like when their brain is attacked, it swells. I've never had my son tested."

Michael: "How do they test that?"

Laura: "Good question. I don't know."

Michael: "Ok. Don't worry."

Laura: "Every time I've had him tested (energetically), it comes up that he has inflammation. Different types, not a medical type test, but energetic tests, it comes up that he has inflammation." *(BioSET and Quantum Biofeedback.)*

Michael: "You don't blend his food or anything do you?"

Laura: "I make him a supplement shake every morning."

Michael: "Supplement shake?"

Laura: "Yeah, I put all of his vitamins, minerals, amino acids, probiotics, everything in his juice and shake it up in a shaker bottle. He has that every morning."

Michael: "Ok. Does he suffer with any temperatures? Has he ever had temperatures?"

Laura: "He has. He used to, he would get really warm."

Michael: "Like his temperature would go up, you mean?"

Laura: "Yeah, he'd get real sweaty, like he was fighting something off."

Michael: "And that was frequent, was it? It would have to be frequent."

Laura: "Yeah."

Michael: "Does he ever scratch his skin?"

Laura: "Yes, he has me scratch his skin every morning. He lifts up his shirt and says, 'Scratch, please.' And I scratch his back, I scratch his belly, I scratch his arms. Yeah, his skin itches."

Michael: "They're bringing all of this up. That's what they're talking about."

Laura: "Ok."

He continued by saying that it was painful when he peed, and that he's been reading more lately, which was true. I gave Michael a few examples of Trevor pointing to words on the TV and reading them to me recently. Michael commented that he had no idea how bad some of these kids had it, how severe it was. I told him that some of the children were completely non-verbal. He was shocked. Then he said:

Michael: "Is there any kind of language therapy used with autistic kids,

like a special therapy?"

Laura: "Yeah, it's called ABA."

Michael: "I don't know what that means."

Laura: "Applied Behavioral Analysis. It's a one on one way of teaching. One therapist, one child, using a lot of visual cues, and repetitive things, asking the same question over and over. We do it with Trevor at home and at school."

Michael: "Is it similar to what they do with the Great Apes?"

Laura: "I never thought of that."

Michael: "You know where they show them pictures of things. It's like association. Is that what it is?"

Laura: "It's similar, yeah."

Michael: "It's very similar then, ok. Is there any kind of reward system?"

Laura: "Yes, they get a reward when they get the answer correct."

Michael: "This is what they do with the Great Apes, how interesting."

Laura: "Yep."

(Applied Behavioral Analysis (ABA) has become the gold standard of treatment for children with autism, popularized by the brilliant psychologist Ivar Lovass at UCLA decades ago. It teaches children behavior modifications as well as language and other skills. This therapy has been very beneficial to many children with autism as it helps them function and interact. However, it doesn't fix the underlying medical issues which caused their diagnosis in the first place for many children. I have had the pleasure of meeting Dr. Lovass's son, Eric, who is a dedicated, compassionate man, following in his father's footsteps, dedicating his life to helping children with autism and their families. Autism takes a multidisciplinary approach to overcome, and ABA has been a big piece of the puzzle for many. Interestingly, Ivar Lovaas died in August, 2010.)

Michael: "Anything weird going on with your boy to do with the sun? Is he saying anything about the sun?"

Laura: "Yeah! He points the sun out to me every day, saying 'Sunset, sunset!' When we're driving in the car, he points and says, 'Sun, sun.'"

Michael: "Is this recent?"

Laura: "Yes. How funny! Yeah."

Michael: "He's been going on about the sun?"

Laura: "Yeah, he'll walk into my office, point out the window and say 'Sunset, sunset' and 'Sunrise' in the morning. He's learning the difference between sunrise and sunset."

Michael: "How weird. Well, that's what they're telling me anyway. That's what he's been doing."

Laura: "Yep."

Michael: "This appears to be your dad bringing this up. I'm asking who's bringing this up and they say, your father, your dad."

Laura: "Ok, hi dad."

Michael: "Is there anything to do with whispering going on? Has he been whispering or talking very quietly to himself?"

Laura: "He's been whispering when he reads. We give him cards to read, and instead of reading it really loud so we can hear him, he whispers to himself."

Michael: "It also is fairly recent, the last 3, 4 months maybe?"

Laura: "Yeah, I can barely hear him; I can see his lips move."

Michael: "That's right. Your father is talking about him whispering. Like he sits and he whispers and you can't make out."

Laura: "Mmm-hmm."

Michael: "I do believe that your husband that died, and your dad, and a few other people are trying to help your son. They are around him and they're trying to... I know they are doing stuff with him as well, to sort of help move things on a bit."

Laura: "Ok."

(This is one of my favorite pictures of my dad with Trevor. It was taken in 2006 at the Milwaukee County Zoo in Wisconsin, when Trevor was six-years-old. Trevor just cuddled up on my dad's shoulder, which made my dad cry. My dad died in 2008, so for Michael to tell me that my Dad was telling him accurate things about my son, years after his death, lets me know that he is around us, watching out for my son.)

Michael: "Did he use clay at all?"

Laura: "In school, they use clay, like a play dough kind of stuff, for therapy. It's therapy-type play dough for small motor skills." (Gluten-free, of course.)

Michael: "Yeah, so they do that in school with him, do they?"

Laura: "Yeah."

Michael: "And how does he respond to that, any improvement there?"

Laura: "Yeah, he likes it. Sometimes they're averse to touching certain things, or have tactile issues, or small motor skill issues."

Michael: "What does he like to touch? What is his favorite thing to touch?"

Laura: "He used to always have to have something in his hand. He likes to hold stones now; like rocks and things."

Michael: "Really hard things. Does he like crystals?"

Laura: "Yeah."

Michael: "But if they're round."

Laura: "Yeah, usually round."

Michael: "Smooth."

Laura: "Yeah."

Michael: "See if you can find one. Just like a quartz ball. See how he responds to that."

Laura: "Ok."

Michael: "And he likes pink, doesn't he?"

Laura: "Yeah, he has a flat, oval shaped flat stone (pink quartz crystal) that he likes to carry around and hold."

Michael: "Ok, so an oval one, maybe that's what I'm seeing. But it looks round. Let's see here. Does he like to fit things into other things? You've got to get him to somehow find out if… You know what it seems like, it seems like he can't, what's the word, get the basics under him, you know?"

Laura: "Mmm-hmm."

Michael: "It's like he can't understand the purpose of certain basic things. Am I correct?"

Laura: "Yeah."

Michael: "Like if you put a thing in front of him with different blocks that fit in different holes, would I be correct in saying that he doesn't understand the purpose of it?"

Laura: "Yeah."

Michael: "That he doesn't know that you fit a square block in a square hole, is that correct?"

Laura: "Yeah. He could probably do it, but it's nothing he would want to do."

Michael: "It wouldn't interest him."

Laura: "Exactly. He was more interested in the wrapping paper than the present."

Michael: "Ok, he's more interested in the wrapping paper than the present. That's really interesting. How can we help him? Well, some kids ordinarily have no desire to build things or make things. I've never understood that, why that is. I always thought that was a basic for any kid."

Laura: "Mmm-hmm."

Michael: "Some kids just don't know, they're hopeless at any of that."

Laura: "Yeah. He never played with blocks or legos or any of those kinds of toys ever. But my other son did."

Michael: "Ok, tell me his favorite thing to do."

Laura: "Watch TV, and play chase or jump on the trampoline. He likes either running games, bouncing, you know large motor-type things, or just hanging out and watching his Sesame Street DVD's. Yes, he's 12, and watches Sesame Street DVD's still. And he watches the same parts over and over and over."

Michael: "Ok, what is it that he watches?"

Laura: "He'll just watch a DVD and replay, rewind, play certain parts. They call it stimming. They like that repetition."

Michael: "What is it that he's watching though?"

Laura: "Sesame Street DVD's, Elmo's World."

Michael: "I know, but what is it that they're doing?"

Laura: "It's different; he has so many different ones. He finds a certain part of a video that he likes, and it might be just a word they're saying that he finds funny, and he just repeats it and repeats it and repeats it."

Michael: "It seems to me that that is very important, that's why I'm asking you."

Laura: "I wish I knew why. He just wants to see the same little part. He won't watch it all the way through."

Michael: "No, you see, it's telling you something, that's what I'm trying to say. It's like you can almost look at it as, it's almost like an obsession."

Laura: "Yeah."

Michael: "It's like revealing something to you, that's how I feel. What is it that's triggering that? There is always something more to it."

Laura: "Yeah."

Michael: "What is it that he's trying to tell you?"

Laura: "I don't know. It's not really funny to me."

Michael: "I know it may not be funny to you, but maybe it's telling you something and you're not picking up on it. Why Sesame Street?"

Laura: "I don't know, it's like he kind of stalled developmentally when all of this crap happened to him, that's what he was watching at the time. I think that there is some safety there or something, or like it's familiar."

Michael: "That's what I'm getting at. There has got to be a reason why he's fixated on that."

Laura: "He won't watch age appropriate stuff; he always goes back to that."

Michael: "You know what, perhaps he's aware of the trauma, but he doesn't know the cause, but he's just afraid. He's identifying with a happy moment just prior to this thing happening to him."

Laura: "Maybe."

Michael: "Like you said, it's like a safety zone."

Laura: "His happy place is in Elmo's World."

Michael: "You need the coping skills to deal with the trauma, but if you're stuck at that young age, how do you get past it?"

Laura: "Mmm-hmm."

Michael: "There's got to be some way to get him past it. Sounds like he's making some progress though."

Laura: "Yes."

Michael: "Does he have a problem being hugged or held?"

Laura: "Yes, he'll turn his body sideways; we call it the back hug. He'll turn his back to hug. Giving a front hug is aversive to him. Most kids with autism are that way. You have to say give me a squeeze, and then he'll put his arms around you and hug you."

(Marti brings up the movie Temple Grandin, and the "hug machine" that she made.)

Laura: "We sometimes do that with pillows with him, we'll put him on the bed and put a big pillow on him and smoosh it and make him laugh."

Michael: "And he likes that?"

Laura: "Yeah, he loves it."

Michael: "It's the one on one contact is difficult though."

Laura: "Yeah."

Michael: "It's interesting, isn't it?"

Laura: "He's getting better though. He goes around and hugs people in our family, Matt's family now, where before he'd say 'no' and whine. Now, he'll do it."

Michael: "Now he does it?"

Laura: "Yeah, he's getting better."

Michael: "What's his taste like? Does he have an aversion to any type of taste?"

Laura: "Yes, he's very particular about what he eats. He has more texture issues I think. He doesn't like certain textures, like thick things. Pudding, that type of texture he'll gag on it."

Michael: "He doesn't like it?"

Laura: "No. "

Michael: "Like if you gave him thick custard, he'd probably gag on it."

Laura: "Yeah."

Michael: "That's very interesting, when I was a kid, I couldn't eat lumpy custard. In fact, I'd sit there the whole dinner hour and wouldn't eat it, and the nuns would make me sit there until I ate it. I couldn't eat it, I would vomit, I would be sick if I eat it."

Laura: "Yeah, he'll gag; the gag reflex will kick in."

Michael: "How interesting. Does he hold his breath at all?"

Laura: "I don't know, I never noticed that. He's a shallow breather."

Michael: "He's a shallow breather, is he? Is that common with autistic kids? Well you know, shallow breathing leads to shallow thinking. The brain doesn't get oxygenized enough. But it's more than that. The deeper you breathe, the deeper you think. That's a yogic tenant."

(We talked for a few minutes about how HBOT was going and how it made me feel before Michael continued with the session.)

Michael: "Have you noticed any kind of rashes on him?"

Laura: "Yes, he's always had skin issues. Even now, he has little bumps on his arms."

Michael: "How about his feet? Any cracking or fissures?"

Laura: "Oh, you know, he used to have cracks between his toes, and I always had to put stuff between his toes, and it would never heal very well."

Michael: "And that was when he was younger?"

Laura: "Even a few years ago, even probably a year ago. It just recently healed up."

Michael: "Did he ever have any burning sensations or an aversion to heat?

Laura: "Not really, he used to like cold water. He would run through the hose and get the biggest kick out of it, when it was super cold. It's like he liked the cold water."

Michael: "I have this sensation like his skin is hot or heated, so that would make sense that he liked the cold."

Laura: "Mmm-hmm."

Michael: "Well he's always drunk enough water, hasn't he?"

Laura: "Maybe not always, but lately, he drinks tons of water, yeah."

Michael: "Marti has drawn a coconut tree, which she thought had to do with hydration."

Laura: "I used to have him on coconut kefir. I would make it myself."

Michael: "Coconut what?"

Laura: "Coconut kefir. You take the water out of a young coconut and it's got all these probiotics and nutrients in it. You ferment it, and it's very healing for the whole body. It's called the Body Ecology Diet. They use that a lot for kids with autism."

Michael: "Why did you take him off of it?"

Laura: "He didn't like the taste of it. I always tried to hide it in stuff. It fermented, and it's like sauerkraut tasting. It's gross."

Michael: "Sauerkraut. Maybe this is the taste thing they were going on about. That's what I was asking you, how he was with taste."

Laura: "Oh, yeah. Sour."

Michael: "So, he didn't like the taste of it."

Laura: "No."

Michael: "Well, Marti has this stuff that's just coconut water that is for hydration she got me. I bet it works. Is there any way to hide it? Try it without fermenting it."

Laura: "I just saw at Whole Foods, they have some coconut drinks, like coconut water.

Michael: "Try it again. There may be a reaction on his part."

Laura: "Ok."

Michael: "They are saying something about blue blood to me. They're showing me the blood and they're saying blue blood. I don't know what they mean by it. I don't understand it."

Laura: "I'll have to look it up."

Michael: "Right. Well they're going on about this and I don't know what they mean, but it comes into this somehow. It is a reaction in the blood. It's the blood reacting in a strange way. That's what I'm seeing. It must cause some sort of mental issues or mental problems."

Laura: "Ok."

Michael: "It has to do with a lack of oxygen."

Laura: "Hmm, they're referring to oxygen again."

(Deoxygenated blood is referred to as blue blood.)

Michael: "Does he suffer with cramps a lot?"

Laura: "I don't know, if he did, he couldn't describe it to me."

Michael: "He couldn't tell you. So he never had a problem with his hands cramping?"

Laura: "He's always doing little weird things with his hands. He'll touch his thumb and middle finger together repetitively. If you touch your thumb and your middle finger, it looks like you're making finger puppets. He does that still with his hand, and kind of twists his hand, you know? I don't know why either, that would be fun to know."

Michael: "Well, you know it's telling you something, see? All of these things are telling you things. That's a neurological thing that is showing itself in the hand."

Laura: "Mmm-hmm."

Michael: "I really strongly feel that water therapy will help him. I just felt like he'd feel at home in the water."

Laura: "Oh yeah, he loves the water."

Michael: "I just feel like he'd benefit greatly from it."

Laura: "He loves the pool, the lake, everything. I just need to teach him to swim."

Michael: "I think that is going to help him a lot. It will help develop his motor skills, his coordination. I think it will just help him a lot, ok?"

Laura: "Ok."

Michael: "Does he like to play fight at all?"

Laura: "I wouldn't say fight, he loves to be chased and tackled and stuff."

Michael: "Likes to be tackled. Does he ever hit things with sticks or anything? Beat on things?"

Laura: "No."

Michael: "No, how interesting. I mean, most kids like to do that kind of stuff."

Laura: "Yeah, he has no interest in any of that. It's like he wouldn't know what to do. He'd just get hit."

Michael: "Like he'd have no idea how to defend himself."

Laura: "Yeah, he'd just kind of duck, probably."

Michael said he wanted to quit for the day, but we continued to chit-chat for a while, but some very interesting subjects came up, which I'd like to share a bit of here.

Michael: "It's almost like your son is in his own little world, and it's like he has very limited ways of telling you what's going on, right?"

Laura: "Yes."

Michael: "But really and truly, everything tells you something. Everything is not as it appears on the surface. Do you see what I mean?"

Laura: "Mmm-hmm."

Michael: "So there are lots of ways to look at things, and most people never do that."

Laura: "Mmm-hmm."

Michael: "When you said when he taps his thumb and finger together, there is a mudra, a Tibetan mudra like that. I don't know what it does mentally, but it does something, and there he is doing that, so what does that mean? Get me?"

Laura: "Yeah."

Michael: "What mentally is going on that causes him physically to do that? He's doing it the other way around, you see what I mean?"

Laura: "Yeah."

Michael: "Or he's doing it subconsciously or some part of him is doing that and consciously he has no idea why he's doing that. You get me?"

Laura: "Yes."

Michael: "I always look around, and see things that are going on or have done in the past a lot and see things that other people don't see simply because they never thought about it. People tend to dismiss things as irrelevant; they do it all the time, because they think that the whole Universe is just this chance thing. They talk about luck and chance all the time, like there is no rhyme or reason for everything. Then the next minute, when they want something to be reasonable, they'll say there is a reason for it. You see what I mean?"

Laura: "Yes."

Michael: "And to me, the word chance and luck are some of the stupidest things ever. There is no such thing. There is no chance, there is no luck. Everything means something, and that's how I look at it. If I was around your son all the time, I'd be watching him like a hawk."

Laura: "Mmm-hmm."

Michael: "And that's kind of what I've been doing in this session. That's what they've been doing. They've been letting me see some of how your son behaves and how he acts because I've never been around an autistic kid. I've never known anyone with one."

Laura: "Yeah, when you're around them all the time, you just think that's part of what they do and who they are. You don't always look deeper. Why is he doing that? You know, you question it, but you know…"

Michael: "Yeah, but you see, it's like applying a whole set of different skills to it that you never would have thought of, you know what I mean?"

Laura: "Mmm-hmm."

Michael: "It's like you have to look at things in a totally different way. There has to be a reason for everything. There has to be reasons why he behaves… It's like with anything, if somebody is talking to me and they are saying one thing, is that really what they are saying to me or are they hiding something?"

Laura: "Mmm-hmm."

Michael: "Are they telling me that to mess with me? Are they telling me the truth or are they hiding what they are saying. See what I mean. You have to do it all the time. You can't trust what people say, you really can't."

Laura: "Mmm-hmm."

Michael: "They're constantly…"

Laura: "Omitting things."

Michael: "Yeah, they are, or arriving at conclusions that have nothing to do with reality. They jump to conclusions about things based on nothing. It is usually based on a desire, rather than any real evidence, see what I'm saying? Then you think, well how did you get from there to there? It doesn't make any sense at all. There are no facts for you having arrived at that conclusion. You're doing it because that's what you want it to be. That's what people do all the time. So, I'm pretty good at looking at things in a hard way."

Laura: "That's good."

Michael: "That's kind of what I'm getting at, that's the way you have to be. You have to be very, very detached. And that might be hard for you because you're his mom."

Laura: "Mmm-hmm."

Michael: "It would be very difficult for you to be very clinical in a way, and very, very detached and looking at this from a really, really different viewpoint, because he's your son and you're so wrapped up in a way. You know what I mean?"

Laura: "Yeah, especially when he was younger. You try to reason away all of his oddities. 'Oh, he's fine; there is nothing wrong with him. That's just the way he is.' A lot of parents are in denial that there is something going wrong or going on with their kids."

Michael: "I don't know, I mean I've never talked to anyone…that's what I'm saying, this is completely new for me. I don't know. Is that what happens?"

Laura: "Oh, yeah. A lot of them don't even get a diagnosis until later because they are in denial the whole time. 'Oh, he's fine, he's just a boy, he'll talk later, he doesn't have any problems.'"

Michael: "Right, ok, now look. Don't ask me why I just said all of this to you, because I don't know, I really don't know. But I know that what I am saying to you is the truth."

Laura: "Mmm-hmm."

Michael: "So, what you're now saying to me is just affirming what I just said to you, about people not being honest really. Let's try something out here. To me, aliens are absolutely real. No question of doubt in my mind, ok?"

Laura: "Mmm-hmm."

Michael: "But when you meet somebody who's religious, they're usually in denial about it. Even if one landed in front of them, they would still be in denial. And they're in denial because it doesn't fit with their comfort, their little world that they live in. It's like a survival technique. Got me?"

Laura: "Yep."

Michael: "Because they haven't dealt with their fear of the unknown."

Laura: "Mmm-hmm."

Michael: "There are so many factors going on that they haven't dealt with and they don't have the tools to deal with it, so they retreat into this little make-believe world. See what I mean, it has nothing to do with reality."

Laura: "Yep."

Michael: "You're dealing with a lot of issues you see I suppose. Am I anything to do with this? Is it my fault? All these kinds of things come into it, right?"

Laura: "Yep."

Michael: "So, what you're telling me is that people live in denial, is that right?"

Laura: "Oh, yeah. I meet people all the time that have children that they suspect something is wrong, but they'll take him to a specialist, and say, 'Well, they say it's not autism.' And they tell me what is going on with the child, I can tell you it is, but they don't want to believe it so they'll label it something else. Sensory Integration Disorder or PDD-NOS, that's a good one."

Michael: "I have no idea what all these are."

Laura: "They label it something else because they don't want to call it what it is."

Michael: "Ok, so this is interesting. So actually the level of autism could be far greater if they all called it what it is."

Laura: "Yeah, but even the word autism is a mislabel. These children have a disease, not a disorder if you ask me. They are sick, they can be cured."

Michael: "It's a physical thing, yes."

Laura: "But most people think it is a disorder. They call it Autism Spectrum Disorder."

Michael: "What do they attribute it to?"

Laura: "They think it is genetic."

Michael: "They think it's some random thing."

Laura: "Oh yeah, it's a genetic thing, or they might have some food issues, or whatever, but it's genetic and there is nothing you can do about it. It's bologna."

Michael: "It's handed down from parent to son, that kind of a thing?"

Laura: "Yeah, even though no one else in the family has that problem. There is no possible way to have a genetic epidemic. But, they think it's genetic. Yeah."

Michael: "Oh, I see. I haven't looked into that area at all. I have no idea how they look at it."

Laura: "Oh, yeah, the government and all the medical people don't want to admit that vaccines or environmental toxins could have anything to do with this. It's genetic; they pawn it off on genetics and tell the parents there is nothing that can be done."

Michael: "So we are dealing with the same thing as with the nuclear stuff, where they totally lie and about the fact that it can kill you."

Laura: "Mmm-hmm."

Michael: "The same thing. Well, this explains a lot. I see."

Laura: "And then the parents are in denial a lot too. They don't want to admit that their child has a problem."

Michael: "Well that makes the problem even worse."

Laura: "And then years go by, and years go by, and they get further and further and further behind. And then by the time they are 6, "Oh, now there's a problem" although it was there all along, they just didn't want to face it."

Michael: "Right. And the trouble is, you see, it cuts across all political agenda, all religious barriers and everything. Because there it is, it's right in front of you. So what we are dealing with is a really big issue,

really."

Laura: "Mmm-hmm. I've been there; I didn't want to believe that my son had something wrong with him. I was going to fix him and cure him, by this year, by the time he was this old. You get on this mission to fix your kid."

Michael: "You know, I'm going to throw something at you that might make you, perhaps maybe you look at it like this anyway, but everyone has their own karmic pattern."

Laura: "Mmm-hmm."

Michael: "Ok, and there has to be a reason why your son is dealing with these issues, on a personal karmic level. And you as his parent have decided to help him with these issues."

Laura: "Mmm-hmm."

Michael: "You agreed to do all of this before he was born."

Laura: "Yeah, I believe that."

Michael: "That's a fact. Ok, so it's very brave of you to do it and go through all of this with him."

Laura: "Yeah."

Michael: "And I'm sure on a deep, deep soul level he's grateful to you for everything you're doing for him, even if he can't express it to you."

Laura: "Mmm-hmm."

Michael: "Ok. You know, half the people that fought in World War II are reincarnated into the exact country that they were fighting against. You know, I lived in England, and half the people there are Germans."

Laura: "Wow."

Michael: "They are German souls. The first car they go out and buy is a BMW or something, you know? These people think like Germans, I've seen it."

Laura: "Mmm-hmm."

Michael: "You know what I mean? They don't feel like English souls to me, a lot of them. Especially as time went by, I felt less and less like I was living in England. I didn't feel the English soul there. And I can see why. Can you see what I'm getting at?"

Laura: "Yes."

Michael: "It's like here. I was an American Indian many times. I feel like America is my home, you see?"

Laura: "Yep."

Michael: "I feel and I think a lot of people feel that way actually. I feel like there are a lot of reincarnated Native Americans, and they are not reincarnating as Native Americans, they are reincarnating as Caucasians."

Laura: "Mmm-hmm."

Michael: "The karmic repercussions for our actions. I mean, what happens to all the people that helped build the bomb and killed all the people in Hiroshima?"

Laura: "I know."

Michael: "I mean, were the Thalidomide kids that started appearing, were they people that had been in Hiroshima who were reincarnated, whose bodies were still not on a higher level, were still not healed? Or were they people that had been involved in the process, and caused it? Was that them coming back?"

Laura: "Mmm-hmm."

Michael: "Or was it any of those people who were involved in those kinds of horrific experiments and everything, were they coming back in those bodies to learn something?"

Laura: "Right."

Michael: "I don't know, but there is a reason for everything. There has to be some sort of personal involvement. Some reason that this is happening on a personal level. See what I'm getting at?"

Laura: "Yeah, I wonder about that a lot, actually."

Michael: "There has to be."

Laura: "I think, 'I must have been a jerk in a past life.'"

Michael: "What? You? No, no, no. No, no, listen."

Laura: "I'm joking."

Michael: "You know we are going to have to maybe speak to this a little bit in the book perhaps about karma, and the real reasons behind a lot of this, you see what I'm getting at?"

Laura: "Yeah, that would be cool."

Michael: "Because if we don't then people are still going to live in denial, you see what I mean? Because they are not going to really, really understand why."

Laura: "Right, or blame themselves."

Michael: "We know these people are out there for decades and decades working on biological weapons, on nuclear weapons. And there have been hundreds of thousands of people involved in all of this. A lot of them have died and gone on. Well, there are karmic repercussions for detonating a bomb."

Laura: "Yeah."

Michael: "You can't detonate a bomb on the surface of a planet, and have no repercussions from it, that's insanity to think that."

Laura: "Mmm-hmm."

Michael: "My master delivered a message from space people that said if you were to fire a missile at any planet, there would be huge karmic repercussions from it. Recently, they fired a rocket at the moon and there were huge repercussions world-wide for that. Because the moon is a beam, and so is the Earth. And when you think about all of the stuff that goes on that they do to the Earth itself. All of the fracturing, the extracting gas and oil; all these things they do to the planet, and the repercussions on people, the poisoning of the environment. Everything, all of it, has repercussions. And anyone enrolled in any of it, will have karmic repercussions attached to them."

Laura: "Mmm-hmm."

Michael: "The consequences of everything that they have done will be felt by them when they reincarnate again."

Laura: "Right. Well usually when they are doing those things, they don't understand anything like that."

Michael: "No, they don't even think about it, no. Albert didn't, neither did any of them."

Laura: "Even if their scientific experiments or whatever they were doing wasn't used for good, even if they had nothing to do with that, you know…"

Michael: "Exactly, then they are involved in it. My yoga master was a conscientious objector in the war. He wouldn't fight. In his mind, he thought, this is how he looked at things; he thought nothing could last forever. Even in the worst attack and England has been invaded, how long can tyranny last?"

Laura: "Mmm-hmm."

Michael: "Alright, so it might be hell for a while, but nothing lasts forever."

Laura: "No."

Michael: "Tyrants die, tyranny ends. But nobody here has had the courage to, in any country except Gandhi in India where they got rid of the British by simply not doing anything, you know what I mean?"

Laura: "Uh-huh."

Michael: "I think that mankind is still not at the point where they'll just try things a different way. They always want to use weapons all the time."

Laura: "Mmm-hmm. Have the biggest and the strongest and beat everybody."

Michael: "It's insanity, it's mad."

Laura: "Yep."

Michael: "I don't know, that's how I always look at it. I think to myself, you cannot be involved in something so horrendous. Everybody involved; anyone that flew the plane that dropped the bomb, any of it. Everyone involved in the process is involved in it and bears responsibility."

Laura: "I kind of feel that that's why a lot of these people have been coming through to help with what's going on."

Michael: "Oh, I know it is. I know that's why. Why else? I am certain of it. I am certain that they realize the consequences. I mean if Winston Churchill can come through and speak through Leslie Flint, a medium that I talk about sometimes, and talk about his concerns over bacteria brought back from space when they go out on their little space adventures."

Laura: "Mmm-hmm."

Michael: "He's very concerned about that because there are bacteria in space. And people think there aren't any bacteria or life forms. Oh, yes there is. You know what I mean?"

Laura: "Yep."

Michael: "And they bring stuff back from the moon. They have no idea what is on the moon, and they bring back this rock back you know, and you don't know what you're bringing back. Do you see where I'm going with this?"

Laura: "Yeah."

Michael: "That there must be reasons for everything. I don't know who your son was, or who he was before, or why this is happening to him. But I don't think that any of us are innocent, if you like."

Laura: "Mmm-hmm."

Michael: "I think that some people deal with more when they can. You see you can only deal with past karma when you are strong enough to deal with it, otherwise it would crush you."

Laura: "Mmm-hmm."

Michael: "You see? When people are dealing with things, it is because they have the strength to deal with it. There are periods, you know, people have lives where they appear to have no problems at all, no stress, no nothing. And you look around and you go, how come I have to deal with so much shit and these people don't have to deal with anything? Right?"

Laura: "Uh-huh."

Michael: "This is how it appears to be. And yet, it could be that either they are shirking their responsibilities and there is stuff they could be doing but they don't or they are having a break. Maybe they had 10 really shitty lives."

Laura: "Ha, ha."

Michael: "You know where karma was piled on like a triple hamburger, you know what I mean? And they are having a little break right now."

Laura: "You get a good life every now and then."

Michael: "I always look at it like this, my master never believed in having breaks at all. His view of things was if you weren't doing anything, then you were doing nothing. If you weren't finding life difficult, then you weren't doing anything."

Laura: "Yeah."

Michael: "So, that's how he looked at things. And he looked at it like karma would be extracted from you."

Laura: "Yeah, maybe."

Michael: "It was difficult to be around him because every little opportunity he could see to extract some karma from somebody and balance their karma, he would do it. Just when you thought you were having it easy, he'd pile it on again. See what I mean?"

Laura: "Mmm-hmm."

Michael: "Now, most people don't have anybody around like that or remotely look at it like that, they just don't. They have no idea about any of this stuff. They just tiptoe through the tulips or they just get crushed all the time because they have no understanding of karma, they are clueless."

Laura: "Usually they haven't had experiences in their life that forced them to look at that."

Michael: "No, they don't even think about it. Most people's understanding about karma is so limited. They don't really understand it. Once you understand it, you begin to see from a very detached standpoint, that there are reasons for everything. There is no point in putting blame on anything. One simply has to understand what is going on and why. Once you understand that, then you can start to change things so that everything is in a positive light. Until you understand why it's going on, there is nothing you can do about anything, you see?"

Laura: "Mmm-hmm."

Michael: "You see, a lot of the stuff that is happening in the world now is happening because of all of the shit we did in World War I and then that piled up and then that led to World War II and then that's piling up. And it's this never ending cycle, because people won't step back and go 'huh?'"

Laura: "Mmm-hmm."

Michael: "We are still ruled by fear. We are still ruled by ignorance."

Laura: "Yep."

Michael: "That's why we keep doing the same stupid shit over and over."

Laura: "That's what I was thinking."

Michael: "That's all it is. I mean, the people in charge of this world, the ignorant masterminds behind all of this, they want stupid people. They don't want intelligent people in the world, because intelligent people will want to lead towards a utopian society. And they don't want that. Their idea of a utopia is a ruling elite."

Laura: "Mmm-hmm."

Michael: "If the space people could come here tomorrow and land, if they were allowed to, they could have crops 12 feet high. We could feed everyone on Earth no problem, easily. Completely and utterly change the face of our world. 10 billion people would not be a problem. All these energy resources that we would need, all the food we would need, all the oxygen problems, all the everything could pretty much be solved overnight."

Laura "Maybe they will intervene. We need some help."

Michael: "That's all I hope for. I hope there will be some huge intervention soon. The way that has to happen is that you have to get the majority of mankind wanting that to happen. And until you get them wanting it and welcoming it and like begging for it, then they can't intercede, you see?"

Laura: "Yep. I am trying to make a difference in what is going on."

Michael: "Oh, you are. We are making a difference; I know we will make a difference here. I am really grateful to you for doing all this, but I think we can make a bit of a difference; it is a hard slog, that's all. I know it is. But as long as you are seeing results, and I think you are seeing results with your son. I know we are going to figure out exactly. It's taking on a big thing; we are dealing with a big issue here."

Laura: "It's hard to fix. That's the whole thing, I thought for sure he'd be fixed by now, and he's not, so I have to keep going."

Michael: "Well, you are going to see incremental improvements. You are. But like I said to you a while back in one of the sessions, don't expect immediate results."

Laura: "I am so happy and grateful for the progress he's made since we've been doing this, and it just fuels my fire even more to keep going in the same direction because I've seen the changes first hand in my own child. And he's happy and he's not upset all the time."

Michael: "Are they pretty dramatic changes then?"

Laura: "Oh, yeah. Everyone that knows him notices, even his aide at school said to me the other day, "He's like a different kid this year." She was his one-on-one aide for the past two years. His teacher told me that he is growing and moving in a direction that is so exciting."

Michael: "The Hyperbaric chamber…when you see other kids doing hyperbaric therapy, it seems weird that all these people who know your child, are they unaware that this hyperbaric chamber…"

Laura: "They know that we did it."

Michael: "Are they ignorant of its implications, then?"

Laura: "It's a pretty new therapy, I would say. It is not very widely used."

Michael: "There is very little known."

Laura: "This disorder, if you want to call it that, this disease, has not been prevalent until the last 10-15 years, and HBOT isn't even approved to be used for autism. It is an experimental treatment for autism."

Michael: "So it's all very experimental, is it?"

Laura: "Yeah, and it's very anecdotal, parents reporting what results they've had from it. Lots of them don't have the money to have a brain scan done before and after, but some have had that done. So it's more based on their behavior and what they can see outwardly, but the people who have had brain scans done, they show a huge improvement in the areas that look like they are dead, light up again. So these neurons are coming back again."

Michael said he was curious what the other medium that channeled the material for my other book brought up that tied in to what he's brought up so far. I told him that she mostly brought through what caused it, not about how to fix it. She quit before we finished. I told him that this was more specific. Just the fact that biowarfare was implicated again three years later really made me certain that it was true. We finished up our conversation with the following:

Michael: "I've spent decades being aware of a lot of this kind of stuff, but I wouldn't know its effects on the population. When you hear about nerve toxins, nerve attacks, gas nerve attacks, nerve weapons, you think that you've got a suit on…you're still vulnerable. Only when you really, really start looking into this stuff, what they've got, and how it affects you. It's very difficult to know what's correct because they keep such a tight lid on the real stuff they have. It's hard to find out what the real effects would be."

Laura: "Right, and I think just bringing it up and knowing that part of it is huge. And like you had said before, there is no way to validate it. How are you going to do that?"

Michael: "That's it you see? That's why I found that all a bit pointless. We all know they have anthrax; they have all of these things. The thing is, you need to get to like how it manifests in the body. You need to be way more specific, and that's all too general."

Laura: "Well, how to fix it and how to prevent it is more pertinent to helping people than trying to prove it. Like the government is going to admit it anyway. Maybe in 30 years, they'll go 'Oops. Oh, yeah, we did that.'"

This session was interesting because it seemed like the other side was aware of the challenge Michael had been having over the past few sessions connecting with spirits that I didn't know, and even from other countries. So, this time, people I did know came through with the information. My late husband, his grandfather, my ex-boyfriend, my friend's brother and my father all came forward, and Albert seemed to be overseeing the whole thing. The information was all mostly about my son specifically, and things that I could immediately validate. It seemed to make a difference in the connection for Michael.

Marti drew some pictures too, here they are:

Doodle Explanations: After the session, Marti explained her doodles. First, the obvious one, the coconut tree, had to do with drinking coconut water. There are many of them out on the market today, and are great for hydration, have electrolytes and other important nutrients, which is what she was feeling. I also know lots of parents of children with autism have had success using coconut kefir, fermented young coconut water, which is part of the Body Ecology Diet. I tried to make it myself, and was not very successful. I couldn't disguise the flavor and get my son to ingest it, so I became discouraged and stopped. It was quite a process, trying to find, crack open, and then prepare the fermented coconut water. But now they sell it, go figure.

I made this photo a bit darker than the rest because it was hard to see the doodle in the top corner. It is of a mushroom cloud, a nuclear explosion. This was drawn two days before the Fukushima nuclear accident. She said that she felt scared about an upcoming nuclear event. Even thought the dates she wrote are not when the actual earthquake occurred, it was during those dates that the radioactive fallout was being detected in the U.S. in rainwater, drinking water and milk. This was the third precognitive picture Marti had drawn prior to the Fukushima nuclear accident.

When Michael was describing the pictures that Marti had drawn, he said, "She's drawn a welder's mask and it looks like he's holding something that's sparking. Well, I did see blue light, for a minute or so, and that's what you see in arc-welding or welding, you see this very bright blue light, a blue-white light. I don't know what this other thing is. A belt with a buckle, perhaps some of these things are symbolic. The arc-welding reference will come up again later and make sense to me. The missile also will make sense later. Not sure about the others yet. But, as we've seen, the doodles don't always make sense immediately. I also don't want to try to fit a square peg into a round hole and make it fit. Time will tell.

***

Chapter Fourteen

"I know not with what weapons World War III will be fought, but World War IV will be fought with sticks and stones."

— *Albert Einstein*

Session Twelve

This session was held on March 22, 2011. Marti drew some pictures during the session. It was only 11 days after the Fukushima nuclear accident, and we had spoken on the phone numerous times because of all of the premonitions about it during our other sessions. This was our first channeling session since then. It is another example of not being able to figure out who was talking to us. It didn't matter because the information was more important than who delivered it. It would be nice to know who she was, but perhaps it will make sense to someone else reading the book, or it will make sense in the future. She was from another country again, so it made finding her even more challenging. Here are the highlights:

Michael: "Interesting, I was seeing like a satellite up in space, orbiting and someone said something like Mira or Myra. I have this sense of being up in space and there's a woman scientist in the room. Now I'm seeing blood being taken or drawn. This might be a little different how I'm going to do this session. I'm just going to say everything, every single thing that I'm getting or seeing without thinking about anything, ok?"

Laura: "Ok."

Michael: "I keep seeing blood being drawn, blood testing. And somebody keeps repeating dopamine, dopamine. So my sense is like a general lowering dopamine levels in people."

Laura: "Mmm-hmm."

Michael: "I'm hearing two things that sound like Mishka and Myra. The woman I see has dark hair, she might be Russian. She's going back and forth with what sounds like Mishka and Myra and I also heard what sounded like Miriam. She's Israeli. It's a lady and she keeps repeating

that she's a scientist. So it has to be a female scientist who is here. She just said 'hello' to me, so I know she's here. Ok, great. Yes, I can hear you, but you sound like you're from a different country or something, you have an accent. She said, 'I'm sorry, yes I do, I will try to speak clearly for you.' What are we going to discuss today? Like a vaccine? Vaccination? What you mean that's coming along? She's saying something about in the near future they are going to try to vaccinate people for something, so this may be some new vaccine they're coming out with."

Laura: "Ok."

Michael: "What is the vaccine for? Depressed people? Well she says under the guise of. So, it's some sort of new vaccine that they are going to try to come out with. Let's hope I'm completely wrong."

Laura: "Hmm."

(There are over 300 new vaccines currently in research and development.)

Michael: "Ok, I'd like to know who you are. Are you Russian or did you work behind the Iron Curtain? I think she might be Jewish Russian, and she was behind the Iron Curtain and she might have moved to Israel. So, she may have been one of these scientists in Israel that did some sort of research thereafter."

Laura: "Ok."

Michael: "Sure sounds like she's saying Miriam or Myra. And there is a K last name. Almost sounds like Kohl, like K-O-H-L. Kohl. Are there 2 k's in your name? I feel like I'm saying two K names, like k,k something. Like k something, k something. I'll try to get it in a second. I'm asking her how she died; I think she died of cancer, leukemia. She's an experimental researcher. I think she's been in the spirit world about 8 years, so she died around 2003, and June or July, maybe July. I think she has a husband and two children. I think she lived in Israel. She's getting louder for me. She's saying 'hello' to you."

Laura: "Hi."

Michael: "Maybe she had some issues with one of her kids and that's why she's here. Maybe she also had problems to deal with, with one of her children. Are there any issues with your children? She mentions her daughter, so I think she has a son and a daughter. Every time I ask her where, she says Israel. So she could be Israeli Jew or maybe her family was from Russia, or she came from Russia."

Laura: "Ok."

Michael: "Oh, an isotope. She's saying something about chelation."

Laura: "Oh, ok."

Michael: "Chelation, chelating something or chelation. Cuz she's showing me a tube with semi-clear liquid in it and she's talking about chelating. She's showing some sort of cellular effect of white blood cells, she's talking about. And she's saying something about a compound effect that she noticed on white blood cells. She keeps talking about something targeting white blood cells. I want to say that there are these little things that are attached to white blood cells. That's what it seems like to me. And she's talking about abnormal bone growth."

Laura: "Mmm-hmm."

Michael: "Or abnormal deformities in bone. So maybe she's also talking about bone marrow here. And she's talking about particulates. Are you talking about radioactive particulates? Isotopes. Every time I ask her that, she says isotopes, and how they break down. And the breaking down of particulates.

(After the session, I looked up chelation for radioactive isotopes, and traditionally, it is done through an IV. I actually found a great product called BioAlgae Concentrates, or BioSuperfood, which contains Chlorella and Spirulina, which chelate radiation. It was used in Russia after the Chernobyl nuclear accident to reduce radiation in people and animals. They measured the levels of radiation in the urine and found a huge reduction within weeks. The Russians studied 25,000 species of algae and came up with the top four, which are included in BioAlgae Concentrates. This is a product I began using for my son, also because it is a Superfood and contains all the vitamins, minerals, amino acids, and fatty acids. I will talk more about this in a future session other reasons. Visit www.bioage.com for more info.)

Michael: "I can hear her pretty well actually. She said something about she understands how difficult this is for me, but not to worry. Maybe we will all grow food in greenhouses."

(It's interesting that he says this here, because BioAlgae Concentrates are grown hydroponically in a sterile environment, away from the mercury pollution in the ocean and the toxins in the air.)

Laura: "Hmm."

Michael: "Maybe her son is Joseph, sounds like Johan. Could be Johan. I think she's in her 50's this woman, late 50's. 58. I think she's won prizes or awards. She talks about a prize for her research. And she talks about Ben Netanyahu; I think he's the prime minister." (Of Israel.)

Laura: "Netanyahu."

Michael: "Netanyahu, yeah. What she's doing is she's showing me what looks like some sort of cap with electrical things attached to it. And it's almost like a thing that regenerates the brain. It's not electrical shock treatment, but it's some sort of, it's almost like a biofeedback thing that looks like a cap, and has lots and lots of wires, and you put it on your head, and it kind of zaps your brain."

(It sounded like she was describing Neurofeedback. They use it as a therapy in autism.)

Laura: "Hmm.

Michael: "What does it do? I think what it does is, one of the things it does is elevates dopamine levels and gives you a sense of well-being. And she says this coupled with nutrients. She's talking about certain particles, isolating certain areas of the brain which leads to depression. Depression doesn't allow the brain or other organs of the body to regain health. To overcome... the word is inertia. She's using the word inertia."

(Inertia means inactivity. Neurofeedback can be used to normalize brainwave activity, and increases dopamine.)

Laura: "Ok."

Michael: "They are all allergic to gluten?"

Laura: "Yeah, well a lot of them are on gluten-free diets."

Michael: "Oh, a lot of them are. What does gluten do?"

Laura: "Well, it acts as an opiate in their system?"

Michael: "It acts as an opiate? You mean, like makes them high? What does it do for normal people?"

Laura: "Nothing if they are not allergic to it. But these kids' bodies aren't processing it right."

Michael: "What's its normal purpose?"

Laura: "It's a protein in wheat. It's hidden in a lot of foods too."

Michael: "So, it's natural?"

Laura: "Yeah, it's part of the food, but these kids' bodies don't process it properly and they become allergic to it and it has an opiate effect in their body. So it's like they get drugged every time they eat it, but it's harmful to their body and brain."

Michael: "It ends up harming them? How does it harm them? Does it make them sleep a lot? Does it make them depressed?"

Laura: "Probably depressed I would think. When my son was on it, he didn't feel pain, it's like he was high all the time. He was lethargic."

Michael: "Oh, he'd become lethargic, would he? I feel kind of sleepy, or lethargic, I see."

Laura: "Drugged. Yeah, he'd fall down, wouldn't feel it. Get in a hot bathtub, wouldn't notice it was hot. It was like his pain receptors weren't working."

Michael: "It would be handy for the military."

Laura: "Yeah."

Michael: "Ok, she said something about it's Kosher, or Kosher. So I know she's Jewish."

Laura: "Kosher foods are gluten-free."

Michael: "Oh, are they? Well she says something about Kosher; she should know she's Jewish."

(I looked up depression and gluten after the session, and lots of people who suffer from depression and anxiety got better after going on a gluten-free diet. Depression is linked to low serotonin levels in the brain. 90% of the production of serotonin occurs in the digestive tract. When a person eats wheat, the stomach breaks down the protein into small peptides which attach to the opioid receptors in the brain, which in turn affects the central nervous system.)

Michael: "Oh, how interesting this is, ok. She seems very nice, she says she's very happy to be here and do this, so I said ok. I'm totally out on a limb with all this stuff I tell you. I'm totally trusting this. Did any of your children have any issues, the same as Laura's? She says not to the same degree, but I think her daughter had some problems. Maybe she's

saying Michaela. She's saying a name like Michael, but it's not Michael. Maybe it's one of her kids, it sounds like Michel."

Laura: "Ok."

Michael: "The gluten seems to bond with a protein. That's what she's talking about. She's talking about this gluten bonding to a protein and something about the protein won't get taken up in the right way. It's weird; she said something about it's sticky. Or it seems to stick where it shouldn't. So it attaches or bonds where it shouldn't. Has it to do with the receptors? Ok, I really have to listen, she says you have to listen really hard, I said ok."

"It's like the brain is fighting off an infection, or misunderstands. There are certain receptors in the brain that are not triggering correctly, or misperceiving something, and it's almost like it attacks itself."

Laura: "Ok."

Michael: "Ok? That's what she says. And I keep seeing the white blood cells as the blood is circulating around, I keep seeing white blood cells. It's like a train coming into the train station, like you have at some airports, where the doors open, and the outside doors open, but they don't line up."

Laura: "Hmm."

Michael: "Is there anything to do with food poisoning?"

Laura: "Food poisoning from botulism, which is in the biowarfare. That's a type of food poisoning."

Michael: "When was the earliest time he had a problem with gluten?"

Laura: "When he was 3 or 4." (It could have been sooner, but that's when I found out.)

We got into a short discussion about the difference between gluten intolerance and Celiac disease. Celiac disease involves an autoimmune response where the body attacks healthy tissue when a person eats wheat/gluten. I found it interesting to learn after the session that Celiac disease also involves the activation of a particular type of white blood cell, the T-lymphocytes, as well as other parts of the immune system, which may increase the risk for GI cancers. I've never done a blood test or biopsy for Trevor for celiac disease; we just did the elimination diet. Then we got back into the session.

Michael: "Ok, well she's going on and on about blood to me, and kept showing me drawing blood and testing blood, understand?"

Laura: "Ok."

Michael: "She kept saying it's in the blood. That's why she kept drawing blood and showing me, not vials, but a needle with full blood in it. She kept insisting that it was in the blood, that's why she kept showing me circulating blood. And I'm seeing red blood cells, but I'm also seeing white blood cells, and she seems to focus on the white blood cells for some reason. Like I said, not all causes are the same. Perhaps she's trying to isolate it down for you."

Laura: "Ok."

Michael: "Who knows, maybe the military has been messing around with all kinds of normal things to try to make their soldiers invincible for a while, who knows what they're up to? Who knows what kind of research they are into and what they're up to, you know what I mean? I know they are totally into drugs and mind-bending substances and all the rest of it. So we don't know what they've been up to, see?"

Laura: "I think what she was saying about the brain, and it's attacking itself. It was fighting an infection, which I think might be the biowarfare, and then it becomes an autoimmune reaction, which means it is attacking its own brain. The body is attacking the brain and it becomes allergic to the foods they are eating. That's what happens to a lot of these kids, they are not allergic to it, and then they acquire these food allergies."

Michael: "That's what I'm saying, it's as though the brain receptors or the things that identify things are saying something is bad when it shouldn't. It's like saying 'Uh-oh.' I can't put it any better than what she said. Like it seems to be sticking. It's sticky. It's a strange term, its bonding where it shouldn't."

Laura: "Mmm-hmm."

Michael: "There's this attraction going on for some reason, it's bonding where it shouldn't. Maybe she's referring to the gluten. Yes. She's referring to the gluten in the blood stream, attaching or bonding where it shouldn't. And there seems to be a reaction where the brain treats this as an invasion. So it's almost like a virus going on, 'Uh-oh' and it starts to attack something it shouldn't. So it's almost like the brain attacks itself. You see what I'm getting at?"

Laura: "Yep, I totally understand that."

Michael: "That's how it seems to occur. Things are attaching in places in the brain where it shouldn't and then the brain wrongly identifies it. It's like you think that your leg doesn't belong to you all of the sudden, and you think it's someone else's leg, so you start attacking it. Trying to leave it behind when you walk out the door or something, you shut the door on it because you think it's not your leg. Do you know what I'm saying?"

Laura: "Yep."

Michael: "I mean obviously it is, but the brain can't identify it correctly. It's like a misappropriation. Things are getting filed in the wrong places. They are misidentified."

Laura: "What's causing that to happen?"

Michael: "Well, this is what we are trying to figure out. It's almost like something; a tiny molecule is triggering it. It seems to be like a chemical that's… Is it like a toxin that's bonding to the gluten? Or genetically altering wheat? Is it something like that? Maybe they are altering the genetics and it doesn't function the same. Because they've changed the molecule, the molecular structure of the wheat. They think they have it the same, but it isn't."

Laura: "That makes sense."

Michael: "Well this is where you look. It's something to do with that then. Look, we don't know what is in the minds of these people that are doing all of this stuff. To me its insanity, because they are playing with things they don't understand, just like nuclear stuff. They have no idea the ramifications of this."

Laura: "Mmm-hmm."

Michael: "You know they think they are so clever. Well there you go; there is one of your answers I think."

I was a bit confused, thinking that there was a virus in the brain and that when a child ate this modified wheat, it saw it as a virus also. Michael clarified:

Michael: "No, it's like a virus, do you understand? It treats it like an invasion, like a virus. She keeps saying, once it's attached to certain receptors, it's like it identifies it as like the flu or something, you know what I mean?"

Laura: "Mmm-hmm."

Michael: "It doesn't go away, cuz it's sticky. I can't put it any better."

Laura: "It's fine, you're doing great."

Michael: "She's talking to a layperson here. I am not a scientist, I don't know this stuff. Not in this life anyway, maybe I knew some before maybe that's why they are able to tell me this stuff, I don't know. All these things are bad. It's a process of elimination. What's affecting one child; there are different effects and different causes. What this lady is doing is identifying one cause here, one branch, got me? I mean, mercury is an entirely different problem all together, but it may produce the same result."

Laura: "Brain damage."

Michael: "I think what they are doing is they are talking about various things that affect the brain, and just like a lot of things, things can look very similar. Diseases, they can have entirely different causes, but they can be very similar to where you can't tell. I mean, I can't tell the difference between a cold and the flu. You know, I thought we just got over the flu, but we didn't have a fever. Our fever didn't go high. You see what I'm saying?"

Laura: "Yes. What's causing the symptoms?"

Michael: "Yeah, the causes can be different, but the symptoms look the same. Maybe it's got to do with the brain misidentifying. Several things can cause the same thing."

Laura: "Right."

Michael: "Variants on it, you see what I mean?"

Laura: "Mmm-hmm."

Michael: "Like chlorine, ok. That's a poison, it's a toxin. And that isolates the pineal gland; you know what that is right?"

Laura: "Yeah."

Michael: "The pineal gland is basically your link to your higher self, it's your little radio antenna that allows the higher consciousness to connect to the physical body. It's where your conscience is. And chlorine, what it does is it builds a little barrier around it, and what's going to happen? You're going to become extremely depressed because you don't have access to yourself, to your consciousness, as much as you'd like, and if it gets completely isolated, you will suffer extreme depression and get very ill. You know what I mean?"

(Chlorine and Fluoride are both pineal toxins, which calcify the pineal gland.)

Laura: "Mmm-hmm."

Michael: "That's one of the things chlorine does. It's like we are at war, you know? And everything they stick in the environment brings about similar results or results just as bad. I mean look at how many people are suffering from mental illness. Look at how many people that are schizophrenic and manic. I think we have some good help here, on this gluten."

Laura: "Mmm-hmm."

Michael: "Do you know how they genetically modify stuff? Cuz I don't."

Laura: "The plants? I'll have to look into it. I know that it's not the same wheat that we used to eat."

Michael: "No it's not. That's what we need to find out."

Laura: "What's different about it? Why is it affecting these children worse than a grown-up eating it?"

Michael: "Interesting, isn't it? See look, the plant because it's genetically altered, may be picking up chemicals from fertilizers or whatever, where tiny molecules from toxic fertilizer or from the atmosphere, or from being sprayed on the plant or whatever, the plant itself will now pick up and include in its genetic makeup those toxins. Got me?"

Laura: "Yeah."

Michael: "Because the plant is different, it could be including things in its makeup that it never would have before. Or way more easily than it would have before."

Laura: "Yep."

Michael: "It's such a subtle way that you don't even notice it. Maybe they are aware of it, maybe they're not. I don't know what their purpose is for doing all of this. We don't know, there are people out there trying to make better crops, but there are people out there trying to do other things too. This is such a deep subject, and we may not find out. You need to have a genetic scientist when you are talking about this stuff, so I can figure it out with them."

Laura: "Mmm-hmm."

Michael: "Let me ask her some direct questions, hold on. I said does the genetically altered food pose a threat? Yes. In what way does it pose a threat? They said it will gradually change the physiology."

(Definition of physiology: The branch of biology dealing with the functions and activities of living organisms and their parts; including all physical and chemical processes.)

Michael: "It will change it quicker in a child, you see, because a child is developing. You understand. Were you eating gluten?"

Laura: "Yeah."

Michael: "When you were pregnant?"

Laura: "Oh, yeah. I've always eaten wheat. Now I'm allergic to it."

Michael: "They are telling me adults become allergic to it, it takes longer."

Laura: "Yeah, I just found out I'm allergic to it, I wasn't before."

Michael: "Genetically altered wheat hasn't been around that long, so older people are not going to be succeptible to it. It's like allergies, why are so many more people getting allergies? Obviously something is changing in the environment. They say that sensitive people are the radar for the general population, do you understand?"

Laura: "Yes."

Michael: "That's the way I look at it. So if they start getting sick, watch out because people that are more robust, that are not as sensitive, are not going to be aware of it."

(Marti asks me if I breast fed my son.)

Laura: "No."

Michael: "No?"

(Marti was reading something online about the immune system and breast feeding, and that breast fed babies are less succeptible to have an adverse reaction to gluten. Bottle fed babies also have a higher rate of autism.)

Laura: "I know all of that, trust me."

Michael: "Ok, listen, all of these things play a part. You can't say, this is it, this is what did it. It's this and then this, and this led to this, and on top of it you had this. It is a bunch of things combining in a way, which makes it worse; it compounds what is going on. Do you follow me?"

Laura: "Yes."

Michael: "You are allergic to gluten but you are not suffering the same way as your son, are you?"

Laura: "No, I just have intestinal issues from it."

Michael: "Right, you're more able to cope. But you see, a child is developing, they are growing at a rapid rate. All sorts of things are still developing, so when things get thrown in the mix, then you have a totally different kettle of fish to deal with. A whole different syndrome."

Laura: "Mmm-hmm. So why do some kids get this and others don't, if they are all eating this and exposed to the same things?"

Michael: "I don't know. A lot of people breast feed, so their immune systems are up. They don't have drugs, you know you were given drugs; you got sick and were given drugs."

Laura: "Antibiotics and painkillers."

Michael: "I see it like a tipping point, you understand?"

Laura: "Mmm-hmm."

Michael: "You're going along, and it gets to a point. It's like stretching an elastic band. Bang! At some point it is going to snap."

Laura: "Right."

Michael: "At some point, you stretch it so far, it loses its elasticity. It's

261

like that. So, there must have been a concoction of things that just happened, too many things in a row."

Laura: "All the vaccines."

Michael: "Yeah, all those things seemed to have happened at once in a short period of time. You almost need a chronology of everything that happened in those first few years; everything you took, everything he ate, and narrow it down. See what I mean? This happened, then that happened, and we were feeding him this, we weren't breast feeding. So we know that breast feeding helps immune systems of children."

Laura: "Mmm-hmm."

Michael: "I wasn't breast fed."

Laura: "Neither was I."

Michael: "I was terribly sickly as a kid."

Laura: "We have five kids in our family, and we thought, 'None of us were breast-fed and we are fine.' I know better now, I can't go back and do it over."

Michael: "Are you saying you're not as fine as you could be?"

Laura: "No, I mean if I could do it over I would have definitely breast-fed both of my kids. But at the time, I was going back to work; I didn't want to have to do all that pumping. And I was bottle fed, so I figured, well I'm fine, and I was bottle-fed."

Michael: "What we are talking about is that there are a lot more factors. There is a lot more mercury around now than when you were a kid."

Laura: "Oh, I know."

Michael: "There is GMO around now that wasn't around when you were a kid. There are all sorts of things around now that weren't around when you were a kid. There is a whole different generation; you see what I'm saying?"

Laura: "Yes."

Michael: "So these are factors that are a thousand or whatever times greater than when we were kids."

Laura: "Yeah."

Michael: "And there were things around when we were kids. We were given injections, like measles vaccines and all that stuff, you know."

Laura: "But now they get thirty-some within the first two years of life."

Michael: "I know, it's insane. I think I got six shots when I was a kid. I remember six needles, and this booster thing. They called it a booster, and I still have this little thing on my shoulder where they did it." *(A scar from the smallpox vaccine.)*

Laura: "Yeah, I have that one too, and then they stopped it."

Michael: "I remember that and a couple other things, and also when I joined the military, I had to have a bunch of shots then. So I probably suffered more."

(Marti says, "The older ones weren't the problem, it's the new ones.")

Michael: "We don't know what they're up to see these days."

Laura: "Now the shots are different. They are combining 3 in one, giving you 3 different shots on the same day with 3 different diseases in each one."

Michael: "It's insanity."

Laura: "It's too much."

Michael: "It's too much, exactly, it's too much. And then you've got 80,000 chemicals, and only 2,000 of which are identified."

Laura: "Yep."

Michael: "You have 80,000 chemicals which no one can identify in our environment now. It's mind boggling. Just think of this, what makes up a car tire? They say rubber hits the road, right? It's not rubber anymore, there is hardly any rubber in it, it's synthetic plastic. Chemicals and plastics. Where does that tire go when it's worn out? It's tiny, tiny particles and chemicals and plastic. Where does it go? It just becomes dust. The brake liners still have asbestos in it, when brakes wear out, where do you think it all went? It went into the air, onto the land. Millions of tons of it."

(This makes me think of the recent study that said that children who live close to freeways have a higher incidence of autism.)

263

Michael: "Mankind is just producing so many chemicals. It is a minefield. Chemicals like when explosives go off, mines blow up, any explosion throws toxins everywhere. You've got tens of thousands of ships that sank in the war with barrels and barrels of toxins and explosives and God knows what in them. Well they don't go away; they are sitting in the ocean down at the bottom of the seabed, slowly breaking down and being released into the ocean. You've got countries dumping nuclear waste in the middle of the Atlantic. That's what Britain did for a long time. Just took it out to sea and dumped it, barrels. So you've got so many toxins and so much really bad stuff."

Laura: "Mmm-hmm."

Michael: "When you burn coal, it releases mercury into the atmosphere, into the water, tons of it. I don't know where this is all going, really. I just think that all the people that drive the wagons out in the Midwest, they don't deal with all this shit."

Laura: "The Amish."

Michael: "Yes."

Laura: "They are healthier than anybody."

Michael: "Our society is very strange. Because in the old days, it was survival of the fittest, and there was no interbreeding, cousins all that stuff. That causes a lot of problems. Then you have Native American Indians, they would put the child out even in the middle of winter all night, if the child survived, they knew he was going to be strong, if he didn't they knew he wasn't going to be a strong child. So it was weeding out the weak. As a society, I believe we need to come to a point where we accept death and transition for what it is, with the knowledge that we will go on and come back. You know, they're so afraid of death in society, and they will keep someone alive because they're afraid of it. This is what it all amounts to basically. We live in a very strange society these days. They don't even think like they used to, it's a very fear based society."

Laura: "Mmm-hmm."

Michael: "Everything we do is out of fear. We are afraid of what we might get, so we make something that will kill us before we get it. We are afraid of having a nuclear war, so we build all these bombs and we detonate 2,000 nuclear bombs, so we don't have a nuclear war. It's insanity. That's how I see it. I think people are insane. They are slowly going insane, en masse. Because they won't be heroic, they won't face fear."

Laura: "Yeah. So are you still connected to this lady?"

Michael: "I think she said what she wanted to say. I think she's pretty cool. She says she's going to come and talk to me again, ok."

Laura: "Ok."

That was the end of the channeling session. Here is the picture that Marti drew:

Doodle Explanations: First, the Chlorine bleach reference. It was interesting that Michael was talking about chlorine affecting the pineal gland, and then Marti drew a pail, and wrote "Chlorine bleach" beside it. Marti felt that part of the meaning was that diapers are bleached with chlorine, and it is harmful. Disposable diapers also contain dioxins, a byproduct of chlorine, used during the bleaching process. Dioxins had come up in a previous session. Dioxins accumulate in the body and impede the immune system. During Trevor's allergy testing with NAET and BioSET, it showed that he is allergic to chlorine. We used disposable diapers, so maybe it had a harmful effect. Chlorine is also in our drinking water, which is part of the reason I have my water filtration machine.

Next, the picture of the baby crib with a spider over it. Marti felt that spider bites were toxic to children with autism, and that it had something to do with Lyme disease too. Lyme disease is not just spread by tick bites; it can be spread by many insects, including mosquitoes and spiders. I remembered back to when Trevor was young and he got this nasty looking ulcerated rash on his outer calf that wouldn't heal. I remember taking him to his useless pediatrician at the time, who didn't know what it was, but wanted me to put a steroid cream on it. When I took him to another doctor, an integrated medicine doctor, he tried to dissuade me from using a steroid because it pushes the disease back into the body, and it will come out in another area. He said that often when you suppress eczema with a steroid cream, the child then develops asthma. Anyway, it eventually cleared up, but left a bad scar on his leg.

When I brought him in for his next BioSET appointment, I asked his practitioner to muscle test him for spider bites. He tested weak to the Black Widow. I remember when he got the rash, it was right after we were at the community pool, and he was walking back and forth along the perimeter of the fence, and let out a loud scream. We didn't know what caused the scream, but then the rash started to develop days later. We thought he rubbed his leg up against some poisonous bush or something that was coming through the slats in the fence. Trevor's BioSET practitioner had me hold the Black Widow vial on his scar and asked if this was the cause of the scar, and the muscle test was weak, meaning yes. I'll be darned. Years later, I find out my son was bitten by a venomous spider, which affects the nervous system. Spiders have always been my nemesis, especially after accidentally having one get into my drink and almost swallowing it alive. It gave me the heebie-jeebies for days. Ok, it still does.

The sink picture had to do with one of the faucets in our house with that particular type of handle, and Marti felt it had something to do with mold. I wouldn't doubt it. Mold is a neurotoxin, and can cause numerous health problems. In fact, I saw a recent study of sinks and buildings that concluded that plumbing surface biofilms serve as reservoirs for human pathogenic *fusarium* fungus species. Michael also felt that the faucet reference had to do with prescription drugs in the water supply. He said that parents of children with autism need to get back to basics, and provide pure water, no GMO food, no gluten, detoxing, good nutrition; creating a purer environment so their kids can recover.

The picture of the baby book: Marti felt looking at Trevor's baby book would help give me some more answers. I believe this was in reference to what Michael was talking about, in finding out everything that my son was exposed to in the first few years of his life before this hit him. Everything adds up and eventually he hit the toxic tipping point.

Here is a short list: In utero, he was exposed to antibiotics and Darvocet that my doctor prescribed, twice mind you, as well as whatever virus was causing my respiratory illness during the pregnancy. He was born with thrush, a fungal infection caused by the antibiotics, but did his pediatrician notice? Of course not. I also have a negative blood type, so I was given a Rhogam shot, containing Thimerosal (mercury) during the pregnancy. Luckily, I had natural childbirth, so no birth drugs were given during labor and delivery. Chalk one up for me. Then, he had the full series of recommended vaccines beginning at 2 months, and given Tylenol afterwards, depleting his glutathione, which helps the body detoxify. He had cradle cap (fungus), he had eczema. He was colicky, and hard to get to sleep. Sounds bad already, but he developed ahead of schedule, he was happy and appeared healthy on the outside to his pediatricians. He was drinking genetically engineered formula (I recently learned) as well as eating genetically engineered baby food and snacks. His skin and hair care products had harmful chemicals in them. You know the typical baby shower gift variety that unsuspecting moms think is perfectly harmless. We used a microwave to warm up his Frankenformula, which alters the proteins making them indigestible. He received more and more genetically engineered vaccines every few months, with Thimerosal (mercury) in some of them. He was a host to many pathogens; viruses, bacteria, parasites and fungus. He had some ear infections and was given antibiotics, further depleting the good bacteria in his GI tract, leading to more yeast and biofilm. Unbeknownst to me until the mediums brought it up, he was also exposed to nuclear and biological warfare as well as numerous chemical toxins in the air, food and water. Other opportunistic infections expressed themselves in him, including the Lyme bacteria, Borellia burgdorferi, and the numerous co-infections that often accompany it.

When my son was 5, I found an alternative medicine practitioner who could test him through the non-invasive modality of muscle response testing, or applied Kinesiology. I learned that he had excessive mercury, yeast, numerous pathogens, including parasites, viruses, bacteria, food allergies, as well as vaccine damage. We cleared miasms (genetic predispositions) homeopathically. We used homeopathic detoxes and cleared his food allergies with NAET, and went on a specific food allergy elimination diet. He was allergic to unusual things like beef, (probably because of the antibiotics, growth hormones, and steroids that they give to the cows and were fed GMO feed.) He got better, but I certainly wouldn't say recovered. I knew I was on to something, but hadn't found all of the answers yet. So, as you can see, it is not just one thing here, it is multiple things compounded. Who knows the synergistic effects of all of these things and more on a developing infant?

On a happier note, regarding the picture of the bicycle. Marti and Michael both felt that Trevor would really like riding a bike. We ended up buying a tandem attachment that goes on the back of another bike. Now we are able to go on bike rides together. Trevor loves it!

***

Session Twelve: After the Session

Even though I didn't know who this woman was talking to Michael, she brought up some very key things. The fact that she lived in another country made it more difficult to find out who she is. Either way, I did some more research into why eating wheat is so harmful to the brain, and found some interesting facts, which actually made me stop eating wheat. I also stopped letting Trevor eat wheat occasionally after he became re-sensitized to it, but mainly because of this new information. Michael said that wheat was a problem, specifically gluten, and the brain was mis-identifying it and attacking it like a virus, and also because the wheat is altered, as well as the plant uptaking molecules from fertilizer or something they spray on the plants. He also mentioned something about white blood cells. I tried to find the connections.

I already touched briefly upon how wheat is different in a previous chapter. Plant breeders have changed wheat in dramatic ways. Modern wheat, the type grown in 99 percent of wheat fields around the world, was once four-feet-tall, but is now a stocky two-foot-tall plant with an unusually large seed head. Accomplishing this involved crossing wheat with non-wheat grasses to introduce altogether new genes, using techniques like irradiation of wheat seeds and embryos with chemicals, gamma rays, and high-dose X-rays to induce mutations.

According to Dr. Davis, author of *Wheat Belly*, Clearfield Wheat, grown on nearly 1 million acres in the Pacific Northwest and sold by BASF Corporation, the world's largest chemical manufacturer, was created in a geneticist's lab by exposing wheat seeds and embryos to the mutation-inducing industrial toxin sodium azide, a substance poisonous to humans and known for exploding when mishandled. This hybridized wheat doesn't survive in the wild, and most farmers rely on toxic chemical fertilizers and pesticides to keep the crops alive.

The intensive breeding efforts that have transformed wheat should not to be confused with genetic engineering or GMO's. Modern wheat has been hybridized (crossing different strains to generate new characteristics; 5% of proteins generated in the offspring, for instance, are not present in either parent), backcrossed (repeated crossing to winnow out a specific trait, e.g., short stature), and hybridized with non-wheat plants (to introduce entirely unique genes).

Intense crossbreeding created significant changes in the amino acids in wheat's gluten proteins, a potential cause for the 400 percent increase in celiac disease over the past 40 years. An estimated 1 in 133 people have Celiac disease. Wheat's gliadin protein has also undergone changes, with what appears to be a dire consequence. Dr. Davis says that the new gliadin proteins may also account for the explosion in inflammatory diseases we're seeing. Early evidence suggests that modern wheat's new biochemical code causes hormone disruption that is linked to diabetes and obesity, and believes that everyone should eliminate it from their diets, that is how bad it is.

I also looked more into pesticides and found that there are over 50 pesticides used on wheat, including known or possible carcinogens, suspected hormone disruptors, neurotoxins, and developmental or reproductive toxins. This information can be found on www.pesticideinfo.org, where the Pesticide Action Network gets its data from the USDA Pesticide Data program. This is another reason why eating organic is so important, even for those who are not sensitive to wheat, if there are any left.

Two jaw-dropping articles really got my attention: *The Dark Side of Wheat* and *Opening Pandora's Bread Box: The Critical Role of Wheat Lectin in Human Disease* by author Sayer Ji. He contends that wheat intolerance is not simply a matter of allergy/genetic intolerance in a minority subset of the human population, but rather a species-specific intolerance, applicable to all of us. He says that a powerful chemical in wheat known as "wheat germ agglutinin" (WGA), is largely responsible for many of wheat's pervasive and difficult to diagnose ill effects. What is unique about the WGA glycoprotein is that it can do direct damage to the majority of tissues in the human body without requiring a specific set of genetic susceptibilities and/or immune-mediated articulations. This may explain why chronic inflammatory and degenerative conditions are endemic to wheat-consuming populations even when overt allergies or intolerances to wheat gluten appear exceedingly rare.

WGA is a lectin. Lectins are the plant's defense against predators, a built-in pesticide. Like man-made pesticides, lectins are extremely small, resistant to break-down by living systems, and tend to accumulate and become incorporated into tissues where they interfere with normal biological processes. Lectins are glycoproteins, and through thousands of years of selectively breeding wheat for increasingly larger quantities of protein, the concentration of WGA lectin has increased proportionately. The poison, ricin, is another lectin, derived from the castor bean casing. WGA is neurotoxic and can pass through the blood brain barrier (BBB) through a process called "adsorptive endocytosis" and is able to travel freely among the tissues of the brain. WGA may attach to the protective coating on the nerves known as the myelin sheath and is capable of inhibiting nerve growth factor which is important for the growth, maintenance, and survival of certain target neurons.

The part of *Opening Pandora's Bread Box* that really raised my antennae said "There are a number of interesting similarities between WGA lectin and viruses. Both viral particles and WGA lectin are several orders of magnitude smaller than the cells they enter, and subsequent to their attachment to the cell membrane, are taken into the cell through a process of endocytosis. Both influenza and WGA gain entry through the sialic acid coatings of our mucous membranes (glycocalyx) each with a sialic acid specific substance, the neuraminidase enzyme for viruses and the sialic acid binding sites on the WGA lectin. Once the influenza virus and WGA lectin have made their way into wider circulation in the host body they are both capable of blurring the line in the host between self-and non-self. Influenza accomplishes this by incorporating itself into the genetic material of our cells and taking over the protein production machinery to make copies of itself, with the result that our immune system must attack its own virally transformed cell, in order to clear the infection. Studies done with herpes simplex virus have shown that WGA has the capacity to block viral infectivity through competitively binding to the same cell surface receptors, indicating that they may affect cells through very similar pathways. WGA has the capability of influencing the gene expression of certain cells, e.g. mitogenic/anti-mitogenic action, and like other lectins associated with autoimmunity, e.g. soy lectin, and viruses like Epstein Barr virus, WGA may be capable of causing certain cells to exhibit class 2 human leukocyte antigens (HLA-II), which mark them for autoimmune destruction by white blood cells. Since human antibodies to WGA have been shown to cross react with other proteins, even if WGA does not directly transform the phenotype of our cells into 'other,' the resulting cross-reactivity of antibodies to WGA with our own cells would result in autoimmunity nonetheless."

This sounds eerily similar to what Michael said during the channeling session, although in a much more scientific manner. The point being, that it backs up what came through in the session. Wheat is bad. The body sees it as an invader and attacks it. It causes an autoimmune reaction in the brain, causing further damage.

In *The Dark Side of Wheat* Ji says that despite common misconceptions, monogenic diseases, or diseases that result from errors in the nucleotide sequence of a single gene are exceedingly rare. Perhaps only 1% of all diseases fall within this category, and Celiac disease is not one of them. In fact, following the completion of the Human Genome Project (HGP) in 2003 it is no longer accurate to say that our genes "cause" disease, any more than it is accurate to say that DNA is sufficient to account for all the proteins in our body. Despite initial expectations, the HGP revealed that there are only 30,000-35,000 genes in human DNA (genome), rather than the 100,000 + believed necessary to encode the 100,000 + proteins found in the human body (proteome). The "blueprint" model of genetics: one gene → one protein → one cellular behavior, which was once the holy grail of biology, has now been supplanted by a model of the cell where *epigenetic* factors (literally: "beyond the control of the gene") are primary in determining how DNA will be interpreted, translated and expressed. It is not the genes, but what we expose them to. What we eat and what we are exposed to in our environment directly affects our DNA and its expression.

The word "gluten" literally means "glue" in Latin. Michael talked about gluten being sticky during the session. What gives gluten its adhesive and difficult-to-digest qualities are the high levels of disulfide bonds it contains. These same sulfur-to-sulfur bonds are also found in hair and vulcanized rubber products. Ji points out in *The Dark Side of Wheat* that wild and selective breeding of wheat has produced variations which include up to 6 sets of chromosomes (3x the human genome worth!) capable of generating a massive number of proteins each with a distinct potentiality for antigenicity. Common bread wheat (*Triticum aestivum*), for instance, has over 23,788 proteins cataloged thus far. In fact, the genome for common bread wheat is actually 6.5 times larger than that of the human genome! With up to a 50% increase in gluten content of some varieties of wheat, it is amazing that we continue to consider "glue-eating" a normal behavior. Ji sums up the adverse effects of wheat on both celiac and non-celiac populations as: 1) wheat causes damage to the intestines 2) wheat causes intestinal permeability 3) wheat has pharmacologically active properties 4) wheat causes damage that is "out of the intestine" affecting distant organs 5) wheat induces molecular mimicry 6) wheat contains high concentrations of excitoxins.

Bread is a comfort food, although it is more of a drug than a food. On a personal note, I knew that I was intolerant of wheat, but I still ate it. It is addicting. I was never tested for Celiac disease through the traditional biopsy, but I have had digestive issues my whole life. When I was a young girl, I remember having such bad stomach pains and discomfort that it brought me to tears. My mom brought me to the doctor, and he came up with the diagnosis of "spasms of the small intestines." I had to take this icky green medicine and was told to avoid eating raw apples, popcorn, and spicy food. Really? Then as an adult, I frequently had cramping and diarrhea after eating certain foods. I went to the doctor again, and was diagnosed with another catch-all diagnosis, Irritable Bowel Syndrome. Could it be that wheat was irritating my bowel all along? After doing extensive muscle response testing with NAET, I learned that I am also allergic to lactose and some other foods as well. I guess this would be the genetic predisposition. I am prone to mood swings and depression. (You would be too if you had my life.) Perhaps wheat was contributing to that.

So, after this session and learning about WGA, I stopped eating wheat, and joined Trevor on his gluten-free diet. I didn't allow Damon to eat it either. I also had done NAET allergy elimination years ago for my food allergies, but I became re-sensitized to it because I continued to eat it. No more. The first thing I noticed was that I no longer woke up with a headache every morning, as I did when I was eating wheat. I used to feel hung over every morning, even when I didn't drink alcohol. My husband kept telling me there was something wrong with me because I always woke up with a headache. I felt so much better in general right away, and I no longer had diarrhea. I didn't know any different my whole life, it was normal to me. I know, too much information, but if it can help others give it a try, I don't care.

Some of the gluten-free breads and cereals are very tasty. There are many gluten-free products on the market to choose from. I no longer have to make everything from scratch, as I did when I first put Trevor on a gluten-free diet 8 years ago. The gluten-free market has exploded since then. Many restaurants also have gluten-free menus now as well. There are also gluten-free bakeries in many cities that cater to this population. It is not a "fad" diet. The health and future health of my family is worth all of the sacrifices we have had to make to stick to this diet. You can't eat fast food, eating at restaurants is difficult and requires research, and traveling takes a lot of planning. We have to bring our own food everywhere we go. Convenience or health, you choose. You either pay the farmer now or the doctor later.

***

Chapter Fifteen

"To the electron: may it never be of any use!"

— J. J. Thomson

Session Thirteen

This session was held on March 29, 2011. Marti drew some pictures again during the session. It began with Michael talking to a guy named John. Michael began:

Michael: "What I'm seeing in front of me is vials, like what you see in a chemistry lab. Like an inch wide or half an inch across, you put blood in or whatever, chemicals and you swoosh it around."

Laura: "Right."

Michael: "That's what I'm seeing, and one of them is red, so I don't know if that's blood? I don't know who this guy is yet. I get researcher, so he must have been a researcher or a medical person. I got 'yes' to that."

Laura: "Ok."

Michael: "Might be UK, so he could be English, maybe he lived in England. I get Cambridge, so he could be a researcher at Cambridge or he lived in Cambridge. I'm just going to go with it and see where this goes, ok?"

Laura: "Ok."

Michael: "Is there such a thing as a Y blood type?"

Laura: "Not that I know of. I think it's A, B, O, and AB."

Michael: "That's weird; I don't know what this Y means."

Laura: "The Y chromosome maybe, there is X and Y."

Michael: "Oh, yeah."

Laura: "Boys have an X and a Y, girls have 2 X's."

Michael: "Ok, well he's given me Y."

Laura: "The Y chromosome?"

Michael: "It has something to do with genetics, yes. Hold on; let me get this straightened out. In the vaccine? Is it a genetically altered vaccine? Rubella. It's Rubella, isn't it?"

Laura: "Rubella, German measles."

Michael: "Rubella, is that genetically altered?"

Laura: "I don't know."

Michael: "I think he is saying something about a mutation of the virus. Like it mutates, a mutation of the virus. So maybe... does it take place in the body or is it before? That's what I'm trying to determine here. Is it something that's already mutated before it's in the body or does it happen when it enters the body?"

(Shortly after the session, an article came out that answered this for me. *Retired scientist Helen V. Ratajczak, PhD., did a comprehensive review of autism research. She had two separate reviews published in the "Journal of Immunotoxicology." In the first review, "Theoretical Aspects of Autism Causes – a Review," Dr. Ratajczak proposes a novel theory regarding the mechanism of action for a vaccine to cause autism stating* that the MMR II vaccine is contaminated with human DNA from the cell line in which the rubella virus is grown. {Meaning it is genetically altered.} This human DNA could be the cause of the spikes in incidence. She also suggests that the human DNA from the vaccine can be randomly inserted into the recipient's genes by homologous recombination {mutation}, a process that occurs spontaneously only within a species. The rubella virus grows in human fetal tissue, from aborted embryonic cells during vaccine production. Dr. Ratajczak theorizes that *when the virus is incorporated into the vaccine, it has human DNA in it, and this vaccine with the human DNA is injected into another human. Because the new DNA is from the same species as the recipient of the vaccine, homologous recombination of the DNA occurs. The body of the recipient recognizes that self has been altered, and the immune response kills the altered self. Now the recipient has an autoimmune response in his body.*)

Michael: "Botulism."

Laura: "Is it combining together and mutating?"

Michael: "Maybe it's a mutated form of botulism? Like a new virus."

(This is the second time this came up in a session, genetically modified botulism. I

mentioned it to Michael and he continued.)

Michael: "Oh, I don't remember. I'm just trying to follow this guy's train of thought here. I'm just looking at what I've written here and I've written what looks like Borium and then there is another b under the y right next to it and then I put botulism. Is this happening because they simply don't know what they are doing or they are stupid or is this deliberate? You know the brain barrier?"

Laura: "Mmm-hmm."

Michael: "I don't know if there is any way to find this out, but was the brain barrier in your son thin compared to other kids?"

Laura: "I have no idea, I wouldn't even know how to…"

Michael: "Is it thinned? The guy I am seeing in front of me has very blue eyes, so I can see the eyes in front of me. He's got a fairly nice face, good-looking face. He just said 'Oh, thank you.' So, a good sense of humor, this guy. He just said, 'I do.' So, am I right here? Am I getting this right?"

Michael: "Huh, this is interesting. Is there any way your kid could have been exposed to some radiation in a big dose? Did he get any kind of treatment that involved any kind of radioactive isotope? Or was he x-rayed a lot?"

Laura: "He got hurt one time when he was 5 or 6, and he had to have an x-ray on his knee. But that was after all of this happened. But we live in Nevada, where they did all this bomb testing, so maybe when the wind blows, does it blow this stuff around again?

Michael: "Does it?"

Laura: "I guess so. According to our doctor, she says when the wind blows; it blows the crap around again."

Michael: "Oh, yeah because you've got Plutonium, which has a half-life of like hundreds of thousands of years."

Laura: "Yeah."

Michael: "It primarily goes into your bones and liver through the lungs. It doesn't get absorbed that much through your digestive tract, but if it does, it goes again into your liver and works its way to your bone marrow. So you get bone diseases. I still can't get rid of the radioactive element. Well they could be talking about other cases, not just your boy. Ok. Cesium. How did they make it? Did this, how do they make it? Did they expose it to this or something? Is it mutated before it entered the body?"

"Oppenheimer."

Laura: "What's that?"

Michael: "He said something about Oppenheimer."

Laura: "Oh, that's the nuclear bomb guy."

Michael: "I know, he's been going on about the radiation and cesium and stuff and he said something about Oppenheimer to me. Maybe he is giving us a clue here. Maybe Oppenheimer was doing some other experiments and it led to a condition or led them to understanding some other medical aspect or something. Cuz they had a lot of medical research going on at the time, they were exposing people to radiation and all kinds of stuff."

Laura: "Right."

Michael: "You know Oppenheimer? Joseph? I put Joseph."

(I finally figured out who the guy talking to Michael was after this comment. At first he said his name was John, and was a scientist who lived in Cambridge, England. He mentioned Oppenheimer and now said Joseph. Drum roll please. Joseph John Thomson, better known as J.J. Thomson was a Nobel Prize winning physicist in 1906, and one of the founders of modern physics, who discovered the electron. He was educated at the University of Cambridge, and taught at the Cavendish Laboratory from 1884-1918. In 1903 he suggested a discontinuous theory of light, foreshadowing Albert Einstein's later theory of photons. One of J. J. Thomson's students at Cavendish Laboratory was J. Robert Oppenheimer. Michael mentioned that he had blue eyes, which is true. Here is a photo of J.J. Thomson.)

Michael: "This virus, what is causing the virus? I'm pretty certain he's telling me it's a virus. That the cause of it is a virus. What I'm not sure about is if it is a genetically modified virus, or if it mutates when it gets in the body for some reason. Follow me?"

Laura: "Yeah."

Michael: "That's the only bit I'm not sure about right now as I talk with him."

Laura: "Or is it part the Rubella vaccine and part the biowarfare genetically mutating together and creating this?"

Michael: "I don't know. Did your son swim at all?"

Laura: "Well, he's trying to learn how to."

Michael: "Where did he swim?"

Laura: "Just in a little kiddy pool, or the shallow end of a lake."

Michael: "A lake huh, cuz I was seeing a lake. What lake?"

Laura: "He swam in a pool outside of our house when we lived in California. We moved here when he was 3 and we went to Pyramid Lake."

Michael: "Pyramid Lake, huh? How often would he swim in Pyramid Lake?"

Laura: "Just in the summer. Although I've recently read about them blowing up depleted uranium bombs north of there and it is down wind of this place. I don't know if that's what they are getting at?"

Michael: "I don't know, I'm seeing radioactive water, see?"

Laura: "Huh, probably Pyramid Lake."

Michael: "And I'm seeing him swimming in what looks like a lake. It's not a swimming pool; it's not a little pool. It looks like a lake to me."

Laura: "It's probably Pyramid Lake. It's downwind from Sierra Army Depot where they blow up depleted uranium."

Michael: "Hmm."

Laura: "I just read about this not too long ago."

Michael: "That's what they are showing me, see?"

Laura: (Sarcastically) "Great. He loves that lake."

Michael: "He could have swallowed some water, or he could have got it on his skin as he's walking in and out. We don't have testing equipment, so there is no way we can go out there with a Geiger counter and check it out. Cuz they are talking about two things, you see. They are talking about the virus and then they are also putting this radioactive element in here. That's why I think he's been exposed somewhere to some radiation."

Laura: "Yep, he has."

Michael: "If the radiation has mutated the virus or if it's just yet another component that has affected him? That's what I'm not sure about. Do you understand?"

Laura: "Yeah."

Michael: "I am certain that the virus is in the brain. I'm certain it's a brain... does it begin and end in the brain or does it begin in the blood and end up in the brain?

(Just the fact that Michael brought up the fact that my son has been in a radioactive lake validated my recent findings about depleted uranium. Sierra Army Depot, in Herlong, CA, is 15 miles upwind from our beloved Pyramid Lake, which is on a Pauite Indian Reservation, just across the state line in Northern Nevada. This is pretty significant coming from a guy who worked with radiation and with Oppenheimer, known for developing the nuclear bomb. According to nuclear whistleblower Leuren Moret, whom

I mentioned in an earlier chapter, she says that "For 40 years, the Sierra Army Depot in Northern California has burned millions of tons of old munitons, including 20 times more DU {depleted uranium} than was used in the Gulf War. The radioactive smoke and ash full of heavy metals, phosgene gas and dioxins contaminated local communities as well as many Native Americans downwind, especially the Pyramid Lake Pauite Reservation. The health problems in those communities have been horrendous." I will discuss this further in the "After the Session" chapter.)

My boys in Pyramid Lake, NV

Michael: "He had vomiting didn't he?"

Laura: "Yeah."

Michael: "When did the vomiting begin and end?"

Laura: "It was just sporadic here and there. He'd get sick a lot, so who knows what was causing all the sickness. If it was stomach flu, I have no idea."

Michael: "He was in a very weakened state and so he was very vulnerable, see what I mean?"

Laura: "Mmm-hmm."

Michael: "Here are the questions I am posing to them. I'm trying to find out if any of this is a deliberate experiment. He says somewhat. The whole vaccine thing. Do you understand?"

Laura: "Mmm-hmm."

Michael: "Because it involves so many people, I think that some are and some aren't. So, some may be a little naïve about it, or are just trying to do the right thing, and others are in it for different reasons, ok? Money, or just plain ignorance, or just don't care, you know?"

Laura: "Mmm-hmm."

Michael: "The second element is I want to know if there is any military involvement for any reason, and I don't really get that either. What I get from them is the sense that it's almost like a haphazard thing in a way, as far as the external elements. If there is any biowarfare that's got out."

Laura: "It's not intentional?"

Michael: "It's not intentional, it's just stupid. It's a bit like the whole nuclear thing, you know what I mean?"

Laura: "Yeah."

Michael: "They know it can happen, but they're just shutting their eyes and sticking their heads in the sand, you know what I mean?"

Laura: "Yeah."

Michael: "They just don't want to confront the hard issues. So they just keep dancing around it, you know. Collateral damage is what they like to call it, you know. They say, 'Oh, we're going to die, but it's all for a good cause' that kind of crap, you know?"

Laura: "Mmm-hmm."

Michael: "We expect some collateral damage. It's like trying to take a hostage out of there, 'Oh, well they might get killed, but we're going to go in anyway.' That kind of stuff. Like that, that's the kind of feeling I get."

Laura: "Yeah."

Michael: "I'm wondering if this Oppenheimer was affected in any way or any of his children or something. This is what is going through my mind at the moment, as to why they are bringing him up in relation to this? Sometimes these people are so removed from reality. It is only when it affects them that they change their minds."

Laura: "Yeah, sure."

Michael: "Let's put it that way. So, some of them, they've got no… they're almost like sociopaths, they have no feeling, no involvement. But something, sometimes can dramatically give them a turnaround and they see things completely different. But it's very rare, it doesn't happen very often. This is what I'm getting with the Oppenheimer guy."

Laura: "When they love someone, it's different; it's not a nameless, faceless person."

Michael: "Exactly, a lot of these people, the extremists, they don't really love anyone; they don't really care about anyone. They have families and stuff but they say things like, "Well, if my son behaved that way, then I'd hang them too." Ridiculous things like that, like sociopaths say. You think, oh, really, wow, that's love. So many of those kinds of people. They are borderline insane. People involved in research, they have no social, they're smart, but they have no feelings…"

Laura: "Emotions."

Michael: "Exactly, no empathy for people, nothing, they're like stone-dead cold."

Laura: "Mmm-hmm."

Michael: "I'm back to these two vials again. I can see one in front of the other one, except the one in front looks red. Which I think is just blood. Is it… blue blood? Is it a weaning out a blood type, a war on a certain blood type? Genetic ideology? Blue blood. This blue blood thing."

Laura: "I know blue blood is lack of oxygen to the blood."

Michael: "Oh, is it? Well they keep going on about blue blood."

Laura: "Yeah, I looked it up cuz it came up once before, that term, and it means a lack of oxygen in the blood. Because it's blue when it doesn't have oxygen and it's red when it has lots of oxygen."

Michael: "They keep going on about blue blood. Did he get starved of oxygen at all when he was little?"

Laura: "I don't know. I don't know if these toxins cause a lack of oxygen, cuz sometimes toxins and viruses can reduce oxygen in the blood, and that would kill the brain cells."

Michael: "Well that makes sense, almost like suffocating the brain.

Especially if the virus was rampant. Wait a minute, maybe that's why I've been asking about his lungs, I wonder if it like somehow prevented his brain from getting oxygen. Like the virus acts as a, don't paralyze the lungs, but somehow prevents it from getting the oxygen it needs, you know.

(He asked me earlier in the session if my son had asthma, and I said no.)

Laura: "Makes sense."

Michael: "You see I'm not sold on the virus (in vaccines) that they are giving kids. I know they call it this, and they say that's what it is, but I don't fully trust that. I'm not sure what the kids are getting are what they say it is."

Laura: "I'm with you."

Michael: "I mean, unless you can get a hold of some and take it somewhere and have it analyzed, and say what i that? An independent source, has anyone done that?"

Laura: "Not that I'm aware of."

Michael: "Or do we just take their word for everything?"

Laura: "Yeah, pretty much."

Michael: "That's something worth looking at. Why do we take everybody's word for everything? Is anyone questioning what's in these viruses?"

Laura: "Yeah, what's in the vial you are just about to stab into my child? Oh, it's this, it's on the label, it's on the insert, that's what's in there."

Michael: "They don't label what's in your bloody food; you think they are going to tell you what's in a virus? That's my point. I don't know how you verify that."

Laura: "Yeah."

Michael: "I think we are getting somewhere here. Ok, blue blood is lack of oxygen, so you mean literally, then? Sort of oxygen starvation taking place. I think we are right on the money there. There is definitely some sort of starvation of oxygen to the brain. It could be to the brain barrier, it could be around the brain and not to do with the lungs or anything, do you understand?"

Laura: "Yeah."

Michael: "Did he have any thyroid issues?"

Laura: "Yeah, he still does."

Michael: "See what I get is on the way up to the brain, the thyroid is near there and that's doing something too. Is it overactive thyroid?"

Laura: "Underactive, hypothyroid."

Michael: "Hypo, that means less, hyper means more, I see."

Laura: "That's the T4, the thyroid hormone, it isn't producing enough, or maybe it's attacking itself, I don't know."

Michael: "T4, uh-huh. Hmm, that's interesting. Does he have lazy eye, or would he ever exhibit lazy eye to you?"

Laura: "No, not lazy eye, but he would look at things really close to his eye, and zoom things past his eye really quickly back and forth in front of his eye, from the corner of his eye."

Michael: "What, like he was trying to see it or something?"

Laura: "Yeah, a lot of kids with autism do that. They call it visual stimming. They move things back and forth really quickly in front of their eye or go right up to the television and look at it really closely."

Michael: "Like look at the dots?"

Laura: "Who knows what they're looking at, but yeah, they get really close to things or move things quickly back and forth in front of their eye. I have no idea why."

Michael: "And what, there is no explanation for that from any doctor? Like an eye doctor can tell you why? There is no explanation anywhere for that, that you've found?"

Laura: "Not that I've heard. They say, oh, that's what they do, they visually stim."

Michael: "No, it isn't just what they do. There is a clue here, this is another clue. You see, I don't feel like he's blind, it's not that, but there is a problem with the eyes, or the way he's perceiving things with his eyes, do you understand?"

Laura: "Yeah."

Michael: "That's what I just got from them. And also hearing."

Laura: "Yeah, very hypersensitive hearing. He covers his ears a lot if things are too loud."

Michael: "So you've got all the senses going on at the brain level."

Laura: "Mmm-hmm."

Michael: "I think when he screams, it is out of sheer frustration. Just sheer frustration is what it is."

Laura: "Yeah, he can't say what he wants."

Michael: "What I feel like is taking breaths and holding my breath, you understand? Like I'm taking a breath and I'm holding my breath and letting out a scream, like that. Did he do that?"

Laura: "I think so. He whines a lot and gets wound up and it escalates."

Michael: "This is interesting; it's absolutely a brain issue here. They've just shown me Humpty Dumpty."

Laura: "Oh, cracked his head."

(I hope we can put him back together again.)

Michael: "Do you have anything you want to ask that is pertinent here, maybe something I haven't thought of."

Laura: "I'd love to clarify, this virus he's talking about in the brain, and it's mutated, is that part vaccine and part environmental coming together and mutating? Where is this virus originating?"

Michael: "Well, to a degree, I feel like it's in the, you see they put the mercury in there to stop the deterioration of the virus. Not deterioration, what's the word? Do you know why they put mercury in?"

Laura: "They say it is a preservative, but I think it's because it has to trigger an immune response in the body, it's called an adjuvant, so something toxic to illicit an immune response, but they say it is to preserve the vaccine."

Michael: "It's to preserve the vaccine, right. It's to preserve the virus. So what happens if it's not preserving the virus correctly? Not that the

virus dies, but that it morphs into something else because it is sitting in this sea of mercury?"

Laura: "Well, the MMR doesn't have Thimerosal, but what if they are all three mutating together, having all three live viruses in one vial?"

Michael: "Yeah, exactly. That's what I'm saying."

Laura: "I never thought of that."

Michael: "I don't trust that what they are putting in is what you're getting. Like once it's injected, it seems to me that it's already mutating. That basically when it gets to the brain, when it's doing the most development, the fatty brain, it's already mutating. And that's why the lymph system is messed up. That's what it seems to be. I don't think all the other factors help. Because he's trying to fight this infection off and if he can't fight it off, at what point... Why do my friend and my ex come down with Graves disease? What triggered it? Is everyone walking around with Graves disease? I don't think so. It's some sort of genetic propensity for that, but something triggered it. Stress triggered it. People say, 'what do you mean stress triggered it?' I couldn't put my finger on what stress is, but it's like a snapping point. And I think that's what is going on here. His body is stressed, they put this in and it's overload, boom, and he can't handle it, he can't defeat the virus."

Laura: "Mmm-hmm."

Michael: "And it's like it's mutated into something else. So it's become something else. It's like a parasite on the brain. Ok, so it's almost like a parasitic infection of the brain."

Laura: "How do we get rid of it? That's my next question."

Michael: "Well I think what you've got left, if the virus is dead, if it's killed off, you've got basically brain damage. So you are trying to repair the brain damage. You see what I'm getting at?"

Laura: "Mmm-hmm."

Michael: "Which is obviously pretty severe, ok? So if it starved the brain of oxygen in the way it works, remember iron was mentioned in the blood?"

Laura: "Mmm-hmm."

Michael: "That the blood wasn't iron rich? Something is starving the oxygen out of the blood. It's like something is stealing it. Has anyone extracted any, like done any samples, gone into kids heads and took samples of the inter-brain cranial fluid or anything like that? Has anybody done anything like that to see what it is?"

Laura: "Not that I'm aware of. I know recently I saw something about post-mortem studies, and this came up in one of the readings, which is why I looked it up."

Michael: "Wait, wait, wait. What?"

Laura: "Post-mortem studies, like if someone with autism dies."

Michael: "I know, but you said it came up in one of the readings."

Laura: "Yeah, forensic pathology came up in one of the readings."

Michael: "Did it? I don't remember."

Laura: "Yeah, so I was looking it up, and this doctor who does a lot of HBOT was saying in a conference speech that I listened to that there was a report that came out that kids with autism have certain viruses in their brain that antibiotics are ineffective on."

Michael: "That's it! We're on the right track here."

Laura: "But he didn't specify which one, I don't know that they have said what it is."

Michael: "Well that's what we need to find out. This is where they are going with this."

Laura: "And Autism Speaks has just started a brain bank of autistic brains, there are not a lot of them that are dead that have donated their brains, that's the problem. But for studies, they are heading this brain bank to do grants to do studies on brains. They have the tissue samples."

(So does the Eunice Kennedy Shriver Brain Bank I mentioned earlier.)

Michael: "Well it's a start. This is what they've been telling me, ok. I think we got further."

Laura: "Yeah. So what other ways are there, I know we talked about some, but what are the most effective ways of repairing all of this damage. And I'm sure there had to be inflammation involved as well. Kill the virus, repair the brain, isn't that what you would do?"

Michael: "Well that's basically it, yeah. So, we are talking about the virus, they are talking about finding a virus in the brain post mortem. Has anybody said what it is?"

Laura: "No, I haven't found that yet, I just heard him talking about it. I'd have to try to find the study, because he said it's a new study."

Michael: "But the only way they are going to find out is for them to do some sort of research on it. You said that no antibiotics will treat it?"

Laura: "Yeah, the virus he was talking about."

Michael: "How did he arrive at that conclusion, do you know?"

Laura: "No, I don't know. I know some viruses they say there is no cure for or way to treat it."

Michael: "Like the herpes virus isn't."

(Antibiotics don't work on viruses anyway, plus they don't cross the blood brain barrier.)

Laura: "Or even Lyme disease is hard to treat, or XMRV (a retrovirus) is really hard to treat."

Michael: "What does Lyme disease do? What is the product of Lyme disease?"

Laura: "It is a bacterial infection; a spirochete is what it is. It is very invasive and causes all kinds of damage in the body."

Michael: "Does it go into the brain?"

Laura: "Yep."

Michael: "What happens when it goes to the brain?"

Laura: "It causes all kinds of different symptoms, and a lot of kids with autism have Lyme."

Michael: "Which you get from a tick bite."

Laura: "Or a mosquito bite." (Fleas and spiders can also carry Borellia burgdorferi.)

Michael: "A mosquito bite. Of course mosquitoes carry the AIDS virus."

Laura: "And all kinds of other bacterial infections too."

Michael: "They carry all kinds of stuff. So he could have got bitten."

Laura: "Yeah, I tested Trevor energetically, and he always tests weak to Lyme."

Michael: "Which means?"

Laura: "He's been exposed to it. And it hides in the body. It's not always detectible because it's a shape shifter and goes into tissue and comes out during times of stress."

Michael: "I did ponder Lyme disease and a tick earlier."

Laura: "Hmm. I mean it could just be another co-factor. A co-existing opportunistic type of infection."

Michael: "See the biggest question you keep posing is why my son as opposed to any other kid, or why just these kids, which is something I don't know if I can answer for you. There's got to be some point in which something becomes so overwhelming that it takes hold more than it normally would, you see?"

Laura: "Yeah. And it kind of came up today with the Y chromosome. Is that why? I've heard that autism is 4-8 times higher in boys than girls, and I've never figured out why. I've never found an answer. Does it have something to do with Y chromosomes or the way the male brain is?"

Michael: "It must be. Otherwise they wouldn't have mentioned the chromosome. It must be. What else would delineate that? It has to be. There is some genetic component to this."

Laura: "I never even thought of that. Because they have a Y chromosome, does it attack boys?"

Michael: "It may. Maybe what this is, it singles out boys. Maybe there is a deformation in the Y chromosome, a genetic mutation in the Y chromosome. I know nothing about genetics, you see?

Laura: "I don't either, not a lot."

Michael: "We are kind of in an area where I couldn't begin to tell you really. I know there is a genetic component; this may explain why certain kids get singled out. And you're telling me more boys than girls, predominantly boys. There's got to be a genetic component there, because

that's what's saying you and not you, this one not that one. Has to be, it's like a computer, it's going to say yes, this one, that one no. Has to be, that's on a genetic level. That's where the decisions are made."

Laura: "So they are succeptible just from being a boy?"

Michael: "Interesting, isn't it?"

Laura: "Yeah, so it attacks boys because they are more vulnerable to it?"

Michael: "Apparently it does, not really a question, it's a fact; it does attack boys more than girls. So that's a genetic component there."

Laura: "So why is it higher in certain states than others? That's another question I have."

Michael: "I don't know. Maybe that's the environmental component."

(Marti says, "There are so many different causes.")

Michael: "Yeah, I know they lump everybody together and say this is autism, just like they lumped Aspergers together, and clearly once you look into it, you can see that Aspergers is not really autism."

Laura: "Right."

Michael: "When we first started looking at this, I just took your word for it and thought, I guess so, but really and truly it's not, it is different. They're just different."

Michael mentions how undetectable forms of radiation, like gamma rays, can cause mutations in the body; they bombard the cells and alter people genetically. The channeling part was over. Marti just drew one picture. She felt that it was something microscopic, perhaps a virus or a neuron, but she felt it had a white center. Here it is:

3/29/11   white center

Session Thirteen: After the Session
<u>Featured Spirits:</u> J.J. Thomson, J. Robert Oppenheimer

I found it interesting that during the session where they talked about a radioactive lake, J. Robert Oppenheimer was mentioned by J. J. Thomson, the main speaker this time. I had never heard of J. J. Thomson, but he was one of Oppenheimer's teachers. Oppenheimer is known as the "Father of the Atomic Bomb" for his involvement with the Manhattan Project, which led to the U.S. dropping two nuclear bombs in Japan. J.J. Thomson discovered the electron, and worked with atoms and sub-atomic particles. He won a Nobel Prize in Physics, as did his son, George Paget Thomson. Because of their expertise, I believed what they were saying. After doing a little research, I learned that Oppenheimer was also friends with Albert Einstein and worked at the Institute for Advanced Study in Princeton, NJ at the same time. He was also friends with other spirits who have made appearances, Werner Heisenberg and Wolfgang Pauli.

Another interesting connection that I learned was that Oppenheimer received the Enrico Fermi Award in 1963, which was presented to him a little over a week after JFK's assassination at the White House by the newly appointed President Lyndon Johnson. Jacqueline Kennedy was still living in the White House at the time, and met with Oppenheimer to tell him how much JFK wanted him to have the award.

I gave many of the validations throughout the chapter, but I did want to talk about the radioactive lake that was mentioned in the session. We loved going to Pyramid Lake in the summertime. Trevor especially loved it and asked to go there. We would find a private section of beach and it was as if we had our own lake. It was much less crowded than nearby Lake Tahoe. When there is the potential for a meltdown that could happen at any time for no apparent reason, privacy is a good thing. It was always a fun time. We'd bring snacks, the kids would splash in the cold water, dig in the sand, run up and down the beach, and get a little sun. If Trevor freaked out, there were no strangers around to give us the stink eye. Good times.

After this session, I was so scared that we never went back there, and instead went to Lake Tahoe last summer. Prior to this session, I had just started reading some articles about depleted uranium, and a few of them mentioned Pyramid Lake, NV being contaminated by detonations of DU weapons at Sierra Army Depot. I also read that there is a DU storage facility at Pyramid Lake itself, uphill of the Pauite Reservation. It is stored out in the open, and can't be buried for 50 years because it is "too hot." I didn't want to believe it, but because it came up in the session, I had to. Here is a little background on depleted uranium (DU), for those who are as unaware as I was.

In an article written by independent scientist, international radiation expert and nuclear whistleblower Leuren Moret titled "The Little Fox is Still, The Dogs of War Have Made Their Kill" in the November 7, 2001 article for the *San Francisco Bay View*, she explains that "The United States now has hundreds of thousands of tons of depleted uranium piled in heaps outdoors at DOE facilities. It is 99.5% of what is left when the most fissionable isotope (one of three) is extracted from naturally occurring uranium. The extracted uranium is used in nuclear weapons or nuclear fuel for nuclear reactors. The 99.5% that is discarded cannot be put back into the mines it came out of because after crushing and processing, the volume is greater than before it was removed from the mines. 'Depleted uranium' does not mean it is not radioactive – it is very radioactive and very dangerous to all living things."

"The Dept. of Defense got the bright idea of using depleted uranium in weapons because (1) it is very dense which gives it greater penetrating power to destroy tanks, etc. (2) it is pyrophoric, which means upon impact, it explodes into fire and smoke creating submicroscopic radioactive particles which travel great distances and can remain suspended until it is 'rained out' of the atmosphere, (3) it is cheap and passes the responsibility for disposal from DOE on to civilians (that means us) and the environment. It is also radioactive and will continue acting internally long after the battlefield has been cleared – with delayed effects which continue acting on soldiers and civilians the rest of their lives. The half life of uranium is 4.5 billion years – in ten half lives radioactivity becomes an insignificant amount. In 45 billion years it will no longer be a danger."

Don't think that it is just here in Nevada, folks. Moret says that "The U.S. has manufactured and tested depleted uranium in 39 states. Communities living near these test ranges will continue to be exposed to health problems. DU is in the arsenal the U.S. and British military forces are using on Afghanistan. The DU which contaminates the Gulf States since the Gulf War can be detected on gamma meters in Greece and Bulgaria on windy days. It's the weapon that keeps giving and keeps killing. Depleted uranium is a boomerang weapon, the radioactive dust makes its way around the planet, carried by the wind and brought down to Earth in rain and snow. Ionizing radiation increases all kinds of cancer, infertility, birth defects, and many other ill effects. There is no safe level of radiation. Future generations will be even more affected. The amount of DU used in Iraq in 2003 is equivalent in atomicity to nearly 250,000 Nagasaki bombs."

The book *Discounted Casualties: The Human Cost of Depleted Uranium* by Japanese journalist Akira Tashiro, with the foreword by Leuren Moret, contains lots of useful information on DU, as well as personal accounts. The website lists the locations involved in the fabrication, assembly, R&D, test firing, storage and demilitarization of sites involved in DU ammunition in the U.S.[23] If you live downwind, move.

After this session, when I took Trevor for a BioSET appointment, I had his practitioner test him for radioactive elements. Not surprisingly, he tested weak (exposure) to many different isotopes including Uranium-

---

[23] http://www.chugoku-np.co.jp/abom/uran/shisetsu_us_e/shisetsu.html#22

238, or U-238 (DU). Some of the others were Uranium-235, Uranium-236, Iodine-131, Strontium-90; all used in nuclear weapons. He also was weak to Uranium Oxide, which is the gas from the explosions. We cleared him from all of these items with acupressure and gave him a homeopathic remedy for radiation with the energy signatures of the isotopes transferred into it. I also had him on the BioAlgae Superfood which helps chelate radiation. Our planet is polluted with radiation from the detonation of nuclear weapons and from making nuclear energy, as well as the accidents, including Fukushima. This testing shows me that my son has been exposed to many radioactive isotopes related to both. This session showed me that Michael was correct, that he was in a radioactive lake, polluted with DU, or U-238.

Because we live in Nevada, although Northeast and upwind of the Nevada Test Site, where the bulk of the nuclear bombs were tested, the wind blows the radiation around the state. We are also downwind from Russia and hit by the radiation from Chernobyl, and recently from Fukushima in Japan. The particles are brought down to Earth by rain and snow in the Sierra Nevada Mountains. The water runs both West to California and East to Nevada. A student at the University of Reno detected specific Fukushima isotopes here in Nevada within weeks of the accident. It was detected in the water, rain and dairy products from cows eating radioactive grass and feed all across the United States.

To see how far-reaching nuclear fallout is, look at the fallout map below from the nuclear explosions from the Nevada Test Site. This map represents areas crossed by three or more nuclear clouds from above ground detonations. It didn't stop at the border; it traveled around the world as atmospheric dust, and remains in the atmosphere today.

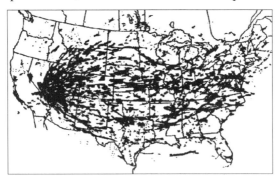

I also saw a map from the National Cancer Institute estimating thyroid doses of Iodine-131 received by Americans from Nevada Atmospheric Nuclear Bomb Test from 1997. The thyroid gland uptakes Iodine-131 and it irradiates it, later causing thyroid cancer. The states along the predominant wind pattern coming from Nevada had the highest rates. I saw another map of cancer mortality rates in relation to U.S. nuclear reactor sites. Not surprisingly, the highest cancer rates are located near the nuclear reactor sites. The maps are easily accessible online. Scientists use radiation to give lab rats cancer for studies, what does that tell you?

The United States has 104 nuclear power plants in 31 states, mostly on the East coast, with a greater population density and higher energy needs. The main pathways for fission products from nuclear power plants are through drinking water and dairy products. The combination of nuclear weapons testing, nuclear power plants, and radiation accidents like Three Mile Island, Chernobyl and Fukushima are steadily increasing the radiation contamination on the planet. We can't escape it because it is in the air we breathe, the water we drink and the foods we eat which are grown in contaminated soil.

According to Greenpeace, since July 16, 1945 there have been 2,044 nuclear weapons tests worldwide, the equivalent of one test occurring somewhere in the world every nine days for the last fifty years. Trying to prevent a nuclear war, we have essentially had one. I believe that nuclear radiation is another piece of the autism puzzle. I feel that, like soldiers that become ill with Gulf War Syndrome after returning home, children with autism have been exposed to the same nuclear, biological and chemical assaults as Gulf War veterans. The difference is that when a developing child is exposed to these things, among others, they stop developing. When a grown adult is exposed to the same disease process, they begin to degenerate.

***

Chapter Sixteen

"Now I am become death, the destroyer of worlds."

— J. Robert Oppenheimer (1904-1967)
(Citing from the Bhagavad-Gita, after witnessing the world's first nuclear explosion)

Session Fourteen

The session was on April 6, 2011. It was just Michael and I this time, and it started off with Michael saying that there was a man there and he thought it was Oppenheimer. He said his name was Bob or Robert. I told him that his full name was Julius Robert Oppenheimer and he went by J. Robert, or just Robert Oppenheimer. The fact that he said his first name validated that it was really him that the last time. Next, my dad came through for a little bit. Then, Michael started asking me about some of the things my son has been doing. First he said they were showing him a piano and asked me:

Michael: "He didn't listen to any Mozart today or anything?"

Laura: "Oh my God. He has a Baby Einstein DVD called Baby Mozart, and he was watching it and listening to it today, and he was carrying around the DVD and pointing it out to me and saying 'Baby Mozart.'"

Michael: "Ha, ha. See, that's what I'm looking for. I need something to know I'm tuned in, see what I'm saying."

Laura: "Yeah, that's funny."

Michael said that they were saying something about a Rabi, or Rabbis, and asked if it had anything to do with my son. I said no, and thought it might be rabbits, which Trevor was pointing to in the yard recently.

(Interestingly, after the session, I learned that one of Oppenheimer's colleagues and good friend was Isador Rabi. They worked together at Los Alamos. Rabi was also a Nobel Prize winner for his discovery of nuclear magnetic resonance. He also worked with Werner Heisenberg, and Wolfgang Pauli. Rabi actually testified on Oppenheimer's behalf at the controversial U.S. Atomic Energy Commission hearing in 1954, which ultimately led to Oppenheimer being stripped of his security clearance. So, I think

Oppenheimer was mentioning his friend Rabi to further validate that it was him.)

Michael mentioned that someone had been watching my son that day and telling him some of the things he was doing, for instance writing about a dog at school, taking a bath with salts in it, and even knew that when I went to wash his hair, there was water and not shampoo in the bottle, which was true because his brother emptied the shampoo and put water in the bottle. He repeated that someone was watching me and then said that my paternal grandmother was there. She told Michael that my son was happier and that he was making jokes, which were both true. He asked if we were planning a trip in about a week a few hundred miles away, and I told him that we were going to drive to Monterey Bay Aquarium for a few days.

He also said that he was seeing a skateboard, and I told Michael that the other day, Trevor was watching America's Funniest Videos with his brother and I, and Trevor pointed to the TV and said "Skateboard." He had never said that before. Then Michael said:

Michael: "Someone is saying they are helping him with diction."

Laura: "Oh."

Michael: "They are helping him with cognition, with his expression."

Laura: "Cool. He's been saying things very clear lately."

Wow! Who knew spirits could do stuff like this? I know my son is very clairaudient, so I'm sure he can hear them. Many children with autism are very psychic. When you lose your ability to speak, it becomes a survival mechanism I suppose.

Next Michael talked about sound therapy and vision therapy and said that swimming would be very good for him by bringing up the name of my friend who is the director of a pool that uses saline instead of chlorine. Michael said that swimming would also be helpful for my son's confidence, because "a certain level of his confidence has taken a bashing too."

The next part of this session made me laugh. Michael says:

Michael: "And now they're saying what sounds like Gary."

Laura: "Ok."

Michael: "I don't know if there is anyone immediate to him (Trevor)

297

called Gary as well."

Laura: "Ha, ha. That's what we call my other son as a nickname."

Michael: "Oh, you call him Gary?"

Laura: "Yeah, Spongebob Squarepants' pet snail is named Gary. And my son Damon is usually pretty pokey, so we call him Gary all the time."

Michael: "Oh, that's funny."

Laura: "His nickname is Gary; he even got the 'Gary Award' from his teacher at school last year, because she thought it was funny."

Michael: "Oh, that's funny."

Laura: "So she gave him the Gary award. Ha, ha." (It was a certificate from the school.)

Michael: "That's funny."

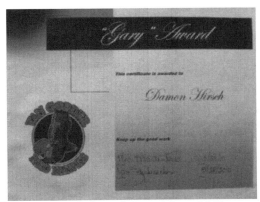

Damon's "Gary" Award from 2010

Next, Michael asked me if I ever took Trevor to the movies. I told him that I hadn't taken him for a few years because they were always too loud for him, and he always wanted to leave. He said that he might like the movies, like a kid's movie. And he mentioned him eating popcorn. Shortly after this session, I gathered up some courage and took both boys to a matinee kid's flick, and as soon as we got there, Trevor asked for popcorn. I probably shouldn't have, but I got some and we all split it, and Trevor sat through the whole movie and was happy and laughing, and pointing out things to me on the screen. It was a great day. Now, I can take both of them by myself, without another adult or an extra car as a backup escape plan. It was the first time in a long time that I felt like a normal family, taking my kids to a movie. What is no big deal for most families was a monumental event for us.

Michael said, "You're doing all the right things, someone said to me." That was reassuring. Then he said, "You know I'm not getting any big stuff tonight about anything. My main feeling with them, I think he's going to make some big improvements. I think that he seems to be getting happier within himself. He seems to be spreading his wings, is the way they put it." This made me smile.

After that, Michael was talking about Trevor riding a bike. He said he could see him riding and enjoying a bike. I told him that Marti drew a bicycle last time. He said that he could also see him listening to music and humming along to it. He asked if he had any books with music that he liked listening to. I told him that he loved "Puff, The Magic Dragon" book and CD set. He plays the CD and reads the book. Michael said, "That's what they're telling me." He listened to it at school as a reward. In fact, he just received two of them for his birthday the previous summer. Here is a picture to prove it. That's Gary in the background. Meow. (Gary the snail meows like a cat.)

July 14, 2010 – Puff the Magic Dragon Birthday gifts.

Michael added, "My overriding feeling is that you have a lot of help, I think from your dad and a few grandparents and the husband. They are helping you with him, you know, they are like around you. Perhaps because he's now starting to make some progress. It's been a long haul where he's sort of been treading water for a long time, you know what I mean?" This was true.

Then, Michael said something that there is no way he could have known. Keep in mind we live in the desert in Nevada. He said:

Michael: "You don't have a…This is strange, you don't have a sailboat?"

Laura: "No, but he's been on a sailboat a couple times. They have a marina here, and they actually do special needs charters and teach people how to sail."

Michael: "Does he like it?"

Laura: "Yeah, he loves it. He's done it twice."

Michael: "That's cool. Yeah, cuz I saw him on a sailboat, a small sailboat. Yeah, that's very stimulating for him, you see?"

Laura: "Cool, I'll have to do that again."

Michael: "It's pushing his boundaries; it's forcing him to do it. He has to be challenged in an environment where he's still comfortable."

Laura: "Yeah."

The picture below is from June of 2009. It is Trevor when he was 10-years-old, with one of the sailing instructors. He did it again the following summer as well. You can see the Sierra Nevada Mountains in the background.

Trevor sailing June, 2009

This past summer, we actually took the boys on rented paddleboats on the Marina a few times. I took Trevor, and Matt took Damon so they could fish off of their boat. Trevor and I just cruised around; I even let him steer a little bit. He was so calm the whole time.

The next part of the session, Michael mentioned that he saw Trevor playing a goalie in soccer. I told him that he had never tried it before. Michael thought he might like it, and that any sporting activity would be good for him. I put it on the to-do list. They have Challenger sports here and in many other states for children with special needs. This next part really made my night. I asked:

Laura: "I just want to know if he is going to fully recover. That's the one thing that…I just can't sleep at night because I worry so much about him."

Michael: "I think he will. I think he will get a lot further than you think."

Laura: "Really?"

Michael: "I see him a bit older, saying to you 'I'm fine mom, don't worry about me.' Like that."

Laura: (Sniff.)

Michael: "He's going to get to a point where he can interact on a more adult level with you."

Laura: "That's my biggest dream in life, is to make sure he's ok."

The next part was pretty interesting, and something I had never really thought about. Michael said:

Michael: "Ok, I'm seeing him in his bedroom, on his bed, and I'm seeing him hanging over the side of his bed. But his head is down, like he's lying on the bed and his head is hanging over the side or something. Has he done that? Is there any type of inversion thing that he does, where he's inverted?"

Laura: "He's very acrobatic, he'll do handstands, he'll do forward rolls, he'll run and do a dive roll, he bounces off a ball and flips, he does trampoline tricks and all of that."

Michael: "So he's is sort of inverted or upside down fairly often then?"

Laura: "Yeah, I call him the ninja."

301

Michael: "Well that's good, maybe that's part of the reason he's doing it. Maybe subconsciously he knows that's helping him."

Laura: "I was a gymnast and my dad was a gymnast, so I think it's in his genes that he has that."

Michael: "Hmm, ok, I just see more blood rushing to the brain, you know what I mean?"

Laura: "Yeah, maybe it's good for him."

Michael: "And spinal fluid going to the brain, you know?"

Laura: "Oh."

Michael: "That's why yogi's stand on their head, to get the subtle spinal fluid to go to the brain, base of the spine, you see?"

Laura: "Oh, ok. I'll have him do handstands all day long."

I was just joking in that last comment, of course, but I did end up buying one of those inversion tables for him after the session. You hook your feet in and slowly go back as far as you want to go, even totally upside down like a bat. Michael talked a bit more about it later, and said just to have him hang upside down for a few minutes. I spotted him the whole time, but he seems to like it. It makes your back feel good too. Michael said that every little thing they bring up helps.

Michael asked me if Trevor liked honey. I told him he never tried it. He said that it was amazing stuff with antibacterial properties that might help him a bit. I had him try it on some gluten-free toast, and he spit it out. Later on, I made some gluten-free granola with raw honey and he loved it, so he got it that way. Make sure it is raw honey, not "funny honey" which is not even honey at all; it's high fructose corn syrup. The rest of the session wasn't directly channeled, but Michael said a few things that almost made me cry. Ok, I cried.

Michael: "I think tonight they just want to reassure you that they are helping you."

Laura: "That's good, because I feel alone a lot in this whole endeavor."

Michael: "Do you?"

Laura: "Yes."

Michael: "Well, my feeling is that they didn't want to talk about anything heavy tonight; do you know what I mean? Cuz it is overwhelming."

Laura: "Yeah."

Michael: "I mean just about the lake and stuff they told you about the lake. 'Oh my God,' you must be thinking,"

Laura: "I know, like I can't take him anywhere."

Michael: "Yeah. Well, my feeling is don't worry, he's going to make a lot of progress, and keep doing what you're doing, and you've got helpers. You've got people helping you."

Laura: "That's good to know."

Michael: "You're not on your own with this, you know. You're just not. You're really are not on your own."

Laura: "How are they helping? I know you said a few things, but what other ways?"

Michael: "You know they have a lot of influence, people in the spirit world. They can do all kinds of stuff, you know. They aren't just sitting there watching. They can impact our lives. Quite literally, move a car out of the way so you don't die. Literally, if they can move a car out of the way, they can certainly do other things, you know what I mean?"

Laura: "Mmm-hmm."

Michael: "Constantly healing people all over the world. Miraculous healings take place every day, purely because the spirit people intercede."

Laura: "I always talk to them, I know that probably doesn't sound weird to you, but I always ask for help. And I know he can hear them and see them. Sometimes, he'll just laugh and look around me, like look behind me. And so many pictures I take of him, there are orbs all over the place in the pictures."

Michael: "Uh-huh."

Laura: "You should see the pictures from my wedding which were taken inside; it looks like it's snowing in my house. It was like a spirit party."

Michael: "Yeah. You'll just get to a point where you just thank them for their help, because you honestly are being helped. I think you just need to know that you are being helped, you're not alone. When sometimes you have to make a decision and it's a tough decision, what you decide to do, you get help with."

Laura: "Mmm-hmm."

Michael: "You really are not on your own, you're never alone. There is always somebody looking in. When I say it, I'm sure that every day you get a visit, especially with him."

Laura: "Yeah, I always ask for signs to for them to show me that they are here, and a touch lamp will be on that nobody turned on. Or I have a ceiling fan with a light on it that goes on in the middle of the night by itself, stuff like that. And I say 'Thank you.' It's like I need that physical evidence."

Michael: "So I just think you need to just know that they are helping you, you know?"

Laura: "I do, but it's good to hear it from you."

Michael: "Yeah, I think you needed that today."

Laura: "I did, I've been transcribing all of these readings, and like you said, it's all this heavy stuff."

Michael: "It is heavy, and you see, for me, I'm used to heavy."

Laura: "Mmm-hmm."

Michael: "You know what I'm saying? So, sometimes I have to catch myself when I am with other people cuz they're just not used to it. My teacher was the most heavy duty person you could ever meet. I mean the stuff he dealt with was so heavy. Dark, dark stuff he dealt with. I'm used to it, but I have to realize sometimes that there are very few people I can talk with about that kind of stuff. And they can't handle it either; they're just not used to it. So, love is everything. That's all there is, there is just love."

Laura: "Mmm-hmm."

Michael: "There is nothing else, there is just love. Everything really is truly, it really is just love, you know."

Laura: "I think I needed this, I mean with everything going on in the world today, and all these things, and dealing with him, I mean, I'm surprised I don't get depressed over this stuff. But I guess I have been dealing with grief and heavy things most of my adult life, and still managed to retain a sense of humor and enjoy life still. I don't let it drag me down in the gutter. But it's still nice to hear stuff like this, that's what keeps me going. Every now and then I just need that happy stuff. Balance."

Michael: "Well you know this kind of little small talk stuff about what he's doing, about what he's looking at, what he likes to do, and what kinds of things he enjoys and all that stuff, what that lets you know is just how involved the spirit people are."

Laura: "Exactly."

Michael: "You know what I mean? That's what it shows you."

Laura: "Yeah."

Michael: "And sharing it with others, when others see that, they go, 'Huh, maybe I'm not alone then.' Even if they've never had a personal experience like this."

Laura: "Yeah."

Michael: "So, I think it all helps."

Laura: "Yeah, for someone who is going to read this, you weren't here in my house today. You didn't know that Trevor's brother's nickname is Gary. You know?"

Michael: "No, I don't know that stuff. That's the kind of stuff they always bring up, you see?"

Michael proceeded to give me another example of doing a session for someone and the spirits brought up seemingly insignificant things, and then he said:

Michael: "I used to think that it didn't matter years ago. I'd dismiss it a lot of times. I'd say, 'What are you telling me that rubbish for? I'm not going to say that, it's stupid, it's kind of meaningless.' And I found that all the little stuff isn't meaningless at all. It's probably the most meaningful stuff I could say to anybody."

Laura: "Mmm-hmm."

Michael: "But I also like the fact that they tell me the big stuff too."

Laura: "Right."

Michael: "So, I think they are both important."

Laura: "I do too."

Michael: "They have different effects on people, you see. They have different purposes."

Laura: "Well, I think the best thing you could have possibly said to me, you said to me tonight, and it made me cry, was that he was going to get farther along than I can imagine."

Michael: "I think so, but it may take a few years."

Laura: "Yeah, the fact that he will be able to say a sentence to me like, 'I'm fine mom, don't worry about me.'"

Michael: "I'm sure he is going to do that."

Laura: "That is what drives me every day, is to make sure that before I kick the bucket that my child is going to be ok."

Michael: "I think so; I think he will show some big improvements. He's already improving a lot."

Laura: "I feel like so much of this is my fault indirectly."

Michael: "No."

Laura: "And I know it isn't, I know it isn't, but part of me still blames myself in a way because I didn't know better. I'm smarter than that, I feel like I should have investigated it more, and not blindly followed what someone else said."

Michael again assured me that it wasn't my fault, and proceeded to tell me a heartwarming true story from a book that he really likes about past life regression. Whenever he's inspired to tell someone a story, there is always something in it for them.

Michael: "This woman is in a trance state, they've hypnotized her and she goes back to another life and she's a little girl, she's in a carriage in like France or something and her mother is in the carriage with her and she's messing around with the door handle as the carriage is going along. And her mother keeps saying 'Leave the door handle alone, stop messing around, sit back in your seat.' And she ignores her, and the door flies open and she falls out of the carriage and the carriage rolls over her legs and breaks her legs. What happens is the hypnotist takes her in between lives and speaks to her soul asks her why she did that?"

Laura: "Mmm-hmm."

Michael: "Why did that happen? And this is her reply: My soul thought that I would learn more if my legs were broken. I would do more. And what happened is she said I was able to overcome pain, because she had lifelong pain. She was crippled, she spent the rest of her life in a wheelchair and she couldn't walk again."

Laura: "Hmm."

Michael: "She overcame pain. She learned to teach children, she became a teacher. She did a lot of things she said she never would have done had she not had that happen to her. So her soul decided to make that happen so that she would advance faster, and learn quicker and do more."

Laura: "Wow."

Michael: "Now you wouldn't think that, would you?"

Laura: "No."

Michael: "Initial impression is shock, 'Wow, I must have done something bad.' All the misconceptions come up, right?"

Laura: "Mmm-hmm."

Michael: "But from that point of view, you can see it was a good thing, see what I mean?"

Laura: "Yeah."

Michael: "This is what people do in life. They see things. You know Marti and I sit here and watch TV and people pass judgements on things and they say things and we look at each other and say, well that doesn't mean that. Why are you jumping to that conclusion? What's that got to do with it? It could mean this instead."

Laura: "Mmm-hmm."

Michael: "That's what people do. They just jump to conclusions; they don't see the big picture. And that's what I want to say to you."

Laura: "Yeah?"

Michael: "You're jumping to conclusions and you're drawing conclusions from something you don't know. You don't know yet why. You don't know who he is to you from previous lives. You don't know what he's, maybe he was a she before, you don't know him completely yet."

Laura: "Yeah."

Michael: "You know him on a certain level obviously. You love him, you're connected. Obviously you know each other, but you don't remember is what I'm trying to say to you, why?"

Laura: "Right."

Michael: "So it's a waste of time beating yourself up over it because you don't know why. It's ok, it must be ok, because it happened. It's meant to happen. There is no chance, there is no chance. That's a crazy word. It's ludicrous; there is no chance in the Universe. Accidents don't just haphazardly, just randomly happen. There is no randomness in the Universe. If there was randomness you wouldn't be able to get a rocket to the moon. But we'll try it today; maybe we'll get it there today."

Laura: "Mmm-hmm."

Michael: "Everything is completely measured. Everything is perfect, everything works perfectly. Everything has a reason and there is perfection behind everything. Everything that happened was meant to happen. And I know that is true because so many times I tell people things that haven't happened yet. And then they happen, good or bad. So if I'm telling them something that hasn't happened yet and then it happens exactly how I said, that means it is predestined, see what I mean?"

Laura: "Mmm-hmm."

Michael: "And I'm talking about things that they don't understand. Not where I say to them you're going to meet a guy that's tall, dark and handsome and you're going to marry them, and then they go find someone tall, dark and handsome and marry them, you see what I mean?"

Laura: "Yeah."

Michael: "It's not like that. I am telling them things that are obscure that they don't understand that later they go 'Oh, my God.' That's the predestined stuff."

Laura: "Right."

Michael: "I mean this accident is probably going to happen another way, you know what I mean?"

Laura: "Mmm-hmm."

Michael: "I think things can be mitigated through grace. I think that things don't have to be as bad, let's put it this way, the pain and suffering can be lessened. The amount of destruction of something can be lessened, you know what I mean?"

Laura: "Yeah."

Michael: "But I think that generally people experience what they experience, you know they are having an experience."

Laura: "Mmm-hmm."

Michael: "What you're doing as his mother, he couldn't ask for a better mother, or father, he really couldn't."

Now you know why I cried. Michael told me another touching story about a mother who lost her son to Leukemia, and came to have a session with them, and the little boy in spirit told his mom that she was going to have a baby girl. A few years later, she did have a little girl, a very psychic little girl, who talks to her brother in spirit and tells her mom what he's saying. Michael said she lost something, but she received a gift as well. I replied:

Laura: "I feel gifted and I try to be grateful every day. But, I think it is part of the grief process, and I've talked about this to other parents of children with autism. Even though you didn't lose your child, they are still alive, you still grieve over the life you thought they were going to have."

Michael: "Yeah, but you see, that's where pain comes from. When we have an expectation about the way it should be and when it doesn't happen, or it isn't that way, that's when we suffer. We are not just living in the moment, you see?"

Laura: "Yeah. And we all feel like we were victimized somehow, on some level. 'How did this happen to me?'"

Michael: "None of us are saints. In truth, nobody is innocent. That's really the truth, if you want to look at it that way. We all have karma that's why we are here. We are all working out our karmic pattern. We are all trying to get back to our pure, enlightened state. And there are only a handful of people on Earth that are in that pure state. The rest of us are trying to get there. And so there is this kind of conundrum really, that there is a part of you that riles against being victimized. I mean there is a part of me I can feel that kind of comes up sometimes, it's like, how dare these people destroy our world? Now I have to be concerned about this, now I have to be concerned about that. All of it, all of the fear and the frustration, all of it. Know what I mean?"

Laura: "Mmm-hmm."

Michael: "But the only place where I ever felt truly peaceful is when I step back from it all way, way deep inside and I don't feel any of that fear, any of it. None of it concerns me. In truth, nothing concerns you. You are a spirit."

Laura: "I know that, but I still have a job to do here."

Michael: "Look, you're doing your best, that's all that can be asked. There is nothing more that can be asked."

Laura: "I always feel like I'm not doing enough."

Michael: "Hee, hee."

Laura: "It's the pressure I put on myself."

Michael: "As my teacher said, love yourself. It took me a long time to figure out what he meant. Love yourself? What does he mean, love yourself?"

Laura: "What did you come up with?"

Michael: "Well, it's hard to love yourself. I think it's harder to love yourself than to love somebody else."

Laura: "Oh, yeah. We are our own worst critic."

Michael: "Oh, yeah. I think that sometimes you have to cut yourself a bit of slack. Just see that you're not perfect, that you're a work in progress. We can't see everything. We don't know so many things. I think that just trust and faith is sometimes all we have."

Laura: "Yeah."

Michael: "You know? I think that you're doing a great job, and that's the end of it."

Laura: "Well, thank you. I needed this tonight. I needed a pat on the back."

Michael: "I think you did, yeah, I think you did. And you know, you are doing something cool too. You are putting all of this energy into this book, and I appreciate that. Cuz I can't help you with it, so I kind of feel a little helpless and I feel bad because you're the only one that can do it."

Laura: "Well, I want to do it. I feel like I have to do it. I feel like I owe it to my child and all of these other children. This is something I can do. This is how I can contribute. And I am grateful to you and Marti for your role in all of this too. And I am just going to try my best to get it done and do it justice and help others. That's the most I can do."

Michael: "We have come up with a lot of people and facts, and details and stuff like that. But there is this deeply, deeply spiritual aspect to this whole thing too."

Laura: "Yeah."

Michael: "Some of that has to be covered probably too. Exactly what we were talking about tonight, like how people feel about it, all of it is super important. Because it's not just nuts and bolts, there are deep reasons for things."

Laura: "Yeah."

Michael: "I don't know what those people in Japan are thinking right now, you know what I mean? There are these people running these (nuclear) plants and stuff, and they probably think they have it all under control, and look what happens?"

Laura: "Mmm-hmm."

Michael: "Now what? What a mess. They don't know what to do. The ocean is getting polluted, the land is getting polluted. The trust level is starting to plummet. It's nuts. In a way, they're looking for someone to blame, they're trying to figure out why is this happening to us. All of these questions are arising, you know?"

Laura: "Yeah."

Michael: "Germany has cancelled the nuclear reactors. They haven't extended the lives of them, they're shutting them down."

Laura: "Good for them."

Michael: "Yeah, that's great. That's what needs to be done. Unfortunately, now they are getting 20% of their power from France, and of course France is mostly nuclear, but they are trying to go all green energy. They were trying to do it over a ten-year period, but now they've decided they're going to go sooner after having watched all this. It's too great a risk."

Laura: "Maybe that's part of this whole thing, is showing on a global scale what can happen."

Michael: "I don't know why it's happening in Japan, I feel sorry for them, I don't know why. Part of me thinks what other people in the world could handle it as good as them. You know what I mean?"

Laura: "Oh, yeah. Could you imagine if this happen in the United States?"

Michael: "Oh, my God, there would be riots. It would be Bedlam, wouldn't it?"

Laura: "Yeah."

Michael: "That's what I think. I just think thank God it didn't happen here. I don't know how they would handle it. It would be anarchy. Well I'm going to say good-night."

Laura: Well, thank you. This was like therapy for me tonight."

Michael: "Yeah, I didn't mind what they wanted to talk about; they didn't want to go into anything tonight. Maybe they will next time; they just seemed to want to talk about this."

Laura: "It was good, it was a message of hope about my son, which I really needed right now, so thank you very much."

***

Session Fourteen: After the Session
Featured Spirit: J. Robert Oppenheimer

This session was mostly my family members talking to Michael, so there wasn't a lot that I needed to look up after this session, but I did want to touch a bit more on some of the subjects that came up. It was nice to have a session where I was comforted in knowing that my loved ones in spirit are around me daily helping me with my son and with decision making on his behalf. It lets me know that my silent prayers for help to them are being answered. The same goes for all of you out there fighting for your children. You are not alone! Know this, and ask for help. I find that after I ask, I meet just the right people or read just the right article, find the perfect book, or someone just happens to mention something to me to help my son. That's how it happens. I notice the synchronicity and say thank you in my prayers.

Also, I wanted to talk a bit more about what Michael mentioned about karma, and about how things happen for a reason, and that there are no accidents. Regarding autism, I've had friends who also have children with autism discuss this subject with me and I've read many heated discussions about the idea of autism being a "gift." I've heard certain people say that children with autism are "crystal children" and are higher spiritual beings who are here to teach us lessons, and all that kind of stuff. Others are just stuck in anger and they don't want to hear any such nonsense.

Let me tell you first hand, autism is no gift. If it is, I'm re-gifting it. All kidding aside, here is my take on this. There certainly are personal lessons that I have learned as a result of having a child with autism, so some good has come out of it. I've become more compassionate, patient, determined, wiser, awakened, enlightened, and as a result, able to help others; all good things. On the other hand, I know my son was damaged and poisoned by many environmental factors that could have been prevented and can be prevented in others. I do not want to have other families go through what we have. It doesn't have to happen, but our thinking needs to change. We are so brainwashed and trustworthy as a society. We are lemmings, sheeple, by and large. The only gift of autism will be for us to wake up and change the way we have been doing things to our children and the planet because of what happened to all of our "autistic" children.

Here is my take on the spiritual component of this. Obviously I am a spiritual person, but also a practical one. I do believe that things happen for a reason. I believe that we choose many people in our lives before we incarnate, and that we have certain experiences to advance ourselves or to balance our karma. That being said, I also believe that that my son and I chose each other, that perhaps he had to experience something like this for his personal growth, and that I am supposed to be helping him. What is happening to these children is a warning to us all of what happens when we let our guards down, and trust profit-seeking entities to control our children's health and the planet. It is a wake up call. Because we are driven by love for our children, we the parents will be the change to provide a better world for them and for generations to come.

So, it is a bit of a double edged sword, really. On one hand, I'm pissed off, as many of us are, because our children are suffering, and our concerns often fall on deaf ears. Or worse, we are seen as the crazy ones because we question medical figures and the government. This is what got us all into this mess to begin with, blind faith and misguided trust. On the other hand, as Michael brought up, from a spiritual perspective, we don't know why all of this is happening, or who we all were in previous lifetimes to each other. I'm sure after we cross over ourselves, it will become clear. But for now, I trust that there is a reason that all of this is happening and why so many wonderful, loving, smart, articulate, courageous, revolutionaries are the parents of these beautiful children. I am privileged to call many of them friends.

Trust me, I know that the grief can sometimes swallow you up, especially anger, but if you can change your perspective and consider that perhaps we are jumping to the wrong conclusions for a moment. Consider that you and your child are not victims, but perhaps because of our experiences we are the way showers, the light workers if you will, and then your pain will not be as severe. Pain happens when your expectations are not being met. None of us planned for this when we decided to have children, but this is what we have been given. I didn't plan on being a young widow after I married Darren either. But, I have come to peace with it, and believe that it was his time to go. If you read *Widowed Too Soon,* you will see my long struggle with understanding this. We can make the world a better place, but sometimes it takes a severe contrast, the worst-case-scenarios, to see what can happen before change can come. Anger gets things done, and so does love.

For now, it is important to channel that anger and/or love in constructive ways, and to use our own gifts for the betterment of these children. We all have unique gifts that we can contribute in our own ways. It will take more than a village to raise these kids. Also, as Michael men-tioned, we as parents need to cut ourselves some slack. We are doing the best that we can under enormous stresses. I truly admire all of you parents who are out there in the trenches day after day. Just do your best, which is all that can be asked of you. That message was for all of us.

The last thing I want to mention here is that it is not just me, but all of us have spirit helpers. No one is alone in this journey, even though it feels like it a lot of the time. Other people don't understand our struggle, our grief, why we do what we do for our kids, we don't feel like anyone is helping them or us, we have other kids that need our attention, the list goes on and on. Just know that all you have to do is ask for help from spirit and it is there. Even if you can't see them or feel them or hear them (some of us can), they hear your prayers, they are helping to heal you and your child. Ask for signs, and be open to them. They may not be as obvious as you'd like, but subtle things speak volumes. A special song on the radio, a butterfly, dragonfly, or rainbow, or any special thing that you see that reminds you of a departed loved one lets you know that they are there. There are also very obvious signs too. Reach out, they are waiting. Trust me on this one.

**

Chapter Seventeen

*"Our scientific power has outrun our
spiritual power. We have guided
missiles and misguided men."*

— *Martin Luther King, Jr.*

Session Fifteen

This session was done on April 20, 2011. It was all three of us again this time. This turned out to be a very interesting session. It began with Michael saying he had someone there named John, and then asked me if there was a Joe Kennedy. I told him that John Kennedy's father is Joe Kennedy. I found out after the session that he also had a brother named Joe, who was also in spirit. Michael said that John and Joe were both there.

Then Michael asked me if I knew if there was someone named Luther who was connected to the Kennedy's. I said, "Maybe Martin Luther King." Michael and Marti both got excited because they were doing a session before mine, and someone named Martin popped in and they couldn't figure out who it was for that person. Marti reminded Michael that he thought it was Martin Luther King during the session, and now here he was again. Sometimes spirits do that, show up to an earlier session. It has happened to me before with them. Then Michael continued:

Michael: "What I did is I said, 'If this is you John, tell me something else.' And he said 'Luther.' And I was just feeling a shot."

Laura: "Yeah?"

Michael: "Ok, hold on. Maybe he is here."

Laura: "Wow."

(*Long pause*)

Michael: "Oh, I'm just going to say it. Ok, I wrote assassination attempt, you see? I didn't want to say it."

Laura: "Assassination attempt?"

Michael: "An attempt, yeah."

Laura: "On who?"

Michael: "On the President."

Laura: "On Obama?"

Michael: "That's why Martin Luther and John are both here." *(They were both assassinated.)*

Laura: "Oh, my gosh. You're going to freak out when I tell you this. The last book I did, that came through also, about Obama getting shot. This is the second time I have heard this."

Michael: "Well, I wouldn't have believed it, unless they just said it to me."

Laura: "I know. When you just said that, I went what? It's in my book if you read it."

(The other medium also brought up Obama getting shot during one of our sessions, which was before he was even elected as President.)

Michael: "I'm not sure if he's going to die, or if it can be thwarted. I don't know."

Laura: "Wow."

Michael: "I am trying to get a timeline from them, that's what I'm doing at the moment, I'm wondering if it's...cuz they put soon."

Laura: "Hmm."

Michael: "Oh, I also got Florida. So I don't know if the attempt may be in Florida, but I put Florida. What was going through my mind was who can I tell about this? I know one FBI agent."

Laura: "Mmm-hmm. Like they'd believe you anyway."

Michael: "I know. I'm asking him when? I reckon it is soon. I wonder if he's going to go to Florida."

I couldn't believe this was coming up again! It gave it more validity in my eyes. Next, Michael said that he was feeling something funny in his jaw and throat, and asked me if I knew if Martin Luther King was shot there. I said I didn't know. After he said it, the sensation stopped. I learned after the session that he was shot in the jaw. Then Michael said he was getting the name Fitzgerald. I told him that was JFK's middle name,

Fitzgerald. They were just giving him more validations that it was indeed them.

Before I continue with the rest of the session, I am going to explain what happened after the session regarding what just came up. Michael was so bothered by the information about Obama, that he contacted the FBI agent that he recently had a session with to see if he could do something to stop it. Michael and the FBI agent agreed to do a phone session on Wednesday, April 27th to see if he could get an exact time, date, and place, etc. The spirit people said something about the Kennedy Space Center and stated that the assassination would take place on Sunday, May 1st. The agent was true to his word, and passed on the information to a friend of his in the Secret Service, who in turn apparently passed it on to those who protect the President. Michael called me to tell me about the session with the FBI agent. He was hoping that the Secret Service would be able to thwart an attempt if they knew about it in advance. He couldn't sit back and do nothing. The Secret Service agent was so impressed with the details of the session (I haven't shared them all) that he said that Michael might be getting a visit by them.

Two days after this session, on April 29, 2011, President Obama went to the Kennedy Space Center in Cape Canaveral, Florida to witness the launch of the Space Shuttle Endeavour, and to meet Congresswoman Gabrielle Giffords, who was shot months earlier. The Endeavour was commanded by Gifford's husband, Mark Kelly. Interestingly, the shuttle launch was delayed, and President Obama went on to visit Tuscaloosa, Alabama, one of the cities hit hard by recent tornadoes. The deadly twisters killed 339 people and caused billions of dollars in damage. I called Michael after I heard the news that the President was in Florida at the Kennedy Space Center. I was hoping that nothing bad would happen. I was so relieved when I heard that the launch had been delayed and that Air Force One was in Alabama.

Two days later, on Sunday, May 1st, President Obama held a press conference where he announced that Osama bin Laden had been assassinated. After the announcement, I talked to Michael, who thought that because of the similarity of the names, Osama and Obama; perhaps he misunderstood or heard it wrong. It had something to do with an assassination and Obama. Or maybe it was two or three separate events. As Michael said, Obama did go to the Kennedy Space Center, and who's to say if attempt on Obama was or wasn't planned and/or stopped? It was just a bit too coincidental that the shuttle launch was delayed. As predicted, Obama's announcement of the assassination of Osama bin Laden was on the exact day mentioned in the session with the FBI agent. Maybe there will be another assassination attempt on Obama, and it just hasn't happened yet, who knows? I just felt this was too important to omit.

Ok, on with the rest of the session. The subject quickly changed to talking about my son. Michael had asked spirit to tell him something about him to make sure he was getting the other stuff right. He asked me if my son liked apples. I told him that he loved them and sometimes ate five in a row. Then Michael said that he was seeing a candle lit in my house. I told him that I just got the Autism Speaks Scentsy warmer candle, and I turned it on every day. A light bulb inside of it melts the wax, so there are no toxic fumes or metallic wick.

Next, Michael asked me if I knew anyone called Gary. I laughed and told him that this came up last time, and that it was my other son's nickname. He said that my husband that died in the car accident was bringing it up and thought it was funny. Then he said that walnuts would be good for my son, and that they are shaped like a brain for a reason, they are good for the brain. This is true; I read that the Omega 3 fatty acids in walnuts buffer the brain from the harmful effects of sugar. Then Michael said that "Gary" just had the flu, and is doing better now. He was sick for two weeks, so I finally took him to his doctor and they tested him for strep, which was negative, and for influenza, which is what he had. He recovered quickly with a homeopathic remedy and Chinese herbs.

This next part was so funny to me I was laughing so hard, I was crying. Michael says to me:

Michael: "You know your husband that's deceased. Is he funny?"

Laura: "Very funny."

Michael: "Does he ever do a weird dance?"

Laura: "Yeah, we used to have dance contests to see who could do the dumbest dance, the craziest dance."

Michael: "He's doing this silly, weird dance in front of me."

Laura: "Yeah. Ha, ha, ha."

Michael: "I'm like, what are you doing? It's like something out of the 20's mixed in with God knows what, I said to him. It's the strangest looking dance I ever saw and he's laughing. 'That's just how I dance,' he says."

Laura: "That's what we used to do and then we'd take pictures of the other one doing their stupid dance."

Michael: "But he's pulling faces too."

Laura: "Yeah. Ha, ha. That's hilarious."

Michael: "You know like how you run on the spot, your hands go up and down and your arms go up and down and then he's doing the splits."

Laura: "Yeah, ha, ha."

Michael: "Just bazaar stuff he's doing in front of me, just wacky looking."

Laura: "Yeah, oh, that's funny."

Michael: "That's pretty funny. Now he's having a beer. He says, 'Hey, member?' like that."

Laura: "Yeah, I remember. That is funny."

(There was no way Michael could have known about this inside joke between the two of us. We would play loud music, and take turns dancing, and made it into a contest to see who could come up with the silliest dance moves, and we took pictures of each other doing it. I have pictures of us that are too embarrassing to show. In some of the pictures, he's making funny faces, and sticking out his tongue.)

Michael: "Now he's saying 'Dave.'"

Laura: "Oh, my God. That's his friend who was driving the car when he died in the accident. I just talked to Dave yesterday."

Michael: "Oh, ok. He said, 'Say Dave.'"

Laura: "Oh, my God. Actually, he Facebook messaged me and said 'I had a dream about you last night that I called you,' and I said back, 'You should call me then.' We are playing phone tag now. Yeah, Dave."

Michael: "Tell Dave he says 'Hi.' Ok?"

Laura: "Alright. He's supposed to call me next. Oh, my God, that's awesome."

Michael: "Is Martin Luther in the room here with me? Are they here? Am I correct about this? Is this true? I think he just said, 'Fraid so.'"

(He was asking Darren if it was Martin Luther King and if he was correct about Obama getting shot. Darren replied, "Fraid so.")

Laura: "Oh."

Michael: "I reckon we are right here."

Laura: "Yep."

Michael: "Huh. Do you know anyone called Jimbo or J.B.?"

Laura: "J.B. There is a guy in the autism community called J.B., he's a writer and he's..."

Michael: "He says it's J.B. J.B he says. What does he do?"

Laura: "He's a writer and he has a son with autism and he's part of Generation Rescue."

Michael: "Oh, have you met him?"

Laura: "No, I've never met him but I really like his work. I was just reading an article written by him the other day."

Michael: "Your husband is talking about him. He must have been looking in."

Laura: "Yeah, his name is J.B. Handley."

Michael: "'I was,' he says. J.B. Handley? Oh, I heard the name Handley."

Laura: "Oh, really?"

Michael: "Yeah, I'm sure I heard him say that earlier on but I had no idea who that was. J.B., he says he's a good guy."

Laura: "He's very smart and a really good writer. He exposes the truth. Maybe I'll meet him someday. I admire his writing and work."

(Again, another example of something Michael could not have known. It was comforting to know that Darren was looking in on me. It was really interesting to me how he got Michael to say an odd name like J. B. to get me to know that he was aware of what I was reading, who wrote it, and that he also knew about J.B. himself. I am truly in awe of how

involved spirit is in our lives.)

Michael: "So your husband…the other guy survived the accident?"

Laura: "Yeah, he was driving and walked away."

Michael: "Yeah, he survived. Had he been drinking?"

Laura: "Yeah, Dave was drinking."

Michael: "Yeah, that's it. Cuz I said why did you say something about beer? He said Dave was drinking."

Laura: "Oh, yeah."

Michael: "Was your husband?"

Laura: "His blood alcohol was zero." (Dave said that Darren had a few beers, but the toxicology report said that Darren's blood alcohol content was zero.)

Michael: "Oh, really?"

Laura: "Yeah, he didn't drink much when he went out. He'd get migraine headaches from drinking a lot. He let people drive his car all the time, and he gave his friend the keys and said 'You drive,' even though he knew he was drinking."

Michael: "Oh, I see. I got ya."

Laura: "And Dave fell asleep at the wheel pretty much. Flipped the car, it landed on Darren's side."

Michael: "It was a pretty new car too."

Laura: "Yeah, he just got it."

Michael: "He said, 'It's my new car too.'"

Laura: "Uh-huh."

Michael: "'Oh well, live and learn,' he said. He's pretty dry. A very dry sense of humor, very droll."

Laura: "Yeah."

Michael: "And could he say things with a straight face?"

Laura: "He'd try but then he'd laugh."

Michael: "He wasn't very good at that then?"

Laura: "No."

(Here were more details about the accident that were accurate, as well as Darren's personality.)

Next, Michael described in detail what was going on at our house the night before, proving to me that Darren was there checking in on us. He joked about there being a fire by me, and I told him that the night before, Matt lit the chiminea on the deck, and left a piece of wood hanging out, and embers were falling on the deck, leaving burn marks. My brother-in-law and I were frantically trying to scoop up the embers before we had a fire on our hands. Michael said that Darren showed himself taking out a lighter, lighting something on fire, and dropping it on the ground in front of him.

Then, Michael accurately said that this happened about 7 o'clock, and that I was playing music in the house. He also said that I watered a long-leafed plant. I told him that I moved it and then watered it because it looked like it was dying, and yes, it was a long-leafed plant. Then, Michael said, "He's showing me a Valentine's Day card, I said "What's that for?" He said, "Well, I went around Valentine's Day. He's showing me a heart. He also wants to let you know that he loves you." I told him that he died on February 11, and his wake was on Valentine's Day. I thought I'd never celebrate Valentine's Day again after that.

Then Michael said something about sharpening our knives, and I told him that all of our knives are dull, and we keep talking about needing to sharpen them. Then Michael said he was smelling pine, and asked if we had owls out here. I told him that last night, we had a big Great Horned Owl in the pine tree on the side of the house. Damon came running in the house to tell me, but it flew away before I got there. There is no way Michael could have known that. These are the little things that let me know that that information could have only come from Darren.

This next part was so crazy to me. Michael was talking about a lake and about fishing. At first, I thought he meant the small lake behind our house, where we often fish. Then he asked me if there was any UFO activity up here recently. He said that it was North of where I live and that there were hills around it, and he saw a flash, which reminded him of the time he saw a UFO. I told him that my brother-in-law told me a story about this guy named Kenny that he met fishing at Pyramid Lake (where the depleted uranium is), who told him that he saw a UFO come out of Pyramid Lake, and that it was so bright that he couldn't look at it, it was like an arc welder's light. (Marti had recently drawn a picture of an arc welder.) The UFO came out of the water, and zipped away and disappeared. Michael validated that the story was true.

I asked Michael if there was an undersea UFO base there. Michael said that he was seeing a narrow canal, like a tunnel, so maybe there was. I told Michael that Kenny also told my brother-in-law that there is a cave at Pyramid Lake that has carved pictures that looks like space people with long fingers, and the surface that covers the drawings is like glass. It's like the rocks were melted or something. I had recently seen an episode of UFO hunters, in which they talked about other places similar to this in which the rocks were melted like glass, and suggested alien influence because of the temperature required to melt the rocks in that manner.

My brother-in-law and I were actually just talking about this subject while we were sitting around the chiminea the night before. I also told him that I wanted him to get me a water and soil sample from the lake to test it for depleted uranium during our next BioSET session. Michael mentioned that the lake was very alkaline, which is true. For him to mention all of this, shows me that this information was coming from spirit. These were all things that happened or were discussed the night before at my house. Michael was not there, and could not have known these things.

My dad came in next to say "hello" and started talking about tornadoes. I told Michael that there was just a string of tornadoes that hit many states including North Carolina, where my dad used to live. I was just talking to my sister about this and asked her if she had checked in with my dad's girlfriend. She said no. Michael then said my dad's girlfriend's name, which I hadn't mentioned. Michael said that there was some concern about a nuclear power plant and a tornado. Evidently, after the tornadoes hit the south, the power was knocked out at the second biggest nuclear power plant, the Brown's Ferry facility in Alabama. It went into automatic shut down, avoiding a nuclear disaster.

Michael asked me if my dad was a weatherman or something, because he was talking about the upcoming hurricanes. I laughed and said, no, but we always joked about it because my dad loved to talk about the weather. He asked Michael to get out his map and showed him where the hurricanes were going to be hitting this hurricane season in Alabama, Florida and Texas. One year, my dad got hit by 3 hurricanes in North Carolina in one season. He had a lot of water damage, and had to replace flooring and other things. So, this was a subject near and dear to his heart.

Then Michael said that my dad was a history buff, and liked World War II shows, as well as Wild West stuff. This was true. I remember when I was a child; my dad would watch those old black and white War shows and Westerns. Then he said, "And did he have a tip of the whiskey now and then?" I laughed and said, "Yes." Michael said that my dad produced a decanter of whiskey, and poured himself some and drank it straight, and he said, "Honey, it's an acquired taste." I laughed again, because after his memorial, we went to my cousin's bar in Wisconsin, where a bunch of us all did a shot of Jack Daniels in honor of my dad because he was known to drink whiskey. It was so disgusting to me, but I did it for him. Blah. Again, Michael could not have known about this stuff.

After this, Michael said that there was someone named Henry there. Then he said the name Thoreau. Henry Thoreau. I told Michael that there was an author named Henry David Thoreau. It was my dad who was mentioning him. Michael said that maybe he's written a book about something we'd be interested in.

Here are the pictures that Marti drew. She wasn't quite sure what they meant at the time, but felt that they had something to do with the assassinnation attempt.

Session Fifteen: After the Session

Featured Spirits: John F. Kennedy, Jr., Martin Luther King, Jr., Joe Kennedy, Henry David Thoreau

After the session, I looked up Henry David Thoreau, and learned that his philosophies of Civil Disobedience and Nonviolent Resistance in-fluenced Martin Luther King, Jr. and his writings also influenced JFK. In his Autobiography, Martin Luther King said of Thoreau's work: "As a result of his writings and personal witness, we are the heirs of a legacy of creative protest." Thoreau stood up for what was right, and went to prison in 1846 for refusing to pay the poll tax in protest of the American War on Mexico. Maybe this is telling us that we need to start asserting a bit of our own Civil Disobedience. The government works for us, not the other way around.

I remembered reading Thoreau's book *Walden* in English Literature in College. I didn't make the connection until months later, but hanging in my laundry room, I have a plaque that I've had for years with the quote *"Happiness is like a butterfly: The more you chase it, the more it will elude you. But if you turn your attention to other things it will come and sit softly on your shoulder…"* Thoreau.

I think that the most interesting part of this session was the prediction of a future event in the same session as very personal things from my loved ones. It was direct evidence that I could validate instantly, which allows your mind to make the leap of thinking that if these things are true, then it is very possible that this other information is also true.

***

Chapter Eighteen

"Mankind must put an end to war, or
war will put an end to mankind."

— John F. Kennedy

Session Sixteen

We didn't have a session together during the month of May. They did however come to Virginia City, NV, for a Ghost Hunting adventure and a gallery session. The gallery session is a group session where Michael brings through spirits and determines who they are there to see, and Marti draws pictures and does the same. I went to the gallery session, and brought a friend of mine, whose boyfriend passed away a few weeks prior. I was so happy to see them, and just so grateful for all they had done for the project. I laughed when I saw Michael because he was wearing a t-shirt with a picture of Albert Einstein on it, and underneath his face it said, "I see dumb people." It was a reference to the movie "The Sixth Sense" where the psychic boy says "I see dead people." He said he bought it years ago after Albert showed up during the session with the young man who asked Albert to come and answer some questions.

During the gallery session, my friend was one of the people who got a reading. Her boyfriend came through, as well as her mom. One of the most validating things for her was that Michael said, "Your mom is telling me her name is Bob. Now I wouldn't normally say a woman is named Bob, but that's what she's telling me." My friend told Michael that her name is Roberta, and they called her Bob for short. My friend was so grateful to them, and it helped her heal her grief and mend the relationship with her late mother.

We had Michael and Marti over for dinner one of the nights they were in town. We had a non-GMO organic meal. I think we were all a bit freaked out from our sessions about GMO's. It is hard to find places to eat that have organic food, so we decided to cook instead of go out to eat. This was the first time they got to meet Trevor. They probably felt like they already knew him. They got to see firsthand what life was like at our house. Trevor stayed in his room most of the time watching TV, except when we ate dinner, he made an appearance. He was doing some of his verbal stimming, and laughing with his brother, and repeating the same thing over and over.

We had a really nice visit, and Michael and Matt got along well. Damon was showing Marti all of his artwork, and she was impressed with his abilities. He's a very good artist, and has been drawing most of his young life. I showed them the swing in our backyard that looked identical to the one Marti drew, and pictures of Darren and I doing our crazy dances. It was nice to see them again in person. We had talked on the phone so much, but I hadn't seen them in eight months. Our joint project had blossomed into friendships as well.

After they went back home and things settled down, we decided to do another phone session on June 2, 2011. It was the trifecta again, Michael, Marti and I. The first thing Michael said was that there was someone there named John Hunter, and he kept hearing "Sir", so maybe a Sir John Hunter. Then he said that he was showing him the central part of the brain that looks like a horseshoe shape that separates the two hemispheres.

Then Michael said "They're talking about Warren, like a report or something." I said, "The Warren Report was to do with Kennedy, and the Warren Commission. Michael said, "You're right, and then they were talking about something being re-opened. He said that he was seeing John in the car, and felt like he was in the hotel where his brother Bobby was shot. He felt that they were both in the room. Then he said, "You know whose case I think they're going to re-open? Bobby."

Next, he asked me if I knew if John had any type of brain disorder. I told him that I've seen his name on lists of famous people with ADD/ADHD. He said that there was also someone named William there.

(After the session, I found that Sir John Hunter was a Scottish surgeon, specializing in obstetrics, and his brother William, was also an anatomist and physician. There is a Hunterian Museum and Art gallery in Glasgow, Scotland, and Sir John Hunter founded a museum in London. Michael felt that this was the guy who had been assisting him with medical diagnosis during healing sessions for many years, but he never knew his name.

I also found an article after the session about Sirhan Sirhan, who was charged with Bobby Kennedy's assassination. The article was from the Associated Press was called "Assassin Maintains He Can't Remember Shooting RFK." The article suggests that

Sirhan was "hypno-programmed," turning him into a virtual "Manchurian Candidate." Sirhan's attorney claimed that thirteen shots were fired; while Sirhan's gun only held eight bullets and that the fatal shot appeared to come from behind Kennedy while Sirhan faced him. Then a few months later, another article came out with a witness saying the same thing, that there were more than eight shots fired, and that the authorities who interviewed her changed her story. They also found an audio tape of the shooting, and experts analyzed it and agreed that there were way more than eight shots fired. So, maybe Michael was right, the case will be re-opened.)

Then, Michael said that Albert was in the room, and that he was saying "Hello" to me. I said "Hello" back. He said that he was there with some of his friends. Michael said that there was a new person there, a brain specialist. Michael says:

Michael: "Ah, this is weird. I'm hearing this noise, it goes from low to high pitch over and over, it's like an oscillating sound. And it sounds like an oscillating sound when they make me think of the central part of my brain, it's really weird. I keep seeing an oscillator on a scope."

Are there any heart functions that are affected in a certain way in kids with autism?

Laura: "Yeah, I think so, in certain kids. Electrical problems, the heart and brain are connected that way."

Michael: "There is some sort of hiccups in the heart or it just doesn't function properly. It's something to do with like a frequency, and now what they are showing me is the heart rate. And I said, so you're saying that this is effecting the heart, are you? And they said "yes." And they keep highlighting this horseshoe-shaped part of the brain. I don't know if I'd call it a gland, but it's like a gland. It's not the pituitary or the pineal. It seems to be a governor for the emotions. Like a gateway for the emotions, your emotional translation."

Laura: "Ok."

Michael: "Disrupted. It doesn't allow the logical side to process the emotional input. The logical side cannot integrate the emotions is the best way I can put it."

Laura: "Ok."

Michael: "What I hear is 'um, going.' And that had something to do with listening or not listening."

Laura: "Ok. A lot of them appear to be deaf and they have a lot of auditory processing problems."

Michael: "What about Trevor, does he?"

Laura: "Oh, yeah. His hearing is supposedly fine, but he's not processing sound properly."

(We've actually done Auditory Integration Therapy for his auditory processing disorder on three separate occasions. It was definitely helpful, but he still covers his ears when there are loud noises or when he anticipates loud noises.)

Michael: "Like right inside, deep inside. It seems to be this also is connected, see. They can't hear."

Laura: "Ok."

Michael: "Does Trevor not look down much? Like down to the right?"

Laura: "Huh, I don't know. I never noticed."

Michael: "They're talking about where the kids look. Is what you spoke about before, whoever it was, about the Y chromosomes, is that relevant? He said "Yes, in development." So the thing with the Y chromosomes, it's very important in their development. What is the other chromosome?"

Laura: "X. Girls get two X's and boys get a Y and an X."

Michael: "Well, is the X missing?"

Laura: "No, having the Y means that they are a male."

(Marti says, "It's like the Y is missing a leg.")

Michael: "Well, are there two Y's?"

Laura: "No. There are two X's in a female, an X and a Y in a male."

Michael: "No, you're not getting what I'm saying. With autism. I don't know why I'm seeing this. I'm not seeing the X; I'm seeing two Y's."

(An X missing a leg would look like a Y, so you'd have YY, not XY.)

Laura: "Hmm. I have no idea."

Michael: "Am I right, Albert? Have I got this right?"

(Interestingly, after the session, I learned that because females have two X chromosomes,

331

if there are problems with one of the X's there is another copy to back it up. If males have a problem or mutation with either their X or their Y chromosome, there is no backup copy. It has been speculated that the reason autism is more prominent in boys is because of a mutation on the X chromosome, where boys don't have a back up copy.)

Michael: "Is there anyone called Arthur immediate to Albert."

Laura: "I'm not sure."

(Arthur Eddington, a friend of Einstein, has come through in past sessions.)

Michael: "Arthur. Curious, I've got this YY thing. I got this sense that one bit of the chromosome was being interfered with, like it was almost being attacked. I know that sounds weird, huh?"

Laura: "I'll have to look back and see what they said about the Y chromosome last time; because I remember there was something about that too."

Michael: "They're bringing this up. I can't remember what they said last time, but there is something about something being attacked, see? Like it's targeting one bit of it."

Laura: "Ok."

Michael: "Oh, now they're putting back in my head something to do with, I don't know if it has to do with sperm? What does it have to do with that? You know what it felt like? I felt like I was in the glandular system basically."

Laura: "Ok."

Michael: "Sir Arthur Conan Doyle is the science fiction writer, right?"

(He and Marti talk about who he is, they both thought of him when the name Arthur came up.)

Laura: "I thought of Arthur Eddington. I think it was Sir Arthur Eddington, actually. He was another scientist, a friend of his."

Michael: "Was he? A friend of…"

Laura: "Einstein's, yeah. Cuz the name Arthur had come up before, and he was the only Arthur that I could find that was associated with him."

Michael: "Oh, interesting. Eddington."

Laura: "Sir Arthur Eddington."

Michael: "Sir Arthur Eddington. I did think of a friend of Albert's too, and I was wondering if he knew Arthur Conan Doyle. Isn't that weird?"

Laura: "Uh-huh.

Michael: And we both thought of Arthur Conan Doyle. But I was thinking that Arthur was a friend of Albert's. So, maybe there are two Arthur's?"

Laura: "Maybe."

(I didn't know who Arthur Conan Doyle was until after the session. He wrote the Sherlock Holmes book series. Interestingly, he was a huge proponent of Spiritualism and mediumship, and even wrote a few books on Spiritualism. I was trying to find out if Albert knew Arthur Conan Doyle, and I found that one of the actors who played Sherlock Holmes, William Gillette, was good friends with Arthur Conan Doyle, and owned a castle, which Albert Einstein took a tour of, so perhaps they did know each other as Michael suggested. I found that not only was John Hunter a "Sir," but both Arthur's were also "Sir Arthur." See why this gets confusing?)

Laura: "The Eddington guy, he helped prove his Theory of Relativity, the light bending thing. He traveled and took photographs of the eclipse and stuff like that."

Michael: "Oh, ok."

Laura: "Maybe he'll tell us who he is."

Michael: "Was there any work done on lasers that came from Arthur's work?"

Laura: "I'm not sure."

Michael: "Sounds like laser. I can hardly hear you. Is this who we think it is? It is. Cuz there is still Arthur Conan Doyle as well. Hmm, I don't know what the significance of this is, it sounds crazy, but I'm seeing meteorites."

Laura: "Sir Arthur Eddington worked in an observatory, he was a scientist."

(He was an astrophysicist and worked at and directed numerous observatories.)

Michael: "Oh was he? Oh, thank God!"

Laura: "Ha, ha, ha."

Michael: "I thought he was showing me meteorites were going to hit the Earth."

Laura: "He looked at the stars and took pictures of the moon and the sun and the stars, that's what he did, the kind of scientist he was."

Michael: "I was looking for a validation from them, and they said Arthur is talking to you. And I said I don't know which Arthur, I'd really like a bit of validation. I'm not sure who's talking to me. Can you tell me something maybe she'll know or that I don't know. And all of the sudden I'm looking into space and they are showing me meteorites."

Laura: "Oh. That's why he took the pictures from the observatory."

Michael: "What?"

Laura: "Eddington took the photos of an eclipse from an observatory to prove Einstein's theory of the light bending."

Michael: "Oh, cuz you didn't say where he took the pictures. So that's good, that's good. You didn't say anything about pictures of space.

Laura: "No."

Michael: "You just said took pictures and I had no idea what you were talking about. Oh, well there you go, there you go. Alright. Yeah!"

Laura: "Ok, that's good."

Michael: "Yeah, I was kind of lost in thought there for a second watching these meteorites and a planetary body and I'm thinking, why am I seeing this? You're not telling me this is going to happen next year or anything, are you? And they were silent on it. So I didn't know what it meant."

(Actually, I was mistaken on where the pictures of the solar eclipse that proved Einstein's Theory of Relativity were taken. Although Eddington worked at different observatories, including the Royal Greenwich Observatory and Cambridge Observatory, he traveled to an island off of Africa and to Brazil to observe and photograph a solar eclipse in 1919. During the eclipse, he took pictures of the stars in the region around the Sun. According to the theory of general relativity, stars with light rays that passed near the Sun would appear to have been slightly shifted because their light had been curved by its gravitational field. This effect is noticeable only during eclipses, since otherwise the Sun's brightness obscures the affected stars. Eddington confirmed Einstein's theory and wrote a number of articles which announced and explained Einstein's theory of general relativity to the English-speaking world.)

Michael: "This may be lasers, some sort of laser, something to do with lasers he's going on about."

(After the session, I learned that the Laser Astrometric Test of Relativity or LATOR, would look at how the sun's gravity deflects beams of laser light emitted by two mini satellites. Gravity bends the path of light because it warps the space through which the light is passing. It was by measuring the bending of starlight by the sun during a solar eclipse in 1919 that Sir Arthur Eddington first tested Einstein's Theory of General Relativity. LATOR would measure this deflection with a billion times the precision of Eddington's equipment.)

Michael: "Pieces of a puzzle, huh? This doesn't make any sense to me, but what I'm getting right now is like something to do with an uneven distribution of water molecules in the brain."

Laura: "Oh."

Michael: (To Marti: "Have you just drawn a molecule?" She says. "Yes." They laugh.) "How weird." (She says it started out differently from that.) Yeah, it's a molecule, she's drawn a molecule. Holy cow!"

Laura: "Oh, my gosh."

Michael: "That's what I just got. But it doesn't make any sense to me, ok?"

Laura: "Ok."

Michael: "An uneven, that's what they said. You know, perhaps this is tied into the military, because most military are men. If you want to debilitate the enemy, you would target men with the virus."

Laura: "Right."

Michael: "Do autistic people have kids, and what happens when they do?"

Laura: "Well, none of them are old enough to have kids yet. The ones that are…"

Michael: "Of course, we don't know yet."

Laura: "There is a different type of autism, which was autism before, which isn't what we are talking about now."

Michael: "It's a different kind of thing. I was wondering about reproductive organs, like how they are affected, that's what I was wondering."

Laura: "Good question."

(Marti says "Sterility.")

Michael: "Sterility, yeah. That's what's been going on in the back of my mind. But when I asked them about your husband, or anyone else who is the father, I didn't really get that was it. So perhaps they are talking about the children themselves."

Laura: "Becoming sterilized."

Michael: "The males, are they sterile? That's what I've been wondering. That's what's going on in my head at the moment you see. Just need to find out, huh?"

Laura: "Yeah, well they link a lot of this stuff to sterility, like GMO food for example causes sterility in animals."

Michael: "Oh, does it?"

Laura: "Oh, yeah."

Michael: "Well maybe the male organ, the testes are a gland and they have a regulatory capacity to the body, so they've been talking about the glandular system in particular. So maybe what this is targets the glands, which would make sense. So, I think we are on the right track here, I think it's affecting the glandular system, which is regulating, you know, I think this is what it is."

Laura: "Ok, I know they've mentioned the T4 and the thyroid before, so I know that's affected."

Michael: "Oh, did they?"

Laura: "Yeah, they specifically brought up…"

Michael: "I don't remember any of it. But this is what they're talking about ok?"

Laura: "Ok."

Michael: "When I say talking, basically what I'm doing right now is I'm just being receptive and they are just sticking this stuff in my head. It's just easier than listening word for word, so they are just showing me."

Laura: "Ok."

Michael: "Does he ever break out in his feet? Or does he have any foot problems?" (To Marti: What are you laughing about? She says "You're saying everything I just drew. I just drew a bandaged foot." He says, "Oh, how weird. She's drawn a foot bandaged up.")

Laura: "Yes, he used to get cracks between his toes."

Michael: "That's it, cracked feet. I was looking at my feet and I was thinking, well they're not cracked. I was seeing my feet cracked or fissured."

Laura: "Yeah, in between his big toe and his second toe. He had big cracks there for a long time."

Michael: "Oh, interesting. Well, Marti has bandaged the front of the foot."

Laura: "Oh, my gosh. What is that from?"

Michael: "I don't know. Interesting isn't it?"

(To Marti – Discussing her drawings. "And this is an iceberg?" She says "Yes." He says, "And that's the water." She says, "What water? I didn't hear" He says, "Well, water, you've drawn icebergs and water, and I said water molecules. She says, "Cuz I started off thinking it was water molecules like one with hydrogen and oxygen and then another molecule, something else attached." He says, "There is another molecule, something else attached to it exactly. That's what I've been thinking all along. Something that is attached. We call it a virus, but I'm not sure it's, it could be this genetically altered virus, it's something that's attaching and it's messing." Marti says, "So I started drawing a person, and then I turned it upside down, and said that's a molecule, so that's when I drew that." He says, "And that's when you drew the molecule. Alright, so we're getting somewhere here." She says, "You know why I turned it upside down too, is that you were talking about the left brain and the right brain, and to me all I think about is that book *Thinking out of the Right Side of the Brain* and you draw and you turn it upside down." He says, "Right, I see. We're getting out of the box there. I get it. What is this Marti?" She says, "That's when I was drawing the X's and Y's and it was strange." He says, "I find that interesting, because that looks scrambled. That looks like an interfered frequency." She says, "I was joining the X's." He says, "Yeah, I know, but to me that looks like an interfered frequency, and I find it interesting that you stuck that right there. You see, I saw the water molecules looked different to me. They seemed different in the construct of the water molecule.")

Laura: "Ok."

Michael: "So, I think we talked about water before didn't we? When you think that we are mostly water, you know whatever affects the water."

Laura: "And the brain is like 90% water."

Michael: "Yeah, there you go, you see?"

Laura: "That is why we have been using alkaline water, the Kangen water machine, to help heal his brain."

Michael: "Maybe that's why the chamber is helping so much too."

Laura: "Yep."

Marti talks a bit more about the other drawings, which I will describe at the end of the session. Then Michael starts talking about Trevor playing soccer again. He said the spirit people were making him think about it again, and how much coordination it takes to kick a ball back and forth and the whole team effort takes so much coordination. There had to be a reason they were brining this up, Michael said. Then Michael said:

Michael: "Obviously whatever this is, is singling out males. How interesting. What's a pathogen?"

Laura: "Bacteria or viruses are considered pathogens."

(Dictionary definition: any disease-producing agent, especially a virus, bacterium, or other microorganism.

Michael: "Well they are saying pathogens. So then it must be a virus. It is definitely this."

Laura: "Ok."

Michael: "And it seems to be targeting, because I'm thinking about why just the boys? And they said it's a pathogen."

Laura: "Is it genetically modified to target just the males?"

Michael: "It may be, I don't know. It's a pathogen, I know that. Skull? Skull? Is that what it is? Oh, a pathogen in the skull, got it."

Laura: "Oh."

Michael: "Cuz it sounded like skull, and I've written it under pathogen. So it must be skull, pathogen in the skull. I think we are right with this virus. I think it's a virus, I think it's a pathogen."

Laura: "Uh-huh."

(Genetic engineering can be used to manipulate a bioweapon to target a specific population, for example boys, who would mainly be the ones fighting in a war. This theory could help explain the higher prevalence of boys vs. girls with regressive autism.)

Michael: "I've been asking them to can we please narrow it down, so we know for sure. That's what I've been asking them. Like, what is it that she needs to know, because I'm kind of worn out doing all of this. I think we're on the right track with a lot of this, aren't we? And they said yeah. And I said, well, is there anything that she wants to know so that we can nail it down, and this is what I've been getting."

Laura: "Ok."

Michael: "Did you ask them anything like this? Was this one of the questions that you were going to ask them?"

Laura: "Yeah, to be more specific."

Michael: "Did you want to know if this is a virus?"

Laura: "Yes, and I want to know where it's coming from."

Michael: "Oh, where it's coming from, I don't know. You mean where it originates?"

Laura: "Yeah, how are they getting it? How are they acquiring it?"

Michael: "I still feel there is a military component to this. I was feeling that while we were doing it."

Laura: "So then it would have to be biological warfare if it's a virus."

Michael: "Well, they're saying "An experiment, an experiment." You know, we get experimented on all the time by these assholes."

Laura: "Yeah."

Michael: "I'm sure it's some form of experiment."

We started talking about the pictures that Marti drew here, so I am going to show it, and then add the rest of our dialogue after that.

Doodle Explanations: Some of these doodles were described earlier in the session, for instance the molecule was discussed when Michael was talking about water molecules in the brain being different, that something was attached to it. I found it interesting how they both got this at the same time. Also, as I previously mentioned, they both came up with the cracks between the toes at the same time. Michael was talking about cracks or fissures between the toes, which often indicates fungus, and Marti drew a bandaged foot. The iceberg, she felt, meant that this is the tip of the iceberg. There is a whole lot more beneath the surface that we can't see. The woman who does our Quantum Biofeedback sessions lives in Lancaster, CA, so I understood that one. As mentioned earlier, the squiggle mark is when Marti started drawing the X and Y chromosomes, and then it became messed up and scrambled. Michael felt that it was a distorted frequency.

The other doodles are discussed below. First we were talking about what the dolphin meant. I said:

Laura: "I know a lot of kids with autism swim with dolphins because they can communicate with them telepathically."

Michael: "Does it make any difference?"

Laura: "Yeah, a lot of people report very calming effects on their children when they are in the water with dolphins."

Michael: "Has Trevor ever done it?"

Laura: "No, but I've always wanted to have him do that."

Michael: "So maybe he will benefit from it."

Laura: "Yeah, it's a therapy that parents do, have their child swim with dolphins."

Next, we started talking about what the child wearing the hat meant. Marti said she felt that it was a French beret, with a feather in it, Medieval almost. Michael said:

Michael: "Makes me think of the plague."

(Marti says, "I thought of that too.")

Michael: "Ha, that's what I'm thinking of, the Black Death, like the plague. Oh, how interesting, ok, alright. Well this is very hard stuff to do, so however we get there, we get there, you understand?

Laura: "Uh-huh."

Michael: "So maybe what they're doing is showing a link to Trevor, as kind of portrayed in this picture and the plague. When you think about it, and this is very deep stuff. But, there has to be karmic consequences for everything."

Laura: "Right."

Michael: "Now, people used to cause the plague in war, it was used as warfare. They'd throw bodies with catapults into cities, and stuff like that and cause the population to die of the plague. It was used as a weapon, way, way back. For thousands of years disease has been used as a weapon."

Laura: "Right."

Michael: "I don't know, but wouldn't it be interesting if you could know. Maybe Trevor at one point, who knows, maybe he was involved in that in some way, you know? Karmically, I'm talking. Maybe this is the consequence. Interesting, huh?"

Laura: "Mmm-hmm."

Michael: "But you know we all suffer the consequences of what we've done before."

Laura: "Right."

Michael: "But not always does it come back, you know, sometimes there are different karmic consequences for something you do. So if you do something that causes someone to die in a particular way, doesn't mean that you're going to die in exactly the same way. And yet, the underlying cause may be similar. See what I mean?"

Laura: "Mmm-hmm."

Michael: "If you are riding a horse and you kill someone, you trample them; maybe you'll be run over by a car."

Laura: "Yeah, in another life."

Michael: "You see? Or suffer the same damage to the same part of your body as was caused, you know. You see what I mean?"

Laura: "Yeah."

Michael: "I find that interesting."

Laura: "Yeah."

Michael: "That's all hypothetical. I just find that interesting. There has to be some, none of us are innocent. There is a reason for this. He's suffering this condition for a reason."

Laura: "Yeah."

Michael: "He's obviously trying to work through something. So, perhaps she's drawn him, for all we know, he could be, there is some link for this, and a reason Marti and I both got the plague. I find that very interesting, because they still don't have a cure for that, you know. We don't know what they've been messing around with."

Laura: "Well, the plague is Yersenia pestis, the bacteria that causes the plague, and it's still around. Even in the Sierra Nevada mountain range, some of the rodents carry it."

Michael: "Really?"

Laura: "Yeah, and I'm pretty sure that Trevor tested positive for it when we did muscle testing for all the pathogens. I remember Yersenia pestis, which is plague. I should look that up."

Michael: "Well, he can't possibly test positive for all of them, what did he test positive for?"

Laura: "Well, that he's been exposed to it. Maybe not that he's showing the symptoms."

Michael: "Has he tested positive for exposure any others?"

Laura: "Oh, yeah. I have a whole list of them."

Michael: "Well, that doesn't make any sense. Logically it doesn't make any sense."

Laura: "Well, when I ask about it, and it's been a couple different practitioners, they say it's in the air. It's biological warfare varieties. The wind blows it all over the world. If different countries are using it or experimenting with it…"

Michael: "I see what you're saying, yeah. It's like the Fukushima thing, nobody is talking about how bad it is, they just keep quiet about it, yet it's worse than Chernobyl. So, there's a prime example of people just oblivious to what's going on."

Laura: "It's another one of those invisible things in the environment that nobody thinks is doing any damage to anybody."

Michael: "Well, what I think they are trying to do is focus on how to heal. Like how did it get in his system?"

Laura: "Yeah, that's what I want to know."

Michael: "That I don't know yet. I still think it has to do with the injections. I still think it's that. But for some reason, it's just targeting the males."

Laura: "That's what I'm kind of confused about."

(Marti asks me if I've ever had his testosterone levels tested.)

Laura: "No, I've never done that. It's probably high though. Most kids with autism have high testosterone levels."

(With BioSET, I checked his hormone levels, and he had excessive testosterone. Often

when boys with autism go through puberty, their "autistic" behaviors worsen.)

Marti talks about an article she was reading about lowering testosterone levels to help behaviors. We talk about the glandular system, regulating the testes and discuss sterility. We agreed that older people who have a diagnosis of autism, it's not the same thing as this. These new kids with "autism" were normal and then became ill, it is a disease. Adults with a diagnosis of autism were not exposed to the same onslaught of toxins at a developmentally fragile time as the children of today did. Then Michael said that they are using the word "Governor" in relation to the glandular system.

***

Session Sixteen: After the Session
Featured Spirits: Sir John Hunter, President John F. Kennedy, Jr., Robert Kennedy, Sir Arthur Eddington, Sir Arthur Conan Doyle.

After the session I learned that the area of the brain that contains the hypothalamus gland and the pineal gland is known as "The Governor" or "The Genius" and is located in the horseshoe shaped part of the brain that Michael brought up during the session. The creator of the BioAlgae Concentrates (BAC), also known as BioSuperfood that I mentioned earlier assisted in writing a book called "Awakening the Genius Within." In it, Michael Kiriac says "When the hypothalamus itself is poorly fed, it does its own job less effectively, contributing to the downward spiral, becoming less and less able to regulate the glands that control all metabolisms and to respond to the requests by the cells to perform the myriad of their other functions." He adds that "BAC increases nutrient absorption, enhances regeneration of all cells, including those of the villi and the microvilli in the small intestine, reduces the load on the cleansing organs of the body, and awakens the hypothalamus. This in turn triggers cellular awakening and metabolic healing in the trillions of cells in your body." When the "Governor" is awakened, the other glands are regulated.

It was also interesting to learn that certain parts of the brain are not protected by the BBB, including the hypothalamus, pineal and pituitary glands. The median eminence of the hypothalamus connects the hypothalamus to the pituitary gland. The median eminence of the hypothalamus is not covered by the blood brain-barrier because hormones secreted by the pituitary gland collect in this region before being secreted into the bloodstream. This area, which is part of the hypothalamic-pituitary-adrenal or HPA axis, would be more succeptible to viruses and bacteria without the protection of the BBB. Inhaled biowarfare would enter the brain directly since the olfactory tract penetrates the blood-brain barrier in the unprotected region of the brain.

After the channeling session, Michael and I continued talking for a bit. Michael started talking about the news, and how there is a mass hypnosis going on to control the minds of the masses. He said that mind control through suggestion is the ultimate weapon. They repeat things, even though they admit what they say if false, they continue to repeat it. If you say it often enough people will believe it. It is done subliminally, right through the TV, and has been happening for decades. The goal is to make the population docile so that they won't react, then they can control the world and do anything they want. He said that the Germans were prolific at it, and then the Nazis came to America and Russia. There are people working on that goal on this planet.

Next, he talked about the biowarfare again, saying that he's certain that it is a release, an experimental thing. Maybe it was an experiment that they didn't mean to let out, but it got out. He compared it to the Black Ops helicopter that crashed at Area 51 recently, and revealed to the world that the technology existed. He said that we are trying to unravel something that has been concocted, like reverse engineering something. There are a lot of pointers that the spirit people are bringing up, and perhaps they are all important. We are just putting it all together.

***

Chapter Nineteen

"As well consult a butcher on the value of vegetarianism as a doctor on the worth of vaccination."

— George Bernard Shaw

Session Seventeen

This session was done on June 9, 2011. It was just Michael and I this time around. Before the session started, I excitedly shared the news with Michael that I just got the news that my application for funding for 40 more HBOT sessions was approved! He told me that my dad and my late husband helped make that happen. I only did 30 sessions the first time around. Now I could do the full 40. According to research I had been reading, between sessions 30 and 40 of HBOT are when stem cells in the brain grow. I was very excited to see what 40 sessions could do for my son.

The channeling session began with Michael saying that he was thinking of Edgar Allan Poe, and was hearing the name Edgar. I told Michael that I liked Edgar Allan Poe's writing. He was one of my favorite writers when I was young. My dad had a book of his poems and stories and I read all of them. I really liked "The Raven," "The Telltale Heart," "The Pit and the Pendulum" and "The Fall of the House of Usher." They were very macabre, and gave me nightmares, but I still liked the stories and his poetic writing style. A common theme in his stories was life after death, and communing with spirits. Likely because his parents died when he was a child and his wife died at a young age. I found it interesting to learn that Poe influenced the writing of Sir Arthur Conan Doyle, the author of the Sherlock Holmes books, who came through in the last session.

(After the session, I learned that many speculated that Poe had Asperger's or autism, and that there is a new school for children with autism called The Edgar Allan Poe Academy in Maryland, near where Poe died.)

When Michael first said the name Edgar, I thought it may have been Edgar Cayce, since he was mentioned in the sessions for my other book, and Michael was just talking to me about him before the session. There was a tabloid magazine that did a story on Michael and Marti, and on the magazine's cover was a picture of Edgar Cayce and his psychic wife. Michael and Marti's story was on the back side of the cover. He repeated that the spirit he was talking to was Edgar.

Next, Michael was talking about HBOT, and how we should listen to music while in the chamber. Then he said:

Michel: "Now they are putting Bernard Shaw in my mind. Well, he's another writer, isn't he?"

Laura: "Bernard Shaw? I've heard the name before."

Michael: "Bernard Shaw. I don't know."

(Marti says, "George Bernard Shaw is a playwright." She was there, but not drawing.)

Michael: "George Bernard Shaw? What is he? A playwright? Huh. Was he ever ill when he was younger, Marti? I think it's Shaw. Bernard Shaw. Bernard Shaw. Did he have any whiskers?"

(Marti says, "Yes.")

Michael: "Did he have like a beard?"

(Marti says, "Yes.")

Michael: "I think Bernard Shaw is here."

(After the session, I found out that Nobel Prize winning Irish playwright Bernard Shaw had smallpox when he was younger. His full name was George Bernard Shaw, but George was his father's name, whom he didn't like evidently, so he preferred to be called Bernard, which is the name he gave to Michael, not George. He did have a long, white beard. I also found that in the 1938 movie of his award winning play "Pygmalion" it says "Screenplay and Dialogue by Bernard Shaw, not George Bernard Shaw. It was just very interesting to us that he didn't give Michael the name George, just Bernard Shaw, which was in fact the name he preferred to be called. Who knew?)

Laura: "Hmm."

Michael: I know he's got a beard, this guy. I'm wondering why he's here. Edgar Allen Poe. It's strange that they would be here. I have a different feeling about it tonight. Like, it's not medical stuff or anything that I'm getting. It's writing. They are both writers. He wrote as well you see. Well, you know sometimes people write in a comedic way to try to get a point across. Interesting, did you hear that?"

Laura: "Uh-huh."

(When Michael said that sometimes people write in a comedic way to get a point across, it really clarified something for me. After the session, I figured out how I had heard of Bernard Shaw. On Glenn Beck Show, which I was passively watching months earlier, it showed George Bernard Shaw, this old guy with a white beard, talking about eugenics, and about Hitler and the gas chamber, and it appeared that Shaw was actually promoting it. After reading more about Bernard Shaw, it was easy to see that he was actually satirizing eugenics, not promoting it. It was scary to see how easily his words were taken literally and out of context. He was making fun of it and showing how ridiculous it was. Writing something in a comedic way to get a point across, as Michael said. I also learned that Shaw was an early opponent of forced vaccination. He was an outspoken opponent of the smallpox vaccine, the only vaccine at the time, and called it a "filthy piece of witchcraft" which did more harm than good.)

Michael: "Well, he's here I think with Edgar Allen Poe."

Laura: "Huh."

Michael: "They said two Edgars. Maybe the other Edgar is Edgar Cayce. Bernard Shaw, yeah."

Michael starting talking about the book we were working on, this book. He said that it was going to be a fairly thick book, and mentioned the name of a book company and a person's name in publishing. He also said that there was going to be something to do with TV coming up soon. He also said that the book would make a good movie. I told him that he had mentioned this once before, and the actor Jude Law. I joked that Jude could play him. Then Michael said that he wondered if Albert ever met Bernard Shaw. He said he was getting the feeling that they knew each other.

(After the session, I searched online to see if they knew each other, and much to my surprise, on the official Nobel Prize website, there is a video of George Bernard Shaw paying tribute to Albert Einstein at an after-dinner speech at the Savoy Hotel in London, England on October 27, 1930. Shaw is standing and speaking into a microphone and Albert is seated to his side. You can watch it yourself at http://www.nobel prize.org/nobel_prizes/literature/laureates/1925/shawdocu.html. They were both Nobel Prize winners, which is what makes me think that the Nobel Prize winner named George who showed up in one of the earlier sessions was George Bernard Shaw.)

Next, the subject changed to my son for a few minutes. Michael said to make sure he was getting enough Vitamin C, staying hydrated, and to have him drink coconut water. Coconut water is full of electrolytes and nutrients and is great for hydration.

He got back into talking about the HBOT facility, saying that he was seeing that it looked like a hospital with strip lights on the ceiling. I confirmed that it was in a medical facility with strip lights on the ceiling. He said that green lighting would be calming and healing for him, and to use violet light on his head for 10 or 15 minutes to stimulate the brain. Even just a flashlight with color over it would work. He said that color therapy isn't used very much, but it works.

Then Michael said to try to get Trevor to drink apple cider vinegar, perhaps with honey to sweeten it. It is good for detoxification and for the blood, he said. I said that I could maybe put it in his bath, but didn't think he'd drink it. I was right, I tried it afterward. It does have many health benefits, however.

Next, Michael was talking to a guy that was a professor/scientist and a politician, but I never did figure out who this guy was. Henri and a French sounding last name like de Laurie. In any event, he said that sweeping changes were coming. I said that I hoped he meant for my son. Michael said:

Michael: "Well, when you said your son, I got "Transformation" so maybe there is going to be a huge change in him."

Laura: "I'll take it!"

(There were a lot of changes in my life shortly following this session. I got a new job right down the road from my house, and we had my mom move back in with us.)

Michael: "Every time I think of stem cells, they use the word "components."I don't know what makes up stem cells, what's the main thing that makes them up but you need to ensure that there is enough of whatever it is to make sure the stem cells grow. You follow me?"

Laura: "Yeah."

Michael: "I don't know what the main ingredients of stem cells are. They keep making me think about that, and the ingredients of what it's composed of. So you just need to ensure that there is enough of that present so there is growth."

Laura: "Well, they say in the Hyperbaric Chamber that between 30 and 40 sessions is when stem cells grow."

Michael: "Right, so you have to ensure that there is a supply within him that he can draw on, so that you get the most out of it. If you don't have the building blocks you can't grow it, even though it would grow. See what I'm getting at?

Laura: "Right."

Michael: "If you don't have enough silica, your hair doesn't grow nice. It will grow, but it won't grow as well as if you had all the right ingredients."

Laura: "Right. So we could supplement him with whatever that is."

Michael: "So, maybe look into that a little and see what you can find out about stem cells, and what stem cells are, where they come from, and what helps them grow."

Laura: "Alright."

(After the session, I looked up supplements that assisted in stem cell growth, and to my amazement, I read that Algae has recently been spotlighted for its potentially positive effects on stem cells. Stem cells begin in bone marrow in the blood. Studies indicate that certain types of algae contain compounds that may facilitate increased release of bone marrow stem cells and increase the placement of stem cells into tissues in need. Stem cells are cells that have the remarkable ability to develop into various cell types in the body, such as red blood cells, muscle cells or brain cells. BioAlgae Concentrates, or BAC, which I've referred to earlier, was renamed BSF or Biosuperfood. Over 200 strains of blue-green microalgae were investigated by Russian researchers. BAC contains the most nutrient and phytonutrient dense algae found on Earth, selected amongst thousands and empirically tested for 20 years. The four microalgae in its proprietary blend are Spirulina Pacifica, Spirulina Platensis, Dunaliella, and Astaxanthin. It is grown indoors hydroponically, so I wasn't concerned about environmental contaminants like mercury and radiation from Fukushima. There are over 5,000 known nutrients in BAC, and many more unknown. The website www.quantumleapwellness.com specifically addressed BAC and stem cell growth saying "BAC will stimulate not only stem cell metabolism, but all metabolisms of life." Adding that "It is smarter to stimulate the producer glands of the brain rather than supplement one specific deficiency or metabolism." I made sure Trevor took this when we did the next round of HBOT.)

Michael: "I think Albert's here."

Laura: "Oh, cool."

Michael: "If this is him, he's giving me the thumbs up. I guess he seems pleased about your son."

Laura: "Ok. Maybe about him getting the therapy." *(HBOT)*

Michael: "Yeah, they're very concerned about these hot particles though."

(There were recently "hot particles" of radiation detected in the Northwestern U.S. from Fukushima. People are exposed to them, breathing them into lung tissue, which cause cancer.)

Laura: "Hmm."

Michael: "Yeah, don't know what to do about that. You don't wear anything special when you go it the chamber, you just wear these gowns with the back open?"

Laura: "Yeah, and there is a connector bracelet that you have to wear that grounds you to the unit so static isn't involved or anything."

Michael: "So there are no sparks. That makes sense. I saw a band, you see?"

Laura: "It's a wristband."

Michael: "I didn't know where it was, I kept seeing this band. 'You have to wear this band,' they said. I said, 'Oh, ok.'"

Laura: "Yep."

Michael was frustrated because he couldn't get the Henri guy's name down. He said he was also seeing these glasses that were brought up once before. He explained:

Michael: "You know what I was seeing? I call it a gadget; I've tried it. It looks like a pair of sunglasses, you put them on and it's got these little red diode lights, like little infrared lights that flicker. The cool thing is, when you put them on and you shut your eyes, you keep your eyes closed and you put these glasses on, and it's like you don't have your eyes shut. You can see scenes, it's like daylight, and you have all this stuff going on in front of you. It's like a movie playing. And you're not doing anything. You've got your eyes shut and yet it's bright, it's like daylight, and you start to see all these cool things. They do some sort of stimulatory effect on the brain. I'll have to look it up, but that's what I kept seeing."

Laura: "Ok, you know what's funny. You've said this once before about these glasses, when we were talking about some other sort of visual therapy or something, and the glasses came up then too."

Michael: "Well, they're bringing this up again, that's what I kept seeing."

(Maybe this technology can be used or incorporated into some kind of visual therapy for children with autism? They brought it up twice, so it must be important.)

We decided to call it a night, but Michael felt that he also had to get working on his book that he's been working on for years. That is why authors were coming through. A kind of "Come on, get it done" he felt.

***

Session Seventeen: After the Session

Featured Spirits: Edgar Allan Poe, George Bernard Shaw, Edgar Cayce, Albert Einstein

This wasn't a very long or mind-blowing session, but it was interesting that while they were talking to us about the book, one of my favorite writers came through (Edgar Allen Poe) and a famous writer that Albert knew (whom we didn't know that he knew until after the session), who just so happens to be an early vaccine opponent.

Shortly after the session, I found out that they were making a movie about Edgar Allan Poe called *The Raven* starring John Cusack, which was pretty shocking by itself. Then in March of 2012, Michael got a call from a producer who was looking to book a medium to contact Poe in the afterlife for an event they were doing in conjunction with the release of the movie in March, 2012. Michael told the producer that he had already contacted Edgar Allen Poe during a channeling session for a book project about autism. The producer ended up going with someone else for the event, but the fact that they contacted Michael about it was another one of those synchronistic moments worth mentioning.

It was also exciting to me that Edgar Cayce came through. He came through a few times during the sessions for *Foundation of Discovery*. I didn't know that Michael and Marti were featured in the same tabloid as Edgar Cayce and his wife, but gives another reason why he would come

352

through. For those who don't know, Edgar Cayce was perhaps the greatest medical intuitive/psychic that ever lived. He was born in 1887 and died in 1945. He was called the "Sleeping Prophet" because he put himself in a sleep-like state when he channeled information about people's medical conditions.

There are volumes of his channeling sessions documented about numerous medical conditions at his foundation in Virginia called ARE: Association for Research and Enlightenment. I was aware of him prior to his appearances in the channeling sessions, and had read a few of his books. His appearance made me feel like we had his support, and he was interested in what we were doing.

After the session, I went to Edgar Cayce's ARE website to see if he ever did any readings on people with autism. Now, remember the time period that he lived; some of his readings are over 100 years old. This is obviously not the same kind of autism we are seeing today. However, I found some interesting things. There were three cases that he did readings for, which weren't specifically called "autism" but were noted on the website. It said:

"Although the above cases vary greatly with regard to symptoms and severity, some common themes are worth noting. In all these cases Edgar Cayce focused on nervous system incoordination involving the sensory nervous system. All these individuals were described as over sensitive (even "super-sensitive"). Nerve pressures were cited as causative factors. Spinal manipulation was consistently recommended, as was the use of the Radial Appliance to assist with balancing and coordinating the system.

Problems with the digestive system and intestinal tract was significant in two of these cases (1179 and 2014). Therapies such as abdominal castor oil packs, diet, and dietary supplements were suggested.

The mental and spiritual aspects of healing were prominent in all three cases. Suggestive therapeutics was usually recommended. The spiritual focus of the family and caregivers was strongly emphasized.

Thus a blending of treatments into a well integrated treatment plan was often recommended by Edgar Cayce for the treatment of autism. Here is a summary of some of the most common treatment recommendations.

TREATMENT RECOMMENDATIONS

Conceptually, the Cayce approach to autism focuses on assisting the body in healing itself by the application of a variety of therapies intended to address the <u>underlying causes</u> of the condition. The mental and spiritual aspects of healing are strongly emphasized.

Here are some general therapeutic recommendations intended to address the <u>underlying causes</u> of autism:

1. MANUAL THERAPY (SPINAL MANIPULATION): Cayce often recommended spinal manipulations to correct specific problems which may be a primary cause of autism. It is difficult to obtain the osteopathic adjustments specified by Cayce. However, a chiropractor may be of help. The frequency of the adjustments will depend on the recommendations of the individual chiropractor or osteopath. The use of an electric vibrator may also be helpful for individuals unable to obtain regular spinal adjustments.

2. ELECTROTHERAPY: Regular use of the Radial Appliance to coordinate nerve functioning and circulation is recommended.

3. INTERNAL CLEANSING: Because autistic symptoms were sometimes linked to problems with the alimentary canal resulting in poor eliminations, hydrotherapy is recommended to improve eliminations through the colon. Hydrotherapy includes drinking six to eight glasses of pure water daily and obtaining colonic irrigations to cleanse the bowel. Following the diet should also assist with internal cleansing. Hot castor oil packs applied over the abdomen are recommended to improve circulation (especially lymphatic) and eliminations through the alimentary canal.

4. DIET: The Basic Cayce Diet is intended to improve assimilation and elimination. The diet focuses heavily on keeping a proper alkaline/acid balance while avoiding foods which produce toxicity and drain the system. Essentially, the diet consists mainly of fruits and vegetables while avoiding fried foods and refined carbohydrates ("junk food"). Certain food combinations are emphasized.

5. SUGGESTIVE THERAPEUTICS: The use positive suggestions during the presleep period and during therapy sessions (such as massage and the Radial Appliance) is recommended to awaken the inner healing response. The spiritual attunement of the caregiver is essential.

6. MEDICATION: The use of a mild natural sedative (such as Passion Flower fusion) may be helpful for excitable children. Laxatives and dietary supplements may be helpful, particularly for individuals with significant gastrointestinal symptoms. Although Ventriculin is no longer available, similar products such as Secretin (made from hog gastric

tissue and available only by physician's prescription) have proven helpful for some persons suffering from autism."

I read all three cases, and interestingly, one of them was a girl, who was advised to take wheat products out of her diet. She got better, went on to become a school teacher and got married. Even way back then, there were some common threads with some of the children today. Edgar Cayce was also called "The Father of Holistic Medicine," which is evident by his treatment recommendations.

***

Chapter Twenty

"The intuitive mind is a sacred gift
and the rational mind is a faithful
servant. We have created a society
that honors the servant and has
forgotten the gift."

— *Albert Einstein*

Session Eighteen

This session was done on June 30, 2011. It was just Michael and I again. Marti was there but didn't draw this time. I had sent Michael a list of questions that I wanted to see if our "friends" could possibly answer or clarify. The session began with us talking, as it usually does, and then we get into the channeling session. However, this time things went a bit differently than our normal sessions do.

Michael began by telling me about an article he read about the polio vaccine and the SV40 virus (simian virus 40) in it causing cancer. I was already aware of this. They knowingly made the polio vaccine that was cultured on monkey kidney cells infected with a simian virus, and millions of people were injected with it. It can be passed down genetically. Michael found it interesting how FDR came through to talk to us, who had polio. FDR brought this up in the channeling sessions for my other book. He warned that two vaccines were dangerous to humanity, the polio vaccine and the MMR vaccine. Michael said that he wonders if this was deliberate or utter stupidity. He also said "I think what we are getting to at the deepest core here is that the vaccines don't work. They are counterproductive. They kill you more than they cure you. They don't work, that is the point. We are making ourselves a weaker race on top of it."

Next, Michael brought up the fact that we know they are using biowarfare, and genetically altering it. He mentioned the recent story that came out about people getting ill from e-coli from eating tainted organic lettuce, and when they studied the strain, it was genetically engineered with the plague virus in it, and engineered to be resistant to several strains of antibiotics. This doesn't occur in nature. Michael felt that this proved that people genetically engineered it and released it. Michael said that vaccines are genetically engineered. Again he said,

Michael: "The question always comes back to 'Is somebody intentionally doing this, or is it just utter stupidity?' I think that is a question that you should put in your book."

Laura: "Mmm-hmm."

Michael: "Because you have people out there engineering viruses deliberately to kill people, very cleverly. We know that. There is no question that they are doing that. And there is no question that they are doing it to slowly kill off people. They have been doing that for centuries. They put poison on arrows so that if the arrow nicked you, it still kills you. They used to throw bodies with catapults into cities with plague on them to kill the population. Germ warfare has been going on forever."

Laura: "Right, yep, I know."

Michael: "So it's not new, they do that. So that answers some of these questions here. Now, 'Why do boys (have autism) more than girls?' (This was one of my questions.) We know it has something to do with the Y chromosome, don't we? Because they alluded to that. Personally, I did not know that."

Laura: "Yeah, I mean it was totally random when it came up. We didn't know what it meant."

Michael: "Exactly, I didn't know what it meant or why they were mentioning it. But now we do, but why? Why does it target the boys? Now your question, 'Why are autism rates higher in certain states?' I don't know."

Laura: "Well, those are just the unanswered questions. I don't even know if they will get answered."

Michael: "Well, they may. It may just by a little bit of groundwork, a little bit of footwork. We need to look at a map and map it on just the United States maybe, and say what is predominant in these places. What are the factors that we can clearly see that we do know about, you know what I mean?"

Laura: "Yeah."

Michael: We know that those guys with the little wooden buggies don't vaccinate and they don't have autism. *(The Amish.)* So we look at that and put a circle on the map and say that's where they live."

Laura: "Right."

Michael: "And we know where the very high rates are, they are here, here, here and here. Then we can find out where they do the most vaccinating. And we can find out, maybe we can plot where laboratories are where they do testing and stuff. So once we plot this stuff out on a map, we can maybe draw some conclusions ourselves. See what I mean?"

Laura: "Yeah."

It was interesting to learn after this session that Utah's autism rate had doubled in six years to 1 in 79. 10,000 children in Utah have been diagnosed with autism. Utah is the state directly downwind of Nevada. So if it is true that biowarfare is escaping from an underground military facility in Nevada, as per the channeled information from my first book, Utah is the first state hit. They are also downwind from all of the nuclear open air testing done in Nevada. I also remember reading a story years ago about how the Great Salt Lake in Utah had a lot of mercury in it, and they blamed it on the mining industry in Nevada, and the wind carrying it there. So, it could be multiple factors.

We started talking about the other medium's channeling compared to what they are telling us now. Michael asked me what was different, and I told him that it was mainly about the biowarfare and where it was coming from. He said:

Michael: "Yeah, I know but that is every conspiracy theory person out there comes up with that. I mean, that's something that you may never get to prove, because nobody is going to own that stuff. What are you going to do? Go out and park your butt outside a gate of a biowarfare (manufacturing facility) and say, 'You killed my son!' You know? It's not going to happen. They are never going to admit to it. You know when a spy dies; they don't even admit that they even existed."

Laura: "Mmm-hmm."

Michael: "Nope, we never had a spy in that country. And the other country will never tell you what they did with them. They are like a non-entity. They'll never discuss it. It's like UFO's. What we are dealing with here is on the level of UFO's. Like every time a UFO is seen, 'Oh, it's wild geese, that's what they saw.' 'It was dust particles in the cloud.'

'Oh, they made it up.' 'They digitally altered it on the computer.' That's all you ever get."

Laura: "Yeah."

Michael: "No matter what is presented, that's all you ever get. And every time you see a show, a program, that's the same shit. My master did so much stuff with the public, he went on television, he did this, he did that. He gave proof of when UFO's would be seen, he did all sorts of stuff. And did it make a bit of difference? No. Not a bit."

Laura: "Hmm."

Michael: "Like I said, I'm not a doctor, so it is very hard for them to explain medical things to me and I'm not a scientist, so I don't know how they are doing things exactly. I just know that they are. It's common sense that they are doing it. We know that they are doing that, there is no question. The military admits that they have been doing it for years, but they are not telling you exactly what. And you are not going to find that out either."

Laura: "And the other thing is I don't want to put any of us in any kind of danger."

Michael: "There is that too. Ha, ha. You know, like I said to you, the spirit people are kind of protective about us, and if they think something will endanger us, they are not about to tell me."

Laura: "Right. I mean, as much as I want to know all the specifics, is it really in my best interest to go spouting off about this that and the other about what the military is doing? Or just alluding to it and letting someone else figure it out later?"

Michael: "Well, I think you are on the right track there, exactly. What we are trying to do is make people more aware of a number of things. One is the danger of vaccines. The dangers of all the things they brought up. Obviously, they are implicit in what is going on. So if people are aware of it...Like if I had a kid, I wouldn't have him vaccinated."

Michael tells me a story about a kid with cancer that he and Marti did healing work on. After the healing, the doctors had him tested again and he didn't have cancer, but they gave him more chemo anyway and it almost killed him. He was a teenager, and if he didn't have the chemo, he could have been taken away from his mom and forcibly given chemo, even though the grapefruit sized tumor he had disappeared. Then, Michael healed him from the chemo. Once he turned 18, the catheter in his chest was making him cough up blood. Michael's spirit helpers told him the catheter was causing the bleeding, and he needed to have it taken out. Michael told the boy that he didn't have cancer, and to go to the hospital and ask for an x-ray, and ask them to remove the catheter and tell them he was done. Because he was an adult now, he could make his own decisions. He did what Michael suggested, the doctors argued with him, even though they found nothing, and told him he was going to die. He is alive and well 8 years later. Michael said:

Michael: "What we are dealing with is ignorance, pure ignorance with people. They are determined to do things the way that, for whatever reason, I don't know what their reasons are, but why should we all have to tolerate it? We don't."

Laura: "Mmm-hmm."

Michael: "They are messing around with everything, and we have got to put our foot down or we are all going to die of something. I mean, what are they doing with Fukushima? Oh, they raised the level of radiation we are suddenly able to absorb. Huh? Really? Oh, we just got that much better at handling radiation, did we? I don't think so."

Laura: "Yeah."

Michael: "And now of course, they are talking about this other reactor that is a plutonium reactor on the other side of the island that they have had this accident with that has been messed up for months now and they haven't been able to repair it. And that's possibly going to melt down too."

Laura: "Oh, my gosh, I haven't heard about that."

Michael: "Oh, you didn't know about that one?"

Laura: "No."

Michael: "Well I kept telling you remember, that there was another reactor, that there was this other plant that was in danger?"

Laura: "Yeah."

Michael: "Well, that's probably it, that one. It's a plutonium reactor; it's

a fast breeding reactor."

Laura: "And the wind will blow it across the entire island."

Michael: "Yeah, it's on the West Coast, right on top of a fault line. It got hit pretty hard a while back by an earthquake and something broke off in the reactor. Actually, it's a very important device, a piece of machinery and it fell into the core. And they haven't been able to get it out of the core ever since. They don't know what to do about it."

Laura: "Lovely."

Michael: "And that is also happening, see. So, we've got all this stuff going on right?"

(He starts reading my questions and answering them.)

"Is there is a main cause of the epidemic of regressive autism?" "You know, they said that there is not just one cause."

"Can vaccines alone cause autism?" "No, I don't think it's just vaccines alone, I think it is a combination."

The next question is *"Can mercury alone cause regressive autism?"* "You know, the mercury doesn't help."

Laura: "Right."

Michael: "What I'm getting at is I'm not a scientist and neither are you, and even if they told me, I probably wouldn't understand what the hell they are talking about. So I think if this gets scientists to look at everything that has been said, maybe some light bulbs will go on in their head and they will immediately figure it out."

Laura: "Scientifically, yeah."

Michael: "Yeah, scientifically, they'll go, "Hmm, I hadn't thought of that." Well, if you put all of this together, maybe it gives you some answer that we are oblivious to."

(From my questions) "Why is the autism rate in military families double that of civilian?" "Well, is it all military or just the ones out in Iraq and Afghanistan?"

Laura: "I think it's active duty."

Michael: "You know that program I told you about where they were saying that it's depleted uranium that is killing them?"

Laura: "Uh-huh."

Michael: "Well, they were given those injections that were never tested, you know, so they were inoculated against all these things and they were never tested."

Laura: "Right. Like the anthrax vaccine."

Michael: "Yeah. The anthrax vaccine? They were given anthrax? Are you kidding me?"

Laura: "Right."

(From an article called "Vaccinations: The Hidden Dangers" in "The Blaylock Wellness Report" from May, 2004, Neurosurgeon Dr. Russell Blaylock says that military person-nel were given approximately 17 vaccines in a short time period during the Gulf War. This includes seven anthrax shots and another series of botulism shots, which don't appear on their vaccination records, but say "Vac. A" or "Vac. B." Blaylock also ad-dresses the multiple causes theory, calling it "synergic toxicity," where two or more toxins combine together and become more dangerous. This is similar to what was described during the sessions for my book "Foundation of Discovery," where it was explained that it wasn't the vaccine alone causing autism, it was the combination of the biowarfare and the vaccine. There are common threads here.)

Michael: "But look, you're not a scientist and neither am I, and what I'm saying is, a lot of this, like if we put what we've got out there, then per-haps someone who takes seriously what we are saying."

(Marti says, "That's exactly what I was thinking.")

Michael: "Like a doctor or something like that, or a neurosurgeon, or maybe some people that we already know who we've had sessions with that are medical people, might step forward. And then we can say let's do a session with them as well and see if they can clarify some ques-tions that they have that may answer these questions here. See what I mean?"

Laura: "Yep."

Michael: "It's what I said to you before, I might say something to them that only they'll understand, in a way that they would understand it. You know, I understand the Theory of Relativity in a basic sense, how I understand it. But if you wrote it out in a mathematical formula, I wouldn't know what the hell you are writing. See what I'm getting at?"

Laura: "Yeah, me too."

Michael: "In my mind, I can see the little germs moving around in the blood and I can see that they attack this cell, I can see that visually. But I don't know what it is actually doing chemically."

Laura: "Right."

Michael: "I couldn't chemically tell you what is going on, I couldn't. I'm not a chemist and I'm not a biologist. See what I'm getting at? But someone that is might be given that piece of information. That's what usually happens. That's how they do things. That's what I've seen happen. You know, that's when they get very specific, when they are dealing with the very person that the piece of information is absolutely meant for. Otherwise you kind of get lost in the mix."

Laura: "That's helpful. I mean, I just want to heal my boy and help these people so desperately."

Michael: "I know you want to heal your boy. Laura, remember I told you early on, don't expect too much here. What we are dealing with sweetie is brain damage caused by these different factors. And nobody wants to even look at it that way."

Laura: "Mmm-hmm."

Michael: "When you talk to people, they want to refer to it as mentally challenged, or this. But they don't want to call it what it is, you know. Because then that means..."

Laura: "Someone is to blame."

Michael: "You know, you're not culpable in this, or you're not responsible. And the reason is you didn't know all these things were going on. You were just as unknowing as all the other people."

Laura: "Yep. Blind faith in the government and the doctors; you trust what they say."

Michael: "Yeah, all of them."

Laura: "You trust that everything is safe, and you are trying to protect your child against diseases that could kill them."

Michael: "We live in such a conditioned society. We live in a society where we have to believe something. If you think that you can't talk to dead people, and you believe that Jesus is going to come and save you, that's what you believe. But unless somebody comes along and shakes your world and says, you know, you can talk to your father, or you can talk to your whomever, and you prove it to them, then they keep believing what they believe. And most people are pretty ignorant about the world."

Laura: "Yep."

Michael: "So they just have to accept what their peers tell them. Luckily, my peer, the man I was fortunate enough to meet was an enlightened being. And he answered all of my questions for me within a year or so. I completely understood what was going on, what it was all about. So, I was lucky."

Laura: "Yeah."

Michael: "But I see so many people who are groping around in the dark, and they know next to nothing. And whew, it's frustrating. I think to myself, God Almighty. I say to Marti, 'I feel like I'm living in a Funny Farm and I'm the only sane person in it sometimes.'"

Laura: "Ha, ha. Yep."

Michael: "I really do. I do feel like that. I just keep going cuz every now and then I get a letter from someone who says 'You changed my life, thank you, don't stop what you are doing.' And that's what keeps me going see, so if I didn't get that, I probably would stop. I'd probably just retire away somewhere with Marti."

Laura: "Well, I would second that motion; you need to keep doing what you're doing because there are not many people left on this planet that are enlightened, and that can change the way things are going. And you are definitely two of those people. And I like to think that I am one of them as well. But the way that things are going…"

Michael: "It can get you down, can't it?"

Laura: "Yeah, people are totally skeptical."

Michael: "Yeah, I know when I found out about this other nuclear reactor this morning, when I was reading about it, I thought, 'Oh my

God,' I was right. I bloody knew there was more than that Fukushima plant. I think there are actually 3 main plants that are having real issues. I think the other sister plant to Fukushima is also having major problems, but they are not talking, they are covering so much of this up. It's just like borderline insanity. Well, you see, the nuclear establishment, the people who support the nuclear establishment, all the scientists who have their fingers and hands in deep pockets, who are making a ton of money out of it and whose livelihood depends on it, they are all like, 'Oh, this is a little bump in the road, now we will do things better, and everything will be safe.' And all this crap, and on and on it goes like some mantra."

Laura: "Right."

Michael: "Because basically their entire livelihood is on the line. There is a possibility if there was a massive public outcry that it would be the end of the line for nuclear power. And these people can't even imagine that. They'll fight tooth and nail against that. Even if we all die, they don't care. These people are just jerks, absolute jerks. These people have no idea how dangerous this stuff is."

Laura: "Nope."

Michael: "You see, the particles that are released... didn't I explain this in one of the sessions we did, how the subtle particles alter the genetic makeup?"

Laura: "Uh-huh."

Michael: "See, DNA isn't just altered by... it's kind of like an atom splitting machine. One of those circular splitting machines they use. I can't think of what they call them now."

Laura: "The particle accelerator?"

Michael: "About the size of a football field, where they move atoms around and they smash them together."

Laura: "Right."

Michael: "There are so many tiny particles that they are finding out about. They're into anti-matter. My master wrote about anti-matter in his book. He talks about anti-matter. This is in 1957 he published his book."

Laura: "Geez."

Michael: "He's talking about anti-matter, all sorts of stuff; cesium, plutonium. He just goes right into it, talks about all sorts of stuff. Only now are they finding, oh yeah, it's true, there is anti-matter, and there's this, and there is that. There are particles that can't even be measured yet. And those particles are the particles whizzing through space that you can't even detect that are released on such a subtle level, and they are what causes the main cancer because they distort the etheric body, your higher body, that's what they go through. And just like a magnet with iron filings, it is like drawing a line through something. I say it like this; if you had a plan and somebody came in the middle of the night and drew some lines on the plan, well the guy that comes in the next day and reads the plan is going to build it just like it looks. He's not going to say, 'What does that line mean?' He's just going to go 'Oh, I guess they want it like that.' He's just going to build it as funky as it looks. If he's not questioning it, he's just going to go, 'Ok, if that's what they want, I'll put a wall there. If they want a widow with a diagonal line through it, I'll put one there. Funky looking window, but if that's what they want.' That's how the physical body reacts to the etheric body. They physical body reacts always to the etheric body. The etheric body is the first vehicle. The physical body always does what the etheric body says, not the other way around. So if you have a distortion in etheric matter, then you will get some sort of cancer or some sort of genetic mutation take place. You see what I mean? You follow me?"

Laura: "Yes, definitely."

Michael: "That's what happens at the airports. There is a big who-ha going on right now because people working at the airport are saying those x-ray machines are giving them cancer."

(Marti says, "Even though this is not being channeled, you probably should put some of this stuff in the book.")

Laura: "I've been recording this whole thing."

Michael: "You've been recording it, have you? I was going to say, I should have put the recorder on."

Laura: "Yeah, for some reason, I hit record. I thought this was going to be good."

Michael: "Well see, this is stuff I've been thinking about all my life. I know it. I can't tell you, I just know what I'm talking about here is correct. So this is something I think needs to be put in the book to also explain what, shall we say, cannot be explained."

Laura: "Right."

Michael: "I was also reading something that came up about the cancer thing. It's just a big scam. A big money pit, it's all it is. For people to make a bunch of money."

Laura: "Yeah, did you see that movie, the Burzynski movie, that guy that was able to cure rare cancer, and the government spent millions of dollars to try to take his technology and say it didn't work and then get the patents for themselves and then they totally screwed it up. The Antineoplastons, Dr. Burzynski."

Michael: "Yeah."

Laura: "He's been doing it since the 70's. It's basically a form of urine therapy. Because there are certain amino acids in healthy people that are deficient in people with cancer, so you can give them this urine therapy or whatever, and the cancer goes away."

Michael: "Mmm-hmm."

Laura: "It was everything that the medical community was looking for, but they wanted to control it. And now he can only do it in clinical trials, he's still working in Texas. But the FDA will only allow him to do clinical trials, but most of the time, only after chemo and radiation has failed."

Michael: "Well, you see, they have their agenda. It's like, you're not going to change all the Archbishops, and I can't think of what they call them. All the people in the Catholic Church, the Archbishops and the…"

Laura: "Cardinals?"

Michael: "Cardinals and all that lot. They have a damn nice life. Lots of nice wine, lots of bowing and scraping, nice life they have. They have no intention of changing things. They like it just the way it is. It's a cash cow."

Laura: "Mmm-hmm."

Michael: "I mean, God forbid we stop fighting. How are we going to make money? All my money is invested in arms manufacturers. Oh, good God, we can't stop fighting, there is too much money to be made. I mean that's the bottom line. With 90% of these people, that's how they look at it. They don't give a flying crap about anything. They don't believe in life after death, when you are dead, you're dead, that's it. They don't really care. And I think that is a huge obstacle for people to deal with."

Laura: "Right."

Michael: "You're dealing with such low intelligence people on the whole. They think they are so damn clever with their science mind and all that crap. But really they are a bunch of idiots, most of them."

Laura: "And they manipulate all their data anyway to show that a drug is safe and it's not."

Michael: "Yeah, well you know, being clever doesn't mean you're intelligent. Cleverness isn't a sign of intelligence. All of these people who say they are geniuses or whatever, most of it is just book learning. It's what they remember in a book. It doesn't mean they are really intelligent. It doesn't mean they really thought things out. They're not thinkers, most people. So sadly, we are living in a world full of people who are just totally fearful. You know, Saudi Arabia just made a statement that if Iran gets nuclear weapons, then we are going to get them too. Because we can't have Iran having them and us not, so we are going to have them as well. I mean how primitive can you get?"

Laura: "Right, perfect word. That's not going to solve anything."

Michael: "It's so bloody stupid, all of it."

Then we got back to my questions I had written.

Michael: (Reading my question) "Why do some children with autism have seizures?"

"Seizures? What do you mean when you say seizures?"

Laura: "A lot of children with autism have epileptic seizures."

Michael: "Well, I can explain epileptic seizures for you. Epilepsy is caused when the astral body can't stay in the physical. So the astral body is involuntarily pushed out of the physical body. I'm pretty certain about that, I've thought about this for decades."

Laura: "Mmm-hmm."

Michael: "I'll tell you what happens when you leave your physical body in your astral body in a conscious projection. There is a tremendous shaking that takes place, a really high vibration, ok?"

Laura: "Ok."

Michael: "It's a bit like being in a container where you are trying to separate two substances. Like if you have rice and salt say, and you vibrate it rapidly, doesn't one move above and one move below. Don't they separate out? Look at it that way, when you put two components in a container, and you rapidly shake it, vibrate it, the components separate. Almost like oil and water separates, ok?"

Laura: "Ok."

Michael: "That's what happens for the astral body to leave the physical body, because the matter is intertwined magnetically. You understand?"

Laura: "Mmm-hmm."

Michael: "So the astral body and the matter of the astral body, the particles and the physical body are blended together, intermixed, interwoven. They never touch, the particles, because then you'd have some sort of explosion or something, you see? But they're magnetically held apart, all the particles. So if you want to separate them, a kind of shaking takes place, in which one passes out through the other. And I've had that experience, so I know and I've read it in books where other people have done it. So I know that is what happens. And if you're conscious of it, you get this shaking."

Laura: "Mmm-hmm."

Michael: "Well, what happens if you're not aware of this and it starts to happen? Then the physical body is going to react to the shaking. See what I'm getting at?"

Laura: "Oh, yeah."

Michael: "So, I reckon that's what's going on. Cuz it's like passing out, they go unconscious. They do don't they? They are almost unconscious, correct?"

Laura: "Yeah."

Michael: "I mean they have no control, right. Ok, have you ever jumped in your bed when you were asleep? Like you fell in your dream or something or you fell off a cliff or something and your physical body nearly fell out of bed?"

Laura: "Yeah."

Michael: "You've done that, right?"

Laura: "Uh-huh."

Michael: "Where you go, "Whoa" and you wake up with a start and your arms flail and you feel like you fell out of bed or something, right?"

Laura: "Uh-huh."

Michael: "Why did that happen? What a violent reaction, right?"

Laura: "Right."

Michael: "In your dream, your astral body was coming back into your physical body very rapidly and the magnetism of the astral wallops, collides with the magnetism of the physical so strongly that the physical body jumps as a reaction. And why I'm telling you that is because that's how powerful the astral body, plus the etheric obviously, because you are in the etheric body as well as the astral, affects the physical when it realigns as it enters alignment again with the physical body. You see, you can't move until your astral body is fully in alignment with the physical. That's why people wake up or become aware when they are asleep and they say, "I can't move." And they start panicking. Have you ever had that happen to you?"

Laura: "No, but when I am woke up out of a dream, I'm totally discombobulated and like I'm in another plane. I totally relate to all that."

Michael: "But can you physically move or does it take you a minute or so?"

Laura: "It takes me a little bit."

Michael: "You know Marti has had those experiences where she's awake, but she wants to scream, and she can't move. She actually lay there one night going mmm, mmm, mmm. In her mind she's screaming, or trying to. I could hardly hear her actually; she said in her mind she was going

"Ahh, help, help." And she couldn't move her body, see? That's what happens when you are not perfectly back in your body yet. See what I'm getting at?"

Laura: "Mmm-hmm."

Michael: "That's what I believe is going on with epilepsy. So, what is causing the body to be pushed out? There is some sort of poison. So, something like a toxin is causing you to have to leave your body. You follow me?"

Laura: "Yeah."

Michael: "That's the mechanism, that's what's going on there. Everything I just explained to you there is what's going on. Now what it is that's doing it? I don't know. But something is not allowing the person to stay in their body. Something is kicking them out."

Laura: "That makes sense."

Michael: "They are becoming unconscious. Now I said unconscious, and you said they are still there, but they are not really, they're border-line unconscious. They have no control. So, you know my cat was doing that before he died?"

Laura: "Really?"

Michael: "He'd be lying there and some noise and he'd start flailing around. And I'd have to hold him and calm him down. But he had no control. Because during sleep, you're that close to death really. You're a whisper away from death when you leave your body. You know when you die, you just permanently leave your body, and you don't come back. So, you're that close to death when you're asleep really, you're a breath away."

Laura: "Mmm-hmm."

Michael: (Reading another one of my questions) *"Is there a genetic predisposition that makes certain children vulnerable?"* "I think there is genetic predisposition, but the genetics are altered. So it is altering DNA, there is definitely altering of DNA."

Laura: "Ok."

Michael: "Is there any kind of cranial pressure exhibited? Has anybody ever talked about intercranial pressure?"

Laura: "Yes, but they call it inflammation. Their brain swells."

Michael: "It does?"

Laura: "They say kids with autism have bigger heads."

Michael: "What?"

Laura: "Yeah, their brain swells…"

Michael: "Wait a second, wait a second. This has never come up before, has it?"

Laura: "No."

Michael: "No, ok. Listen, you remember that doctor I talked about last time? Sir John Hunter? I think he's here. Basically in my mind, right now I am asking this question about genetic predisposition. And they came up with intercranial pressure. 'There is intercranial pressure,' they said. I said 'Oh, I didn't know about that.' So their brains swell?"

Laura: "Mmm-hmm."

Michael: "Huh. Wow, now that's a very weird visual thing they just gave me."

Laura: "What's that?"

Michael: "Someone said it's almost like the brain is at war with itself. And what I see as I'm looking at a head, like inside someone's head, it looks like a lot of doors opening and shutting, like slamming. It's almost like the brain is battling itself. It's like it's trying to what I thought, eradicate something, or get something out. But there is another part of it that is saying "No, don't." You understand?"

Laura: "Yeah."

Michael: "So what I'm seeing is like doors opening and shutting very fast, like slam, slam, slam, slam. Lots and lots of them, and it's happening inside the brain. It's like signals are being sent out, do one thing, and then another signal comes back and says 'no, don't do that.' But counter commands. Like opposite commands. That's what I'm seeing. Like it's in a state of it can't make its mind up."

Laura: "Uh-huh."

372

Michael: "Definitely like a poison, it's definitely, this whatever it is that's in the brain, this virus, it's like a poison."

(Long pause...) "You there?"

Laura: "Yeah."

Michael: "Yeah, I was kind of deep in thought there for a second, just kind of contemplative. So I moved the page of questions down, and I looked up again and I was at question 6. "In one session they were talking about gluten affecting the brain that the body saw as an invader and attacking like a virus." I was trying to contemplate what they were just showing me and I looked up and that's what I'm looking at."

Laura: "Uh-huh."

Michael: "Oh boy. Is there a large portion of kids that come down with cancer who have autism?"

Laura: "Some do, yeah."

Michael: "Is the cancer rate any more with kids with autism or is just the same as the average population?"

Laura: "I'm not sure about that. I know some of them have both autism and cancer. Or have autism and then get cancer."

Michael: "I'm looking at the questions about gluten/wheat/GMO and what role does nuclear radiation play."

Laura: "Oh."

Michael: "I think that is a separate issue. I think the radiation; I don't think that is linked. I think that it is simply another just a grave danger. Just a general health danger."

Laura: "Ok."

Michael: "Are there any therapies with honey?"

Laura: "I don't know, but that came up in one of our other sessions about giving Trevor honey."

Michael: "Oh, it did?"

Laura: "Yeah, he tried it and he spit it out."

Michael: "Spat it out? How funny, I wonder why he spat it out?"

Laura: "I don't know, maybe I just didn't give it to him in a way he would like it."

Michael: "Well it looks like honey. There is Royal Jelly. This stuff called Royal Jelly. You ever heard of that?"

Laura: "Yeah."

Michael: "Has he ever tried that?"

Laura: "He's only tried honey."

Michael: "Hold on, let's see what the properties of Royal Jelly are."

Laura: "Maybe I'll try it again, a different way."

Michael: (Long pause, he went to his computer to look it up.) "Wow! Ok. Maybe this is it. You see, there is someone standing, I don't know who it is, it may be that doctor, (Sir John Hunter) and he's standing there and he's pouring this liquid stuff and it looks like honey. And he's pointing at his head and I said 'Yeah?' And he poured something in and he drank it. So I said, 'Ok, what is it? It looks like honey.' He stuck it in my head 'Royal Jelly.' So I'm looking up Royal Jelly. I don't really know what Royal Jelly does but I got down here and I'm reading Wikipedia Royal Jelly, this is what it says; 'Royal Jelly has been reported as possible immunomodulatory agent in Grave's disease, it's also been reported to stimulate the growth of Glial cells, the natural stem cells in the brain!'"

Laura: "Oh!"

Michael: "There you go! Interesting, huh?"

Laura: "Yeah."

Michael: "Try him on that."

He said to muscle test him for it before I gave it to him because some people are allergic to honey and other bee products. He wasn't allergic to it, after I tested him. Royal Jelly is what the Queen Bee produces to feed the worker bees, and it has many nutritional components, ironically including many of the "B" vitamins. Michael ended the session by saying "Sometimes the way they do it is to let this flow go and start talking and out comes the answer, you know. That's what I've done many, many times. You don't always have to sit there and stare at someone (in spirit) and see what they say. I can just talk and out it comes."

***

Session Eighteen: After the Session
<u>Featured Spirit:</u> Sir John Hunter

After the session, I found an interesting study that backed up what Michael mentioned about Royal Jelly. It was called "Stimulatory Effects of Royal Jelly on the Generation of Neuronal and Glial Cells- Expectation of Protection Against Some Neurological Disorders" by Shoei Furukawa from the Laboratory of Molecular Biology, Department of Biofunctional Analysis, Gifu Pharmaceutical University in Japan. The summary stated that "Patients suffered from neurological disorders of the brain such as Alzheimer's disease and Parkinson's disease have been greatly increasing with the development of an elderly society. We tested royal jelly as a practical alternative medicine for these diseases, because it is the source of the queen honey bees marvelous vitality and fertility, and widely known as a health food. We examined its activity on neural stem cells cultured from rat embryonic telencephalon. The royal jelly promoted generation of all three types of cells composing the central nervous system, neurons, astrocytes and oligodendrocytes. The action of 10-hydroxy-2-decenoic acid (decenoic acid), an unusual fatty acid of the royal jelly, and AMP N_1-oxide, a compound newly found in the royal jelly by authors, were also examined, and we found that decenoic acid promoted neurogenesis and AMP N_1-oxide, astrogliosis. These results demonstrate that several components of royal jelly differently affect the fate of neural stem cells, suggesting the unique activity of royal jelly as a whole is responsible for the summing up of the activities of its components."

There are other natural compounds with proven nerve-regenerative effects. They include curcumin, Lion's Mane Mushroom (which I give Trevor), Apigenin (found in vegetables like celery), blueberry, ginseng, Huperzine, Natto, Red Sage, Reservatrol, Royal Jelly, Theanine, Ashwaganda, and Treigoneline (found in coffee).[24] This same article stated that in a 2010 study published in the journal *Rejuvenation Research*, they found that a combination of blueberry (which Marti drew and said to blend into a drink), green tea, and carnosine have a neuritogenic (promoting neuron

---

[24] Ji, Sayer, "Six Bodily Tissues That Can Be Regenerated Through Nutrition" *Wake Up World*, (June 8, 2012).

regeneration) and stem cell regenerative effects in an animal model of neurodegenerative disease.

***

Chapter Twenty-One

"People like us, who believe in physics, know that the distinction between past, present, and future is only a stubbornly persistent illusion."

— *Albert Einstein*

Session Nineteen

This session was held on July 7, 2011. It was all three of us again this time. Before the session began, Michael began by talking about the MMR vaccine and said he's still hedging toward that one being a problem. He asks me if anyone has tested the vaccines to see if something is in it, like the SV-40 in the polio vaccine. I told him, "Not that I know of." He said that what the spirit people seem to be doing is showing us the general direction to look, and it's backing up what a lot of people are already exploring. What they're saying is you're on the right track with that. He also said that there is definitely criminality at work here.

Michael told me that they just did a session where Michael Jackson came through. They were doing a session for a woman who was a singer, and a man named Michael came through, with a last name that started with a J., who said he was a singer. The person having the session had a connection to him. There were other validations that it was him, but it was someone else's private session, and not my place to discuss it. There is a reason I am bringing it up, as you will see later on. Michael said that Michael Jackson is one of those people like Albert and the others, who are around the Earth a lot, and just trying to do what they can to help the world.

The channeling session was another short one, and began with Michael saying that someone was there by the name of Yuri. He was having a hard time with the last name and said it ended in "sky." I told him that name came up before and I couldn't find out who he was. He said he was Russian and was a doctor. He also heard UB and the number 42. He got the feeling that there was going to be some sort of accident to do with a nuclear submarine in Russia and couldn't get it out of his head.

He only mentioned a few things about Trevor; one was "Is there anything special about your boy's tongue? Does he have any problems with his tongue?" I mentioned that he was born with thrush, a white-coated tongue, which is a fungal infection. This is a tip-off that the child has a compromised immune system and should not be given vaccines in my opinion. I remember pointing it out to the doctor in the hospital when he was born and he told me it was milk. I told him it wouldn't rub off; he didn't think it was anything to worry about. It took a few months for our regular pediatrician to recognize it as thrush, and then he was put on an antifungal medication.

Then Michael said that he kept seeing ice cubes in Trevor's mouth. I told him that he chews on ice cubes whenever we go to the movies. He asked if he's ever been in ice bath or something. I said no, but he likes cold water, and doesn't notice how cold it is. It's like his pain receptors are off. Michael cut in: "Oh for God's sake, I can't get this submarine out of my mind. I think there is going to be some sort of accident with this sub. He's talking to me, he keeps saying, 'Terrible accident, terrible accident' he keeps saying. There is going to be a collision or something. We cut the session short for the day because Michael got hung up on the submarine accident. Marti, in the meantime, had been drawing some pictures, and they start to describe them to me. Here are the doodles:

MICRONOLOGIST

Doodle Explanations: Michael said that he thought of South Korea when he saw the helmet picture. I told him that a study just came out about the autism rate in South Korea being the highest anywhere, 1 in 38. He said that was relevant. Marti says it's related to war because of the helmet. I said maybe it's because of biological warfare. He said maybe North Korea is making something. I said and it's probably blowing in the wind.

(After the session, I looked into it and according to www.nti.org, The 2010 Defense White Paper by South Korea's Ministry of National Defense, estimates that North Korea possesses the causative agents of anthrax, smallpox, and cholera, among others. North Korea is upwind of South Korea. North Korea has many biowarfare manufacturing facilities, as well as chemical and nuclear weapons facilities. You can see an interactive map on the website as well.)

Michael said, "It's got to be germ warfare. The missing component I believe is the germ warfare, it has to be that." We talk about the synergistic effects of multiple toxins. Michael said he wonders if they are targeting boys with germ warfare. This had come up in a previous session. Nobody knows why boys get autism so much more than girls.

We talk about Temple Grandin not having the same thing that my son has, but they call it the same thing, autism, which is a problem. Michael says she is nothing like Trevor. He regressed and lost skills, and has physical problems, an illness. They lump it all together. Michael says that certain diseases appear to the same, but the cause is entirely different, even though the symptoms are the same. He suggested that maybe the virus blocks oxygen to the brain. He was seeing red blood cells and something attached to red blood cells which act like a carrier or transporter. "This virus is not natural," he said.

Michael thought the plant looked like an Aloe Vera plant. Marti said, "I don't know if Aloe Vera is the same as the Century plant, but I thought I heard Century." The Century plant is known as *Agave Americana*. Maybe there are some healing benefits of the plant that I don't know about. Other agave varieties, including Aloe Vera are used to help heal colon diseases.

The building with a telescope was an observatory. I found this interesting because a few times during past sessions, Arthur Stanley Eddington had come up. The picture looks like the kind of observatory he worked at. Remember, during the sessions, different spirits can come through to each of them separately. I also saw a picture of Albert standing in front of an observatory that looked just like this. So, that was a validation to me that it was indeed Eddington, and he was coming to Marti this time instead of Michael.

The word Micronologist, Marti said could be Microbiologist, but she thought she heard an "n" in there. Microbiology is the branch of biology that deals with microorganisms that are invisible to the naked eye and their effects on other living organisms. This includes bacteria, viruses and fungi. Perhaps this is another piece of the puzzle that needs further investigation. They were not sure what the tennis match or the hand with the long nails meant at the time.

***

Chapter Twenty-Two

"I believe that this nation should commit itself to achieving the goal, before this decade is out, of landing a man on the moon and returning him safely to the Earth."

— John F. Kennedy (1961)

Session Twenty

We did this session two days after the last one, on July 9, 2011, since Michael was having an off day. It happens. So, it was just Michael and I this time. The session began with Michael saying there was someone named John there, and he wasn't sure if it was John Kennedy or Sir John Hunter, the doctor. Then he said that my dad was there, asking if I was planning to take a trip somewhere. I told him that my sister just invited us to go to Cocoa Beach, Florida over Christmas, and when I looked on the map to see where it was, I was shocked to see that it was right by the Kennedy Space Center. He said my dad was holding up car keys and talking about a trip. I told Michael I just looked it up online that morning. He said, "That would make sense why I just mentioned Kennedy then." Michael said that my dad thinks that it is going well with HBOT and is hoping for good results.

Michael asked me if there was a Matt. I told him my husband is Matt. My dad said to say "hello" to him. Then my dad suggested that I do a blood test on Trevor, saying that it would reveal something to me. He said it might help me narrow things down. He also said that Sir John the doctor was there as well. Next, he brought up chlorophyll. I told Michael that one of the supplements he was on had chlorophyll in it. It was a microalgae, but it was taken from a lake in Klamath Falls, Oregon. After Fukushima, I didn't want to give it to him anymore because it is down-wind of Japan. The BioAlgae Superfood I've been mentioning is grown hydroponically indoors and contains chlorophyll. Chlorophyll has so many health benefits; it is like blood to plants. It helps oxygenate the body. It is also found in other products, like Moringa and is also sold separately.

Then Michael asked me if Trevor still had a yeast issue. I said I think he might, because since we started HBOT, I noticed a rash in the fold of his arms, and I had read that HBOT can aggravate yeast. Michael said that they were showing him bread to get him to talk about yeast. He said that he still has a persistent low-level yeast problem that is flaring up. I told him that I gave him a homeopathic yeast remedy yesterday and the rash went away. He said to keep giving it to him.

Michael asked me if Trevor ate meat and if we cut his meat into really small bites. I said yes, because he doesn't always chew his food very well. He said my dad was showing him cutting meat into small bites and Michael wondered why. This let me know that my dad is around us and knows what is happening.

Michael asked me who Jack was. I said that Jack Kennedy is John Kennedy. He was there too. Then he asked me if anyone around me was suing a medical company or if I had any plans to do so. I said no. He mentioned something about an affidavit. I feel that parents of harmed children should be able to be compensated for what happened to their child, but the way the system is set up protects vaccine manufacturers and the government from liability. The taxpayers fund the vaccine court, but very few have successfully been compensated. If the damage is said to be "autism" they deny it, but if there is another diagnosis, for instance mitochondria disorder, but the child also has a diagnosis of autism, the family was compensated. It is all semantics. Perhaps this will happen someday.

The subject quickly changed, and he said that there was someone there named William, connected to Sir John. Sir John Hunter's older brother's name is William, and was a Scottish anatomist and physician, and was the outstanding obstetrician of his day (1718-1783). He had come up in a previous session. This validated that it was him, having it come up again. Then Michael said:

Michael: "Oh, I think Albert is here. He's saying 'Hello.'"

Laura: "Oh, hello."

Michael: "It's kind of funny; he's treating you like a friend, like a friend who is saying hello."

Laura: "Huh."

Michael: "This is very interesting. I believe it's Albert, but he's holding

what looks like a metal rod. It looks like a rod, and he's holding it, and it seems to be, it's like an electrical thing. I don't know if this is this device that I once saw at a Holistic Fair. You hold these rods and it's some sort of medical tool to analyze what is going on in your body. I don't know if you've ever heard of it, but it is used for analysis of what is going on in the body."

Laura: "Ok."

Michael: "It's weird; I keep seeing electricity into my hands from these rods, like it has a stimulating effect."

(I didn't figure this out until after the session, but I believe he was referring to an EAV machine, or Electroacupuncture According to Voll, also known as Electro Dermal Screening. We went to see a few alternative/integrative medicine doctors who used an EAV machine for various testing in the body. If you are sick, it can tell you what virus you have, what organs are being affected, and many other things. You hold a metal rod in one hand and the doctor used another metal pointer on acupuncture points on the hands to get a reading on a computer screen. It was a very effective, non-invasive way of testing, especially for a child with autism with limited language.)

Michael: "You know your son's hands? Is he good at doing things with his hands, or does he have difficulty with his hands at all?"

Laura: "He has difficulty with fine motor skills, yeah."

Michael: "Does he really? With his hands?"

Laura: "Yeah, he just recently was able to button and zip his own clothing. He never was able to do it for many, many years." *(This started after we began HBOT.)*

Michael: "Well this is interesting. It's almost like a reverse, using the hands to stimulate the brain."

Laura: "Oh…"

Michael: "Instead of trying to get the brain to work to get the hands to work, you stimulate the hands that stimulate the brain. Like a reverse process. You understand?"

Laura: "Uh-huh."

Michael: "That is what Albert is talking about here."

Laura: "Oh, wow."

Michael: "Ok? You stimulate the hands and the hands transmit the stimulation to the brain, and the brain then says, 'Oh, I didn't know those nerves were there.' Like that, you know what I mean?"

Laura: "Ok. Yeah."

Michael: "Oh, I'd forgotten about that little muscle, that kind of thing. Getting the brain to be aware, like that, you see what I mean? Like reverse."

Laura: "Oh, interesting angle."

Michael: "Yeah, that's what I'm seeing."

Next, Michael said that if it was cool in the HBOT chamber we should ask for another blanket. It was cold actually, and we always shared a thin sheet. He said that being warmer is better for blood circulation, being cold constricts blood vessels. He said we'd get better results if he was warmer. The next time we went in I asked for an extra blanket. We were in the middle of our 40 HBOT treatments during this session. Every little thing helps, he added. Michael changed the subject and said:

Michael: "Now they're saying the word "Colic" to me. And I had a breathing feeling. Almost a tightness of breath when they said the word 'colic.' I don't know what colic is."

Laura: "Colic is what they call a baby who is very fussy and cries a lot and has stomachaches. Trevor was a very colicky baby." *(Lots of crying causes the breathing to change.)*

Michael: "Was he?"

Laura: "Yes."

Michael: "Well, every little thing is meaningful."

Laura: "Mmm-hmm. That's validating."

Michael: "Your dad knew him when he little, right?"

Laura: "Yeah."

Michael: "Well I think this is coming from your dad. This colic...Oh, and you just said that in the chamber he's been breaking out again. I wonder if the colic is linked to..."

Laura: "Yeast?"

Michael: "Yeast, yeah."

Laura: "Could be, they all have stomachaches, and that's where the yeast overgrowth is, is in their gastrointestinal tract."

Michael: "I wonder if the colic is linked to yeast?"

Laura: "Makes sense to me. He had it since he was a baby. He had thrush, and that's yeast."

Michael: "Maybe colic is yeast. Maybe yeast is what causes most colic?"

Laura: "Maybe."

Michael: "Seeing as how we are talking about conditions, perhaps they're going to bring up things that cause other things too, just because they can. They might bring up, by the way, this does this, that causes that. That sort of thing."

Laura: "Mmm-hmm."

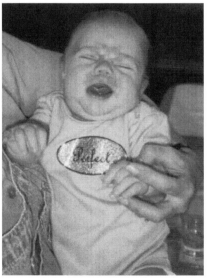

Colicky Trevor, 6 weeks old.

Next, they said the word "Neuropathy" to Michael, and he said he didn't know what that meant, but that's what they were saying. I looked it up afterwards, and learned that **Neuropathy** is a collection of disorders that occurs when nerves of the peripheral nervous system (the part of the nervous system outside of the brain and spinal cord) are damaged. The condition is generally referred to as **peripheral neuropathy**, and it is most commonly due to damage to nerve axons. Neuropathy usually causes pain and numbness in the hands and feet. It can result from traumatic injuries, infections, metabolic disorders, autoimmune disorders and exposure to toxins. Neuropathy can affect nerves that control muscle movement (motor nerves) and those that detect sensations such as coldness or pain (sensory nerves). In some cases – autonomic neuropathy – it can affect internal organs, such as the heart, blood vessels, bladder, or intestines. Sound familiar, parents? Just a minute ago Michael was talking about Trevor having difficulty with his hands.

Then, Michael asked me if I gave Trevor silica. I told him only in the Bioplasma, which is a homeopathic remedy of cell salts, including silica. Michael said that he needed more of it, adding that silica pushes things out. He said "Under a microscope, it looks like little arrowheads. And it pushes impurities out of the body; that's what it does; it works from the inside out. It works its way to the surface of any organ or the body; the skin which is an organ, but it pushes from the inside out. That's its function. It's little like arrowheads and it pushes impurities out of the body." I actually found a wonderful source of silica that actually gets rid of parasites and other toxins in the GI tract, called Diatomaceous Earth, which I started using for him later on. It must be the food grade variety. After that, Michael said:

Michael: "Did your dad smoke?"

Laura: "My dad smoked, yeah."

Michael: "Oh, did he?"

Laura: "50-some years."

Michael: "Yeah, I'm smelling smoke."

Laura: "Yeah, that's him."

Michael: "So did Einstein as well. I think we have a bunch of smokers here."

(One of the pictures Marti draws in a later session is of a camel. My dad smoked Camel cigarettes his whole life.)

Michael: "Your dad's saying he seems happier."

Laura: "Yeah, he does. He laughs, smiles, plays more, and interacts more."

Michael: "Was he doing something with a rope the other day? He doesn't skip?"

Laura: "No, but we have a few jump ropes and my other son was jump roping the other day."

Michael: "Was he?"

Laura: "Yeah. We were doing our little boot camp, where we dance and run down the stairs and stuff, and Damon was jump roping."

Michael: "Oh, well your dad is showing me jump roping."

Laura: "Yeah, that's probably Damon. Maybe we will try Trevor doing it or something."

Michael: "It would help his motor skills."

Laura: "Mmm-hmm."

Michael: "It works the other way around, you see? It's like a para-sympathetic affect, you know what I mean?"

Laura: "Uh-huh."

Michael: "I think people just think that the brain does everything, but it doesn't. Your nerve endings are the extension of your brain. It's actually brain matter. The nerve is brain matter. So you can look at it as little filaments of the brain in the fingers and hands and the feet. They are feelers of the brain, you got me?"

Laura: "Uh-huh."

Michael: "So, if you are stimulating them, the brain works better."

Laura: "Ok."

Michael: "Stimulation, see what I mean. In fact, they're using the word tactile. Tactile stimulation. Ok?"

Laura: "Ok."

Michael: "And that will help him as well, a lot. Maybe there is not enough of the right tactile stimulation taking place to help him."

Laura: "Ok."

Michael: "Ok? So, you're in the chamber with him, and you're lying down? Do you hold his hand?"

Laura: "No, but he'll have me tickle him and scratch him, and play and laugh."

Michael: "Oh, that's good. I was going to suggest that stimulation takes place while he's in there."

Laura: "Oh. What? Like massage his hands or something?"

Michael: "Yeah, something to make his brain more aware of his fingertips. His muscles, got me?"

Laura: "Ok, I'll try that."

Michael: "Does he use a squeeze ball?"

Laura: "No, but that's a good idea though."

Michael: "He might like that, a squeeze ball."

Laura: "Ok."

Michael: "Does he use the potty much? Does he pee a lot?"

Laura: "Yeah. Generally, he does. He drinks a lot of water."

Michael: "They are showing me his kidneys, and talking about him going to the potty a lot."

Laura: "Yeah, he does."

Michael: "Good, maybe he's trying to eliminate, maybe that's part of it, he's aware that he's got to try to eliminate. Well that's good."

Laura: "Uh-huh."

Michael: "Now they are bringing up bromine again."

Laura: "Ok."

Michael: "I forgot what bromine does."

Laura: "I had a question, if it is bromine, like in bread, or the toxic bromine that's in the water supply system."

Michael: "It's in the water."

Laura: "Ok, cuz they brought that up once before, and I wasn't sure which bromine they were talking about."

Michael: "No, I think it's in the water. Cuz I was just going to ask you if you used a water purifier, but I already know that you do. So I think it is the bromine in the water, ok? They are saying to me, 'Without doubt.' So that's it, ok?"

Laura: "Ok."

Michael: "Oh, so you had a question about that, did you?"

Laura: "Yep, I did."

Michael: "You never asked that question on your list."

Laura: "No, it was one of the other ones that I didn't put on the list."

Michael: "Well, there you go, you see, they answer your questions but, now they really answered it. You didn't know which bromine. I didn't even know there were two bromines. You see, it's a slow process. This is a big problem. There a lot of things that need to be figured out. So, that's interesting."

(After the session, I looked a bit more into bromine in drinking water, and found out that it is used as a disinfectant in the water supply. It also reacts with the organic material in the water and creates toxic by-products, known as DPB's (disinfection by-products). It is an unintended by-product of water purification and generates hundreds of different compounds. Some are genotoxic, which damage DNA, some are carcinogenic, causing cancer, and others cause birth defects. Bromine is also a byproduct of hydraulic fracking, and ends up in the water supply.)

Michael: "I don't know why they are showing me his hair. I almost feel like analyzing his hair."

Laura: "For toxins or what?"

Michael: "Yeah. Do people do that?"

Laura: "Yeah."

Michael: "They do? Have you ever done it?"

Laura: "No."

Michael: "You know what I think they are doing? They're saying this: Why limit your toxicity tests to just one thing or two things?"

Laura: "Ok."

Michael: "If you do it with multiple things, you'll have multiple markers."

Laura: "Right."

Michael: "You have a blood test, you have a hair test, you do all the tests, and that helps you too."

Laura: "Yep."

Michael: "Ok?"

Laura: "That's a good idea. I've mainly been doing energetic testing because I don't trust the medical community anymore."

(Marti says, "It still needs to be accepted by the medical community.")

Laura: "Right."

Michael: "You can't just do a one-sided thing here; there are legitimate people out there. Not everyone is narrow minded or tainted, you know?"

Laura: "Yeah. Or they only trust doctors and medical tests. If they see it on a medical test, they'll believe it."

Michael: "Exactly. So, every little thing helps, you know? Also, they are showing me checking his eyes. Has he been to an iridologist?"

Laura: "You know, it's funny, I went to one a long time ago, but he wouldn't sit still long enough for him to look in his eyes."

Michael: "Right, well I think now he may. Plus technology is advanced, they can take pictures now."

Laura: "Yeah. I know a lot about iridology, I looked into it, had an appointment for him, he just wouldn't sit still."

Michael: "Well, that was a long time ago."

Laura: "Yeah, many years ago."

Michael: "Look into it again."

(Iridology is a safe, non-invasive, diagnostic technique that is performed by looking at the iris of the eyes through a special device. The eyes are the windows to the soul, and mirrors of the body, and iridology can detect the condition of various organs and tissues in the body.)

Michael: "Does he have acupuncture at all?"

Laura: "He does acupressure. It's the same thing; same acupuncture points, but just not needles. That's how we clear him of all of his stuff, all his toxins, is through acupressure. That's good, right?"

Michael: "Yeah."

(We used NAET, Nambudripad's Allergy Elimination Technique), for both Trevor and I, which uses acupuncture or acupressure in children to eliminate food and environmental allergies. We also use a similar technique called BioSET, or Bioenergetic Sensitivity and Enzyme Therapy, is an energy-based allergy elimination method that is based on Chinese medicine and acupuncture principles.)

Michael: "I'm asking about the weapon stuff. And when I dwell on that, I get the botulism."

Laura: "Ok."

Michael: "So I think that is weaponized. I think it's botulism."

Laura: "Yeah, they said that before."

Michael: "Well I'm asking again, and that's what they are bringing up. This definitely seems to be fired as a canister or some sort of small missile. That's how it's dispersed."

Laura: "Hmm."

(Marti's doodles from session eleven show a picture of a small missile or bomb that landed in the dirt, and in the next session that she doodles, she draws another military bomb on a launcher.)

Michael: "You know that horseshoe part of the brain? The hypothalamus is in the middle of that, is it?"

Laura: "Mmm-hmm."

Michael: "Well, when I dwell on that, what I see is like a virus like the herpes virus."

Laura: "Ok."

Michael: "You know it stays... doesn't herpes stay in the jaw area? And then when it flares up, but it is always there. It's almost like that. You understand?"

Laura: "Ok."

Michael: "So perhaps this virus, I don't know if there is a way to get it out completely, or if you just have to be able to get it down so that it doesn't do any harm. You know what I mean?"

Laura: "Yes, like suppress it like they do with the herpes viruses."

Michael: "Yeah, get the body to suppress it enough, you know what I mean?"

Laura: "Mmm-hmm."

(It's interesting, when I did the sessions with the other medium, she brought up a future medicine to treat autism and compared it to how they suppress the herpes virus as well. A lot of children with autism also have various human herpes viruses, and there are eight of them, including Epstein Barr virus, HHV-6, shingles, and cytomegalovirus. Many of them go dormant in the nerves. Trevor had muscle tested weak to Epstein Barr and HHV-6 during a BioSET session.)

We were wrapping up the session for the night, and Michael finished the session by saying: "Everything is about clues really, at the end of the day. All science is things being highlighted, things being conjectured, things being pointed at, and you arrive at a certain conclusion. That's what we are on; it's kind of like an egg hunt in a way. That's what we're doing. It's all a process of elimination. Well, they brought that up, that's interesting, well that concurs with this, and that makes sense because blah, blah, blah. It's a process. Narrowing things down."

***

Session Twenty: After the Session:
Featured Spirits: President John F. Kennedy, Jr., Sir John Hunter, William Hunter, Albert Einstein

The other character that showed up was my dad. It was so great to see how my deceased loved ones kept showing up with all of these scientists and medical people. It gave it more credibility in my mind, because I could instantly validate what my loved ones were saying, where I often had to look up the things that the spirits that I didn't know were telling me afterward.

One of the things that came up in this session that I put into effect afterward was the suggestion to massage Trevor's hands during our HBOT sessions. The first day I did it, after we got out and were getting dressed, he put on his own socks for the first time in his life. I was so proud of him. Talk about instant gratification! It's like his hands suddenly worked better and he could perform these small motor skills that he previously struggled with. I didn't really know what I was doing, but I massaged and squeezed each finger, rubbed the palm of his hands, and even ran Reconnective Healing energy on them while we were in there. Something good happened.

I also kept him on his homeopathic yeast remedy, called Aquaflora for the remainder of the sessions, and made sure he got his probiotics daily. I asked the technician who was assisting us if it was common for yeast to flare up during HBOT, and he said that oxygen helps everything grow more, so it was common. Here is a picture of the two of us in the Hyperbaric Oxygen chamber. We have our extra blanket to stay warm. The water was for Trevor to pop his ears on the "dive" and when we "resurfaced." A few times, because of the pressure, if I forgot to unscrew the top of the bottle on the way up and the water squirt out of the top all over us. Good times.

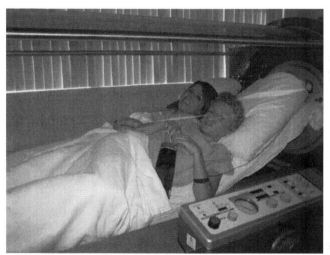

Trevor and I during HBOT.

Chapter Twenty-Three

"You know I do really hate to say it
The government don't wanna see
But if Roosevelt was livin'
He wouldn't let this be, no, no…

All I wanna say is that
They don't really care about us
All I wanna say is that
They don't really care about us

Some things in life they just don't
wanna see
But if Martin Luther was livin'
He wouldn't let this be."

— Michael Jackson's "They Don't Care
About Us"

Session Twenty-One

This session was held on July 16, 2011. It was just Michael and I this time again. Michael started the session by asking me:

Michael: "Is your boy more loving?"

Laura: "Yes."

Michael: "I know it sounds like a strange question, but…"

Laura: "Yeah, this is kind of weird, the other day, he got out of the pool because his brother made him cry, and I brought him in the house because he was screaming. And he came over, put his arms around me and laid his head on my shoulder, and was crying on my shoulder. He turned to me for comfort! I almost cried because I can't remember the last time he did that. Usually he comforts himself and settles himself down, and if you try to hug him he pushes you away."

Michael: "Oh, wow."

Laura: "Yeah, so I was like, 'Oh, my God, he's turning to me for comfort!'"

Michael: "Um, this may sound crazy but I think Michael Jackson's

here."

Laura: "Oh, really? Cool!"

Michael: "Yeah and he's saying... he's talking about love. And you know he loved children. And that's what he said to me. He said her son is more loving."

Laura: "Awe. Yes, he is."

Michael: "I think he wants to help in some way. I think he's here. He's saying 'Yes.' So I think I do have Michael Jackson here. That's interesting."

Laura: "Oh, wow."

Michael: "It's because he loves kids, you know."

Laura: "Mmm-hmm."

Trevor giving me a kiss.
He was more loving.

(I've always enjoyed Michael Jackson's music. I used to watch the Jackson 5 cartoon as a kid even. My gymnastics team learned and performed the "Thriller" dance. I even have some Michael Jackson mixes on my iPod that I play during my Pilates classes sometimes. This is why I mentioned the other person's session where Michael told me about Michael Jackson showing up. Neither Michael nor I believed the allegations against him involving children that were so public. He was never charged, and the father of one of

the boys committed suicide later on. I was pretty shocked when I was looking up his song lyrics that he mentions both Roosevelt and Martin Luther King in his song that I quoted "They Don't Care About Us" because both of them have also come through during our sessions. This song is one of my angry songs that I play when I think about what our government and medical establishment are doing to our children. I also found it interesting that Michael Jackson used to have a Hyperbaric Oxygen chamber himself. When we went to HBOT, I often fell asleep inside, and joked with the technician afterward that I took a "Michael Jackson nap." He told me that the chamber that he had was the model previous to the one we were in from the same company.)

Michael: "The doctor is here again. (Sir John Hunter) So let's see what he's got to say here. Do you feed your kids salads?"

Laura: "Trevor doesn't eat salad."

Michael: "He doesn't eat salad?"

Laura: "No."

Michael: "Why?"

Laura: "I don't know. He eats cucumbers and tomatoes and things that go on a salad, just not the lettuce."

Michael: "He doesn't eat leaf stuff?"

Laura: "No, maybe I should try. We're having a salad tonight with dinner."

Michael: "I think you should. There is this sense that maybe you're a little too easy on him because everything has been so difficult, but I think he needs greens. He needs like spinach or did you ever use dandelion leaves?"

Laura: "No, I've never tried them."

Michael: "Well I'm going to because you know what I found out the other day?"

Laura: "What?"

Michael: "Dandelion leaves are the number 6 herb in Chinese medicine. It has an incredible amount of stuff in it. It is an anti-oxidant, it does so many different things, it's incredible. The leaves, you can use them like lettuce leaves. They have the pompom thing."

Laura: "Right."

Michael: "So check into that ok?"

Laura: "Ok."

(In Chinese Medicine, dandelion is used to treat stomach problems. Dandelion leaves act as a diuretic, increasing the amount of urine the body produces. The leaves are used to stimulate the appetite and help digestion. Dandelion flower has antioxidant properties. Dandelion may also help improve the immune system. Herbalists use dandelion root to detoxify the liver and gallbladder, and dandelion leaves to support kidney function. They are also testing dandelion root extract to cure certain blood cancers.)

Michael: "How's his tummy been lately? Do you ever rub his tummy, or does he ever rub his tummy?"

Laura: "Yeah, he sometimes has a tummy ache and will tell me 'tummy ache,' but I don't know that he's complained about it recently."

Michael: "Oh he hasn't had any recently, that's good."

Laura: "I've been treating him for yeast again since last time it came up that he has yeast. So maybe he does, because it affects your gastrointestinal tract."

Michael: "I am seeing something but I'm not exactly sure what it is. I'm seeing a tube with blue in it. Someone is holding up this kind of vial. It looks like a tube, you know, like a test tube and it has blue liquid in it. Oh, blue for lack of oxygen."

Laura: "Oh, like blue blood, they brought that up before."

Michael: "They did?"

Laura: "Yeah, blue blood. And last time they told me I should have his blood tested. For what I don't know, toxins I think."

Michael: "You see, I feel like holding my breath. So, it's like lack of oxygen or I don't know what this is, but it's blue blood."

Laura: "Ok. They brought that up a few times, and I'm still not sure what…"

Michael: "Has he been looking you in the eye more?"

Laura: "Yes."

Michael: "Would he avert his eyes before, but now he looks at you in

the eye."

Laura: "Yeah, he used to not look at other people in the eyes more, and I see him directing questions to people and looking at them, at school even."

Michael: "So, he's doing that more, he's making more eye contact."

Laura: "Yeah."

Michael: "That's what he's talking about. Has he ever hung upside-down?"

Laura: "Not really, but he goes upside down when he's on the trampoline, handstands."

Michael: "That's slightly different. You don't have one of those back machines, do you?"

Laura: "No, but I know what you're talking about, my friend has one."

Michael: "Well the thing is, I'm thinking it would also help get more blood to his brain, stimulate his brain more."

Laura: "Oh, that makes sense."

Michael: "Yogis do headstands and they do that and it gets the spinal fluid, the subtle spinal fluid to go to the brain. It's a brain stimulation. It's what it does. And what we're trying to do is stimulate his brain. He might like it, hanging upside down, just for 5, 10 minutes, something like that."

Laura: "Ok, I like them too."

Michael: "Ok, it's something else you can do there. He'll probably enjoy it and it would be good for him. So try that. It's not a big expense. I've got one, you guys can use it as well."

Laura: "Ok."

Michael: "I think there is someone here with the name Croft. C-R-O-F-T."

Laura: "Ok."

Michael: "He also seems to be someone like a Sir. Sir something Croft. Either Alan Croft, or Albert Croft. Alexander, could be Alexander Croft.

I've written Alan, but it could be Alexander. Alex, Alexander. He feels like a medical person too, to me."

Laura: "Ok."

Michael: "Alexander Croft. (I never did find out who this is.) What I'm seeing is bone structure. But I'm seeing skeletal structure. How is the bone marrow in autistic kids?"

Laura: "I don't know."

Michael: "Is it normal?"

Laura: "I don't know, I don't see how it could be."

Michael: "Maybe that would be something to look up. They're using the word 'inhibited.' There may be something there we need to look at."

Laura: "Ok."

(Stem cells are produced in the bone marrow. If bone marrow is somehow "inhibited", it would affect stem cell growth. I have heard of people having successful stem cell therapies with children with autism. Many were in other countries. It helps oxygenate the blood and boost the immune system, so does HBOT.)

Michael: "What's scurvy?"

Laura: "Vitamin C deficiency."

Michael: "There's a Vitamin C deficiency, is there?"

Laura: "He's taking a Vitamin C supplement because he's low in it."

Michael: "Do his nails look alright?"

Laura: "Now they do, but they used to be a little messed up."

Michael: "Did they? What did they look like?"

Laura: "They were really weak and he'd bite them all the time."

Michael: "I was going to say, 'Did he bite them?'"

Laura: "Yeah, he bit them off all the time."

Michael: "Ah, well that meant he needed silica. When people chew skin or nails they're trying to get silica."

Laura: "Oh, ok."

Michael: "See, this is skin and bones stuff, see? We're getting into this a little bit here. There seems to be some sort of low, maybe it's production of... is it white cells or red cells? Huh, he's back to showing me this blue... this must be very important, this..."

Laura: "Vial of blue blood?"

Michael: "This blue blood thing. He was never starved of oxygen was he, at any point?"

Laura: "Not that I know of. Unless at birth. I know that if they clamp the umbilical cord too soon it cuts off the supply of oxygen from the cord to the baby."

Michael: "Has that ever happened?"

Laura: "Well, they call it Early Cord Clamping, and it's very common in births now, they cut and clamp the cord right away. That's the only thing I can think of."

Michael: "Why do they do that?"

Laura: "To hurry through the birth process. They don't let it happen naturally, and let the baby get everything out of the cord before they cut and clamp it, they do it really prematurely."

Michael: "And what is the reason for that?"

Laura: "To speed up the process so the Doctor can get out of there, I don't know."

Michael: "It's for their convenience; it's not so much for the kid."

Laura: "Yeah, they call it Early Cord Clamping, and it prevents the oxygen from fully getting into the baby from once they start breathing air."

Michael: "Early Cord Clamping, huh. Because he's a pediatric doctor, Sir John..."

Laura: "William was the pediatrician, obstetrician, he delivered babies."

Michael: "William did, ok. Well, it makes sense that these things would concern them. These things didn't happen in their day."

Laura: "No."

Michael: "Well your son must be growing really fast. You're having to get him more clothes?"

Laura: "I just had to buy him a whole new wardrobe and new shoes."

Michael: "Well that's what they're talking about."

Laura: "Yeah, he got all clothes for his birthday, and shoes cuz he outgrew everything."

(Trevor is small for his age, but he went three years without hardly any growth. It was nice to see him growing finally. It was interesting that they brought it up. My kids are three years apart and are the same height.)

Next, my mom's mom came through and talked about painting the inside of the house. I told Michael that my mom just asked me to help her paint her room a different color. I told her it would have to wait until we were done with HBOT. He said that my Grandma wanted to say "hello" to my mom. The fact that she was aware of our painting conversation lets me know she's around. Then a friend of Michael's named Jim came through. Before Jim died, he told Michael to expect him to bug him every now and then. Michael said:

Michael: "Is there Scottish in your family?"

Laura: "Yes."

Michael: "Is that on your mother's side?"

Laura: "Yeah, my mother's side." (My grandma who was there is Scottish.)

Michael: "You see Jim's dad is Scottish, and he said 'Well, they are a lot Scottish.'"

Laura: "My mom's grandparents were born in Scotland."

Michael: "Yeah, well Jim's dad was in the Scott's Guard, he was a major. Jim would always talk about that. I think this is my friend Jim."

Laura: "Huh."

Michael: "He keeps saying he's just here to help, he's here to help. Marti, Jim's here. He's saying "Hello" to you. I don't have any what? Altoids, hee, hee. It is that Jim. And of course, that Doctor is Scottish."

Laura: "Yep."

Michael: "That makes sense; that makes sense that Jim would be buddies

with him. He'd be talking away with him."

Laura: "Yep, both the brothers were Scottish."

Michael: "That makes sense to me. We have a few of Scotts in the room, see?"

Laura: "If it's not Scottish, it's crap! That's a little joke." *(From a SNL skit with Mike Myers.)*

(Marti was looking up Early Cord Clamping on the computer after it came up and she explained how it can be very detrimental. She said that by clamping the cord too early the baby doesn't get T-cells.)

Michael: "Interesting, isn't it? This is quite important for them to bring it up."

Laura: "Yeah, that's the only lack of oxygen that he could have had, as far as I know, is if they did that. And I know that it is very common in modern births."

(Marti added that "They want to quickly get the baby, suction it and make it breathe and that's not necessary really. They're still getting oxygen through the umbilical cord.")

Michael: "Oh, I see, so there is no need to really rush it. Why do the people allow them to rush it then? Because you're in a hospital environment and you have no control?"

Laura: "No, they just do their thing, you're lying on the bed, and they do what they do, and they hand your baby once it's all clean and pretty."

Michael: "Ok, so here we are in an unnatural environment then. Well maybe this Doctor is concerned about this and thinks we should get back to a more natural...it seems a bit unnatural all of this."

(Marti says, "The placenta gets released naturally, but you still have to cut the cord eventually, but it doesn't have to be cut straight away.")

Michael: "That's more info than I'd like to know. I've never been at a birth, never had kids. This must be fairly important for them to bring this up."

(Marti says, "It also deprives the baby of a lot of blood, they have a low capacity of blood.")

Michael: "Low capacity of blood, that has to be why they're bringing this up. It's like a lack of blood."

Laura: "And oxygen."

(Marti says, "It deprives the baby's body of up to half of the blood volume.")

Michael: "Half of the baby's blood volume, up to half the blood volume. That's a lot. Bloody hell, that's crazy! Wow!"

Laura: "It could be just another thing that's sets them up, and then you start jacking them."

Michael: "It's another thing, see. Boy, that needs looking into, I think that's fairly important what they are getting into here."

Laura: "Is that what they are talking about?"

Michael: "I think so. Cuz it has to do with right at the birth. If you've only got half of your blood, you've only got half of your oxygen. Plus it's so, that's crazy. You wouldn't take blood from a baby, would you? You wouldn't take half of their blood for a blood bank? That's nuts."

Laura: "There is a lot of information on the web about Early Cord Clamping. One of my friends thinks that's one of the major causes of setting a kid up to become autistic."

Michael: "It is a big thing, yeah."

(Marti says "The immune system being compromised because the baby isn't getting it from the mother.")

Michael: "It's crazy. I think it comes back to this we have to keep every-one alive mentality. Rushing everything, it's just nuts. Sticking kids in incubators, no matter what."

Laura: "Well this is healthy babies, full term. That's just the birth practice; they just try to rush through so they can get on to whatever they're doing next. You're in and out in a day from the hospital because your insurance only pays for you to be there for a day."

Michael: "Because of your insurance."

Laura: "Uh-huh."

Michael: "So if you had the money, you could stay two days."

Laura: "Some insurance pays for two days, but now it's like one day in the hospital to recover from childbirth. It's insanity."

(Marti says, "Even when you have stitches.")

Laura: "Yeah, you have no time to recover your own body, much less, 'Here's your baby, good luck with that.' And they shove you out the door."

Michael: "That's crazy."

Laura: "Everything is scheduled and rushed."

Michael: "In France it is completely different."

(Marti says, "They even help you take care of the baby afterward.")

Laura: "That's how it should be."

Michael: "Ok, well this is pretty important what they're bringing up."

Laura: "That's a good validation, I've thought of that before, and wondered myself if that has something to do with…"

Michael: "It does have a lot to do with it."

Laura: "Making them vulnerable from the get go."

Michael: "Yeah, of course it would. I don't know about any of this. I don't have kids; I don't know a thing about childbirth, so this is all news to me. But it makes total sense."

Laura: "Yep."

Michael: "When you think how much that compromises your kid, and with all the other things stacked up, it's a wonder they survive at all."

Laura: "Mmm-hmm."

Michael: "I'm not getting anything else now. I think they've stopped. It wasn't a lot but it was something."

Laura: "I think it's getting down to the nitty gritty now. They're giving us all these things that people can do to prevent…"

Michael: "It's preventative."

Laura: "Having a child vulnerable for a new parent. Don't do this, don't do this. And then what happens if your child is damaged, how you can help them and fix what happened to them."

Michael: "That's right; they seem to be giving us the preventative things and what you can do to help your kid. They haven't gone into any bio-warfare stuff with me. I don't think there is anything we can do about that. Everybody really knows that they are doing this stuff, but nobody wants to think about it. So I can't see, unless there is a mass outcry that anybody is going to do anything about it."

Laura: "Mmm-hmm."

Michael: "That's something that has to be done through some big collective movement."

Laura: "Right."

Michael: "You know what I mean? Everybody for fifty years has been worried about a nuclear war, well, we've already had one. They've detonated 2,000 nuclear bombs. So, you've already had a war. The entire planet is contaminated. And nobody even thinks about it. They walk around going 'I hope we don't have a nuclear war.' We've already had one."

Laura: "Yeah, just because your town didn't get blown to smithereens."

Michael: "Exactly, just because you didn't lose your town…"

Laura: "The radiation is still there, you just can't see it."

Michael: "Absolutely, and nobody thinks about it because their town hasn't gone, but they're all dying from it."

Laura: "Yeah."

Michael: "You're dealing with, on the whole, no matter how clever they are, most people are not thinkers. They don't think about things."

Laura: "They don't have time to think about bigger issues."

Michael: "That's part of it, keep everybody busy."

Laura: "You've got to work every day of your life, never get a vacation, dealing with your sick kids constantly."

Michael: "Yeah, exactly."

Laura: "Trying to make ends meet."

Michael: "That's right, that's part of the strategy. Keep all the people who are capable of thinking far too busy so that they can even think about it."

Laura: "They don't have any free time to devote to a good cause."

Michael: "No. The whole medical field is so messed up too. The whole thing is insane, it really is. No medical care for millions and millions of people in America. It is like a back-water, third-world African country to me. It's crazy."

Laura: "And then the stuff that insurance does cover doesn't help anybody. It's like, "Here's your drugs, go home. Let's put a band-aid on that.""

Michael starts to tell me about a healer called John of God, and how he does his healings, adding:

Michael: "A lot of great healers do that, they say 'Here, it's a special amulet, take it home, it's been blessed, and it will heal your kid.' But really it's the healer doing it, the person just has this belief and it allows the healing to take place, and they don't block it. That's how a lot of Yogi's do healing. I think there is some of that going on with your boy by the way."

Laura: "Oh, yeah?"

Michael: "You understand? Because you're getting interaction with these spirit people, so what you've got is an environment where he can be healed easier as well, do you understand? So there is some healing taking place too."

Laura: "Yeah, that makes sense. I always ask for help, I say 'Whatever you guys can do up there, help me out here.'"

Michael: "And you're doing the right thing. Because even thought they can help, they have to be asked. Nobody in the spirit world can do something unless they're asked."

(Recently, Trevor was having a meltdown, and I had him lying down in his bed and ran some Reconnective Healing energy on him to calm him down, as I often do. In my head, I asked anyone in spirit to help me out. Trevor said out loud, "It's Grandpa." I said, "Do you see Grandpa?" He said, "Yes." I said, "Is Grandpa helping you?" Again, he said "Yes." He calmed down quickly, and I thanked my dad for his help. Trevor has shown on numerous occasions his ability to hear my thoughts telepathically. For instance, I was putting him to bed and saying a little gratitude prayer, and in my head I said "Thank

you" and Trevor said out loud "You're welcome." It caught me off guard, but showed me that he could hear my thoughts. Why else would he say "You're welcome" out of the blue? I asked him "Did you say "You're welcome?" He laughed and answered, "Thank you, you're welcome." I've heard many similar stories of the psychic abilities of children with autism.)

Laura: "I've been begging for help for years. When I feel like I'm on my last leg I pray, 'Somebody please!' And a miracle always seems to happen, something comes up, I'm drawn in the right direction, something I find or someone I talk to. That's how it's always happened. And then I thank them, 'Thank you to whoever sent me this person.'"

Michael: **"That's exactly how it happens because I was like that when I was a teenager and that's when I came across my master because I was looking so much for the answers to things."**

(He tells me the story about how he met his master in England.)

Laura: "I'm still on that healing path and however it happens, I'm just open to whatever it is. I have to let go of my ideas of how he's going to be healed and in what timeframe and just allow it to happen in the way it's supposed to for him. Which is hard for people to do when they're desperate."

Michael: **"Yeah, there are so many things to address. We haven't even got into karmic things. Maybe we should touch on that a little bit in the book. There has to be some karmic reason why this is happening to him outside of the fact, there has to be a reason for everything."**

Laura: "I wonder about that myself."

Michael: **"There has to be some karmic cause for it."**

Laura: "And why all these kids would sign up for this at the same time."

Michael: **"Well, why did everybody sign up to be gassed in gas chambers?"**

Laura: "I don't know."

Michael: **"I knew somebody that thought they had been a Jew in their last life, and had been gassed, and I asked them why do you think you did, and they said because they thought that they were someone in the life before that where they were affluent, and kind of didn't care much. So when they came back, they decided they were going to be a Jew and** be put in a Concentration Camp as a sort of atonement for their other life."

Laura: "Hmm, wow."

Michael: "This sort of makes sense in a way, but is pretty harsh from a soul point of view. But these are the decisions that people make."

Laura: "Right."

Michael: "So, maybe if we word it right, maybe we can keep it simple and just get people to think about karma a little bit. Cuz it does play into it, absolutely nothing happens by chance."

Laura: "I think all of these kids are going to awaken everybody enough to make some changes and change the path that we're on."

***

Session Twenty-One: After the Session
Featured Spirits: Michael Jackson, Sir John Hunter, William Hunter

I always try to incorporate the suggestions that come up during the sessions if I can. I tried to give Trevor some lettuce, but he wasn't having it. I'll keep trying. I also went out and bought one of those back stretcher devices that Michael brought up. You hook your feet in it and slowly invert yourself, and can go all the way upside down like a bat if you wish. I've had Trevor try it a few times. He seemed to like it, and I could see the blood rushing to his head because his face turned red. I just did it for a few minutes. I tried it myself too. It feels good on the back as well. I'll have to do it more frequently.

I find it so interesting that every session we do, another piece of the puzzle is added. I almost don't want to stop, because I never know what will come up next. This time, Early Cord Clamping was discussed. Think about it, if half of the baby's blood volume is stopped from getting into his body, along with oxygen, T-cells, stem cells, and other important factors, and then the baby is given a Hepatitis B shot, the day it is born, which is filled with toxins, it sets them up for disaster from day one. They say that nature's first stem cell transplant happens at birth. But not when the cord is immediately clamped, the transfer doesn't happen.

***

Chapter Twenty-Four

"The significant problems we have cannot be solved at the same level of thinking with which we created them."

— Albert Einstein

Session Twenty-Two

This session was done on July 23, 2011. It was all three of us again this time, so Marti was drawing her doodles again. The session began with Michael stating that Albert was there, as well as my late husband, Darren and his grandmother Helen and his grandfather Frank. He said that my husband had dark, almost black hair, and that he had blue eyes, which were true. Michael said there was someone named John there as well.

Michael said that there was someone there with a mustache, and then he figured out it was Albert. He said:

Michael: "Did Albert Einstein have a mustache?"

Laura: "Yeah, he did."

Michael: "He does, doesn't he?"

Laura: "Yes."

Michael: "I said, 'Who is this guy with the mustache I can see here?' And he keeps saying, 'Al. He keeps saying, 'Al, Al.' I said are you 'Al?' He said, 'The guy with the mustache that you're looking at is Al.' I said, 'Albert?' He said, 'Yeah.' So Albert is here, ok. He's saying 'Hello' to you."

Laura: "Hello."

Michael: "He's very polite, you know."

Laura: "Yeah."

Michael: "He said, 'How are we doing then? Doing good?'"

Laura: "Uh-huh."

Michael: "Who is this other person then? Does Albert have a brother?"

Laura: "No, just a sister. He did have a friend named John though, an associate."

Michael: "Named John. Oh, ok. Well I've already said John. So that's John, an associate of Albert's."

Laura: "Ok. I'm pretty sure I know who this is."

Michael: "I don't, but he's back to this 'J' name again, as I speak with Albert, you see. So what I think he's doing is he's making me realize that the John is connected to him. Is John a Professor?"

Laura: "Yep. Ha, ha."

Michael: "He said 'John's a Professor.' I said, 'Ok.'"

(John von Neumann was a Professor at Princeton University's Institute for Advanced Study, and was a friend of Albert's. They were two of the first four faculty members there. John also came through a few times in the sessions for my other book. I didn't name him specifically in the book because I didn't give Albert's identity, so if I mentioned John von Neumann was an associate, people would have been more apt to figure it out. I knew a bit about him from looking him up when he came through before.)

Laura: "Yes."

Michael: "He said I haven't talked to him yet before."

Laura: "No, you haven't."

Michael: "Is this right? I said have I spoken to him before and he said 'No.' Is this guy English or American?"

Laura: "Neither. He's not American, but he worked at Princeton."

Michael: "Well, let's put it this way, he can speak English. He's speaking English to me, this guy."

Laura: "Yes."

Michael: "Did he live in Germany then?"

Laura: "I'm pretty sure he was German or Austrian, one of those."

(He was born in Budapest, Austria-Hungary, and also lived in Germany and the U.S.)

Michael: "He seems German to me, this guy, this Professor. Is he a peer of Albert?"

Laura: "Yes."

(John von Neumann lived and taught at the University of Berlin, Germany.)

Michael: "Did Albert study under him, or did he confer with him?"

Laura: "Yes."

Michael: "Confer. Ugh, I don't know who this John is."

Michael was having a difficult time with his last name, but was getting all of the letters, so I eventually just told him it was two names, von Neumann. Michael audibly asked Albert why John was there. Then he said:

Michael: "Is he a physicist, this John?"

Laura: "Yes."

Michael: "I said what does he do? He's a physicist, he said."

Laura: "Yes."

(He was a principal member of the Manhattan Project as a nuclear physicist who helped design the Atomic bombs that were dropped in Japan.)

Michael: "So, he's like a Theoretical Physicist?"

(He was a Theoretical Physicist, and one of the greatest mathematicians in history, among other things.)

Laura: "I know he helped build the first computer, a total brainiac, and a Professor, Physicist, Mathematician."

Michael: "Yeah, this guy is into theoretics, you see?"

Laura: "And a friend of Einstein's."

Michael: "I wonder why he keeps doing this. He keeps tapping his pipe, emptying it in front of me. He's standing in front of me, he took his pipe out and he's tapping it out, emptying the ash out of his pipe. Something about ash, something about the waste. Tobacco or the waste of tobacco or something. I asked him 'have we done all that we can do with the autism?' He says, 'we've covered most of it.'"

Laura: "Ok."

Michael: "It seems to me like they are looking for a breakthrough here to do with the vaccine thing. He's talking about people trying to control everything through vaccines. He seems to feel like your boy is doing

fine, they've done the best they can do at the moment and they are waiting to see the outcome at the end of this stint (Of HBOT). He likens it to an experiment actually, if you don't mind the use of that word."

Laura: "We are the Guinea Pigs."

Michael: "Yeah, you'll have to look at it that way he says. They're trying an experiment to see what they can do."

Laura: "Ok."

Michael: "Did he calm down a lot quicker last night?"

Laura: "Oh, yeah. After we hung up the phone, he was fine in like 20 seconds. You heard how he was screaming."

Michael: "Yeah, I said to Marti I don't know how she deals with it, I think it would drive me insane, all of that."

Laura: "Oh, yeah."

Michael: "So in the past he would have gone on a lot longer, would he?"

Laura: "Oh, yeah, hours sometimes."

Michael: "Oh my God."

Laura: "Yeah, it's enough to drive you nuts."

Michael: "Well that's what I was thinking, 'Oh my God, this might go on for hours.' Well that's what he just said, Albert."

Laura: "Yeah?"

Michael: "Now he's showing me something on his lapel, almost like a badge, or like a pin. Almost looks like a pin from some sort of organization. And he's saying the name 'Ken.' What's that pin you're showing me? It looks like a pin, but it's blue. A Naval pin? What is this? I can see like an anchor or a smile. What I'm seeing almost looks like an anchor or it's the nose and a smile, you know what I mean? It's got this downward thing. What is this you're showing me? A ship? It's got a Naval feeling about it. A ship, a boat. It's got a blue background, so it's a boat. It's something about a boat that he's going on about. I see the blue background, it seems to be an anchor, but it's a boat with a sail. So it's a boat. Was anyone in the Navy connected to you?"

(At first I thought that Darren's grandfather might have been in the Navy, but then after the session, I learned that he wasn't, but both Albert and John von Neumann were consultants for the U.S. Navy. In fact, it was John von Neumann's Navy consults which led to his involvement with the Manhattan Project. He was a key player who worked directly with Oppenheimer. When I looked up someone named Ken associated with von Neumann and the Navy, I learned that John von Neumann was a consultant in developing IBM's NORC (Naval Ordinance Research Calculator), the first Super Computer, the most powerful computer in existence from 1954-1963. Another man who worked on the NORC was Ken Schreiner, who was the Logic and Control designer, who also submitted many photos of the NORC and people who worked on it. Von Neumann gave the inaugural address, and I saw photos of the event, which also included Oppenheimer, and Isidor Rabi, who was mentioned in an earlier session. The following picture is John von Neumann's ID badge from Los Alamos, during his work on the Manhattan Project.)

John von Neumann's Los Alamos ID badge.

(Michael said that someone there died of cancer. I found out after the session that John von Neumann died of cancer. In 1955, von Neumann was diagnosed with what was either bone or pancreatic cancer. A von Neumann biographer Norman Macrae has speculated: "It is plausible that in 1955 the then-fifty-one-year-old Johnny's cancer sprang from his attendance at the 1946 Bikini nuclear tests." Von Neumann died a year and a half later. He was also a witness to the first atomic bomb blast near Socorro, New Mexico. He was apparently very involved in many aspects of the atomic bomb, including being part of the target selection committee, in which he oversaw computations related to the expected size of the bomb blasts, estimated death tolls, and the distance above the ground at which the bombs should be detonated for optimum shock wave propagation and thus maximum effect.)

Then my late husband came back into the conversation, Michael said:

413

Michael: "Is his father alive?"

Laura: "Yes."

Michael: "I said, 'Where is your dad?' He said, 'Alive.' I wonder why this granddad is so strong here and why he's here."

Laura: "I don't know."

Michael: "Is he a very cool guy?"

Laura: "Yeah, I really liked him."

Michael: "Is he someone who likes to help others?"

Laura: "Yeah."

Michael: "He seems like he wants to help in some way. I think they've been working on your boy, you know?"

Laura: "Cool. He needs all the help he can get."

Michael: "Remember when I said that he might be getting this healing taking place as well?"

Laura: "Mmm-hmm."

Michael: "I think they're working on him as well, and I think this man is one of them."

Laura: "Thanks Grandpa Frank!"

(Shortly after our wedding, Darren and I drove down to Georgia to visit Frank and I will never forget how sad he was when we had to leave, he was crying. He was such a sweet man. I even mentioned him in my other book, "Widowed Too Soon." Grandpa moved back to Illinois where we lived, and he and Darren were rebuilding an old muscle car together, and were pretty close. Darren died a short time later. After Darren died, I went to visit Grandpa Frank, and he was still so angry about is wife Helen dying, and I remember not wanting to be like him and hang onto my grief the way he had for decades. He died within a year of Darren.)

Michael: "Hmm. The word Cabal keeps coming up."

Laura: "Cabal? What the heck is that?"

Michael: "It's like a bunch of conspirators."

Laura: "Oh."

Michael: "Does your boy eat chocolate?"

Laura: "He likes chocolate. He eats it every now and then. Should he?"

Michael: "Albert likes chocolate."

Laura: "Oh."

Michael: "I wonder if chocolate is being genetically modified."

Laura: "Hmm. If it has milk in it, if it's milk chocolate it probably is."

Michael: "They're genetically altering milk aren't they?"

Laura: "Yeah, I only buy the chocolate from Switzerland, the Lindt chocolates because I know they are not GMO."

Michael: "Most milk is GMO?"

Laura: "Yeah, it's got the RbST, the recombinant bovine growth hormone, unless it's organic or it says they don't use growth hormones."

Michael: "I think that's where they are going with the chocolate."

(Recombinant bovine growth hormone is genetically engineered and in dairy products that are not certified organic or stated that they don't use growth hormones. Also, chocolate has sugar in it, so unless the sugar is from sugar cane, it could be derived from genetically engineered sugar beets.)

That was the end of the channeling session, and they started talking about the pictures that Marti had drawn. Here is the doodle page:

Doodle Explanations: I already mentioned that my dad smoked Camel cigarettes for 50 years, so that's what the camel means to me. It is also interesting to me that back in 1949, there was a TV commercial that said "More doctors smoke Camels than any other cigarette" and they encouraged patients to smoke. Tobacco companies also claimed that cigarettes didn't cause cancer, until proven wrong and then they were held liable.

It is a similar situation that we are currently dealing with regarding vaccines. Vaccine proponents claim that studies show that vaccines don't cause autism, when in truth there have never been human studies on the combination of all the vaccines a baby is mandated to get, nor has there been a vaccinated vs. non-vaccinated study regarding autism. Most of the money in autism research goes to dead-end genetic research. "Tobacco science" which faulty scientific papers are often called, written by paid-off scientists and those with conflicts of interest is rampant in the medical field today. It is just a matter of time before the truth catches up to them. They don't want to be wrong, because they will be liable for damaging an entire generation of children.

The picture of the star with "True Grit" underneath it had to do with

John Wayne, who had come through once before, and has come through to Michael in other sessions with other people who had family members who personally knew him.

Regarding the champagne bottle with the circle around the cork: Marti said that she heard a cork pop while drawing it. Michael said that it's got nothing to do with the bottle or the cork. He says it's like once you take the cork out, you can't put it back in. Once you take the top off, that's it. Once you let the genie out of the bottle, you can't put it back in. I told him that I say that exact thing about GMO's. He got that feeling around a virus in the bottle. He feels like bacteria on the cork. Has to do with an organism. Once you take the cork out, it's too late.

The picture of the bicycle: Marti said felt like an old fashioned bike. I told her that we were just talking about getting Trevor an adult trike (a big three wheeler) that very morning. Michael was getting the old fashioned feeling about it and said that the trike is a good idea, and that there was a safety issue with a regular bike. I was looking online earlier that morning at the Schwinn adult trike, which is an old fashioned style three-wheeled bike, and a friend of mine posted a picture on Facebook with her son with autism riding the very same bike and she said he loved it, and mastered it in one day.

The doodle of the purple military beret: Michael said that the military in India wear purple berets, and she put a rocket under that. He added that "India used to be under British rule and their uniforms haven't changed much. India and Pakistan might come to blows in a serious way. Pakistan might collapse as a state." Finally, I have no idea who Daniel Weisburg is, but as I have learned, perhaps that will make sense later.

***

Session Twenty-Two: After the Session:
Featured Spirits: Albert Einstein, John von Neumann

After the channeling session, we talked for a bit as usual. He said that his overwhelming feeling in this is that things have to play out a little bit in the world and that the Murdoch thing with the medical companies was happening in order to address some of these issues. Michael said that the spirit people were saying they are hopeful that there will be some breaks like this that this cabal, the organized group of people who are covering up their criminal actions. (He was referring to a recent story about Rupert

Murdoch, who owns News Corp., the second largest media conglomerate in the world, and was being charged with phone hacking and other crimes.)

News Corp. systematically destroyed the reputation of Dr. Andrew Wakefield, and lied about his work, resulting in a retraction of Wakefield's *Lancet* paper and the revocation of his medical license.) In 1998, the Lancet published Wakefield's peer-reviewed paper, a case series on twelve children receiving treatment for bowel dysfunction at the Royal Free Hospital in London. The paper called for further study of a possible association between bowel disease and developmental delay, including cases of autism. It also noted that eight of the children's gastrointestinal and autistic symptoms began shortly after they received the MMR vaccination. When Dr. Wakefield's findings questioned the safety of the MMR vaccine, it threatened Big Pharma's profits, and Murdoch's own connections to drug companies. Dr. Wakefield's work has been replicated, but you won't hear about that on the fake news.

Shortly after this session, one of Dr. Wakefield's co-authors of the controversial "MMR paper" Prof. John Walker-Smith, who also lost his medical license, was exonerated of all charges of professional misconduct by the GMC, the U.K's medical regulatory board, that had ruled against both he and Wakefield over the 1998 paper. Wakefield filed a defamation lawsuit against the people who falsely accused him of fraud. They tried to make an example of him as a warning to others who questioned the "cabal."

Michael said "A big fire has to be lit to galvanize everybody together. Everyone has their toe in the water, trying to do something, but there are no big lawsuits against vaccine manufacturers." I told him that people are trying to get something going. I told him about the vaccine court, the 83 canaries, which are families that went to the "vaccine court" claiming that their child had brain damage from vaccines, not autism, although some of them had a diagnosis of autism. It's the same thing. They had to keep quiet after the payout, but were now coming forward. Michael added that it was to limit someone else's ability to pursue it. He said that we need one big movement to squish this for good. This hasn't happened yet. He said that we have to galvanize people; it's all he's been thinking about. He's angry about it. We need a mass lawsuit with top lawyers out there, or it's going to go on and on.

I told Michael that in the other book I did with the other medium, a person named John came through who was a friend of Einstein's, which is why I had looked him up before. Michael said that maybe Albert brought him along to show it was Albert. It gets harder each time because they have to tell him new things.

Michael relayed a story to me of his master doing a transmission of a very powerful being and that millions of others in sprit were waiting to hear what he had to say. He felt that this was similar because they all know each other and are concerned about what's going on here on Earth, and they'll all come back at some point. He talked about Winston Churchill speaking through Leslie Flint, and was concerned about viruses coming from space on a meteorite or something, and there would be no defense for it because it's alien to us. The spirits are concerned because they are doing things that we've never done that really threaten us.

HBOT

Since they mentioned in the session that they were seeing what happened with this stint of HBOT, it is a good time to address it. After the session, Michael and I started talking about the changes I've seen in Trevor since we started HBOT. I told him that I've noticed that he's been more verbal, he's singing more, he's more affectionate, he does math for fun, he's playful, he calms down faster after meltdowns, which are becoming less frequent. I started an HBOT Diary, and these were some of the other things I noted: While we were in the chamber, we watched Baby Einstein videos, mainly for the classical music, and during the sessions, Trevor would point to and label everything on the TV. He was also pointing to and reading words off of the TV at home as well as signs, calendars, and anything else he recognized words on. He started asking for help and saying what he wanted instead of just whining. His small motor skills improved a lot. During the first 30 session, he started to unbutton and button his own shirts without prompting. He also started to buckle and unbuckle his own seatbelt in the car.

During the second 40 sessions, he put his own socks on and straightened them out by himself. At school, he passed my friend Jenny and her son Austin, a classmate, in the hallway, and Trevor waved to him and said "Hi Austin" without prompting. She called me to tell me the good news and how she's noticed changes in him. She did HBOT with Austin because she saw the changes in Trevor, and saw similar improvements. Trevor also started saying words more clearly. He used to say "luh" instead of "love," but during HBOT, he started to say it correctly, and often hugged me and said "I love you" as clear as a bell. I cried.

His memory seemed to improve, because when we corrected him on how to say something, he'd remember it the next time and say it correctly. He used to say lines from movies that were barely recognizable, but because we knew them from hearing them over and over, we knew what he was trying to say. For instance, he used to say the line, "Don't tell me not to worry, wolves eat little animals like us for lunch" from *Sesame Street's Peter and the Wolf* something like "Not to worry, wup ea lil abacis fo lu." After HBOT, we slowly told him how to say it word by word, and now he says it perfectly.

Now, he certainly wasn't "recovered" from doing HBOT, but there were definite improvements, which is all I could hope for. Anything that makes his life better and easier is worth it. Actually, two of my friends also saw similar gains in their sons from HBOT. Motor skill improvements, language gains, emotional regulation. Many children with autism who do HBOT see similar things according to Talk About Curing Autism's website www.tacanow.org. There are good articles about HBOT for autism on their site. During the first 30 sessions, we did 1.3 atmospheres (ATA) during the hour dive, which was a brain injury protocol. During the second 40 sessions, we tried Dr. Paul Harch's protocol, (www.hbot.com) which gradually increases the atmospheres up to 1.75 ATA throughout the 40 sessions. The higher the atmospheres, the deeper the dive. Dr. Harch's website also has SPECT scan imaging before and after HBOT for traumatic brain injuries and other applications.

During the sessions, I added Michael's suggestions: supplemented him with Royal Jelly and Biosuperfood (microalgae), treated his yeast, kept him warm, listened to classical music, and massaged his hands. Hopefully those extra things made the experience the most beneficial for him. I would like to do this therapy again in the future for sure, once a year if I can.

***

Chapter Twenty-Five

*"The release of atom power has changed
everything except our way of
thinking...the solution to this
problem lies in the heart of mankind.
If only I had known, I should have
become a watchmaker."*

— Albert Einstein

Session Twenty-Three

This next session was unplanned. We hadn't done a session in many months, because I needed to catch up and start writing. We stayed in touch and talked on the phone often. I was working five days a week and taking care of two kids, which didn't leave me much time to work on the book, but I was slowly getting it done. Michael called me on February 18, 2012. He told me that he was doing a session the night before with someone who was a patent clerk from Germany. He said that Albert showed up with his pipe in his hand and said that it was him. Albert was also a patent clerk from Germany, and there were many similarities between Albert and the man having the session. Anyway, Albert told Michael during the session that he and I needed to do another session together, and there was a sense of urgency. Because of our schedules, we actually did it later that night.

The session started out with a person who was associated with Albert, and Michael said there was a name like "Von Strapp", or Von Staph." I told him that name had come up before. Michael said, "Did it really?" I told him that I couldn't figure out who he was. Michael tried to get the name again, and I told him that this was the guy that I thought was the mustard gas inventor. I couldn't think of his name, but I told Michael that I was just reading about mustard gas earlier that night. I just read an article about it which said they renamed it Sulfur Mustard, because it is a liquid which becomes a gas when detonated. There was a lot of it stockpiled in many locations. Michael said that he heard them say sulfur. Michael said that it had to be him. I told him his name started with a W, but sounded like a V because it was German, I couldn't think of it off the top of my head. As I went to my notes to look his name up, Michael continued:

Michael: "He must have known the Kaiser."

Laura: "He worked at the Kaiser Wilhelm Institute."

Michael: "There is something about Kaiser. So he worked at Kaiser Wilhelm Institute?"

Laura: "Yes, and so did Einstein."

Michael: "I know he knows Albert. Is this Sarin nerve gas? There is going to be some sort of attack in the very near future. I don't think it's mustard gas, maybe it's a nerve gas."

Laura: "On us?"

Michael: "No. I think he's saying the name Roland."

(After the session, I looked it up, after I found his name, and learned that he was influenced by a man named Roland Scholl.)

Michael: "He keeps talking about an attack. Maybe this is why they wanted to talk. There is going to be some sort of gas attack, but I don't know what. Did he develop any other forms of gas do you know? After mustard gas."

Laura: "I don't know."

(I looked it up after the session, and I found that he later worked on arsenic compounds, thiophene compounds and the formation of petroleum.)

Michael: "Do you know if his research then went into medicine?"

Laura: "I'll have to look him up more."

(After the session, I learned that after doing autopsies on soldiers that died from mustard gas in WWI and after chemical warfare in WWII, researchers noticed decreased white blood cell count. They investigated nitrogen mustard as a therapy for Hodgkin's lymphoma and other types of lymphoma and leukemia, and this compound was tried out on its first human patient in December 1942. The results of this study were not published until 1946, when they were declassified. These studies led to the development of nitrogen mustard called "HN2" which became the first cancer chemotherapy drug, mustine.)

Michael: "He just said that Albert is here and that they are friends. So let's see where we go with this. Albert is saying good evening to you."

Laura: "Good evening. His name is Wilhelm Steinkopf. *(I found it in my notes.)*

Michael: "Steinkopf. It is interesting, it looks like pf. That's it. Do you know how he died? Don't say, do you know?"

Laura: "No."

Michael: "Some sort of heart issue, like heart disease, or heart issues. And he's saying Peter."

(I could only find that his health was fragile due to his work with mustard gas and related substances.)

Michael was trying to ask them questions as to where and when the attack was going to happen. He thought they were telling him that it was on America, but it looked like Iran was doing it. He repeated that they were saying the name "Peter" and didn't know if it was a General, or what. Then they said "Marshall." Is this like the Marshall plan or is this someone Albert knows? He keeps saying "There is going to be an attack. They are certain of this. I think it is going to be in Iran. I think we are going to attack Iran." Then he said "Arthur" and asked if Albert knew Arthur Conan Doyle. I mentioned that Arthur Eddington has also come up a few times. He said that he seems to be well known. I told him that he helped prove Einstein's Theory of Relativity.

Michael said that there must be a big event coming because they were talking about the deployment of forces both here and abroad. He was having a bit of trouble because he was having daydreams about someone trying to kill Obama with a large bomb from a distance. People within this country would be doing this. He was having a hard time believing some of the things he was hearing. It was a big attack, being orchestrated from within. I said, "Another 9/11 false flag attack?" He said, "Something like that."

He mentioned he was getting the name Erhardt, or Earnheardt, and the first name William, and said the William could start with a "V" like "Villiam" and also a name like "Kesh." Michael asked Albert to tell him something so we would absolutely know it was him, and then he said:

Michael: "Was Albert into pocket watches at all? I know that sounds like a funny thing that they could bring up."

Laura: "I don't know."

Michael: "Do you know if there is some significance to some special pocket watch or gold pocket watch?"

Laura: "I'll have to look that one up."

Michael: "With perhaps an inscription upon it? And something to do with a design center, or an artist, a special artist. Is it Kopech? Kopek?

(Immediately after our session, Michael and Marti turned on the TV and there was a movie on called I.Q., starring Walter Matthau and Meg Ryan. In the movie, Matthau plays Albert Einstein, and at the beginning of the movie, he has a pocket watch. They just had to laugh. After the session, I researched Albert and pocket watches. I found that he had many pocket watches, one of them was designed by Patek and Czapek, Michael almost got the name, which later became the famous Patek Phillipe watch company. Evidently both Albert and Marie Curie had a Patek Phillipe pocket watch, and Albert's watch is on display at the Patek-Phillipe museum in Geneva, Switzerland. Albert's Omega pocket watch is on display at the Omega museum in Switzerland. He also owned a Longines pocket watch which is kept at the History Museum in Bern, Switzerland. Most surprisingly, I found that a Longines wrist watch belonging to Albert was auctioned off in 2008, and was accompanied by photos of him wearing the watch. It sold for $596,000. Here is a picture of the gold inscribed watch from the auction.)

The session continued with my dad showing up, and Michael asked me if my dad had cancer, to which I replied, "Yes." Michael said that my dad was bringing up Friday, and the 2nd or the 22nd. I wasn't sure what those days and dates meant. Michael was trying to figure out who "Peter" was. He asked them if it was some sort of bomb. Then he said "Richmond" and asked if it was a place? He asked me if there was a city called

Petersburg. I looked it up on my phone and found that there was a Petersburg, VA, and also a Richmond, VA. He was thinking it was Virginia. I noticed that the two cities were close. Richmond is the state capital and Petersburg is south of it.

(Interestingly, after the session, I read that in Virginia, there are numerous underground COG facilities, or Continuity of Government facilities, including Mt. Weather, home of FEMA's headquarters, which is 46 miles from Washington D.C., and reportedly connected via underground access in case of a National Emergency. Mt. Weather reportedly contains a working duplicate of the Executive Branch of the Federal Government. I read that there are 96 underground COG facilities in Pennsylvania, Maryland, West Virginia, Virginia, and North Carolina. I also found it interesting that there was a recent 5.9 earthquake in Virginia that was felt in 22 states. There was a seismology comparison between an earthquake and a nuclear detonation compared to the Virginia earthquake, and the pattern was clearly that of a nuclear detonation. I don't know how much of that is accurate, but after the messages from the session, it makes one wonder.)

My dad was talking for a little while, and Michael asked me if he lived in Virginia, I told him close, North Carolina. Michael brought up the name James Walker, and that he had to do with Albert, and not my dad.

(After this session, I looked up James Walker and there were so many of them. When I called Michael to tell him about the watches, he said that he also got the middle initial "J" with James Walker, so he looked him up; he found that James J. Walker was the Mayor of New York. I looked him up after our phone conversation and found a picture of Albert with Mayor Walker, because when Albert came for a visit to the United States, he received the official welcome to NYC at City Hall from Mayor James J. Walker on December 13, 1930. Look for yourself. Also interesting, was I found out that James Walker was also connected to FDR, who was the Governor of New York at the same time, and FDR pressured him to resign. The State Supreme Court upheld the Governor's right to remove him from office.)

Michael was getting stuck, so he asked Marti what she drew. She drew a portrait and a doodle page. Here they are:

<u>Doodle Explanations:</u> First of all, we didn't know who the person in the portrait is with the child's hand, so maybe someone else will claim it later. The screw-type drill, Michael felt was a type of bunker busting bomb, which bores its way through the ground and then explodes. He mentioned that Iran recently procured some of these, and they can go hundreds of feet down before they blow up. They are programmed and launched from a distance.

Marti felt like the person in the rain poncho that was running had something in their hand, and that the key was depicting a copy being made. The Café with the tunnel, Michael felt was an underground entrance or bunker but it looks like something else when you look at it, sort of hidden in plain sight.

***

Session Twenty-Three: After the Session:
Featured Spirits: Wilhelm Steinkopf, Albert Einstein, Arthur Eddington, Mayor James J. Walker

This is an example of a future event being told to us, so until it actually happens, I can't really validate it. However, some of the other things that were mentioned during the same session, I was able to validate afterward. I already mentioned these things in the text, but it shows me that if certain things turned out to be true, there is a good possibility that the other things they said are also true. This is the theme of many of these sessions. If message A is true, then message B may also be true. Of course, since Michael is not a scientist, nor am I, some of our interpretations may be off. Hopefully, someone who is a scientist or researcher can take some of these clues and use them in a way to help our children and their future. That is my hope in sharing this information.

***

Chapter Twenty-Six

*"There are two ways to live your life.
One is as though nothing is a miracle.
The other is as though everything is a
miracle."*

— Albert Einstein

A Miracle

There was a big gap in time from this very last session we did in February, 2012 and the previous one done in July, 2011. I really needed to spend some time working on putting the book together, and doing some more research. I didn't want to get too far behind. During this time off, something amazing happened. This had nothing to do with the channeling sessions, but it helped my son, so I feel it is worth mentioning. The fact that it happened during the time that we were working on this book leads me to believe that it is all connected.

I received a phone call from my good friend and hairdresser Tara, who told me that a former client of hers had this mineral solution of some kind that she cured herself of Leukemia with and that many children with autism had also been cured with it. Tara was going to go to the woman's house to talk to her because Tara's husband was in the military and just returned from spending two years in Afghanistan. I had been telling her about depleted uranium and biowarfare, and she wanted to see if this mineral stuff could help detox him from toxins he was exposed to over there. Tara invited me to go with her and without hesitation, I told her yes, which is totally unlike me. Normally, I'd sarcastically think, "Yeah, right, they've cured autism with this stuff." Typically, I would think it was a scam, but for some reason, I didn't this time.

It was the first week of October, 2011, and Tara and I drove separate cars, and I met her and followed her there. On our way there, I called her and asked her for more details. It turned out that I already knew the woman! Her name was Janet, and she used to own a healing center in town where I used to take Trevor for Far Infrared Sauna sessions. I really liked her and felt comforted that I already knew and trusted her. I asked Tara more about the treatment Janet used and she said it was some sort of mineral product. I asked her if it was MMS, Miracle Mineral Solution, which my friend Melanie had been talking to me about for a year and I blew it off. Tara said that it sounded familiar. After I hung up the phone, I was in awe that MMS was coming up again, and I knew that there had to be a reason I was going. Maybe this was a way to get me to listen because I was getting tired of Melanie talking about it all the time.

When we got to Janet's house, she recognized me and we shared a hug. She was so happy to see us and share her information with us. It turned out that it was indeed MMS, and Janet passionately told us her story. She had Leukemia for the second time, and after trying MMS, she was cured in 18 days, and the following day, she flew down to the Dominican Republic to train with the founder of MMS, Jim Humble, to learn how to use it and share it with others. At the MMS training, she met a woman named Kerri Rivera and her husband, who have a son with autism. They ran a DAN! based HBOT clinic in Mexico, where Kerri is the Medical Director, and she was the one having children with autism recover in a short time using MMS.

Janet showed us a PowerPoint presentation of her trip and about MMS, and gave us instructions on how to use it. We made a donation to Reverend Janet's church (so sad) for the "cleansing water" and talked to her individually about our situations. While we were there, another woman showed up that Janet had been helping to treat her lung cancer. She told us that Janet saved her life. She was sent home from our local hospital 6 months earlier with 5 days to live, and then began the MMS cancer protocol with Janet after learning about it through a mutual friend. The woman was now alive and well, and in remission. We saw the x-rays of her 20 lung tumors before and after MMS. They disappeared. She was in tears as she told her story. She had over $750,000 in medical bills doing chemotherapy, radiation, and all the other things the allopaths told her she had to do, and then they sent her home to die because they couldn't do anything more for her. The MMS costs $30, and it cured her. She said that she went back to the hospital that sent her home to die and saw her doctor in the hallway and he looked at her as if he were seeing a ghost. Her testimonial was very riveting.

Janet told me more about Kerri, and said that she had recovered 17 children from autism using MMS. I knew that I had to try this for Trevor. After I got home, I contacted Kerri and decided to use her autism protocol, instead of the one that Janet suggested for regular folks. For my sensitive boy, I used Kerri's protocol, which is much slower. If Kerri's protocol cured autism, I wanted to do it that way. Actually, as of this writing in May, 2012, Kerri has 40 recoveries in 20 months using MMS. No one else can say that, with any treatment modality! She collects their ATEC scores (Autism Treatment Evaluation Checklist) from the Autism Research Institute to show recoveries as well as other evaluations. On a scale of 0-180, an ATEC score of 10 or under is considered recovered from autism. It measures a child's abilities in the following areas: speech/language/ communication, sociability, sensory/cognitive awareness and health/ physical/behavioral. Kerri ran her autism clinic for four years using the DAN! Protocol (Defeat Autism Now), which uses lots of supplements, and she only saw two recoveries. She started using MMS in August, 2010, and has already seen 40 recoveries, mainly in South America.

Kerri and I became fast friends, and truly I admire her determination, dedication, integrity, and enormous heart. She wants to rid the world of autism, one child at a time, and hopefully hers and mine are among them. She started helping families in the U.S. via a Facebook private group, which started in February, 2012. She is so generous with her time and expertise. She also started a website, www.mmsautism.com which has her protocols and information in English. She recently started doing webinars to answer parents' questions. I watched one recently with Andreas Kalcker, a scientist who did a documentary about MMS. He talked a lot about the problem with parasites and how to get rid of them.

Through talking to Kerri, I learned that she personally knew Bernard Rimland. She actually translated the DAN! Protocol into Spanish for the Autism Research Institute. Much to my surprise, when I was researching Bernard Rimland to try to validate some of the things he told us during the channeling session he showed up in, I realized that Kerri is in the picture with him on his Wikipedia page! The photo is in this book in Bernard's chapter. I was shocked! When I called Michael and Marti to tell them about this "coincidence" he said, "Perhaps Bernard sent you to her." Marti sarcastically commented, "No, it's all just a coincidence." They know how these things happen, they see it every day.

My psychic friend Melanie was trying to get me to use MMS because she knew it would help Trevor, but stubborn me, I heard her say the word "chorine" and thought "Hell, no!" I'm not giving him chlorine. Even though

MMS is not chlorine, the word itself was scary enough for me to reject it initially. I was doing HBOT and other things, so I didn't want to add another thing and not know what was helping him or aggravating him. I kick myself now for not trying it sooner, but it seems that the Universe found another way to get it to me, through my friend Tara. I am going to give another disclaimer here, I am not giving medical advice for anyone else here, I'm just telling a story of what happened to me and my son. Use your own judgment. Check out the science at www.factsheetproject.org/MMSFactsSheet.pdf.

MMS

You are probably wondering what exactly is MMS, and how can it cure diseases like cancer and autism? I'll begin with the MMS story. MMS stands for Miracle Mineral Supplement, or Miracle Mineral Solution, or Master Mineral Solution, it's all the same thing. Jim Humble was a chemist working in South America when he discovered his water purification drops had anti-bacterial/anti-fungal properties when activated with something acidic (citric acid or vinegar). He cured hundreds of people of Malaria. MMS was administered to about 75,000 people in non-US countries by Jim Humble before it was released for wider use in 2006. From his own website, www.jimhumble.biz, he explains that MMS (actually chlorine dioxide gas, which is one molecule of chlorine and two molecules of oxygen) has been known and widely used since 1947 as a powerful germicidal agent. It is capable of exactly targeting nearly all bacteria, viruses, fungi, yeast, and blood-borne diseases, while doing no harm to normal human living cells.

The way it is taken as a supplement is that you activate equal parts of sodium chlorite (NaCLO2) and citric acid, which brings the combined ph level to under 5, causing the sodium chlorite to become unstable and release chlorine dioxide gas (CLO2); then you add water to it and drink it. MMS is not bleach. Household bleach is sodium *hypochlorite*, not sodium chlorite; there is a massive difference here. MMS stays in the body for one to two hours at the most, so you take numerous doses per day. Protocols vary, depending on the nature of the illness. Do not try this on your own. Get with someone who is trained on how to use MMS, especially for autism, and Kerri is the go-to person for that.

Is it safe to ingest? As published in the December 1982 installment of the peer-reviewed journal, "Environmental Health Perspectives", a study entitled "Controlled clinical evaluations of chlorine dioxide, chlorite and chlorate in man" stated: "By the absence of detrimental physiological responses within the limits of the study, the relative safety of oral ingestion of chlorine dioxide and its metabolites, chlorite and chlorate, was demonstrated." The three phases of this controlled double-blind clinical evaluation of chlorine dioxide and its potential metabolites in human male volunteer subjects were completed uneventfully. This really eased my mind.

In her presentation, Kerri explains that chlorine dioxide is an oxidizer, compounds capable of reacting with and changing or destroying other materials. Oxygen and ozone are also oxidizers. Because of its structure, chlorine dioxide has an electrical potential that will accept 5 electrons from some other molecules, thereby destroying the other substances. The pathogen is destroyed by destroying some of its molecules. In this reaction, both the chlorine dioxide and the substance being oxidized are destroyed, leaving only basic components that are neutral and freely wash out of the body. Chlorine dioxide itself becomes neutral oxygen atoms and chloride, which combines with sodium to become table salt in the body. MMS oxidizes pathogens because of the positive charge of the chlorine dioxide molecule and the negative charge of the pathogen. The strength of an oxidizer is measured in volts. Healthy cells have a voltage of 1.3 and chlorine dioxide has a voltage of 0.95. Pathogens have a lower voltage than chlorine dioxide. No pathogen has ever become resistant to it.

There are other considerations that are important while using MMS. For instance, you need to remove the use of antioxidants like Vitamin C, while using MMS, because they cancel each other out. One is an oxidant, the other an antioxidant. Also, you need to use distilled water or neutral ph water, not alkaline water or dirty tap water. Diet is also very important. There are separate parasite and seizure protocols as well. I am just giving the basics here. Kerri is the person that I mentioned earlier who uses Quinton Marine Plasma in her protocol. Quinton works on the electrical system of the brain. It is very similar to our own blood plasma. It also kills pathogens. It is not regular ocean water. Check it out at www.original quinton.com.

I found it very interesting that the U.S. Government used chlorine dioxide to clean up the anthrax after the 9/11 anthrax mailings at four different locations. From the EPA's website, there is an article titled *"Anthrax Spore Decontamination using Chlorine Dioxide."* It says that

"Chlorine dioxide kills microorganisms by disrupting transport of nutrients across the cell wall. Chlorine dioxide smells somewhat like chlorine bleach. Chlorine dioxide should not be confused with chlorine gas. They are two distinct chemicals that react differently and produce by-products that have little in common." The by-product of chlorine dioxide is sodium chloride, which is table salt in the body. If our own government used chlorine dioxide to inactivate *Bacillus anthracis* spores they must have demonstrated the efficacy of the product against bacillus spores. To me, this was huge news because of the implications during the channeling sessions about biowarfare being a causative factor in autism, anthrax being one of the agents.

Our government also uses chlorine dioxide to remove bacteria from meat and vegetables prior to shipping. It is also used in some municipal drinking water treatment facilities to kill pathogens. It is approved and recommended by the United States Environmental Protection Agency (US EPA) as an environmentally friendly drinking water additive to replace chlorine (which is known to form carcinogenic by-products, as does bromine). It is a highly effective, eco-friendly microbiocide that carries a number of important regulatory approvals from several international organizations including the US EPA, FDA and UK Government for many of its uses.

From a company in the UK that sells chlorine dioxide for water treatment called SafeOx, they state on their website that chlorine dioxide is a strong bactericide and virucide at concentrations as low as 0.1 ppm. It will eliminate both planktonic and sessile bacteria; disinfect surfaces; and rapidly destroy problematic biofilm. With minimal contact time, it is highly effecttive against many pathogenic organisms including bacterial spores, Legionella, Tuberculosis, MRSA, VRE, Listeria, Salmonella, amoebal cysts, Giardia cysts, E. coli, and Cryptosporidium. Importantly, chlorine dioxide also destroys biofilm so bacterial re-growth is significantly impeded. This is for water treatment, which is intended for human consumption.

Viruses, bacteria, fungus, parasites and other pathogens can be removed from the body when MMS releases chlorine dioxide gas into the blood stream. And here is the best part, because it is a gas, it crosses the blood brain barrier! That means that it is capable of killing pathogens in the brain. That was one of the things that came up in these channeling sessions, there are pathogens in the brain. MMS also boosts the immune system, detoxes chemicals, is anti-inflammatory, and oxidizes heavy metals. These are all issues that children with "autism" struggle with. The way that MMS neutralizes heavy metals is by removing the electron shells of heavy metal compounds (i.e. ethyl/methyl mercury) and destroying the molecules. They are returned to their neutral state and the body is able to remove them via the natural pathways of elimination.

Children with autism have a lot in common with people with cancer. Recent studies have come out that show that a large percentage of cancer is caused by viruses. People with cancer are also very toxic, and have not only viruses, but other pathogens; bacteria, fungus, and parasites. This is why MMS works with so many illnesses, it kills pathogens. Many of the problems in autism are merely symptoms, but what is causing the symptoms? Pathogens and toxins in the brain and body.

Kerri has had many people send her their children's lab results after using MMS and they return to normal again. ABA therapy is not going to eliminate pathogens in the brain and GI tract, sorry. These children will not recover on ABA alone. Don't get me wrong, ABA helps them communicate, but they are still very ill.

Our MMS Story

I will start with the autism testimonial for MMS that I wrote for scientist and MMS documentary star Andreas Kalcker's upcoming book. I wrote:

"I believe that regressive autism is a disease, not a developmental disorder, and therefore can be cured. My older son, now 13, was a normal, healthy baby and then regressed and was diagnosed with autism at the age of 3. One in 54 boys in the United States has a diagnosis of autism currently. After his diagnosis, I knew I had to fix him because he wasn't born that way, something happened to him.

I tried every alternative autism therapy out there. Some of them helped him improve, others not so much. He has steadily improved over the years, regaining some of what he had lost, but there was still something missing. After various types of testing, I discovered that my child was a very sick boy, and had numerous pathogens in his body; fungus, bacteria and viruses along with mercury and other toxins. I believe that many of these pathogens are in the brain, which is why traditional antifungal, antibiotic and antiviral medications don't work. They don't cross the blood-brain barrier because the molecules are too large. Mercury also collects in the fatty tissue of the brain.

I believe that the reason MMS works with regressive autism is because it turns into a gas in the body and crosses the blood-brain barrier, killing pathogens in the brain as well as the gastrointestinal tract. It also oxidizes heavy metals. Prior to MMS, the most effective therapy we had tried was Hyperbaric Oxygen Therapy (HBOT), which is also a gas that crosses the blood-brain barrier, healing the damage done by pathogens and toxins.

I was introduced to MMS a month ago, and within days of starting it, my son began to transform before my eyes. He began using sentences that he's never said before. His behavior improved dramatically. He was also more social and playful. For example, he was reading a book to me before bed (which he hadn't done in years), and when his brother walked into the room, he said "(Brother's name), can you read?" and handed him the book. When his brother tried to take the book, he playfully pulled it back and wrestled his brother for the book before finally giving it to him and let him read it.

My son also began pointing everything out and saying what it was ("There is our old house" "There are the horses"), telling me that he wanted to go to certain places ("I want to go to the aquarium" "I want to go to Pump it Up"), asking for new food items that he didn't eat before and putting them in the grocery cart himself, telling me what he wanted to do ("I want to take a bath please"), asking for help with specific things ("I need help with my blanket please"). These are a few of the new sentences he's said within a month of taking MMS. He used to just say a few words to get what he wanted.

The most incredible thing happened a week ago; I was able to enroll him in a new private school for children with high functioning autism and Asperger's syndrome. In the new school, he has to sit at a desk with one teacher leading the class. Prior to this, he was in a specialized self-contained classroom with a one-on-one aide, partially included in regular education. Now, he is able to listen to verbal directions and write down answers on his paper. He has had no behaviors or transition issues. A few months ago, this would not have been possible. He had anxiety and disrupting tantrums due to his illness and inability to communicate fully.

He is not completely done healing yet, but I have never seen so much improvement so quickly in all the years I have been trying to heal him with other modalities. MMS has given me so much hope. I would like other parents to know that it is never too late. You just need the right piece of the puzzle. MMS has been the missing piece. I am so grateful to have found it. I can now see that a full recovery is possible."

That was just my son's first month on MMS. He has continued to make more progress each month. He is so much more calm and happy. He is doing and saying new things all the time. His sentences have lengthened, he now says, "I want to go to Monterey Bay Aquarium with Uncle Joey, go for a ride in the car." He's been helping me cook and do laundry. He writes down jokes and reads them in front of his class at school, and is now doing multiplication. He's very affectionate and follows me everywhere. He watches the screensaver on my computer changing pictures and tells me who is in the pictures and where it is spontaneously, without prompting. I can take him anywhere now and he's great. He asks to go to many more places and do things. For instance, he says, "I want to go to gymnastics" "I want to go to Santa Barbara Zoo" "I want to go sledding" "I want to go to Trader Joes" to name a few. He points out things he sees, "I see the moon" "I see the night." He remembers things and has preferences that he's expressing, it's huge for him. He's not recovered yet, but he's getting closer every month.

With Kerri's encouragement, we also started using MMS enemas on him. An enema bypasses the stomach, gets the MMS into the bloodstream faster and kills pathogens in the colon. I was extremely hesitant to try it at first, never having done one before, but I've seen lots of biofilm and even parasites coming out of him, and it brought on more improvements. Biofilm is what pathogens form around themselves to protect the colony. Think of the slime on your teeth in the morning. Many kids with "autism" have loads of biofilm in their GI tracts.

The SafeOx website also says that chlorine dioxide, like ozone, is a dissolved gas that penetrates biofilm by molecular diffusion. However, unlike ozone, chlorine dioxide is stable and soluble, allowing it to travel to the base of the film where it attacks microorganisms and destroys the biofilm at its point of attachment. Other oxidizers react mostly on the surface of the biofilm to form an oxidized layer, like charring on wood. This precludes further penetration. No other biocide has proven to control biofilm better than chlorine dioxide.

A lot of us moms on the MMS autism Facebook page have had lots of laughs talking about the sensitive subject of enemas, but we have all seen major gains in our kids as a result of doing them. Enemas are such a taboo subject in this country, but health starts in the colon. Our ancestors did them all the time, as well as "de-worming" from parasites. We've stopped doing a lot of these preventative and healing treatments, maybe it's time to bring them back.

Some brave moms in the MMS autism Facebook group took some disturbing pictures of the parasites and worms coming out of their children (in their poop) after beginning the parasite protocol, using MMS enemas, Diatomaceous Earth, and a few other medicines and supplements. One mom even posted a video of live worms found in her son's diaper. It was alive and wiggling on a Q-tip. This is not mucus or undigested food as some doctors have tried to explain away. You don't need to live in a Third World country to have parasites. They are acquired from fecal matter found in the dirt and on playgrounds, from our pets, undercooked beef, pork and fish and even from the mom. We are potential hosts to over 1,000 varieties of parasites, many of them are microscopic. Our kids are the perfect hosts with unhealthy GI tracts, who are fed lots of supplements to keep the parasites alive. Publishing pooparazzi pictures is where I draw the line, but I have plenty of them. Having long slimy, stringy, wormy-looking creatures in your poop is not normal! They're parasites. Any yes, you need to look for them.

Parasites are clearly another problem plaguing many of these kids. They are opportunistic infections in an unhealthy GI tract. Does your child act crazy around the full moon? Think parasites. That's when they breed. Ironically, a few of the moms who have seen and photographed parasites coming out of their child did a parasite test with their GI specialists, and the test came back negative. This is not uncommon. Trevor did a BioSET session after we began the parasite protocol because I wanted to make sure he had them before I did it. We muscle tested him for parasites and he was weak to a few different species. One of them came from under-cooked meat, the other from a bug bite. We had done homeopathic detoxes in the past for parasites, but obviously they didn't clear up, or he was re-infected. I added a homeopathic parasite remedy from our practitioner to his MMS parasite protocol. I would rather do homeopathy than pharmaceuticals.

We also use MMS in the bath, where the skin absorbs it into the muscle and bloodstream, as well as breathing it in takes it to the lungs and the brain. We alternate days of enemas and baths. Kerri has been an absolute angel, helping us through this process with MMS. I don't know how long Trevor will have to be on the protocol. "Until the miracle happens" is what Janet first told me. Kerri's son had been on the protocol for nearly a year, and keeps improving. Some others recovered within months. The younger kids seem to recover faster, since they haven't been chronically ill as long.

When I found out that Kerri was going to be a speaker at the Autism One/Generation Rescue conference in Chicago, IL in May, 2012, I knew I had to go and meet her. Many of the other MMS autism Facebook group from the U.S. also went to the conference to support Kerri and MMS. A lot of them had also started using Kerri's parasite protocol, which she developed with Andreas Kalcker. It was so nice to meet these fellow warriors and compare notes and have some fun!

I met Kerri two days before her presentation and we were like long, lost friends. I recognized her in the hallway at the conference and when I showed her my nametag, we shared a long, knowing hug. Kerri and I and the other MMS moms hung out and even did Karaoke and danced that same night. What an incredible group of kindred spirits.

Kerri's presentation was very well attended, and her MMS fan club was there to cheer her on. Her wonderful, supportive sister introduced her. There were many tears shed, including Kerri's, as she told her story and described the recoveries of the children she has used the MMS protocol with. This is what all of the parents were there for. We wanted to recover our kids. She was a breath of fresh air in a sea of same old, same old presentations. She offered hope to everyone there. She was swamped with questions afterward, and many of us veteran MMS moms helped field some of the questions. This was just the beginning. After the conference our private MMS Facebook group quickly grew.

The weekend after I returned from the conference, Trevor was my "date" and we attended a fundraising dinner/dance/auction for his school. To my amazement, he slow danced with me for the first time in his life, putting his hands on my hips, with mine on his shoulders, swaying side to side during the mother/son dance. He also danced to fast songs with me and his classmates, and even did the YMCA dance. I was so proud of him and was moved to tears. He also won an award at school in his classroom for "Most Improved Academics." He was blossoming before my eyes, and coming out of the disease that has had a chokehold on him for over a decade.

I recently remembered something from the first sessions that I did with Albert through the other medium, bringing this process full circle. He told me that when my son was 14 years old, he would look to the rest of the world like he was okay. He turns 14 on July 14, 2012; his golden birthday. This is going to be the year I've been praying for and working toward since his diagnosis at age 3. It has been a long haul; a marathon of trial and error. I have known since day one that the things I did or didn't do for him was going to determine his future. This is a lot of pressure, but it kept me motivated to find the answers to heal him. The danger in looking for the truth is that sometimes you find it, and don't like what you see. Sometimes you need to go against the grain to make a difference and forge your own path.

The rest of my family also used MMS as a general 21 day detox, and now we do a maintenance dose twice a week. I believe that we all have human pathogens that we are not aware of, so it did us all some good. We are all breathing the same air, drinking the same water, and eating the same food. I had to go slow like Trevor, because I had a few side effects, which can be nausea, vomiting, and diarrhea if you go too quickly. I had the latter, plus a bad headache after a few days on the protocol. You just need to drop back the dose a little bit. After doing my detox, I felt much more clear-headed, and my chronic diarrhea went away. I feel it was a combination of removing wheat, eating a non-GMO diet, detoxing with MMS, and taking Diatomaceous Earth that helped me. I didn't know how bad I felt until I felt better.

My sister started taking it as well, because she was diagnosed with MS several years back, which I told her was probably a misdiagnosis, and suggested that she get tested for Lyme disease. One test came back positive, and one negative, so her ignorant doctor decided that it was negative, and put her on a month of antibiotics just in case. When she came out to visit me, we muscle tested her with BioSET for the bacteria that causes Lyme and all of the co-infections, and she was weak to all of them. After taking MMS, she had no more symptoms that led her to go to the doctor in the first place, including blurry vision in one eye. Since Trevor also tested positive for Lyme (Borellia burgdorferi) and many co-infections, as many kids on the spectrum have, I'm hoping that MMS will also take care of these pathogens as well. Janet also knows a woman who recovered from chronic Lyme disease using MMS. I heard her speaking at a meeting; her mom had to dress and bathe her prior to MMS, now she's independent and has her life back. As I've previously mentioned, Borellia burgdorferi is also genetically engineered.

MMS has so many uses; I think it should be a staple in every home. Every time I start to feel a cold coming on, I take a few doses, and the cold doesn't progress and goes away. With all of the genetically engineered foods and various engineered flu viruses they are messing around with, it is a good thing to have on hand. It is the most powerful pathogen killer on the planet. It is a bit controversial because it is not an FDA approved drug that Big Pharma is making money on, which is why Jim Humble had to move out of the country and start a church in order to heal people. They will approve chlorine dioxide for other uses, but not as a medicine. Just because it hasn't been "evaluated" by the FDA, doesn't mean it isn't safe. Remember, every drug that has been recalled was once approved by the FDA.

Don't believe everything you read, there is a lot of misinformation out there about MMS, even on Wikipedia, every time Jim tried to post something on there, it was deleted minutes later. Anything that works that you can make in your kitchen is a threat to the drug companies and everyone entwined with them. Their weapon is fear. Again, just follow the money. Who are you going to believe, people whose livelihood and ego are at stake, or people whose children have been damaged by the lies and only want to help other people avoid the same fate with nothing to lose?

***

Chapter Twenty-Seven

*"Condemnation without investigation is
the height of ignorance."*

— Albert Einstein

If I Knew Then What I Know Now

This book is a cautionary tale. Hopefully others can learn from my mistakes so that they don't have to walk in my shoes. I had a healthy baby, and then he became "autistic." I don't want to see this happen to anyone else. It is absolutely devastating with potentially lifelong implications. It takes a tremendous amount of restraint for me to keep my mouth closed when I learn that someone I know is going to have a baby boy. I want to sound the alarm, but I've learned that they need to be the one to ask me for my opinion. I have had quite a few new moms and grandmothers ask me questions about vaccine safety and what I think causes autism, knowing that I have a child with regressive autism. I always tell them the truth that vaccines are part of the cause of autism, as well as the other dangers.

Regarding vaccines, I tell these new moms that it's a subject where you're damned if you do, and you're damned if you don't. I do my best to give them information to investigate vaccines on their own without completely frightening and alienating them. I truly feel sorry for the new moms today. There is so much more to think about in order to protect your children from harm. It is not just about childproofing anymore. This is life or death, or brain damage. These new moms usually have well-meaning but clueless relatives telling them that vaccines are safe and save children from diseases. If you truly look into it, you will see right through the corrupt propaganda. Follow the money. In my opinion, if someone is pro-vaccine, they haven't done the research and read the studies, or they work for a vaccine manufacturer. It is a political issue, not a medical issue. I list some good educational websites about vaccines in the "Resources" section at the end of the book.

There are dozens of studies out there that prove the link between vaccines and autism, but you will never hear about it on the fake news because medical companies/vaccine manufacturers own them and pay for their advertising. Nor will they hear it from their vaccine pushing pediatricians, because their livelihood and reputation are on the line. They try to make concerned parents out to be anti-vaccinating nut jobs, threatening the safety of everyone else, while pushing their herd immunity lies. If vaccines worked, an unvaccinated child is not a threat to a vaccinated one. Most people who end up contracting childhood communicable diseases have been vaccinated against the disease. My advice? Educate yourself and take a stand; your baby's future is riding on it. Your marriage is riding on it, your financial future is riding on it, your other children's childhood is riding on it, your own physical and mental health is riding on it. Get the picture?

The media releases many obfuscating studies on a regular basis on all of the things that supposedly increase the risks of having a child with autism. Let me tell you, I don't have any of them. I am not obese; I'm underweight if anything, I only gained 25 pounds during the pregnancy. Trevor's father was not old, he was only 24 when Trevor was born, and I was 29. I took prenatal vitamins with folic acid. I didn't take antidepressants when pregnant. I exercised almost daily; bike riding, prenatal yoga and walking. (For the most part) I ate a healthy diet. I had natural childbirth, no birth drugs. He was born 10 days past his due date, so he was not a preemie. I didn't live near a freeway. I didn't eat mercury-laden fish. You get the picture. Cradle cap, eczema, and thrush are all warning signs that something is going on inside the baby. It means candida, allergies, and a weakened immune system. Do not inject more toxins and diseases in them!

I believe that there are genetic predispositions for autism such as allergies, gastrointestinal problems and autoimmune diseases. The culprits are not the causes suggested in the studies that they put out there to throw you off the vaccine trail. Anything but that! That's the piece that's hidden in plain sight. In my own family, we have allergies, asthma, cancer, rheumatoid arthritis (autoimmune), osteoporosis (linked to gluten intolerance), and thyroid issues. On my husband's side, although he wasn't vaccinated for religious reasons and is relatively healthy, he has some Asperger's characteristics. Here is my equation for regressive autism: genetic predisposition, plus multiple environmental toxins, plus immune system deficiency, plus recommended vaccine schedule, plus genetic engineering in numerous applications never before seen on the planet equals regressive "autism."

We live and we learn. I honestly feel that Trevor saved his younger brother Damon from the same fate. Because I wised up and stopped playing Russian Roulette with Damon's life, he was spared. How many children have to be sacrificed before we all wise up? Until it happens to your own child, you remain blissfully unaware. I stopped vaccinating Damon at 15 months, and he never got the MMR vaccine. He was starting to have some symptoms that Trevor also had as a baby, thrush at birth, cradle cap, and eczema. He got sick a few times, and it went to his lungs. His pediatrician said it was bronchitis the first time, and then asthma the second time. He tried to get me to use a nebulizer on him and a steroid inhaler. Damon flat out refused to partake, and I didn't give him the meds. He was constipated so badly that he bled when he pooped. (Sorry, sweetheart.)

I started taking him to our integrated medicine doctor as well. Damon was allergic to dairy, the cause of the constipation, as well as other foods, and he had candida. We used homeopathy to treat him, removed dairy, and cleared his allergies with NAET. Everything went back to normal and he is a brilliant, healthy child. He did not have "asthma" either. Had I used a steroid to push the disease back in his body, maybe he would have. Had I followed the "recommended" vaccine schedule and the allopathic way of drugging symptoms, I would probably have two children with "autism." After removing GMO and wheat from his diet, his emotional and attention issues also cleared up.

If I were going to have a baby today, here is what I would do differently, knowing what I know from my own experience, research and the channeled information regarding autism. Again, I am not a physician; this is my opinion, not medical advice. Since I am not a doctor, I am an idiot.

1. Before I got pregnant, I would clean up my diet; I would not eat wheat or genetically engineered foods. I would detoxify my body with MMS, or another detoxifier, especially from yeast/candida and mercury. I would have my mercury fillings safely removed. I would take probiotics and organic whole food prenatal vitamin supplements. I would stay away from mercury in fish and seafood. I would drink plenty of purified water and I would exercise.

2. I would not take any medication during the pregnancy, especially antibiotics. I would consult a homeopath and use homeopathic remedies for any problems, as they are non-toxic and safe to use during pregnancy.

3. I would use a holistic doula for labor and delivery, and I would have natural childbirth, so that my baby could get the benefits of ingesting good bacteria from the birth canal which strengthens the immune system.

4. I would not allow them to clamp the umbilical cord early. This allows stem cells, T-cells and oxygen to fully enter the baby's body.

5. I would not allow any vaccinations for myself or the baby. The exception would be if a woman needs a Rhogam shot, because she and the father have different Rh factors (negative or positive). If the Rh factors are different, the mother could form antibodies against the baby's blood, which can be fatal. Just make sure there is no thimerosal/mercury in it. They claim there is no thimerosal/mercury in Rhogam now, but read the insert. The alternate to Rhogam was HypRho-D, which also contained mercury until 1996, when it was reformulated to a mercury-free version called BayRho-D. The autism rate is higher for Rh negative mothers who received the mercury-filled Rhogam shots during pregnancy. Educate before you vaccinate. Just look at the ingredients. That should change your mind immediately. Who would knowingly inject genetically engineered diseases, human and animal DNA, antibiotics, heavy metals and toxic chemicals directly into their newborn baby's bloodstream? I list some good websites in the "Resources" chapter with accurate information, not vaccine propaganda. No shots, no school is also a lie. Don't let them bully you. There are exemptions in every state, medical, religious, and sometimes, philosophical. I cannot stress the importance of this. If you take one thing from this book, let it be this. As George Bernard Shaw so eloquently put it, vaccines are a filthy piece of witchcraft. We have been lied to for corporate profit, and our babies are pawns in their game. The truth will come out.

6. I would breast feed as long as possible. A healthy baby trumps vanity. I'd take saggy boobs over a sick child any day.

7. The baby's food and drinks would be all organic, gluten-free and non-GMO. I would make my own baby food from organic fruits and vegetables. I would limit sugar consumption. No fast food. No soda, ever. I would also invest in a good water filtration system.

8. I would make sure the baby's environment is non-toxic. This includes everything the baby drinks and eats from, plays with, wears, sleeps on, and is exposed to. This is a long list, including cooking on the stove, not in

the microwave, glass and stainless steel cookware not plastic and Teflon, no chemical home cleaners, no chemicals in the baby's hygiene products, laundry detergent, dishwashing liquid and dishwasher tablets, plastic toys, toys with lead, organic cotton clothing and bedding. No disposable diapers with chlorine and other harmful chemicals. There are many safe alternatives on the market. See www.ewg.org for harmful chemicals.

9. I would use homeopathy for medicine, except in life threatening cases or broken bones. Homeopathy is a complete system of medicine, capable of treating many of the diseases that vaccines are supposed to prevent, without the toxic additives and side effects. It is excellent for treating acute symptoms, and is safe for children. It is energy medicine, and it works. I highly recommend reading about the history of homeopathy in this country and how the drug cartel took over medicine in this country. Most medical schools in the U.S were homeopathic before the drug companies took over.

10. I would keep household toxins to a minimum. We must make educated choices. There are many harmful toxins we don't even think about: paint with volatile organic compounds, cheap furniture that off-gasses formaldehyde, carpets with volatile organic compounds, mold, EMF. There is so much to think about. There are good home air filters out there as well. (See the resources section for suggestions.)

If I knew then what I know now and had a child that was normal and then was diagnosed with regressive autism, what would I do differently? My son is now 13, so he was at the beginning of the autism epidemic, before a lot of the current treatments were being used. I had no road map to follow, so I had to make one. I read everything I could, and used my knowledge and intuition as to what I felt would help him. Sometimes, I got help from spirit during some of my sessions with mediums along the way. For instance, I was told he was allergic to wheat and I needed to get it out of his diet during a reading. Then I had him tested and he was indeed allergic to it, along with tons of other things. I was also told numerous times through numerous mediums by my deceased relatives that Trevor was going to be okay, so I trusted that, and it kept me motivated.

So, I will start with the therapies that I have done with him so far that I felt were helpful, followed by the things I would do things differently today. When Trevor was five, I ditched his worthless pediatrician, we went to two integrated medicine doctors and used NAET for allergy testing, and cleared him of his allergies. We used homeopathy to detoxify him from fungus and yeast, heavy metals, parasites, bacteria and viruses. Anytime he got sick, we'd use homeopathy or Chinese herbal remedies. I read many books on homeopathy and took an online class, and used homeopathy for most of our medical needs. I added a few supplements such as digestive enzymes, probiotics, and a vitamin/mineral combination. I mostly stuck with homeopathy. He did Auditory Integration Training 3 times, which helped somewhat, but again, this does nothing to address the pathogens causing most of the symptoms, and his sound sensitivity always returned. ABA (Applied Behavioral Analysis) has been very helpful to help him learn and to speak. We have had various tutors coming to the house for the past eight years. I recently started using a system similar to NAET called BioSET, to test for and clear pathogens, toxins, and allergies. This has been very helpful as well. HBOT was also very beneficial, as I've already stated.

If I had to do it over, I would definitely do MMS right away, including enemas and a parasite protocol. I feel that pathogens and toxins are what are causing most of the autistic symptoms in the first place. I would definitely do dietary intervention, including eliminating all food allergens and wheat, and I would feed my child all organic and non-GMO food. I would do HBOT during and/or after MMS. I would invest in a good water filtration system. Alkaline water is great to reduce acidity, unless doing MMS; the antioxidants in the alkaline water cancel out MMS. I would limit the amount of supplements, because they feed the pathogens. Instead of adding supplements for every nutritional deficiency, ask what is causing these deficiencies in the first place; pathogens. For example, parasites deplete vitamin B12 and iron. Supplementing them does not eliminate what is causing the deficiency, it is feeding them more. Deficiencies are effects, not causes. I would use homeopathy. I would do ABA. I would do NAET or BioSET for allergy elimination and testing. I would make sure he got plenty of exercise and got out and had new experiences. Recovery means getting back to basics: detoxify, get rid of pathogens, healthy food, clean water and oxygen. Most of all I would give him lots of love.

I also learned how to do hands-on-healing to help Trevor, naively thinking that I could magically heal him. That didn't happen, but it has definitely come in handy in his recovery. I started with Reiki, becoming a Reiki Master, and then advanced to Reconnective Healing. If I had to do it over, I would just do Reconnective Healing. It is easy to learn and do, and contains a higher bandwidth of frequencies, including those of Reiki. I can't tell you how many times I've used it to calm both of my kids down, reduce fevers, and heal boo-boo's. It's a great tool, and anyone can learn it. You can also use it on yourself, and lord knows we moms need it with all we are dealing with. You can also do distance healing, so if Trevor is in his bedroom trying to calm himself down to go to sleep, I can be in my room running energy on him from a distance. There is nothing more healing than a mother's touch, this just amps it up many notches, giving the child the perfect combination of energy, light and information that they need in that moment. You can learn to do it yourself in Dr. Eric Pearl's book *The Reconnection- Heal Others, Heal Yourself* or by attending one of his seminars which are listed at www.thereconnection.com.

I won't go into all of the things we tried that were not very helpful, but believe me, there were plenty of them. There was lots of wasted money and time involved. We were a family that was pretty well off before Trevor developed autism. I had money from a life insurance policy when my late husband died and was able to provide us with a nice home, vehicles and everything a child could ever dream of. Matt made a nice living and I could stay at home when my boys were young. My mom lived with us to help us out. This was my dream come true. After having a child with autism who was excluded from health insurance because they consider it "genetic," we had to pay for everything out of pocket. We took out a line of credit on our home to pay for therapies. When my husband and I split up, things got worse, and I pretty much lost it all trying to help my child. The Autism Society of America estimates that the lifetime cost of raising a child with autism is $3.5 to $5 million. I know that we spent at least $25,000 out of pocket each year on various therapies (spending our savings and going further into debt). You do the math. The waiting list in many states for financial assistance for children with autism is often years long. They can't wait. If you have the money, you spend it, if you don't, you go into debt.

Because of my responsibilities to my children and their school schedule, I am unable work full time, and I also rely on my mom for help. Like so many of us, my husband and I each had to file for bankruptcy and we lost two homes and the money we put into them. The financial toll of autism is only one of the effects. So if it could happen to us, it could happen to anyone. I always said I would live in a cardboard box if it meant recovering my child. When I had the financial means, I used it to try to do everything in my power to get my son back. We probably wouldn't be in this financial situation today if I knew then what I know now. You know what they say about hindsight. Besides, home is where the heart is.

***

Chapter Twenty-Eight

When Einstein died on April 18, 1955 he left a piece of writing ending in an unfinished sentence. These were his last words:

"In essence, the conflict that exists today is no more than an old-style struggle for power, once again presented to mankind in semi religious trappings. The difference is that, this time, the development of atomic power has imbued the struggle with a ghostly character; for both parties know and admit that, should the quarrel deteriorate into actual war, mankind is doomed. Despite this knowledge, statesmen in responsible positions on both sides continue to employ the well-known technique of seeking to intimidate and demoralize the opponent by marshaling superior military strength. They do so even though such a policy entails the risk of war and doom. Not one statesman in a position of responsibility has dared to pursue the only course that holds out any promise of peace, the course of supranational security, since for a statesman to follow such a course would be tantamount to political suicide. Political passions, once they have been fanned into flame, exact their victims ... Citater fra..."

Summary

As the saying goes, all good things must come to an end. We had to wrap things up at some point, but hopefully, this is just the beginning. Even though my initial hope of having Albert finish drawing the formula for the cure for autism did not happen, I could not be happier with what did happen. My hope in doing these channeling sessions was to get some information from those in the spirit word who have an expanded vantage point than ours here on Earth. I knew this was possible from my many years of personally investigating mediumship. If they could tell me about my life, why couldn't they tell me about autism? My intention was to get the answers from spirit about what is causing the autism epidemic and what we can do to fix it and also prevent it. If we know what the causes are we can avoid them in future generations. I do not want what happened to my son to be in vain.

Michael, Marti and I were honored and humbled to do this work and put this book together. It would not have been possible without our joint talents, and without the assistance of all of the spirits who came forward in these sessions. We were all astounded during the process, not only by whom was coming through, but by what they had to say. I am forever grateful to all who participated. I cannot thank you all enough, you know who you are. I am especially grateful to Michael and Marti who volunteered their time and talents to help humanity. Karma will be extra good to them for this. I love you guys.

It was interesting to me that many of the spirit people who came through were scientists, people in the medical field, political figures and parents; the same groups of people that are involved in autism on Earth. Many of these scientists had their work used for the war effort, the nuclear bomb in particular. Many of them worked on the Manhattan Project and for Germany and Russia's nuclear weapons programs. Perhaps this is some sort of atonement for them. Again, we had no idea who many of these people were until I looked them up after the sessions, and then finding all of the connections to each other were just incredible. Learning these connections and then finding all of the pictures of them together was like unraveling a mystery and a history lesson all in one. History was my least favorite subject in school, now it was interesting.

The messages themselves were the biggest part of these sessions. Sure, it was fun and exciting talking to famous dead people along with my departed loved ones, but the messages are what this was all about. Remember, Michael knew next to nothing about autism before these sessions, which was a good thing. A lot of the messages were things that many people in the autism community have been talking about for a while now. But for a person who knows nothing to get this information from spirit, it validates that these things are correct. For instance, that vaccines and mercury are causative factors, especially the MMR vaccine.

Also, many of the problems that children with autism have were mentioned, which Michael personally knew nothing about, so for him to come up with those items proved that the information was not coming from him. I hope that the sheer weight of evidence will be enough to convince people that this work is legitimate. These are not just good guesses. These are impossible odds that he could get all of these things correct. Add Marti's art to the mix, and the odds get even more impossible.

Instead of summing up the information from all of the sessions, I would like to focus on the new pieces of the autism puzzle that were revealed during the sessions, which have to do with genetic engineering and biological warfare. I look at this information as a huge warning. Our food supply (GMO's), vaccines, and the biological warfare being created that is in the air are all genetically engineered. Think about that for a minute. Our DNA is being altered and mutated. These problems didn't exist when most of these spirits were alive, or even when I was young.

We also didn't have all of the toxins on our planet that we have today when these spirits were alive. According to CNN, the EPA has tested only about 200 of the 80,000 chemicals in use. We didn't inject our newborns with 30-plus untested vaccines filled with toxins, genetically engineered pathogens, and human and animal DNA. We were not eating genetically engineered food. Genetically engineered biowarfare was not floating around the planet for everyone to inhale. Depleted uranium was not in the environment. Our birthing practices have changed and are unnatural. Children today are born with over 200 chemicals in their bodies according to the Environmental Working Group. Twenty five percent of us live within four miles of a hazardous waste site. No one knows what the combination, or synergistic toxicity of all of these items is in an infant or a developing child.

All of these things and more create the perfect storm. There is not just one cause of autism, there are many factors, and it is different for each child depending on their exposures and vulnerability. There are so many things that are different now and our children and future generations are in big trouble unless we collectively make some changes. It is the parents who still have fully functioning mental capacity that need to make these changes. When one in six children has a developmental disorder, we are the ones who have to step up to the plate. Sadly, it's getting worse. People need to wake up. This is not going to get better until we make changes, folks. Albert Einstein said that the definition of insanity is doing the same thing over and over and expecting different results. I couldn't have said it better myself.

We need to educate the new parents so that they don't make the same foolish mistakes that the rest of us have. This is a global pandemic, an emergency, but no one seems to be too concerned until it happens to them. Until the government and medical community recognizes that autism, in most cases, is not a genetic disorder, it is going to be a grass roots effort of parents educating other parents and telling their stories, in the hopes that they take heed and do their homework. You can lead a horse to water, but you can't make them drink. The truly brave ones will listen to their intuition and to those who have been there before them, and not to the propaganda. If this information can help save one child from the horrors that our family has been through, then it will have been worth it.

My hope in sharing this information is that perhaps medical researchers, scientists, or people who are connected to the spirits who came through in these sessions will contact us and want to have their own session, which will hopefully bring forth more information. It is extremely difficult to do a session when most things can't be validated because you don't know the person in spirit personally. Not being able to validate information sometimes stops the session prematurely. The right information will be given to the right person, so I also hope that someone who can make a difference and understand detailed medical or scientific information will also be interested in having a session. Or perhaps they can make more sense out of some of the information that came through already. I tried my best to make sense of the messages, but it's quite possible that they have other meanings that I don't understand, but someone else will. I'm just one person.

I don't think it is my place to contact the living relatives of some of these spirits and say, "Yeah, your dead father came through in a channeling session, would you be interested in seeing what else he has to say?" They need to want to do it; it can't be forced upon them. But, I'd love to write a sequel someday based on what happens after this book comes out. To be continued...?

There is one final thing I had to add to this story. As I was putting the finishing touches on the book, and waiting for Marti to finish the cover, my younger son Damon, who was in 4th grade, had a school project in which his teacher assigned him a person to write a biography about. He had to read all about the person, draw a picture of them, write a structured poem about them, and present it in front of the class wearing a costume. His teacher chose Albert Einstein for Damon's biography. What are the odds? I had to laugh at the synchronicity once again. Michael and

Marti had a good laugh as well when I told them.

I helped him do his research and taught him some of the things I had learned in my own research on Albert. Prior to him coming through in these sessions, I knew very little about him myself. I knew that he was a genius who was famous for E=MC² and that he had wild hair. Turns out, he was also a wonderful human being. I'd like to share what Damon wrote and the picture he drew of Albert. Here is what his poster looked like:

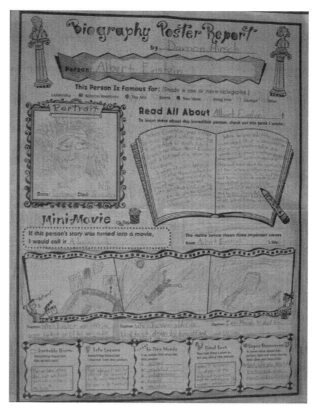

It is hard to read the words, but I especially liked how he wrote that Einstein didn't talk until he was 3 or 4, and that he was "A bit autistic when he was born." In the section with the movie about Einstein's life, called "A Special Life," Damon drew a scene of him not talking when he was little and his mom saying "Oh, Son, is there something wrong?" The second scene is when he was older, and Damon said that he liked to sit down by himself and think about space. The third scene was at his gravesite, and the caption reads "Even though he died, his soul lives on."

Damon knows about my book and that Albert and others have come through to talk about autism. Not that he would tell his teacher that, of course. Can you imagine?

The five words that Damon chose to describe Albert were genius, peaceful, independent, famous, and thinker. In the final fact section, Damon wrote "Albert Einstein loved playing the violin and figured out that the notes were like number patterns in a song." Finally, in the Life Lesson section Damon wrote "For almost all his life, all he wanted to do was think. And he was a bit autistic." He made the poster at school, all on his own, mind you. I was so impressed, and thought it would be a very fitting ending for the book. Damon's poem about Albert gives some insight into who he was as a person. For those who don't know much about him, here is some 10-year-old insight. The following is the picture he drew and the poem that he wrote:

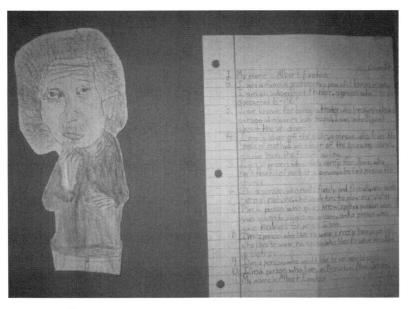

My name is Albert Einstein.

I am a famous Professor, a peaceful loving man, I am an independent thinker, a genius who discovered E=MC².

I am known for being a thinker who knows a lot, a person who wants war to end, I am intelligent about the Universe.

I am a lover of the violin, a person who loves the levels of math; I am a lover of the amazing science, one who loves the fun of sailing.

I am a person who feels sorry for the Jews, who feels fearful of nuclear weapons, who feels passion for science.

I am a person who needs family and friends, who needs time in nature, who needs time to play my violin.

I am a person who gives knowledge, a person who gives vision to people who learn, and a person who gives kindness for people I love.

I'm a person who likes to wear crazy hair, a person who likes to wear no socks, who likes to wear wrinkled up clothes.

I'm a person who would like to see world peace.

I am a person who lives in Princeton, NJ.

My name is Albert Einstein.

***

For Trevor, my starfish...

Trevor, holding a starfish in Monterey, CA.

The Starfish Story
Adapted from "The Star Thrower" by Loren Eiseley

*One day a man was walking along the beach when he noticed
a boy picking something up and gently throwing it into the ocean.*

Approaching the boy, he asked, "What are you doing?"

*The youth replied, "Throwing starfish back into the ocean.
The surf is up and the tide is going out. If I don't throw them back, they'll die."*

The man said, "Son, don't you realize there are miles and miles of beach and starfish all along it? You can't possibly make a difference!"

After listening politely, the boy bent down, picked up another starfish, and threw it back into the surf. Then, smiling at the man, he said, "I made a difference for that one."

Resources

(Laura's list, she's not affiliated with any group, she just likes them.)

Autism Websites

Autism Research Institute (ATEC scoring)- www.autism.com
Generation Rescue (Jenny McCarthy's group) www.generationrescue.org
Talk About Curing Autism- www.tacanow.org
Autism One- www.autismone.org
National Autism Organization- www.nationalautismorganization.com
Age of Autism online newspaper-www.ageofautism.com
Autism File Magazine- www.autismfile.com
Thinking Mom's Revolution blog- www.thinkingmomsrevolution.com
Autism Media Channel- www.autismmediachannel.com

Vaccine Information

National Vaccine Information Center- www.nvic.org
International Medical Council on Vaccination- www.vaccinationcouncil.org
Vax Truth, Inc. - www.vaxtruth.org
Smart Vax. - www.smartvax.com
Sane Vax, Inc. - www.sanevax.org
Fourteen Studies- (The studies used to promote the false assertion that vaccines don't cause autism) - www.fourteenstudies.org
Dr. Sherry Tenpenny- www.drtenpenny.com
Sheri Nakken- (Former nurse who teaches online homeopathy and vaccine information classes.) www.wellwithin1.com

Diet/Nutrition

Nourishing Hope- Diets for autism- www.nourishinghope.org
Institute for Responsible Technology- www.responsibletechnology.org
Non-GMO Shopping Guide and free phone app. - www.nongmoshoppingguide.com
Non-GMO Project- www.nongmoproject.org
Organic Consumers Association- www.organicconsumers.org
The Organic Center- www.organic-center.org
Local Harvest- Local Organic Foods- www.localharvest.org
Organic Foods shipped to your home- www.boxorganix.com
Body Ecology Diet- www.bodyecology.com
Weston A. Price Foundation- www.westonaprice.org

Health/Medical

MMS- www.jimhumble.biz

Kerri Rivera's MMS website- www.mmsautism.com
MMS/Diatomaceous Earth- www.keavyscorner.com
BioSuperfood- www.bioage.com
Supplements for children with autism - www.klaire.com,
www.kirkman.com
King Bio Natural Medicine, homeopathic remedies- www.kingbio.com
HVS Laboratories Homeopathic detoxosodes- www.nutri-pharma.com
Homeopathic books and home medicine kits- www.homeopathic.com
Doris Rapp- Environmental Medicine, author and pediatrician-
www.drrapp.com
Nambudripad's Allergy Elimination Technique- www.naet.com
BioSET- www.drellencutler.com
HBOT Treatment Centers by State- www.healing-arts.org/children/

Education/Language

Lovaas Center for Behavior Intervention- www.lovaas.com
CARD-Center for Autism and Related Disorders- www.centerforautism.com
Teach 2 Talk DVD's- www.teach2talk.com

Others

Michael Parry's blog- www.mysticmike-mysticmike.blogspot.com
Natural News- www.naturalnews.com
Reconnective Healing- www.thereconnection.com
Environmental Working Group- www.ewg.org
Organic clothing and sleepwear- www.hannaandersson.com
Organic food and products- www.allorganiclinks.com
Thrive: What on Earth will it take? - www.thrivemovement.com
The Greater Good movie- www.greatergoodmovie.org
Skin Deep- EWG's Cosmetic Database- www.ewg.org/skindeep
Allergy Kids- www.allergykids.com
Dr. Joseph Mercola- www.mercola.com

About

Laura Hirsch- Laura was born and raised in Wisconsin and graduated from the University of Wisconsin-Whitewater with a Bachelor of Arts in Speech Communications. This is Laura's third book. She is also the author of *Widowed Too Soon: A Young Widow's Journey through Grief, Healing, and Spiritual Transformation;* an autobiography about her experience of becoming a young widow which led to her investigation of mediumship as a therapeutic avenue for grief; as well as *Foundation of Discovery: The Cause of Autism – Channeled.*

Laura and her husband Matt are the proud parents of two beautiful children, Trevor and Damon. In 2001, at the age of 3, their older son Trevor was diagnosed with autism. Laura knew that he was not born that way, which started her quest for answers to bring her son back. Her love and devotion to her son led her back to mediumship to find the answer to her question, what happened to my child, and how can I fix him?

Laura is active in the autism community and participates in local autism fundraisers and events. She volunteers her time to help other parents. Her passion is to educate people about autism from her unique perspective and to be a voice for children with autism, whose voices were taken away. You can contact Laura through her website: wwwtheothersideofautism.com.

Michael and Marti Parry- This incomparable husband and wife team combine the mediumistic ability of Michael with the rare psychic artistry ability of his wife, Marti. In the same caliber as other renowned psychic mediums, Michael is able to make a connection with relatives and friends that have passed over to the other side with incredible accuracy. Equally astounding is the artistic talents of Marti, who has the uncanny ability to draw friends and loved ones that have passed away without ever having seen them, personally or through pictures, or even a description! When you put two such dynamic personalities together with such distinctive talents, the skeptics are left speechless.

They are the best in the business and have appeared on both National and Cable television programs. They have also been interviewed on numerous radio programs and been featured in several newspapers and magazines. A few examples are: A&E's *Paranormal State*, SciFi Channel's *Proof Positive*, and The Biography Channel's *My Ghost Story and Psychic Investigators.*

Although they have a full schedule with lectures, workshops and conventions, they still make time to help others deal with the loss of a loved one. They do this as a means to help others deal with their grief and start them along a path of healing. They freely gave their time and talents to work with Laura Hirsch to get information from spirit to help children with autism. They are true humanitarians. They are down to Earth, funny and extremely knowledgeable about all things spiritual and supernatural. If you would like to experience a private or group session firsthand and connect with lost loved ones, you can contact them through their website: www.spiritart.com.

Made in the USA
San Bernardino, CA
25 November 2014